Fâṭima, Daughter of Muhammad

Islamic History and Thought

10

Islamic History and Thought provides a platform for scholarly research on any geographic area within the expansive Islamic world, stretching from the Mediterranean to China, and dated to any period from the eve of Islam until the early modern era. This series contains original monographs, translations (Arabic, Persian, Syriac, Greek, and Latin) and edited volumes.

Fâṭima, Daughter of Muhammad

Second Edition

Christopher Paul Clohessy

Gorgias Press

2018

Gorgias Press LLC, 954 River Road, Piscataway, NJ, 08854, USA

www.gorgiaspress.com

2018

ISBN 978-1-4632-3939-8

Library of Congress Cataloging-in-Publication Data

A Cataloging-in-Publication Record is available from the Library of Congress.

Printed and bound by CPI Group (UK) Ltd, Croydon, CR0 4YY

TABLE OF CONTENTS

PREFACE

Unless otherwise stated, all quotations from the Qur'ân are taken from the English interpretation of Muhammad Marmaduke Pickthall.[1] Bearing in mind that every translation is an interpretation, I have at times compared his translation with that of other English interpreters of the Qur'ân, and these will be named in the text when they occur.

The system of transliteration, given at the start of this work, has been followed throughout the text, except in instances in which other authors have been quoted, in which case the said author's system of transliteration has been respected.

Unless otherwise stated, all translations of the Arabic texts are my own.

All sources have been referenced in order of their antiquity, in this way providing a graph by which to examine the periods in which Fâṭima's influence grew steadily. Where necessary, the Shîʿî and Sunnî transmitters have been carefully distinguished in order to avoid confusion.

Except when quoting from other works, all dates are given according to the Islamic calendar (*hiǧra*), followed by a backslash and the Gregorian equivalent.

---

[1] PICKTHALL M.M., *The Meaning of the Glorious Qur'ān*, Dar al-Kitab Allubnani, Beirut and Dar al-Kitab al-Masri, Cairo (n.d.).

SYSTEM OF TRANSLITERATION

ء	-	ʾ	ض	-	ḍ
ب	-	b	ط	-	✹
ت	-	t	ظ	-	ẓ
ث	-	th	ع	-	ʿ
ج	-	ğ	غ	-	ġ
ح	-	ḥ	ف	-	f
خ	-	ẖ	ق	-	q
د	-	d	ك	-	k
ذ	-	ḏ	ل	-	l
ر	-	r	م	-	m
ز	-	z	ن	-	n
س	-	s	ه	-	h
ش	-	sh	و	-	w
ص	-	ṣ	ي	-	y

<u>Long Vowels</u>:

آ	-	â
و	-	û
ي	-	î

<u>Short Vowels</u>:

أ	-	a, u
إ	-	i

ABBREVIATIONS

1ST/7TH CENTURY

Shîʿa

QHL: Ibn Qays al-Hilâlî (d. c. 80/662: cf. MODARRESSI H., *Tradition and Survival,* 2003: 82, 424) in his *Kitâb Sulaym b. Qays* (CRCIS, Qum 2000).

3RD/9TH CENTURY

Sunnî

HSH: Abû Muḥammad ʿAbd al-Mâlik Hishâm b. Ayyûb al-Ḥimyarî Ğamâl al-Dîn (d. 218/834: cf. GAS I: 297) in his *Sîrat Muḥammad Rasûl Allâh* (2 vols., Maṭbaʿat Muṣṭafâ al-Bâbî al-Ḥalabî, Cairo 1955).

SʿD: Muḥammad b. Saʿd Kâtib al-Wâqidî (d. 230/845: cf. GAL I: 136, GAL S. I: 208) in his *Kitâb al-ṭabaqât al-kabîr* (11 vols., Maktab al-Ḫanğî, Cairo 2001).

ḤNB: Abû ʿAbd Allâh Aḥmad b. Muḥammad b. Ḥanbal al-Shaybânî al-Ḏuhlî (d. 241/855: cf. GAL S. I: 309) in his *Musnad* (12 vols., Dâr al-fikr, Cairo 1995).

DRM: ʿAbd al-Raḥmân b. ʿAbd Allâh al-Dârimî al-Samarqandî (d. 255/869: cf. GAL S. I: 270) in his *Sunan* (2 vols., Maṭbaʿat al-iʿtidâl, Damascus 1931).

BUḪ[1]: Abû ʿAbd Allâh Muḥammad b. Ismâʿîl b. Ibrâhîm b. Muğîra b. Bardizbah al-Buḫârî al-Ğuʿfî (d. 256/870: cf. GAL S. I: 260) in his *Ṣaḥîḥ* (9 vols., al-Maktaba al-salafiyya, Medina) and **BUḪ[2]**: in his *al-Adab al-mufrad* (Maktaba dâr al-salâm, Riyadh 1997).

MSL: Abû al-Ḥusayn Muslim b. al-Ḥağğâğ al-Qushayrî al-Nîsâbûrî (d. 261/875: cf. GAL S. 1: 265) in his *Ṣaḥîḥ* (5 vols., Maktaba dâr al-salâm, Riyadh 2007).

MĞA: Abû ʿAbd Allâh Muḥammad b. Yazîd b. Mâğa al-Qazwînî (d. 273/886: cf. GAL S. I: 270) in his *Sunan* (2 vols., Dâr iḥyâʾ al-kutub al-ʿarabiyya, Cairo 1952).

ADD: Abû Dâwûd Sulaymân b. al-Ashʿaṯ al-Azdî al-Siğistânî (d. 275/889: cf. GAL S. I: 270) in his *Sunan* (5 vols., Maktaba dâr al-salâm, Riyadh 2008).

TRM: Abû ʿÎsâ Muḥammad b. ʿÎsâ b. Sahl al-Tirmiḏî (d. 279/892: cf. GAL S. I: 267) in his *Sunan* (6 vols., Maktaba dâr al-salâm, Riyadh 2007).

BLḎ[1]: Abû al-ʿAbbâs Aḥmad b. Yaḥyâ b. Ğâbir al-Balâḏurî (d. 279/892: cf. GAL S. I: 216, GAS I: 320) in his *Kitâb ansâb al-ashraf* (vol. I, Dâr al-maʿârif, Egypt 1959, vol. IVa, University Press, Jerusalem 1971, vol. V, Magnes Press, Jerusalem 1936), and **BLḎ[2]**: in his *Kitâb futûḥ al-buldân* (Maṭbaʿat lağnat al-bayân al-ʿarabî, Cairo n.d.).

Shîʿa

RṬB[1]: Abû Ğaʿfar Muḥammad b. Ğarîr b. Rustam al-Ṭabarî (c. 224/839: cf. GAL S. I: 217 and GAS I: 540) in his *Dalâʾil al-imâma* (CRCIS, Qum 2000), and **RṬB[2]**: in his *Bishârat al-muṣṭafâ* (CRCIS, Qum 2000).

ṬAY: Abû al-Faḍl Aḥmad b. Abî Ṭâhir Ṭayfûr (d. 280/893: cf. GAL S. I: 210) in his *Balâğât al-nisâʾ* (CRCIS, Qum 2000)

YQB: Aḥmad b. Abî Yaʿqûb b. Ğaʿfar b. Wahb b. Wâḍih al-Kâtib al-ʿAbbâsî al-Yaʿqûbî (d. 284/897 or 292/905: cf. GAL S. I: 405) in his *Târîḫ* (2 vols., E.J. Brill, Leiden 1969).

4TH/10TH CENTURY

Sunnî

NSA[1]: Abû ʿAbd al-Raḥmân Aḥmad b. ʿAbd al-Raḥmân b. Shuʿayb al-Nasâʾî (d. 303/915: cf. GAL S. I: 269) in his *al-Sunan al-kubrâ* (6 vols., Maktaba dâr al-salâm, Riyadh 2007), and **NSA[2]**: in his *Kitâb al-ḫaṣâʾiṣ fî faḍl ʿAlî b. Abî Ṭâlib* (Maktab al-âdâb, Cairo 1986).

YṬB[1]: Abû Ǧaʿfar Muḥammad b. Ǧarîr b. Yazîd al-Ṭabarî (d. 310/923: cf. GAS 1: 232 and GAL S. I: 217) in his *Ǧâmiʿ al-bayân ʿan taʾwîl al-qurʾân* (16 vols., Dâr al-maʿrifa, Cairo 1969), and **YṬB[2]**: in his *Kitâb aḫbâr al-rusul wa-l-mulûk* (39 vols., in English translation, State University of New York Press, New York 1989).

Shîʿa

KLY: Muḥammad Yaʿqûb b. Isḥâq al-Kulaynî al-Râzî (d. 328/939: cf. GAL S. I: 320) in his *al-Kâfî fî ʿilm al-dîn* (8 vols., Dâr al-kutub al-islâmiyya, Tehran 1968).

NUM: Abû ʿAlî Muḥammad b. Ibrâhîm b. Ǧaʿfar al-Nuʿmânî (4TH/10TH century, pupil of al-Kulaynî: cf. GAL S. I: 321 and GAS I: 543) in his *Ġaybat al-Nuʿmânî* (CRCIS, Qum 2000).

MSD: Abû al-Ḥasan ʿAlî b. al-Ḥusayn b. ʿAlî al-Masʿûdî (d. 345/956: cf. GAS I: 333) in his *Murûǧ al-ḏahab* (4 vols., Publications de l'Université Libanaise, Beirut 1965).

KFI: Muḥammad b. Muḥammad al-Ashʿaṯ al-Kûfî (c. mid-4TH/10TH century: cf. MODARRESSI H., *Tradition and Survival*, 2003: 416) in his *al-Ashʿaṯiyyât* (CRCIS, Qum 2000).

ḪAṢ., Abû ʿAbd Allâh al-Ḥusayn b. ʿAlî b. al-Ḥusayn b. Ḥamdân al-Ḫaṣîbî Zayn al-Dîn (d. 346/957 or 3658/968: cf. GAS I. 584) in his *al-Hidâya al-kubrâ*

QQM: Abû al-Qâsim Ǧaʿfar b. Muḥammad b. Ǧaʿfar b. Mûsâ b. Qûlûya al-Qummî (d. 369/979: cf. GAL S. I: 953) in his *Kâmil al-ziyârât* (Mu'assasat al-nashr al-islâmî, Qum n.d.).

RQM: ʿAlî b. Muḥammad b. ʿAlî al-Ḫazzâz al-Râzî al-Qummî (d. 381/991: cf. GAL S. I: 322 and GAS I: 543) in *Kifâyat al-aṯar fî-l-nuṣûs ʿalâ al-aʾimma al-iṯnâ ʿasharî* (CRCIS, Qum 2000).

ṢDQ[1]: Abû Ǧaʿfar Muḥammad b. ʿAlî b. al-Ḥusayn b. Mûsâ b. Bâbûya al-Qummî al-Ṣadûq (d. 381/991: cf. GAL S. I: 321 and GAS I: 544) in his *Kitâb al-amâlî fî-l-aḥâdîṯ wa-l-aḫbâr* (CRCIS, Qum 2000); **ṢDQ[2]**: in his *Ikmâl (kamâl) al-dîn wa-itmâm (tamâm) al-niʿma fî iṯbât al-ġayba wa-kashf al-ḥayra* (CRCIS, Qum 2000); **ṢDQ[3]**: in his *Man lâ yaḥḍuru-hu al-faqîh* (CRCIS, Qum 2000); **ṢDQ[4]**: in his *Kitâb al-ḫiṣâl* (CRCIS, Qum 2000); **ṢDQ[5]**: in his *ʿUyûn aḫbâr al-Riḍâ* (CRCIS, Qum 2000); **ṢDQ[6]**: in his *Maʿânî al-aḫbâr* (CRCIS, Qum 2000); **ṢDQ[7]**: in his *Faḍâʾil al-ashhur al-ṯalâṯa* (CRCIS, Qum 2000); **ṢDQ[8]**: in his *ʿIlal al-sharâʾiʿ wa-l-aḥkâm* (CRCIS, Qum 2000); **ṢDQ[9]**:

in his *Ṣifât al-shîʿa* (Ansariyan Publications, Qum 2001); and **ṢDQ[10]**: in his *Faḍâʾil al-shîʿa* (Ansariyan Publications, Qum 2001).

FUR: Furât b. Ibrâhîm b. Furât al-Kûfî (d. 310/992: cf. **MOD**.: 413 and GAS I: 539) in his *Tafsîr Furât b. Ibrâhîm al-Kûfî* (CRCIS, Qum 2000).

5TH/11TH CENTURY

Sunnî

ḤNA: Muḥammad b. ʿAbd Allâh b. Muḥammad al-Ḥâkim al-Nîsâbûrî b. al-Bayyiʿ (d. 404/1014: cf. GAL S. I: 276; Brockelmann incorrectly reports his death at 404/914 and names him al-Nîsâbûrî as opposed to al-Naysâbûrî, found in other texts) in his *Kitâb (Talḫîs) al-mustadrak ʿalâ al-ṣaḥîḥayn* (5 vols., Dâr al-ḥarmîn, Cairo 1997).

ṮLB: Abû Isḥâq Aḥmad b. Muḥammad b. Ibrâhîm al-Ṯaʿlabî al-Nîsâbûrî al-Shâfiʿî (d. 427/1035: cf. GAL S. I: 592) in his *Kitâb ʿarâʾis al-maǧâlis fî qiṣaṣ al-anbiyâʾ* (al-Maṭbaʿa al-ʿâmira al-sharafiyya, Cairo 1954).

IṢH: Abû Nuʿaym Aḥmad b. ʿAbd Allâh b. Aḥmad b. Isḥâq al-Iṣbahânî (or al-Iṣfahânî) al-Shâfiʿî (d. 430/1038: cf. GAL S. I: 616) in his *Ḥilyat al-awliyâʾ wa-ṭabaqât al-aṣfiyâʾ* (11 vols., Dâr al-kutub al-ʿilmiyya, Beirut 1967).

BĠD: Abû Bakr Aḥmad b. ʿAlî b. Ṯâbit al-Ḫaṭîb al-Baġdâdî (d. 463/1071: cf. GAL I: 329) in his *Târîḫ Baġdâd* (14 vols., Dâr al-kitâb al-ʿarabî, Beirut n.d.).

BRR: Abû ʿUmar Yûsuf b. ʿAbd Allâh b. Muḥammad b. ʿAbd al-Barr al-Namarî al-Qurṭubî (d. 463/1071: cf. GAL S. I: 628) in his *al-Istîʿâb fî maʿrifat al-aṣḥâb* (4 vols., Maṭbaʿat Nahḍat Miṣr, Cairo n.d.).

Shîʿa

AYY: Abû al-Naḍr Muḥammad b. Masʿûd al-ʿAyyâshî al-Sulamî (d. 401/1009: cf. MODARRESSI H., *Tradition and Survival*, 2003: 410 and GAS I: 42) in his *Tafsîr al- ʿAyyâshî* (CRCIS, Qum 2000).

MFD[1]: Muḥammad b. Muḥammad b. Nuʿmân al-Baġdâdî al-Karḫî al-Mufîd (d. 413/1022. cf. GAL I: 188 and GAL S. I: 322) in his *al-Irshâd fî maʿrifat ḥuǧaǧ Allâh ʿalâ al-ʿibâd* (CRCIS, Qum 2000); **MFD[2]**:

in his *al-Iḫtiṣâṣ* (CRCIS, Qum 2000); **MFD**[3]: in his *al-Ifṣâḥ fî-l-imâma* (CRCIS, Qum 2000); **MFD**[4]: in his *al-Fuṣûl al-muḫtâra* (CRCIS, Qum 2000), and **MFD**[5]: in his *al-Amâlî li-l-Mufîd* (CRCIS, Qum 2000).

ĞQM: Shâdhân b. Ğibrîl al-Qummî (d. 420/1029, cf. MODARRESSI H., *Tradition and Survival,* 2003: 429) in his *al-Faḍâ'il* (CRCIS, Qum 2000)

NĞA: Abû al-ʿAbbâs Aḥmad b. ʿAlî al-Nağâshî (d. 450/1085: cf. GAL S I: 556) in his *Kitâb asmâ' al-riğâl* (CRCIS, Qum 2000).

ṬFA[1]: Abû Ğaʿfar Muḥammad b. al-Ḥasan b. ʿAlî al-Ṭûsî *Shayḫ* al-Ṭâ'ifa (d. 458/1066: cf. GAL I: 405 and GAL S. I: 706) in his *Tahḏîb al-aḥkâm* (CRCIS, Qum 2000); **ṬFA**[2]: in his *al-Amâlî fî-l-ḥadîṯ,* (CRCIS, Qum 2000); **ṬFA**[3]: in his *Kitâb al-ġayba* (CRCIS, Qum 2000) and **ṬFA**[4]: in his *Kitâb asmâ' al-riğâl* (CRCIS, Qum 2000).

FNR: ʿAlî Muḥammad b. Aḥmad b. ʿAlî al-Fattâl al-Nîsâbûrî al-Farisî (c. mid-5TH/11TH century: cf. GAL S. I: 708) in his *Rawḍat al-wâʿiẓîn wa-tabṣirat al-muttaʿiẓîn* (CRCIS, Qum 2000).

6TH/12TH CENTURY

Sunnî

ZMR: Abû al-Qâsim Maḥmûd b. ʿUmar al-Zamaḫsharî (d. 538/1144: cf. GAL I: 290) in his *al-Kashshâf ʿan ḥaqâ'iq al-tanzîl wa-ʿuyûn al-aqâwîl fî wuğûh al-ta'wîl* (4 vols., al-Maktab al-ḫabâriyya, Cairo 1953).

QIḌ: Abû al-Faḍl ʿIyâḍ b. Mûsâ b. ʿIyâḍ al-Yaḥṣubî al-Sabtî al-Mâlikî (d. 544/1149: cf. GAL S. I: 630) in his *Ikmâl al-muʿallim sharḥ ṣaḥîḥ Muslim* (9 vols., Dâr al-wafâ' 1998).

SHR: Abû al-Fatḥ Muḥammad b. ʿAbd al-Karîm al-Shahrastânî (d. 548/1153: cf. GAL S. I: 762) in his *Kitâb al-milal wa-l-niḥal* (Dâr al-maʿrifa, Beirut 1968).

ḪWZ: Abû al-Mu'ayyad Muwaffaq Aḥmad b. Abî Saʿîd Isḥâq al-Ḫawârizmî (d. 568/1172. cf. GAL S. I: 623) in his *Maqtal al-Ḥusayn* (Dâr anwâr al-hudâ, Qum n.d.).

AKR: Abû al-Qâsim ʿAlî b. al-Ḥasan b. Hibat Allâh Ṯiqat al-Dîn b. ʿAsâkir al-Shâfiʿî (d. 571/1176: cf. GAL S. I: 566) in his *Târîḫ madînat Dimashq* (80 vols., Dâr al-fikr, Beirut 1995).

Shîʿa

ṬBR[1]: Raḍî al-Dîn Abû ʿAlî al-Faḍl b. al-Ḥasan Amîn al-Dîn al-Ṭabarsî (d. 548/1153: cf. GAL S. I: 708) in his *Iʿlâm al-warâ bi-aʿlâm al-hudâ* (CRCIS, Qum 2000); **ṬBR**[2]: in his *Kitâb al-iḥtiğâğ ʿalâ ahl al-liğâğ* (CRCIS, Qum 2000); **ṬBR**[3]: in his *Makârim al-aḫlâq* (CRCIS, Qum 2000) and **ṬBR**[4]: in his *Mağmaʿ al-bayân fî tafsîr al-qurʾân* (6 vols., Dâr maktabat al-ḥayât, Beirut n.d.).

RWD[1]: Quṭb al-Dîn Abû al-Ḥusayn Saʿîd b. Hibat Allâh b. Abî al-Ḥasan al-Râwandî (d. 573/1177: cf. GAL S. I: 624) in his *al-Ḫarâʾiğ wa-l-ğarâʾiḥ fî-l-muʿğizât* (CRCIS, Qum 2000); **RWD**[2]: in his *Nawâdir al-Râwandî* (CRCIS, Qum 2000), and **RWD**[3]: in his *Qiṣaṣ al-anbiyâʾ* (CRCIS, Qum 2000).

SHB: Abû Ğaʿfar Muḥammad b. ʿAlî b. Shaḥrâshûb al-Mâzandarânî al-Surrî Rashîd al-Dîn (d. 588/1192: cf. GAL S. I: 710) in his *Manâqib âl Abî Ṭâlib* (5 vols., Manshûrât ḏawî al-qurbâ, Tehran 2000).

7TH/13TH CENTURY

Sunnî

ĞWZ[1]: Abû al-Faḍâʾil Ğamâl al-Dîn Abû al-Farağ ʿAbd al-Raḥmân b. al-Ḥasan ʿAlî b. Muḥammad b. ʿUmar b. al-Ğawzî (d. 597/1200: cf. GAL S. I: 914, GAL I: 500) in his *Kitâb al-mawḍûʿât min al-aḥâdîṯ al-marfûʿa* (3 vols., Dâr al-fikr, Cairo 1983), and **ĞWZ**[2]: in his *Ṣifat al-ṣafwa* (Dai'ratu'l-ma'rif'il-Osmania, Hyderabad 1968).

RAZ: Faḫr al-Dîn Abû ʿAbd Allâh Muḥammad b. ʿUmar b. al-Ḥasan b. al-Ḫaṭîb al-Râzî (d. 606/1209: cf. GAL S. I: 920) in his *al-Tafsîr al-kabîr* (16 vols., Dâr al-kutub al-ʿilmiyya, Tehran n.d.).

ATH[1]: Abû al-Ḥasan ʿAlî b. Abî al-Karam Aṯîr al-Dîn Muḥammad b. Muḥammad b. ʿAbd al-Karîm ʿIzz al-Dîn Muḥammad b. al-Aṯîr al-Shaybânî (d. 630/1233: cf. GAL I: 345) in his *al-Kâmil fî-l-târîḫ* (9 vols., al-Ṭabâʿa al-munîriyya, Cairo 1934) and **ATH**[2]: in his *Usd al-ġâba fî maʿrifat al-ṣaḥâba* (5 vols., al-Maṭbaʿat al-islâmiyya, Tehran n.d.).

QRṬ: Shams al-Dîn Muḥammad b. Aḥmad b. Abî Bakr b. Farḥ al-Anṣârî al-Qurṭubî (d. 671/1273: cf. GAL S. I: 737) in his *Kitâb al-ğâmiʿ li-aḥkâm al-qurʾân* (20 vols., Dâr al-kutub al-miṣriyya, Cairo 1967).

RḤB: Muḥib al-Dîn Abû al-ʿAbbâs (Abû Muḥammad Abû Ğaʿfar) Aḥmad b. ʿAbd al-Raḥmân al-Ṭabarî al-Makkî al-Shâfiʿî (d. 684/1295: cf. GAL 1: 361) in his *Ḏaḫâʾir al-ʿuqbâ* (Dâr al-maʿrifa, Beirut 1974).

BḌW: Abû Saʿd ʿAbd Allâh b. ʿUmar b. Muḥammad b. ʿAlî Abû al-Ḫayr Nâṣir al-Dîn al-Bayḍâwî (d. 685/1286: cf. GAL I: 416) in his *Anwâr al-tanzîl wa-asrâr al-taʾwîl* (Maṭbaʿat Muṣṭafâ al-Bâbî al-Ḥalabî, Cairo 1926).

Shîʿa

BṬQ: Abû al-Ḥasan Yaḥyâ b. al-Ḥasan b. al-Ḥusayn b. ʿAlî al-Ḥillî al-Wâsiṭî b. al-Biṭrîq (d. 600/1203: cf. GAL S. I: 710) in his *al-ʿUmda fî ʿuyûn al-aḫbâr fî manâqib amîr al-muʾminîn* (CRCIS, Qum 2000).

ḤDI: ʿIzz al-Dîn ʿAbd al-Ḥamîd b. Hibat Allâh al-Madâʾinî b. al-Ḥadîd (d. 655/1257: cf. GAL S. I: 497) in his *Sharḥ nahğ al-balâġa* (20 vols., Dâr iḥyâʾ al-kutub al-ʿarabiyya, Cairo 1959–1964).

ṬSṬ1: Raḍî al-Dîn Abû Mûsâ Abû al-ʿAbbâs ʿAlî b. Mûsâ b. Ğaʿfar b. Muḥammad b. Muḥammad b. Ṭâʾûs al-Ṭâʾûsî al-ʿAlawî al-Fâṭimî (d. 664/1266: cf. GAL S. I: 911) in his *al-Taḥṣîn li-ibn Ṭâʾûs* (CRCIS, Qum 2000); **ṬSṬ2**: in his *al-Ṭarâʾif fî maʿrifat maḏhab al-ṭawâʾif* (CRCIS, Qum 2000); **ṬSṬ3**: in his *Kitâb al-iqbâl bi-l-aʿmâl al-ḥasana* (CRCIS, Qum 2000); **ṬSṬ4**: in his *Kitâb al-yaqîn bi-iḫtiṣâṣ mawlâ-nâ ʿAlî bi-imârat al-muʾminîn* (CRCIS, Qum 2000); **ṬSṬ5**: in his *Falâḥ al-sâʾil* (CRCIS, Qum 2000) and **ṬSṬ6**: in his *Kitâb al-luhûf fî qutlâ al-ṭufûf* (Dâr anwâr al-hudâ, Qum 2002).

NAM: Nağm al-Dîn Ğaʿfar b. Muḥammad b. Ğaʿfar b. Hibat Allâh b. Namâ al-Ḥillî (d. 680/1281) in his *Muṯîr al-aḥzân wa munîr subul al-ashğân*

IRB: Bahâʾ al-Dîn Abû al-Ḥasan ʿAlî b. ʿÎsâ al-Irbilî b. al-Faḫr (692/1293: cf. GAL S. I: 713) in his *Kashf al-ġumma fî maʿrifat al-aʾimma* (CRCIS, Qum 2000).

8TH/14TH CENTURY

Sunnî

TYM: Abû al-ʿAbbâs Aḥmad b. ʿAbd al-Ḥalîm b. al-ʿImâd b. ʿAbd al-Salâm ʿAbd al-Raḥmân b. Muḥammad b. Taymiyya Taqî al-Dîn al-Ḥarrânî al-Ḥanbalî (d. c. 728/1328: cf. GAL S. II: 119) in his *Minhâğ al-sunna al-nabawiyya fî naqḍ kalâm al-shîʿa wa-l-qadariyya* (4 vols., Dâr al-kutub al-ʿilmiyya, Beirut n.d.).

TIB: Shams al-Dîn Muḥammad b. ʿAbd al-Raḥmân al-Ḫaṭîb al-Tibrîzî al-ʿUmarî (c. 737/1336: cf. GAL S. II: 262) in his *Mishkât al-maṣâbîḥ* (3 vols., Dâr al-fikr, Beirut 1979).

MZZ: Abû al-Ḥağğâğ Yûsuf b. al-Zakî ʿAbd al-Raḥmân b. Yûsuf Ğamâl al-Dîn al-Mizzî al-Quḍâʿî al-Kalbî al-Shâfiʿî (d. 742/1341: cf. GAL S. II: 66) in *Tahḏîb al-kamâl fî asmâʾ al-riğâl* (15 vols., Mu'assasat al-risâla, Beirut 1983).

ḎHB[1]: Abû ʿAbd Allâh Muḥammad b. Aḥmad b. ʿUṯmân b. Qaymâz Shams al-Dîn al-Ḏahabî (d. 748/1348: cf. GAL S. II: 45) in his *al-ʿIbar fî aḫbâr al-bashar muntaḫab al-târîḫ al-kabîr* (3 vols., al-Turâṯ al-ʿarabî, Kuwait 1960) and **ḎHB[2]**: in his *Mîzân al-iʿtidâl fî tarâğim al-riğâl* (4 vols., Dâr iḥyâʾ al-kutub al-ʿarabiyya, Cairo 1963).

KṮR[1]: Abû al-Fidâʾ Ismâʿîl b. ʿUmar b. Kaṯîr ʿImâd al-Dîn b. al-Ḫaṭîb al-Qurayshî al-Buṣrawî al-Shâfiʿî (d. 774/1373: cf. GAL S. II: 48) in his *al-Bidâya wa-l-nihâya* (14 vols., Cairo 1930) and **KṮR[2]**: in his *Tafsîr al-qurʾân al-ʿaẓîm* (7 vols., Dâr al-fikr, Beirut 1983).

Shîʿa

ḤLL[1]: Ğamâl al-Dîn Ḥasan b. Yûsuf b. ʿAlî b. Muṭahhar al-Ḥillî al-ʿAllâma (d. 726/1325: cf. GAL S. II: 206) in his *Nahğ al-ḥaqq wa-kashf al-ṣidq*, CRCIS, Qum 2000 and **ḤLL[2]**: in his *Kashf al-yaqîn fî faḍâʾil amîr al-muʾminîn* (CRCIS, Qum 2000).

9TH/15TH CENTURY

Sunnî

HAY: Nûr al-Dîn Abû al-Ḥasan ʿAlî b. Abî Bakr b. Sulaymân b. Ḥağar al-Hayṯamî (d. 807/1405: cf. GAL II: 91, GAL S. II: 82) in his *Mağmaʿ al-zawâʾid wa-manbaʿ al-fawâʾid* (10 vols., Maktab al-qudsî, Cairo n.d.).

SQL[1]: Abû al-Faḍl Aḥmad b. ʿAlî b. Muḥammad b. Ḥağar Shihâb al-Dîn al-ʿAsqalânî al-Kinânî al-Shâfiʿî (d. 852/1449: cf. GAL S. II: 72) in his *al-Iṣâba fî tamyîz al-ṣaḥâba* (4 vols., al-Maktaba al-ğâriyya al-kubrâ, Egypt 1939); **SQL[2]**: in his *Lisân al-mîzân* (7 vols., al-Alami Library, Beirut 1971); **SQL[3]**: in his *Fatḥ al-bârî* (16 vols., Dâr al-ḥikma al-ʿilmiyya, Beirut 1997) and **SQL⁴**: in his *Tahḏîb al-tahḏîb* (12 vols., Dâr Ṣâdir, Beirut 1968).

ṢFI: ʿAbd al-Raḥmân b. ʿAbd al-Salâm al-Ṣaffûrî al-Shâfiʿî (c. 884/1479: cf. GAL S. II: 230) in his *Nuzhat al-maǧâlis wa-muntaḫab al-nafâʾis* (al-Maṭbaʿa al-maymuniyya, Egypt 1896).

Shîʿa

ÂML: Zayn al-ʿÂbidîn ʿAlî b. Yûnus al-Bayyâḍî al-Nabâṭî al-ʿÂmilî (d. 877/1472: cf. GAL S. II: 133) in his *al-Ṣirâṭ al-mustaqîm ilâ mustaḥaqq al-taqdîm fî al-imâma* (CRCIS, Qum 2000).

AḤS: Muḥammad b. ʿAlî b. Ibrâhîm b. Abî Ǧumhûr al-Aḥsâʾî (878/1473: cf. GAL S. II: 272) in his *ʿAwâli al-laʾâliʾ al-ʿazîziyya fî-l-aḥâdîṯ al-dîniyya* (CRCIS, Qum 2000).

KFM¹: Taqî al-Dîn Ibrâhîm b. ʿAlî b. al-Ḥusayn al-Kafʿamî (895 or 905/1498: cf. GAL S. II: 133) in his *Kitâb al-miṣbâḥ* (CRCIS, Qum 2000) and **KFM²**: in his *al-Balad al-amîn* (CRCIS, Qum 2000).

DAY: Ḥasan b. Abî al-Ḥasan al-Daylamî (d. 840/1437: cf. GAL S. I: 261, although Brockelmann provides no dates) in his *Irshâd al-qulûb* (CRCIS, Qum 2000)

10TH/16TH CENTURY

Sunnî

SYṬ: Abû al-Faḍl ʿAbd al-Raḥmân b. Abî Bakr Kamâl al-Dîn b. Muḥammad b. Abî Bakr Ǧalâl al-Dîn al-Suyûṭî (d. 911/1505: cf. GAL S. II: 178) in his *al-Durr al-manṯûr fî-l-tafsîr bi-l-maʾṯûr* (6 vols., Dâr al-kutub al-ʿilmiyya, Beirut 1990).

MTQ: ʿAlâʾ al-Dîn ʿAlî b. Ḥusâm al-Dîn ʿAbd al-Malik b. Qâḍîhân al-Muttaqî al-Hindî al-Qâdirî al-Shâḏilî al-Ǧawnpûrî al-Madanî (d. c. 977/1569: cf. GAL S. II: 518) in his *Muntaḫab kanz al-ʿummâl* in the margins of *Musnad Ibn Ḥanbal* (6 vols., al-Maktab al-islâmî, Beirut 1969).

Shîʿa

ABḎ: Sharâf al-Dîn ʿAlî al-Ḥusaynî al-Astarâbâḏî (pupil of ʿAlî b. al-Ḥusayn b. ʿAbd al- ʿÂlî al-Karakî al-Muḥaqqiq al-Ṯânî, d. 946/1538: cf. GAL S. II: 575) in his *Taʾwîl al-âyât al-bâhira fî faḍl al-ʿitra al-ṭâhira* (CRCIS, Qum 2000).

11TH/17TH CENTURY

Sunnî

IṢM: ʿAbd al-Malik b. al-Ḥusayn b. ʿAbd al-Malik al-ʿIṣâmî (d. 1111/1699: cf. GAL S. II: 516) in his *Simṭ al-nuǧûm al-ʿawâlî* (4 vols., al-Maṭbaʿa al-salafiyya, Cairo 1961).

Shîʿa

SHT: al-Qâḍî Nûr Allâh al-Marʿashî al-Shûshtarî (d. 1019/1610: cf. GAL S. II: 607) in his *al-Ṣawârim al-muḥriqa fî dafʿ al-ṣawâʿiq al-muḥriqa* (CRCIS, Qum 2000).

ḤRR¹: Muḥammad b. al-Ḥasan al-Ḥasanî b. ʿAlî b. Ḥusayn al-Ḥurr al-ʿÂmilî al-Mashġarî (d. 1099/1688: cf. GAL S. II: 578) in his *Tafṣîl wasâʾil al-shîʿa ilâ taḥṣîl masâʾil al-sharîʿa* (30 vols., Mu'assasat âl al-bayt, Qum 1994), and **ḤRR²**: in his *al-Ǧawâhir al-saniyya al-aḥâdîṯ al-qudsiyya* (Mu'assasat al-ʿalamiyya, Beirut 1982).

BḤR: Hâshim b. Sulaymân b. Ismâʿîl b. ʿAbd al-Ǧawâd b. ʿAbd al-Raḥmân al-Ḥusaynî al-Baḥrânî (d. 1107/1695: cf. GAL S. II: 506) in his *al-Burhân fî tafsîr al-qurʾân* (4 vols., Mu'assasat al-wafâʾ, Beirut 1983).

12TH/18TH CENTURY

Sunnî

ṢBB: ʿAbd al-ʿIrfân Muḥammad b. ʿAlî al-Ṣabbân (d. 1206/1792: cf. GAL S. II: 399) in his *Isʿâf al-râġibîn* in the margins of *Nûr al-abṣâr fî manâqib âl bayt al-nabî al-muḫtâr* (al-Maṭbaʿa al-ʿâmira al-sharafiyya, Cairo 1898).

Shîʿa

BAḤ: ʿAbd Allâh b. Nûr Allâh al-Baḥrânî al-Iṣfahânî (d. 1110/1698: cf. GAL S. II: 504) in his *ʿAwâlim al-ʿulûm wa al-maʿârif al-aḥwâl min al-âyât wa-l-aḫbâr wal-aqwâl* (CRCIS, Qum 2000).

MǦL: Muḥammad Bâqir b. Muḥammad Taqî b. Maqṣûd ʿAlî Akmal al-Maǧlisî al-Iṣfahânî (d. 1110/1700: cf. GAL S. II: 572) in his *Biḥâr al-anwâr* (110 vols., Dâr al-kutub al-islâmiyya, Tehran 1924–1935).

13TH/19TH CENTURY

Sunnî

SHL: Mu'min b. Ḥasan Mu'min al-Shablanǧî (d. c. 1301/1883: cf. GAL S. II: 737) in his *Nûr al-abṣâr fî manâqib âl bayt al-nabî al-muḫtâr* (al-Maṭbaʿa al-ʿâmira al-sharafiyya, Cairo 1898).

14TH/20TH CENTURY

Shîʿa

NṬR: al-Ḥâǧǧ Mîrzâ Ḥusayn b. Muḥammad Taqî al-Nûrî al-Ṭabarsî (d. 1320/1902: cf. GAL S. II: 832) in his *Ḫâtimat mustadrak al-wasâʾil* (CRCIS, Qum 2000).

ṬBṬ: Muḥammad Ḥusayn al-Ṭabâṭabâʾî (d. 1983) in his *al-Mîzân fî tafsîr al-qurʾân* (21 vols., al-Kutub al-islâmiyya, Tehran 1977).

LIST OF ABBREVIATIONS

A.D.	*Anno Domini*
b.	*bin* (son)
bb.	*bâb* (chapter)
B.C.	before Christ
bk.	book
bt.	*bint* (daughter)
c.	*circa*
CE.	common era
cf.	confer
ch.	chapter
Col.	The Letter to the Colossians
CRCIS	Computer Research Center of Islamic Sciences
d.	died
Dan.	The Book of Daniel
DENZ.	*Enchiridion symbolorum definitionem et declarationum de rebus fidei et morum*
ed.	editor
edn.	edition

edns.	editions
eds.	editors
eg.	for example
EI^2	Encyclopaedia of Islam, 2ND Edition
et al.	and others
etc.	*etcetera*
Ez.	The Book of Ezekiel
ff.	following
GAL	*Geschichte der arabischen Literatur*
GAS	*Geschichte der arabischen Schrifttums*
Gen.	The Book of Genesis
Ibid.	*ibidem*
Jdg.	The Book of Judges
Jn.	The Gospel of Saint John
Kgs.	The Book of Kings
lit.	literally
Lk.	The Gospel of Saint Luke
L.G.	*Lumen Gentium*
Mach.	The Book of Machabees
MIDEO	*Mélanges de l'Institut Dominicain d'Études Orientales du Caire*
Mk.	The Gospel of Saint Mark
MOD.	Tradition and Survival. A Bibliographical Survey of Early Shī'ite Literature
Mt.	The Gospel of Saint Matthew
n.	number
NCE^2	New Catholic Encyclopaedia, 2ND Edition
n.d.	no date
Nm.	The Book of Numbers
nn.	numbers
n.n.	no number
n.p.	no publisher
nt.	footnote

pl.	plural
Q.	Qurʾân
Rev.	The Book of Revelation
Rm.	The Letter to the Romans
SEI	The Shorter Encyclopaedia of Islam
sic	thus
St.	Saint
sing.	singular
trans.	translator
v.	verse
vol.	volume
vols.	volumes
vv.	verses

INTRODUCTION

Muḥammad died in June 11/632, according to some texts with his head cradled on the lap of his young wife ʿÂʾisha, daughter of Abû Bakr.[1] From the shadows, his only surviving daughter Fâṭima glared balefully through her tears at the widow-to-be. There was already little love lost between these two women, and now ʿÂʾisha had ostensibly ousted Fâṭima from her father's side at a crucial moment. Fâṭima would die a few months later, but not before ʿÂʾisha had suffered her wrath, banned from her deathbed and her funeral. Nor would ʿÂʾisha be the only one; Abû Bakr himself would experience Fâṭima's vehemence during the last months of her life, not only for his usurpation, in Shîʿî eyes, of the power that rightly belonged to others, but also for his treatment of Muḥammad's daughter over her inheritance.

The aim of this work is to appraise the life of Fâṭima, daughter of Muḥammad, at the level of the copious extant Arabic texts, noting throughout the vast discrepancies that exist between the Shîʿî and Sunnî sources and interpretations. It will be primarily in the Shîʿî texts of *aḥâdîṯ* that we will happen upon a Fâṭima who is startlingly unique and set apart from all other women.

> On the Day of Resurrection, a herald will call from the middle of the throne: "O people of the Resurrection, lower your gaze, for Fâṭima the daughter of Muḥammad is crossing with a shirt stained with the blood of al-Ḥusayn." She will embrace the leg of the throne and say: "You are the Omnipotent, the Just! Judge between me and those who killed my son. God will

[1] ʿAbd Allâh Abû Bakr (d. 12/634), the first to succeed Muḥammad in leadership of the community. The Shîʿa hold that Muḥammad died leaning on Abû Bakr, and not on ʿÂʾisha.

> judge by my *sunna*" – and then she will say: "O God, grant me intercession on behalf of whoever weeps over his misfortune!" And God will grant her intercession on their behalf.

This pious story, elements of which are found in similar forms in many of the major collections of Shîʿî *aḥâdît*, together with those *aḥâdît* that describe in some detail the entry of Fâṭima, arrayed in vestments of light, into Paradise, offers us several noteworthy clues as to how the Shîʿa envisage her, and provides us with a framework in which to read their conception of the more mundane aspects of her life. On earth she was impoverished and weak, but her reward in heaven will comprise incalculable riches, including jeweled habitations, not for her alone but also for her adherents (*shîʿa*). On earth she was neglected, marginalized, maltreated and divested of justice, but in heaven all the populace of that place will bow their heads in deference to her, and her company will be the angels and those richly blessed by God. On earth she wept and grieved after the death of her father Muḥammad; even after her own death, her grieving continues unceasingly over the murder of her son al-Ḥusayn and the ill-treatment afforded Muḥammad's family, the 'people of the house' (*ahl al-bayt*). But on the Day of Judgment she will be vindicated, the first to enter Paradise, and all her tears will be wiped away, as a dreadful punishment is meted out to her son's murderers. There in that place, this modest and frail woman, who laboured under such a burden of weakness during her life, will be endowed with untold power, making intercession before God for those who love and adhere to her.

I have chosen four salient features of Fâṭima's life through which to consider her position, above all in Shîʿî Islam:

1. Her birth, and specifically the annunciation and supernatural intervention surrounding her conception and parturition as recounted in the Shîʿî *aḥâdît*, teaching and piety.

2. The miracle stories recorded by the Shîʿa concerning the annunciation, conception and birth of her son al-Ḥusayn.

3. Fâṭima as the 'woman of sorrow', and particularly the crucial Shîʿî concept of her necessary grief and mourning, intimately connected with the martyrdom of her son al-Ḥusayn.

4. The intercessory prerogatives of Fâṭima, envisaged as a consequence of her high standing and a reward for her sufferings, giving her startling powers on the Day of Judgment.

These four categories will be considered primarily through the corpus of Shîʿî *aḥâdîṯ*, teaching and popular piety, including the reinterpretation of Fâṭima's life and role from the writings of more contemporary scholars like ʿAli Shariati (d. 1977).

A methodical examination of Fâṭima as she is defined in the Shîʿî sources presents us at once with an enigma and a number of attendant questions. The enigma arises from the paucity of references to her in the earliest extant texts,[2] weighed against prolific references in later sources; the dilemma between Fâṭima as an ordinary woman (if being the daughter of Muḥammad and the wife of ʿAlî b. Abî Ṭâlib, she could be described as such) and Fâṭima the 'sinless virgin', chief of the women of paradise (and ostensibly even of the women of the world), the converser with angels and the heavenly intercessor. The questions turn around this very issue; when did Fâṭima receive these titles and this status? Why do some of the earliest texts, such as the treasured *Nahǧ al-balâġa* (the collection of sermons and speeches of her husband ʿAlî), *al-Ṣaḥîfa al-saǧǧâdiyya* regarded as the oldest prayer manual in Islamic sources and ascribed to her grandson ʿAlî b. al-Ḥusayn (Zayn al-ʿÂbidîn), and the *Sîrat Muḥammad Rasûl Allâh* edited by the Sunnî scholar Ibn Hishâm,[3] scarcely mention her?

---

[2] In fact, she is acknowledged a number of times, for example, by al-Hilâlî in his *Kitâb Sulaym b. Qays*. This is held by some (but certainly not all) scholars to be the oldest surviving Shîʿî text, the author dying around the year 80/662. In this text Fâṭima is already referred to as 'the mistress of the women of paradise'.

[3] She is mentioned in connection with ʿAlî's nickname 'father of dust'; one interpretation (among a number) of this nickname recounts that when ʿAlî was angry with Fâṭima he would not speak to her but would sprinkle dust over his head. Guillame notes that whenever Muḥammad saw dust on ʿAlî's head, he knew that they had been arguing. She is referred to again in the incident of the washing of the swords after the battle of Uḥud. She is described as screening her father with his garment while he washed. Finally, she is named in connection with the incidents imme-

Indisputably, running deeply through the Shîʿî ethos was the steady realization that they would never attain to the power they maintained was their due, and the concomitant turning increasingly to a supernatural, other-worldly power; this would profoundly colour their conception not only of Fâṭima but of all the *ahl al-bayt.* From about the 4TH/10TH century, in tandem with the rise of several minor and some major Shîʿî or pro-Shîʿî dynasties (the Fâṭimid of Egypt[4] and the Bûyid of Iran[5]), Fâṭima's image changes progressively but considerably. The Fâṭimids asserted descent from her, and it was during the Bûyid period in Persia that public mourning for her martyred son al-Ḥusayn was first performed in that country, with public commemorations of Karbalâʾ ordered by the Bûyid leader Aḥmad b. Bûya around 350/962. From this time, she becomes increasingly more flawless and ever less an ordinary woman. With the 10TH/16TH century, the rise of the Ṣafavid dynasty[6] and the encyclopedic collection of *aḥâdîṯ* by al-Mağlisî in his *Biḥâr al-anwâr* ('The Oceans of Lights'), her translation into a woman of substantial import and holiness is complete; a number of titles are conferred upon her, each a manifestation of one or more of her saintly attributes.

In order to underscore the quandary, it would be helpful to scan four fundamental trends. Her image is not much altered since Ṣafavid times, barring one major exception, in the form of ʿAli

---

diately after her father's death. She is also singled out in a fragment of the lost biographical work of Mûsâ b. ʿUqba, in a *ḥadîṯ* which runs: "The Apostle used not to make an exception for Fâṭima." This is understood by some as a reference to the *ḥadîṯ* in which Muḥammad says that if Fâṭima were to steal he would cut off her hand. All of these incidents are examined in this work. Cf. GUILLAME A., *The Life of Muhammad. A Translation of Ibn Ishaq's Sirat Rasul Allah*, Oxford University Press, Oxford 2006: xiv.

[4] 297/909 – 567/1171. Cf. BOSWORTH C.E., *Islamic Surveys 5. The Islamic Dynasties*, Edinburgh University Press, Edinburgh 1967: 46.

[5] 320/932 – 454/1062. Cf. BOSWORTH C.E., *Islamic Surveys 5. The Islamic Dynasties*, 1967: 94.

[6] 907/1501 – 1145/1732. Cf. BOSWORTH C.E., *Islamic Surveys 5. The Islamic Dynasties*, 1967: 172.

Shariati's celebrated book, *Fatima is Fatima*.[7] A French-educated sociologist, and extremely popular in Iran since the 1970s, Shariati propounded his own very distinct vision of Islam and of society in general. The 'West' represented corruption, imperialism, capitalism and commercialism. The 'East' had experienced a splendid past, but had degenerated in the hands of dictatorial leaders and opportunist clerics. The Iranian Pahlavî dynasty[8] had created a class of women with no identity, distorted and cut-off from their origins, heritage and fate. The good Muslim woman had become confused and disorientated, not wanting to be like her mother, but not knowing what she wanted or who she was. Into this state of affairs Shariati introduced his archetypal woman, Fâṭima, as a role model for Muslim women, as the woman that Islam would want every woman to be. Shariati's Fâṭima is not the 'Queen of Heaven', and is wholly without supernatural attributes; in some ways inimitable, but always entirely human. By her own will and sound judgment, she had chosen to be loyal, devoted, compassionate and ready to sacrifice herself for her family and her true fate. All women in Iran, posited Shariati, should adhere to her example and be, like her, an object of sacrifice. This image was taken up enthusiastically by women during the Iranian Revolution, only to be discarded and critically questioned by most women two decades later.

A second trend arises virtually as a reaction against Shariati, as we encounter fresh contemporary debates around Fâṭima's personality. Rosiny[9] recounts a deliberation between two Lebanese Shîʿî theologians representing two distinct tendencies; Ǧaʿfar Murtaḍâ al-ʿÂmilî, representing the conservative 'historical school' and Muḥammad Ḥusayn Faḍlallâh, spiritual leader of *Ḥizbullâh* and a modern reformist. The discussion centers around the incident, shortly after the death of Muḥammad and the nomination of Abû

[7] SHARIATI A., *Fatima is Fatima*, The Shariati Foundation, Tehran (n.d.).

[8] 1344/1925 – 1399/1979. Cf. BOSWORTH C.E., *Islamic Surveys 5. The Islamic Dynasties*, 1967: 180.

[9] ROSINY S., "The Tragedy of Fāṭima al-Zahrā' in the Debate of Two Shiite Theologians in Lebanon" in R. BRUNNER and W. ENDE (eds.), *The Twelver Shia in Modern Times*, Brill, Leiden 2001: 207–219.

Bakr as the first of the four 'rightly-guided Caliphs' (*râshidûn*), usurped, in the Shîʿî view, from ʿAlî; it appears that the intention of Abû Bakr, ʿUmar[10] and some others, angered by ʿAlî's refusal to pay allegiance (*bayʿa*), was to take him by force to the mosque and compel him to do so. An armed group went to the house of ʿAlî and Fâṭima, threatening to set fire to it. They forced their way in, ostensibly seriously injuring Fâṭima in the process, possibly even beating her and thereby causing the miscarriage of her unborn son.[11] There are numerous reports of this incident, each of them diverse and recounting disparate information.

Although he does not contest some sort of attack, Faḍlallâh refuses to allow himself to be influenced by the narratives about the physical violence perpetrated against Fâṭima, claiming that the stories are weakly documented or contradictory, and that there are too many legends that are embellished and difficult to substantiate. He censures many of the texts about Fâṭima, such as those which recount her being created out of light; instead, he wants the transmitters to accentuate her political, religious and social activities, so that she could become a model for the modern activist female Muslim. Fâṭima's life demonstrates that it is possible for women to enter fully into the cultural and social *milieu*, and offers a paradigm for imitation. Faḍlallâh depicts the *ahl al-bayt* as comprising human beings with explicable reasons for their actions and habits, and underscores the human traits of the Shîʿî holy ones, so as to offer them as prototypes for contemporary life.

Al-ʿÂmilî defends the miraculous aspects of Shîʿî belief about Fâṭima, portraying her as a badly tyrannized woman (*al-maẓlûma*). He regards the mystical (some would say mythical) aspects of Fâṭima as crucial to Shîʿî belief, so that minimizing or denying them would in consequence seriously demoralize the faith. He calls attention to many of these *aḥâdîṯ*; among them, her creation from a fruit of paradise, her conversing with her mother from the womb,

---

10 ʿUmar b. al-Ḫaṭṭâb (d. 22/644), the second to succeed Muḥammad in leadership of the community.

11 This is the claim of the Shîʿa: but cf. **ḤNB**., vol. I, *Musnad ʿAlî b. Abî Ṭâlib*, n. 769: 211–212, n. 953: 250–251, where his birth is recorded, and n. 1370: 335 where it is omitted.

her preservation from menstruation, and her never having shed blood when giving birth.

A third, much older trend, and an example of the extreme 'divinization' of Fâṭima, is her assessment in the creed and liturgy of the Nuṣayrî sect (also known as the ʿAlawî),[12] which developed from a radical Shîʿî group[13] and which has been dominant in Syria for the last thirty or more years.[14] The crux of heterodox Nuṣayrî belief consists in the deification of ʿAlî b. Abî Ṭâlib, husband of Fâṭima and cousin of Muḥammad, thus decisively placing this sect amongst the extremists (*ġulât*), a category pertaining to groups positing that a particular person is God or that a particular person is a prophet after Muḥammad. A number of Nuṣayrî texts are extant; these include *Munâẓarat al-shayḫ al-Naṣṣâbî tataḍammanu aḫaṣṣa ʿaqâʾidi-him bi-l-tawḥîd* (a 7TH/13TH treatise on Nuṣayrî 'trinitarian' theology) and al-Ṭabarânî's *Maǧmûʿ al-aʿyâd* (on the Nuṣayrî liturgical calendar).[15] An astonishing and radical picture of Fâṭima emerges from these and other texts; credited with a special status as the mother of ʿAlî's sons and a member of the 'holy family', she is regarded as the patroness of the nineteenth and twenty-third nights of the month of Ramaḍân. As regards the 'night midway through the month of Shaʿbân' (*laylat al-niṣf min shaʿbân*), which is associated with the 'night of power' (*laylat al-qadr*) and is regarded as one of the most important nights of the year for divine blessing, al-

---

[12] Cf. KRAMER M., "Syria's Alawis and Shi'ism" in M. KRAMER (ed.), *Shiʾism, Resistance and Revolution*, Westview Press, Colorado 1987: 237–254.

[13] The Nuṣayrî began as a group (after the death of the tenth Imâm) under the leadership of Muḥammad b. Nuṣayr al-Namîrî, about whose teachings (mostly extremist) there are diverse opinions. In fact, the real founder of the sect was Ḥusayn b. Ḥamdân al-Ḫaṣîbî, and they remain politically active in Syria. Cf. MOMEN M., *An Introduction to Shiʾi Islam. The History and Doctrines of Twelver Shiʾism*, Yale University Press, New Haven 1985: 58.

[14] Cf. BAR ASHER M. B. and KOFSKY A., *The Nuṣayrī-ʿAlawī Religion. An Enquiry into its Theology and Liturgy*, Brill, Leiden 2002.

[15] Abû Saʿîd Maymûn b. al-Qâsim al-Ṭabarânî (d. 426/1034: cf. GAS I: 584, where the work is unrecorded).

Ṭabarânî posits that six nights of Ramaḍân are consecrated to Fâṭima, who is further identified as the person of the 'night of power' and the 'night midway through the month of Shaʿbân'. Fâṭima is named with her masculine title – *al-Fâṭir.* One author notes:

> The need to present Fāṭima substantially as a masculine divine entity historically disguised as a female is a common Nuṣayrī motif deriving from the tension created by introducing a feminine element into the divine realm.[16]

Under that masculine title, and together with her sons, she is identified with Muḥammad, his substance and his light (*ḥaqîqa muḥammadiyya wa-nûr muḥammadî*). In the Nuṣayrî view, the historical appearance of Fâṭima in the form of a female took place merely to confound those who are weak of mind.

For al-Ṭabarânî, the 'night midway through the month of Shaʿbân' is even more important than the six distinguished nights of the month of Ramaḍân; and while the divine power manifested on this night is identified with Muḥammad, the night itself is identified with Fâṭima, who is conceived of as the inner mystery of Muḥammad; the two are in essence one and the same, in a sort of hypostatic identity. It is thus, with Muḥammad identified with the divine power and Fâṭima conceived of as his essence, that she is equated with 'night of power'. It is only the feeble-minded who regard Fâṭima as an ordinary woman of flesh and blood; she is named *Fâṭir* because she is the one who created the creatures and shaped them. The angels who brought down God's decrees on that night were possessors of the true knowledge of Fâṭima. For al-Ṭabarânî therefore, the theological weight of the 'night midway through the month of Shaʿbân' lies with Fâṭima, who is the feminine manifestation of the masculine second person of the deity (her father Muḥammad). She remains an ongoing presence in Nuṣayrî religious history and consciousness (through the medium of the Imâms and perhaps even their own religious leaders) and is under-

---

[16] BAR-ASHER M. B. and KOFSKY A., *The Nuṣayrī-ʿAlawī Religion. An Enquiry into its Theology and Liturgy*, 2002: 144.

stood as exercising an eschatological role in preparing for the coming of the redeemer. It could, writes our author,

> ...be argued that...the festival of mid-Shaʿbān is primarily a celebration of Fāṭima as the divine mother, the consort of the supreme deity, ʿAlī, and the mother of his divine descendants. It could further be argued that in this symbolism Muḥammad as the second person of the trinity becomes somewhat redundant, which may help to explain the strong emphasis on the absolute identity of Fāṭima and Muḥammad, stressing the feminine aspect of the masculine deity.[17]

A final trend is encountered among Western orientalists, for our purposes best represented by two: Louis Massignon (d. 1962), attracted by Fâṭima as he was by other Islamic personalities, found numerous, if not obvious, parallels between Fâṭima and Christian figures, and developed them positively in his writings.[18] Almost wholly opposed to Massignon (and predating him) is the Jesuit priest Henri Lammens (d. 1937), with his curiously idiosyncratic vision of Islam;[19] he accepts solely the fact that Fâṭima existed, scathingly rejecting the *aḥâdîṯ* and theology constructed around her, and dismissing her as a lackluster, unattractive and disconsolate creature, a source of annoyance to her father and of irritation to her husband.[20] In this, he fairly echoes the traditionalist Sunnî historian Ibn Kaṯîr, who remarked that Fâṭima was merely a woman

---

[17] BAR-ASHER M. B. and KOFSKY A., *The Nuṣayrī-ʿAlawī Religion. An Enquiry into its Theology and Liturgy*, 2002: 146.

[18] MASSIGNON L., "Der Gnostische Kult der Fatima im Schiitischen Islam" in *Opera Minora* Tome I, Dar al-Maaref, Beirut 1963: 514–522; "La Mubahala de Médine et l'Hyperdulie de Fatima" in *Opera Minora* Tome I, 1963: 550–572; "La Notion de Voeu et la Dévotion Musulmane à Fatima" in *Opera Minora* Tome I, 1963: 573–591; and "L'Oratoire de Marie à l'Acqa, vu sous le Voile de Deuil de Fatima" in *Opera Minora* Tome I, 1963: 592–618.

[19] Cf. LAMMENS H., "Fatima and the Daughters of Muhammad" in Ibn Warraq (ed. and trans.), *The Quest for the Historical Muhammad*, Prometheus Books, New York 2000: 218–329.

[20] Ibid.

"who could not hope for infallibility"[21] (expressing the concept of 'infallibility' with the Arabic *ʿiṣma*, a term much employed for Fâṭima by the Shîʿa, who use it in the sense of 'impeccability' and 'infallibility').

Our task is to unearth the authentic Fâṭima, who must lie somewhere between the heterodox Nuṣayrî, the traditionalists represented by Ǧaʿfar Murtaḍâ al-ʿÂmilî (and the whole corpus of Shîʿî *aḥâdîṯ*), the disparate Western orientalists and the revolutionary, sometimes almost secular Shariati. Considering the age of the majority of sources available, the line between historicity and hagiography is bound to become hazy. Supposedly, one could use a sort of *via negativa* to arrive at the element of truth around which the hagiographers have constructed their narratives. However, it is precisely here that Lammens' scathing attack on Fâṭima must be judged, at the very least, to be reductionist.[22] He dismisses the whole body of Shîʿî *aḥâdîṯ* as spurious and, in contrast, appears to accept uncritically the Sunnî corpus as authentic, since he uses it to bolster his anti-Fâṭima stance. However, he fails to see that she has, in many Sunnî *aḥâdîṯ*, a distinct status, at the very least as the member of a very exclusive and revered household, and that a substantial number of Sunnî *aḥâdîṯ*, as we shall discover, exalt her standing somewhat more radically.

1. The Primary Shîʿî and Sunnî Arabic Sources

The primary Arabic sources for this study are chiefly the collections of *aḥâdîṯ*, both Shîʿî and Sunnî, but these are copious, and I have made a strict selection, within a number of categories, so that this text does not grow cumbersome. A full list of these sources is provided. If I have deliberately chosen to use what appears to be an inordinate number of Sunnî sources for an ostensibly Shîʿî study, it is in order to examine the authentic status of Fâṭima among Sunnî transmitters and scholars. Among the Sunnî collections of *aḥâdîṯ*, I

---

[21] **KṮR¹**., vol. V: 249.

[22] Nabia Abbott accuses him of the same sort of extremism concerning his view of ʿÂʾisha: cf. ABBOTT N., *Aishah the Beloved of Mohammed*, Saqi Books, London 1988: xviii.

have used Ibn Ḥanbal in his *Musnad* and three of the 'six books' (*al-ṣiḥâḥ al-sitta*):[23] al-Buḫârî in his *Ṣaḥîḥ*, Muslim in his *Ṣaḥîḥ* and al-Tirmiḏî in his *Sunan*. All of these contain whole chapters devoted to the merits of Fâṭima, as well as chapters on ʿAlî and the *ahl al-bayt*. Among the other Sunnî authors, I have selected two who, although sometimes accused of being crypto-Shîʿa, remain firmly in the Sunnî camp: al-Nîsâbûrî in his *Kitâb (Talḫîs) al-mustadrak ʿalâ al-ṣaḥîḥayn* (and in which he devotes a whole chapter to Fâṭima and her virtues), and al-Ḫawârizmî in his *Maqtal al-Ḥusayn*. Al-Ḫawârizmî is a Ḥanafî Sunnî transmitter who has great devotion to the family of Muḥammad, making him a rich source for research into Fâṭima.

The books of Shîʿî *aḥâdîṯ* are no less plentiful, and I have selected a careful number. Firstly, al-Hilâlî in his *Kitâb Sulaym b. Qays*; this work, in a single volume, is reputedly the oldest extant Shîʿî text in terms of *aḥâdîṯ*,[24] and is therefore an extremely valuable source for discerning Fâṭima's early status among the Shîʿa. Another very early work and thus invaluable source is Ibn Rustam al-Ṭabarî's *Dalâʾil al-imâma*.[25] As noted below, this al-Ṭabarî is a Shîʿa, not to be confused with his Sunnî counterparts of the same name.

---

[23] That is, the six collections confirmed by the consensus (*iǧmâʿ*) of the Sunnî.

[24] Kohlberg notes that the *Kitâb Sulaym b. Qays* was named after its supposed author, the pro-ʿAlid Sulaym b. Qays al-Hilâlî al-ʿÂmirî, who died during the governorship of the Umayyad al-Haǧǧâǧ b. Yûsuf (75/694 – 95/714). The Shîʿî bibliographer Ibn al-Nadîm (d. 385/995 or 388/998) regarded it as the first Shîʿî work, but later Shîʿî scholars took a much more skeptical view (shared by Goldziher), and some openly declare it a fabrication. Cf. KOHLBERG E., "Shīʿī *Hadīth*" in A.F.L. Beeston et al., (eds.), *Arabic Literature to the End of the Umayyad Period*, Cambridge University Press, Cambridge 1983: 301.

[25] According to Modarressi, this work is also known as *Musnad Fâṭima* or *Manâqib Fâṭima wa-wuldi-hâ*. Cf. MODARRESSI H., *Tradition and Survival. A Bibliographical Survey of Early Shīʿite Literature*, vol. 1, Oneworld, Oxford 2003: 21–22.

Al-Kulaynî's[26] *al-Kâfî fî ʿilm al-dîn* is one of the 'four books' regarded as canonical by Shîʿî scholars; written over a period of twenty years, it comprises over sixteen thousand *aḥâdîṯ* transmitted through the *ahl al-bayt*, and encompasses the entire doctrine of the Imamate. I have used chiefly three works by *Shayḫ* al-Ṣadûq,[27] since in his works we find the largest grouping of early *aḥâdîṯ* about Fâṭima; these are his *Kitâb al-amâlî fî al-aḥâdîṯ wa-l-aḫbâr*, his *Ikmâl (kamâl) al-dîn wa-itmâm (tamâm) al-niʿma fî iṯbât al-ġayba wa-kashf al-ḥayra* (dealing mostly with the occultation and return of the twelfth Imâm), and his *Man lâ yaḥḍuru-hu al-faqîh*. This latter text, comprising nearly six thousand *aḥâdîṯ*, many of them legal, is another of the four canonical Shîʿî books. I have utilized *Shayḫ* al-Mufîd[28] in his *al-Irshâd fî maʿrifat ḥuğağ Allâh ʿalâ al-ʿibâd* (much of which is devoted to biographical details of ʿAlî b. Abî Ṭâlib), Ibn Shahrâshûb[29] in his five volume *Manâqib âl Abî Ṭâlib* and *Shayḫ* al-Ṭâʾifa[30] in his *al-*

---

[26] The dates of al-Kulaynî's life are problematic. His date of birth is unknown, and the date of his death in Baghdad is disputed. 328/941 is the date agreed upon by al-Nağâshî and al-Tûsî, while others insist upon 327/940. Of a certainty he lived during the time of the minor occultation (*al-ġayba al-suġrâ*) of the twelfth Imâm. The work took twenty years to complete. Cf. AKHTAR S.W., *The Early Imāmiyyah Shiʾite Thinkers*, Ashish Publishing House, New Delhi 1988: 12. Cf. also MADELUNG W., "al-Kulayni" in H.A.R. Gibb et al. (eds.), *EI*², E.J. Brill, Leiden 1993, vol. Va: 362–363.

[27] Born around 306/918 in Qum, he traveled extensively gathering *aḥâdîṯ*, and was a prolific writer, with approximately three-hundred works to his name.

[28] Born around 336/948 or 338/950, he studied in Baghdad under al-Sadûq, as well as under a number of prominent Muʿtazilî scholars. His intelligence was noted by Shîʿa and Sunnî alike, but he was expelled for a time from Baghdad after serious Shîʿî-Sunnî clashes.

[29] Born around 489/1096, he was a popular preacher in Baghdad for a while, but finally settled in Aleppo. Although he was a prominent jurist, he is best remembered for his biographical works.

[30] Born in 385/955, he studied in Tûs, and then continued his studies in Baghdad under al-Mufîd (among others). He was soon the leading scholar in Baghdad, teaching a large student body. Although his most

Amâlî fî-l-ḥadît. I have also examined two works by Ibn Ṭâʾûs,[31] *Kitâb al-iqbâl bi-l-aʿmâl al-ḥasana* and *al-Ṭarâʾif fî maʿrifat madhab al-ṭawâʾif*, and two by al-Ḥillî al-ʿAllâma,[32] *Kashf al-yaqîn fî faḍâʾil amîr al-muʾminîn* and *Nahğ al-ḥaqq wa-kashf al-ṣidq.*[33]

Almost as highly regarded as the 'four books' is the encyclopedic collection of *aḥâdît* entitled *Biḥâr al-anwâr* by al-Mağlisî;[34] in over one hundred volumes, it is a principal source for all Shîʿî-related research, and among all other Shîʿî texts and sources, I have used it as the dominant and elemental one. In a sense, al-Mağlisî ought to be classed as a secondary source, since his is a compilation of earlier works. Additionally, he must be used with great caution; al-Mağlisî is an ardent gatherer of *aḥâdît*, and pays scant attention to grading them in terms of their reliability. His work therefore comprises a fusion of *aḥâdît*, some of which are transmitted by the ma-

---

important collections of *aḥâdît* are extant, the burning of his library during Shîʿî-Sunnî clashes in Baghdad may have resulted in the loss of some of his writings.

[31] Famous as a poet and an ascetic, he was born in 589/1193 and lived in Baghdad for a quarter of a century, as well as for short period in Nağaf and Karbalâʾ. A number of his works are extant.

[32] Born in 648/1250, he studied under Ibn Ṭâʾûs, as well as a number of other Shîʿî and Sunnî scholars, and is the author of numerous books (possibly up to five hundred), especially in the area of jurisprudence. Cf. JAFRI S.H.M., "al-Hillī" in in H.A.R. Gibb et al. (eds.), *EI*², 1993, vol. IIIa: 390.

[33] Momen mistakenly imputes the work *Kashf al-yaqîn* to Ibn Ṭâʾûs (cf. MOMEN M., *An Introduction to Shiʾi Islam. The History and Doctrines of Twelver Shiʾism*, 1985: 314). In fact, the work of Ibn Ṭâʾûs is entitled *Kitâb al-yaqîn bi-iḫtiṣâṣ mawlâ-nâ ʿAlî bi-imârat al-muʾminîn* (cf. GAL S I: 911). The work *Kashf al-yaqîn fî faḍâʾil amîr al-muʾminîn* is by al-Ḥillî al-ʿAllâma, who was a pupil of Ibn Ṭâʾûs (cf. GAL S II: 207; MOD: 421).

[34] Born in Isfahân in 1038/1628, his teachers included his own father. He became the foremost Shîʿî scholar of his era, and is remembered for his campaigns against the Sunnî, the Ṣûfî mystics and the mystical philosophers. His collection of *aḥâdît* is among sixty books accredited to him.

jor Shîʿî sources and others of which are not.[35] His forty-third volume is devoted entirely to Fâṭima, and is thus indispensable.

Finally, I have used al-Qummî in his *al-Faḍâʾil* and al-Ṭabarsî in his *Ḫâtimat mustadrak al-wasâʾil*. This latter work is a supplement to another work of al-Ḥurr al-ʿÂmilî (*Tafṣîl wasâʾil al-shîʿa ilâ taḥṣîl masâʾil al-sharîʿa*), in which al-Ṭabarsî added material he thought important and omitted by al-Ḥurr al-ʿÂmilî.

I have made use of five Sunnî historians, and two from among the Shîʿa. The Sunnî are al-Ṭabarî in his *Kitâb aḫbâr al-rusul wa-l-mulûk*, al-Baġdâdî in his *Târîḫ Baġdâd*, Ibn Kaṯîr in his *al-Bidâya wa-l-nihâya*, Ibn ʿAsâkir in his *Târîḫ madînat Dimashq* and Ibn al-Aṯîr in his *al-Kâmil fî-l-târîḫ*. Their Shîʿî colleagues are al-Yaʿqûbî[36] in his *Târîḫ* and al-Masʿûdî in his *Murûǧ al-ḏahab*.

Among the Sunnî scholars of exegesis (*tafsîr*), I have utilized the writings of al-Ṭabarî in his *Ǧâmiʿ al-bayân ʿan taʾwîl al-qurʾân*, al-Zamaḫsharî in his *al-Kashshâf ʿan ḥaqâʾiq al-tanzîl wa-ʿuyûn al-aqâwîl fî wuǧûh al-taʾwîl*, al-Râzî in his *al-Tafsîr al-kabîr*, al-Qurṭubî in his *Kitâb al-ǧâmiʿ li-aḥkâm al-qurʾân*, Ibn Kaṯîr in his *Tafsîr al-qurʾân al-ʿaẓîm* and al-Suyûṭî in his *al-Durr al-manṯûr fî-l-tafsîr bi-l-maʾṯûr*. Because the exegetical stress of this work concerns the Sunnî interpretation of Fâṭima, I have taken into consideration only three Shîʿî exegetes: al-Ṭabarsî in his *Maǧmaʿ al-bayân fî tafsîr al-qurʾân*,[37] al-Baḥrânî in his *al-Burhân fî tafsîr al-qurʾân* and the more contemporary al-Ṭabâṭabâʾî in his *al-Mîzân fî tafsîr al-qurʾân*.

In order to highlight the person of Fâṭima in Shîʿî devotion, I have also included two manuals of spirituality among the sources: Ibn Qûlûya al-Qummî in his *Kâmil al-ziyârât* and Ibn Ṭâʾûs in his *Kitâb al-luhûf fî qatlâ al-ṭufûf*.

Lastly, among the works of biography and biographical compilations, I have examined three Sunnî authors: Ibn Hishâm in his

---

[35] However, as Kohlberg notes, al-Maǧlisî is scrupulous about naming his sources. Cf. KOHLBERG E., "Shīʿī *Hadīth*" in A.F.L. Beeston et al., (eds.), *Arabic Literature to the End of the Umayyad Period*, 1983: 307.

[36] Some scholars question al-Yaʿqûbî's Shîʿî credentials; if he was not, in fact, a Shîʿa, he had intensely strong Shîʿî dispositions.

[37] Brockelmann entitles the work *Maǧmaʿ al-bayân li-ʿulûm al-qurʾân*. Cf. GAL S. I: 708

Sîrat Muḥammad Rasûl Allâh, Ibn al-Aṯîr in his *Usd al-ġâba fî maʿrifat al-ṣaḥâba* and Ibn Saʿd in his *Kitâb al-ṭabaqât al-kabîr*.

2. THE SECONDARY SHÎʿÎ AND SUNNÎ ARABIC SOURCES

In terms of secondary Arabic sources (which may be regarded as such since, like al-Mağlisî, they are really compilations of early works), I have selected the following four texts: al-Fayrûzâbâdî in his three-volume *Faḍâʾil al-ḫamsa min al-ṣiḥâḥ al-sitta*, a compilation of all the Sunnî *aḥâdîṯ* about the *ahl al-bayt*; Muhammad al-Qazwînî in *Fâṭima al-Zahrâʾ min al-mahd ilâ al-laḥd*, a one-volume compilation of the words of Fâṭima and the *aḥâdîṯ* about her; Muhammad al-Mûsawî in *al-Kawṯar fî aḥwâl Fâṭima bt. al-nabî al-aṭhar*, a compilation in seven volumes of the life and virtues of Fâṭima according to the *aḥâdîṯ* of the Shîʿa;[38] and ʿAlî ʿÂshûr in *Fâṭima bt. Muhammad, qudwa li-l-nisâʾ*, a one-volume compilation of *aḥâdîṯ* about Fâṭima from the Shîʿî sources.

3. TWO PROBLEMATIC TEXTS

Two texts remain slightly enigmatic. The first text is that of Ibn al-Ḥadîd in his *Sharḥ nahğ al-balâġa*; while some claim that he was a Shîʿa, it is not utterly certain that he was. In a passage that concentrates on his brother, he is mentioned ambiguously by Modarressi,[39] who notes in passing that he transmitted from his uncle Abû Muḥammad Murâzim b. Ḥakîm al-Madâʾinî, who in turn transmitted from the fifth and sixth Imâms, but does not name the nephew's work. Brockelmann is equally imprecise. Some claim that al-Ḥadid was a Muʿtazila, but not a Shîʿa. In spite of a dearth of evidence, I have chosen to retain him among the Shîʿa, even though on a number of occasions, he carries *aḥâdîṯ* that are out of line with the Shîʿî stance, thus putting himself out of the Shîʿî ambit. Examples of these, listed later, are the alleged attempt at a second mar-

---

[38] These volumes are unfortunately not without textual errors in their transmission of *aḥâdîṯ*, and although they serve as a useful reference point, cannot be regarded as textually reliable.

[39] MODARRESSI H., *Tradition and Survival. A Bibliographical Survey of Early Shîʾite Literature*, vol. 1, 2003: 308, 319, 353.

riage by ʿAlî during Fâṭima's lifetime, and the contention that ʿAlî's popularity began to wane after Fâṭima's death. At other times I have quoted him among the Sunnî, simply because in that instance his opinion concurs with theirs.

A second textual problem is founded upon a discrepancy between Brockelmann and Sezgin in terms of al-Ṭabarî. Following Sezgin, we note that there are at least three authors by this name, and Sezgin himself warns of the danger of confusing them:

a) Abû Ğaʿfar Muḥammad b. Ğarîr b. Rustam al-Ṭabarî (c. 224/839: Cf. GAL S. I: 217 and GAS I: 540). According to Sezgin, he is the author of three works: *Dalâʾil al-imâma*, *Kitâb al-mustarshid fî imâmat ʿAlî b. Abî Ṭâlib* and *Bishârat al-muṣṭafâ*. Brockelmann also imputes to him *Ğâmiʿ al-bayân fî tafsîr* (or *ʿan taʾwîl*) *al-qurʾân* and *Kitâb aḫbâr al-rusul wa-l-mulûk*, although according to Sezgin these are the work of another author by the same name: in fact, Rustam al-Ṭabarî is a Shîʿa.

b) Muḥib al-Dîn Abû al-ʿAbbâs (Abû Muḥammad Abû Ğaʿfar) Aḥmad b. ʿAbd al-Raḥmân al-Ṭabarî al-Makkî al-Shâfiʿî (d. 684/1295: Cf. GAL S. I: 615), the author of *Kitâb al-riyâḍ al-naḍira fî faḍâʾil al-ʿashara* and *Ḏaḫâʾir al-ʿuqbâ fî manâqib ḏawî al-qurbâ*.

c) A third author, whom Brockelmann seems to confuse with Rustam al-Ṭabarî, but whom Sezgin lists as a separate author: Abû Ğaʿfar Muḥammad b. Ğarîr b. Yazîd al-Ṭabarî (d. 310/923: Cf. GAS 1: 232 and GAL S I: 217). According to Sezgin, he wrote *Kitâb aḫbâr al-rusul wa-l-mulûk* and *Ğâmiʿ al-bayân fî tafsîr* (or *ʿan taʾwîl*) *al-qurʾân*.

4. A NOTE ON THE USE OF THE SOURCES

The bulk of this research is based upon the Shîʿî and Sunnî books of *aḥâdîṯ*; together, these comprise a corpus that raises an abiding quandary in terms of validity and reliability. The key issue of authenticity has engrossed both Muslim and non-Muslim scholars, although they have used dissimilar approaches and methodologies and have arrived at different conclusions. For our purposes, we cannot limit ourselves just to facts, nor can we merely accept all *aḥâdîṯ* as accurate. Writes Mahmoud Ayoub:

> What criterion, then, must the historian, and especially the historian of religion, use in examining the various traditions pur-

> porting to relate an event of great significance for the religious life of so many people over so many centuries...? It will not do...to limit ourselves to the bare facts as we see them, because even they have to be arbitrarily chosen. Nor can we, to be sure, take all traditions to be factual data. We must, however, choose our facts, often including those facts which, while to us they do not seem historically valid, were nonetheless considered as such by the community...[40]

Gustav Weil (c. 1848 and followed by Aloys Sprenger in 1861) was probably the first Western scholar to suggest that a considerable part of the corpus of *aḥâdîṯ* must be regarded as unauthentic. But it was Ignaz Goldziher (d. 1921) who pioneered the first critical study of authenticity; he concluded that a large proportion of the *aḥâdîṯ* came from a period much later than Muḥammad, and must thus be regarded as spurious. His argument was developed by Joseph Schacht (d. 1969), who argued that at least the legal *aḥâdîṯ* must be rejected as false. All of this critical analysis led to the development of three schools of thought: those who followed Goldziher and Schacht (including John Wansbrough and Michael Cook), those who attempted to refute them (including Nabia Abbott and Fuat Sezgin) and those who sought a middle path, or synthesis of the two extremes (including Harald Motzki and Fazlur Rahman).[41]

In opposition to the proposals of Goldziher and Schacht, Nizamuddin Ahmad writes:

> We consider the project of Goldziher/Schacht and their followers, to be rather ill-founded. Our own view is in agreement with the scholars of *usûl al-fiqh* (both Sunnī and Šīʿī), namely that from the standpoint of epistemology the overwhelming

[40] AYOUB M., *Redemptive Suffering in Islam. A Study of the Devotional Aspects of ʿAshura in Twelver Shiʿism,* Mouton Publishers, The Hague 1978: 137.

[41] Cf. HALLAQ W., "The Authenticity of Prophetic Hadîth: a Pseudo-Problem" in *Studia Islamica* LXXXIX, 1999: 75–76.

> majority of the *hadīth* merely engender probability rather than certainty.[42]

Ahmad then refers his readers to the work of Wael Hallaq,[43] who has examined and attempted a way out of the dilemma. He derives his conclusion from what he calls "legal methodology, properly known as *usūl al-fiqh*", from "the perspective of epistemology which seeks to order the types of *hadîth* on a spectrum that ranges from the dubious to the certain, by way of the central category of the probable."[44] He examines three basic strands of *ḥadîṯ*: the so-called *mutawâtir* (a widely-transmitted *ḥadîṯ*),[45] the *wâhid* (which fails to meet the requirements of a *mutawâtir ḥadîṯ*) and the *tawâtur al-maʿnawî*, which he categorizes as "nothing more than a collection of *hadîths* of the *âhâd* type."[46] It is Hallaq's contention that the *wâhid* types of *aḥâdîṯ* (and thus the *tawâtur al-maʿnawî*) – and these form the overwhelming bulk of the corpus of *aḥâdîṯ* – never reach beyond the level of probability, and that Muslim jurists and traditionalists readily admit that they are therefore open to fabrication and error. The gist of his solution is that Goldziher and Schacht have wasted their time, since Muslim jurists and traditionalists have always admitted the insecure epistemological nature of the corpus of *aḥâdîṯ*, conceding that, bar a small number of *aḥâdîṯ*, the vast majority engender only probability. Hallaq concludes that probability – as the jurists and traditionalists themselves admit – allows for fabrication and error.

Since the aim of this work is not primarily a critical analysis of the Shîʿî and Sunnî texts *per se*, but a critical examination of the life

---

[42] AHMAD N., "Twelver Šīʿī *Hadīth*: From Tradition to Contemporary Evaluations" in *Oriente Moderno* XXI (LXXXII), 1–2002: 130.

[43] HALLAQ W., "The Authenticity of Prophetic Hadîth: a Pseudo-Problem" in *Studia Islamica* LXXXIX, 1999: 75–90.

[44] Ibid.: 78.

[45] Hallaq defines this as "any report that reaches us through textually identical channels of transmission which are sufficiently numerous as to preclude any possibility of collaboration on a forgery." Cf. ibid.: 78.

[46] HALLAQ W., "The Authenticity of Prophetic Hadîth: a Pseudo-Problem" in *Studia Islamica* LXXXIX, 1999: 82.

of Fâṭima at the level of those texts, they have been read expressly as religious texts, and treated as sacrosanct documents which employ a specifically numinous language, and around which a distinctive theology and spirituality have been constructed. Just as sacred history cannot be read in the same manner as secular history, so too religious or sacred texts must be studied within the confines of their own *genre*. I have thus taken the texts at face-value, and have read them for their value as primary Islamic religious documents. The corpus of Islamic *aḥâdîṯ* is divided into various categories: for the purposes of this work, it is worth noting that while many Islamic religious texts fall into juridical or legalistic categories, a large proportion of the Shîʿî *aḥâdîṯ* concerning Fâṭima and examined in this thesis, fall rather into the category of edification.

CHAPTER ONE.
FÂṬIMA IN HER CONTEXT. HISTORICAL AND BIOGRAPHICAL NOTES

This chapter aims to present the reader with a simple biographical outline for Fâṭima, relying primarily on the Sunnî sources available to us, in an attempt to provide an historical context for the chapters that follow.

2.1. THE QUANDARY OF DATING AND SOURCES

The clear disagreement about Fâṭima's date of birth is startling, a source of polemics between the Shîᶜa and the Sunnî, and a controversial point upon which to begin a study of her life. It is also the starting point for Lammens' disparagement of the stories surrounding her person.[1]

Harald Motzki[2] specifies the *impasse* of any biographical study of Muḥammad as, on the one hand, the infeasibility of writing an historical biography without being accused of using the sources uncritically, and on the other, the impossibility of constructing such a biography when the sources are critically used. Part of the problem is a dire shortage of source critical studies (which compare differing accounts in order to detect the changes wrought by transmission). The biographies of Muḥammad written until now have

---

[1] LAMMENS H., "Fatima and the Daughters of Muhammad" in Ibn Warraq (ed. and trans.), *The Quest for the Historical Muhammad*, 2000: 218–329.

[2] MOTZKI H., (ed.), *The Biography of Muḥammad. The Issue of Sources*, Brill, Leiden 2000: XIV–XV.

used the earliest sources available (like Ibn Hishâm and Ibn Saʿd); but these in themselves date from the 3RD/9TH century and are therefore moderately late in terms of Muḥammad's own lifetime. Nevertheless, as the context for an assessment of Fâṭima's life, the following Common Era Islamic dates, provided by Rahman,[3] may prove useful:

a) **c. 570–571**, the birth of Muḥammad.[4] The biographical data (*sîra*) and collections of *aḥâdîṯ* offer three reference points for his life, although considering the age of the sources, they must be treated with caution. He was apparently twenty-five years of age when he married Ḫadîǧa (therefore, around 595).[5] Ḫadîǧa was a woman of forty years at the time of the marriage.[6] Muḥammad was thirty-five when, ten years later, the Quraysh tore down the Kaʿba

---

[3] RAHMAN H. U., *A Chronology of Islamic History 570–1000 CE*, Mansell Publishing Limited, London 1989.

[4] Calculations that Maxime Rodinson declares to be 'dubious' put the birth of Muḥammad somewhere between 567 and 573, with 571 as the commonly accepted date. Cf. RODINSON M., *Mohammed*, Penguin Books, London 1971.

[5] **HSH.**, vol. I: 87 (which notes that some say he was twenty-one, or thirty, or thirty-seven), **SʿD.**, vol. X, *Ḏikr Ḫadîǧa*, n. 4926: 17, 18, **BLḎ1.**, vol. I, *Mabʿaṯ rasûl Allâh*, n. 187: 103–104, **BRR.**, vol. IV, *Kitâb al-nisâʾ*, bb. *al-ḫâʾ*, n. 3311: 1818 (which notes that some say he was twenty-one or twenty-four), **ĞWZ2.**, vol. I, *Ḏikr tazwîǧ rasûl Allâh*: 25, **ATH1.**, vol. II: 24, **KṮR1.**, vol. II: 294. Among the Shîʿa, cf. **YQB.**, vol. II: 19 (which notes that some say he was thirty), **MSD.**, vol. III, bb. 71, n. 1461: 15.

[6] **HSH.**, vol. I: 87 (which notes that some say she was forty-five), **SʿD.**, vol. X, *Ḏikr Ḫadîǧa*, n. 4926: 16 (which claims that she was born fifteen years before the 'Year of the Elephant', dated as well before 570, and that some claim she was twenty-eight when she married Muḥammad) and n. 4926: 17–18 (he also reports a strand that held her to be twenty-eight on her marriage day, since she was born fifteen years before the 'Year of the Elephant' and Muḥammad thirteen years before it. For the dating of the 'Year of the Elephant', cf. BUHL H and WELCH A. T., "Muḥammad" in H.A.R. Gibb et al. (eds.), *EI²*, 1971, vol. VIIa: 361), **BRR.**, vol. IV, *Kitâb al-nisâʾ*, bb. *al-ḫâʾ*, n. 3311: 1818, **ĞWZ2.**, vol. I, *Ḏikr tazwîǧ rasûl Allâh*: 25; vol. II, *al-Muṣṭafayât min ṭabaqât al-ṣaḥâbayât*: 1.

in order to reconstruct it,[7] and forty years of age when the prophetic call came, in 610.[8]

b) **c. 600**, the birth of ʿAlî b. Abî Ṭâlib, making him (as maintained by the Sunnî scholars) five years older than Fâṭima.[9]

c) **c. 605**, the birth of Fâṭima (as asserted by the Sunnî scholars). According to the Sunnî historian al-Ṭabarî,[10] Fâṭima was the youngest child of Ḫadîǧa and Muḥammad, born five years before Muḥammad's prophetic call and the start of the revelations, while the Quraysh were still reconstructing the Kaʿba. This would put her date of birth in about 605, when Muḥammad was approximately thirty-five years of age, (the first revelations coming down in 610). In these details, al-Ṭabarî is in almost complete harmony with the majority of Sunnî authors who write of Fâṭima's birth.[11] Not all

---

[7] **SʿD.**, vol. X, *Ḏikr banât rasûl Allâh*, n. 4927 (*Fâṭima*): 27, **BLḎ[1].**, vol. I, *Binâʾ Quraysh al-kaʿba*, n. 178: 99, vol. I, *Azwâǧ rasûl Allâh*, n. 865: 404, **YṬB[2].**, vol. VI, n. 1130: 51, **ATH[1].**, vol. II: 24, **KṮR[1].**, vol. II: 294, **IṢM.**, vol. I, bb. 5: 424–5.

[8] **SʿD.**, vol. X, *Ḏikr Ḫadîǧa*, n. 4926: 18, **TRM.**, vol. IX, bk. 50 (*Kitâb al-manâqib*), bb. 6, n. 3625: 233, **BLḎ[1].**, vol. I, *Mabʿaṯ rasûl Allâh*, n. 187: 103–104, **YṬB[2].**, vol. VI, nn. 1139–1141: 60–61 (which notes that some say he was forty-one or forty-three), **IṢM.**, vol. I, bb. 5: 424–5. Among the Shîʿa, cf. **MSD.**, vol. III, bb. 71, n. 1461: 15, bb. 70, n. 1458: 12 (there were five years between the building of the Kaʿba and the prophetic call).

[9] **SʿD.**, vol. X, *Ḏikr banât rasûl Allâh*, n. 4927 (*Fâṭima*): 20, **BLḎ[1].**, vol. I, *Azwâǧ rasûl Allâh*, n. 865: 404, **IṢM.**, vol. I, bb. 5: 424–5.

[10] **YṬB[2].**, vol. XXXIX, nn. 2434–2437: 166–169. In vol. IX, n. 1767: 127 he names eight children: al-Qâsim, al-Ṭayyib, al-Ṭâhir, ʿAbd Allâh, Zaynab, Ruqayya, Umm Kulṯûm and Fâṭima.

[11] **SʿD.**, vol. X, *Ḏikr banât rasûl Allâh*, n. 4927 (*Fâṭima*): 20, 27, **BLḎ[1].**, vol. I, *Azwâǧ rasûl Allâh*, n. 865: 404, **ḪWZ.**, Part 1, bb. *Faḍâʾil Fâṭima al-Zahrâʾ bt. rasûl Allâh*, n. 1: 89 (including a *ḥadîṯ* positing that Fâṭima was born when Muḥammad was forty-one years old), **ǦWZ[1].**, vol. I, bb. *fî faḍl Fâṭima*: 414; **ǦWZ[2].**, vol. I, *al-Inât min awlâd*: 57, vol. II, *Fâṭima bt. rasûl Allâh*: 2, **KṮR.**, vol. VI: 332, **SQL[1].**, vol. IV, bb. *ḥarf al-fâʾ*, n. 830: 365, where he carries a *ḥadîṯ* that holds her birth as 'one or more years' after the prophetic calling, **SQL[4].**, vol. XII, *Kitâb al-nisâʾ*, n. 4434: 441,

the transmitters agree that she was the youngest of the girls, and it is virtually impossible to establish how many children Muḥammad actually had and whether Fâṭima was the youngest daughter (except by attempting to discover which daughter was married first). Ibn Hishâm, Ibn Kaṯîr (from Ibn Isḥâq and Ibn Hishâm), al-ʿIṣâmî, al-Balâḏurî, Ibn ʿAbd al-Barr (from Ibn Isḥâq), al-Ğawzî and Ibn al-Aṯîr name her as the youngest daughter.[12] Others, reporting differing strands, place her third in a list of six children,[13] or first or second in a list of four girls.[14] Ibn Saʿd posits Zaynab as the eldest girl, followed by Ruqayya and Umm Kulṯûm, all of them marrying before the prophetic call; al-Ğawzî concurs with this, while Ibn ʿAbd al-Barr reports one strand which names Zaynab as the eldest.[15] There is therefore no absolute consensus between the Sunnî scholars; al-Ḫawârizmî and Ibn ʿAbd al-Barr carry *aḥâdîṯ* saying that Fâṭima was born when Muḥammad was forty-one, but these fit in with neither the Sunnî nor the Shîʿî contention.[16] Adding to the dilemma is an unusual *ḥadîṯ*, carried by the Shîʿî transmitters Ibn Shahrâshûb and al-Mağlisî, which insists that Ḫadîğa was a virgin

---

IṢM., vol. I, bb. 5: 424–5, **SHL.**, bb. *faḍl fî ḏikr manâqib ʿAlî b. Abî Ṭâlib*: 42–43.

[12] **HSH.**, vol. I: 190, **BLḎ**[1]., vol. I, *Azwâğ rasûl Allâh*, n. 861: 396, **BRR.**, vol. IV, *Kitâb al-nisâʾ*, bb. *al-ḥâʾ*, n. 3311: 1819, n. 4057: 1893, **ĞWZ**[2]., vol. II, *Fâṭima bt. rasûl Allâh*: 2, **ATH**[2]., vol. V, *Fî maʿrifat al-aṣḥâba*: 519–520, **KṮR**[1]., vol. II, *Faṣl fî taswîği-hi*: 294, **SQL**[1]., vol. IV, bb. *ḥarf al-fâʾ*, n. 830: 365.

[13] **KṮR**[1]., vol. II: 294 (in a report from Ibn ʿAbbâs).

[14] **BRR.**, vol. IV, *Kitâb al-nisâʾ*, bb. *al-ḥâʾ*, n. 3311: 1818. Ibn ʿAbd al-Barr is reporting from three different chains of transmission.

[15] **SʿD.**, vol. X, *Ḏikr banât rasûl Allâh*, n. 4928 (*Zaynab*): 31, *Ḏikr banât rasûl Allâh*, n. 4929 (*Ruqayya*): 36, *Ḏikr banât rasûl Allâh*, n. 4930 (*Umm Kulṯûm*): 37, **BRR.**, vol. IV, *Kitâb al-nisâʾ*, bb. *al-ḥâʾ*, n. 3311: 1818, **ĞWZ**[2]., vol. I, *al-Inâṯ min awlâd*: 57.

[16] **BRR.**, vol. IV, *Kitâb al-nisâʾ*, n. 4057: 1893, **ḪWZ.**, Part 1, bb. *Faḍâʾil Fâṭima al-Zahrâʾ bt. rasûl Allâh*, n. 74: 128, **SQL**[1]., vol. IV, bb. *ḥarf al-fâʾ*, n. 830: 365.

when Muḥammad married her, and that her daughters Ruqayya and Zaynab were in fact the children of her sister.[17]

The number of Muḥammad's children remains an indecisive question. While there is little doubt that he had four daughters by Ḫadîğa[18] (even though their order is not clear), his sons are more difficult to enumerate. All his children, except for the short-lived Ibrâhîm, born of his Coptic wife Mâriyya around the fourth year

---

[17] **SHB.**, vol. I, bb. *fî aqribâ'i-hi wa ḫaddâmi-hi*: 206, **MĞL.**, vol. XXII, bb. 2, n. 5: 191. Ibn Shaḥrâshûb writes: "It was transmitted by Aḥmad al-Balâḏurî and Abû al-Qâsim al-Kûfî in their books, and al-Murtaḍâ in *al-Shâfî*, and Abû Ğaʿfar in *al-Talḫîṣ*, that when the Prophet married Ḫadîğa she was a virgin. This is confirmed in the citation in the two books *al-Anwâr* and *al-Bidʿ*, that Ruqayya and Zaynab were the daughters of Hâla, the sister of Ḫadîğa." The work *al-Shâfî* refers to *al-Shâfî fî al-imâma* by al-Murtaḍâ (d. 436/1044: cf. GAL S. I: 704), while Abû Ğaʿfar's *al-Talḫîṣ* is almost certainly *Shayḫ* al-Ṭûsî's summary of al-Murtaḍâ's *al-Shâfî* entitled *Talḫîṣ al-shâfî*. As for al-Balâḏurî, in his treatment of Muḥammad's marriage to Ḫadîğa in his *Kitâb ansâb al-ashraf*, he not only insists that Ruqayya and Zaynab were born to Muḥammad from Ḫadîğa, but also writes of her marriages and children prior to her marriage with Muḥammad (cf. **BLḎ**[1]., vol. I, n. 168: 95, n. 175: 97–99, nn. 860–863, 867: 396–401, 406). Sezgin attributes two works to Abû al-Qâsim ʿAlî b. Aḥmad al-Kûfî (d. 352/963): *al-Istiğâṯa fî bidʿat al-ṯalâṯa* and *al-Âdâb wa-makârim al-aḫlâq* (cf. GAS I: 543), while Brockelmann names him differently and imputes to him only *al-Istiğâṯa fî bidʿat al-ṯalâṯa* (cf. GAL S. I: 320). In fact, Abû al-Qâsim had a massive literary output; al Nağâshî lists around fifty books (although not *al-Istiğâṯa fî bidʿat al-ṯalâṯa*), but also informs us that towards the end of his life, Abû al-Qâsim slipped into extremism and severely damaged his faith (**NĞA.**, bb. 691: 265). Ibn Shaḥrâshûb seems here to be referring to his *Kitâb al-bidʿ*. The work *al-Anwâr* is hardly indentifiable. The contention that Ruqayya and Zaynab were the children of Ḫadîğa's sister is also carried by al-ʿÂmilî (cf. **ÂML.**, vol. III: 82). Nevertheless, many Shîʿî texts speak of Ḫadîğa's two husbands prior to Muḥammad, and the children she bore them: cf. **ṬFA**[2]., bb. 12, n. 37–1031: 463; **ṬBR**[1].: 139; **IRB.**, vol. I: 402, 510; **MĞL.**, vol. XVI, bb. 8: 171, vol. XXII, bb. 3, n. 20: 300.

[18] Cf. for e.g. **RAZ.**, vol. XIV, Part 27, *sûrat al-Shûrâ*: 186, **KṮR**[2]., vol. V, *sûrat al-Aḥzâb*: 469–470 for lists of four sons and four daughters.

after the emigration (*hiǧra*), were born of Ḫadîǧa.[19] Al-Ḫawârizmî reports four sons: al-Qâsim, al-Ṭâhir, al-Muṭahhar and al-Ṭayyib (or ʿAbd Allâh).[20] However, most other authors raise some doubts about the names and the number, suggesting rather that there were two sons, al-Qâsim and ʿAbd Allâh, both of whom died in infancy, and that the names al-Ṭâhir and al-Ṭayyib are alternative names for ʿAbd Allâh.[21] Almost all the sources are in agreement that all of Muḥammad's children predeceased him, with the exception of Fâṭima.[22]

---

[19] **SʿD.**, vol. X, *Ḏikr Ḫadîǧa*, n. 4926: 19, **ḪWZ.**, Part 1, ch. 5, *Faḍâʾil Fâṭima al-Zahrâʾ bt. rasûl Allâh*, n. 77: 130; **ǦWZ²**., vol. I, *Ḏikr awlâd (Muḥammad)*: 57, **ḎHB¹**., vol. I: 10.

[20] **ḪWZ.**, Part 1, bb. *Faḍâʾil Fâṭima al-Zahrâʾ bt. rasûl Allâh*, n. 77: 130.

[21] **HSH.**, vol. I: 190, **SʿD.**, vol. X, *Ḏikr Ḫadîǧa*, n. 4926: 17, where we are told the children were: al-Qâsim, ʿAbd Allâh (who was also called al-Ṭâhir), al-Ṭayyib, Zaynab, Ruqayya, Umm Kulṯûm and Fâṭima, **BLḎ¹**., vol. I, *Azwâǧ rasûl Allâh*, n. 866: 405, **YṬB²**., vol. VI, nn. 1127–1129: 47–49, **BRR.**, vol. IV, *Kitâb al-nisâʾ*, bb. *al-ḥâʾ*, n. 3311: 1819, **ǦWZ²**., vol. I, *Ḏikr awlâd (Muḥammad)*: 57. W. Montgomery Watt names two sons, al-Qâsim and ʿAbd Allâh, but suggests that they might be one and the same person. He posits that it is generally believed that al-Ṭâhir and al-Ṭayyib were other names for ʿAbd Allâh (cf. WATT W.M., "Khadīdja" in H.A.R. Gibb et al. (eds.), *EI²*, 1971, vol. IVb: 898–899). Armstrong writes of 'at least' six children, naming al-Qâsim and ʿAbd Allâh as the two sons (cf. ARMSTRONG K., *Muhammad*, Victor Gollancz Ltd, London 1992: 81). Lings agrees; he names six children, starting with the short-lived al-Qâsim, followed by Zaynab, Ruqayya, Umm Kulṯûm and Fâṭima, and then another short-lived son, whom Lings fails to name (cf. LINGS M., *Muhammad, his life based on the earliest sources*, Inner Traditions International Ltd, New York 1983: 37).

[22] **BLḎ¹**., vol. I, *Azwâǧ rasûl Allâh*, n. 861: 396, **ḪWZ.**, Part 1, bb. *Faḍâʾil Fâṭima al-Zahrâʾ bt. rasûl Allâh*, n. 77: 130. Among the Shîʿa, cf. **MSD.**, vol. III, bb. 72, n. 1485: 22–23.

d) **c. 610**, Muḥammad receives the first revelations.[23] Alone in his cave on retreat, Muḥammad, if not already a monotheist then fast getting there,[24] was shaken by a heavenly voice. It was not the voice of God, for Islam, indomitably preserving the transcendent mystery would never permit such a thing, but the voice of an angelic intermediary. His first command to Muḥammad was not to write anything down, but to «*Recite, in the name of your Lord who created, created mankind from a clot*» (Q. 96: 1–2).

Different accounts suggest Q. 74 as the first revelation; whichever it was, the first divine communication was followed by a disconcerting pause (*fatra*), perplexing not only for Muḥammad but also for our understanding of this crucial event for, as some authors point out, this pause (of up to three years) means that Muḥammad did not at once set about obeying the divine command.[25]

e) **c. 619**, the death of Ḫadîǧa, and Muḥammad's 'night journey' (*isrâʾ*) and 'ascension' (*miʿrâǧ*). The date of Muḥammad's journey to heaven (and, in terms of being the mother of Fâṭima, the date of Ḫadîǧa's death) becomes pivotal and something of a stumbling block when we turn to the Shîʿî dating of Fâṭima's birth. The consensus of the Sunnî scholars is that Ḫadîǧa died (before Abû Ṭâlib by anything between three and fifty-five days)[26] in Mecca at the age of sixty-five, ten years after the first revelations to Muḥammad,

---

[23] Cf. for e.g. **SʿD**., vol. X, *Ḏikr Ḫadîǧa*, n. 4926: 18, **TRM**., vol. IX, bk. 50 (*Kitâb al-manâqib*), bb. 6, n. 3625: 233, **BLḎ**[1]., vol. I, *Mabʿaṯ rasûl Allâh*, n. 187: 103–104, **YṬB**[2]., vol. VI, nn. 1139–1141: 60–61 (which notes that some say he was forty-one or forty-three), **IṢM**., vol. I, bb. 5: 424–5. Among the Shîʿa, cf. **MSD**., vol. III, bb. 71, n. 1461: 15, bb. 70, n. 1458: 12 (there were five years between the building of the Kaʿba and the prophetic call).

[24] Rodinson maintains that there are "clear indications in his later life to suggest that, like everyone else, he practiced the religion of his fathers" and that Muḥammad was not an instant monotheist. Cf. RODINSON M., *Mohammed*, 1971: 48.

[25] Cf. BUHL H and WELCH A. T., "Muḥammad" in H.A.R. Gibb et al. (eds.), *EI*[2], 1971, vol. VIIa: 363.

[26] **ATH**[1]., vol. II: 63–64.

three years before the *hiğra* and before the prayer was made obligatory.[27] Ibn ʿAbd al-Barr brings in a contradictory strand, placing her death at the age of sixty-four, seven years after the prophetic call, three to five years before the *hiğra* and three years, or thereabouts, before the 'night journey'.[28] In this, Ibn ʿAbd al-Barr stands alone, agreeing neither with the Sunnî nor the Shîʿî system of dating. The Shîʿî historians appear to agree with the Sunnî dating of her death (al-Yaʿqûbî giving her age as sixty-two).[29]

2.2. DATING FÂṬIMA BY THE NIGHT JOURNEY

The 'night journey' is more challenging to date, but decisive in terms of Fâṭima. The majority of Sunnî sources (and those biographers who follow them) place the 'night journey' after the death of Ḫadîğa and Muḥammad's visit to Ṭâʾif, between one and three years before the *hiğra* to Medina, and when Muḥammad was aged around fifty-one.[30] Again, the Shîʿî historians appear to agree with the Sunnî dating, although while al-Masʿûdî places Ḫadîğa's death before Muḥammad's 'night journey' (in common with the Sunnî commentators), al-Yaʿqûbî dates her death after it.[31]

In terms of the expressions 'night journey' (*isrâʾ*) and 'ascension' (*miʿrâğ*), it is not entirely clear whether we are dealing with one single event (the *miʿrâğ* following on the heels of the *isrâʾ*) or two entirely different journeys. Nor can we be sure of the dating; Bev-

---

[27] **SʿD.**, vol. X, *Ḏikr Ḫadîğa*, n. 4926: 19, **BUḪ¹.**, vol. V, bk. 58 (*Kitâb manâqib al-anṣâr*), ch. 43, n. 236: 153, **BLḎ¹.**, vol. I, *Azwâğ rasûl Allâh*, n. 867: 405, **YṬB².**, vol. VI, n. 1156: 76, n. 1199: 115, **BRR.**, vol. IV, *Kitâb al-nisâʾ*, bb. *al-ḫâʾ*, n. 3311: 1818, **ĞWZ².**, vol. II, *al-Muṣṭafayât min ṭabaqât al-ṣaḥâbayât*: 1, **ATH¹.**, vol. II: 63–64, **IṢM.**, vol. I, bb. 1: 286.

[28] **BRR.**, vol. IV, *Kitâb al-nisâʾ*, bb. *al-ḫâʾ*, n. 3311: 1818, 1825.

[29] **YQB.**, vol. II: 34, **MSD.**, vol. III, bb. 72, n. 1466: 18, n. 1476: 23, bb. 73, n. 1485: 27–28.

[30] **BLḎ¹.**, vol. I, bb. *fî qiṣṣat al-miʿrâğ*, n. 586: 200, **ATH¹.**, vol. II: 33, **IṢM.**, vol. I, bb. 1: 286. Cf. ARMSTRONG K., *Muhammad*, 1992: 138, LINGS M., *Muhammad, his life based on the earliest sources*, 1983: 101.

[31] **YQB.**, vol. II: 25, 34, 36, **MSD.**, vol. III, bb. 72, n. 1476: 23, bb. 73, n. 1485: 27–28.

an[32] posits that the two stories allude to two wholly different situations, and that the event of the ascension must be understood as having occurred near the beginning of Muḥammad's prophetic career, as a sort of initiation (through a rite of purification in which his breast was opened and his heart cleansed).[33] This theory was in accord with that of Schrieke[34] (who holds that *al-masǧid al-aqṣâ* is located not in Jerusalem but in God's heavenly sanctuary) as well as with Horovitz and Hartman.[35] Writing in the Encyclopaedia of Islam, Knappert[36] offers a clarification of the following Qur'ânic passage:

> «*Glorified be He Who carried His servant by night from the Inviolable Place of Worship to the Far Distant Place of Worship the neighbourhood whereof We have blessed, that We might show him Our tokens*» (Q. 17: 1).

According to Knappert, the oldest explanation, not found in more modern commentaries, finds in this passage an intimation of Muḥammad's ascension to heaven and preserves the original meaning of that event; the word *isrâ'* is used as synonymous with *miʿrâǧ* and the expression *al-masǧid al-aqṣâ* is interpreted not as Jerusalem but as 'the furthest place of worship' (heaven). Several versions of

---

32 BEVAN A. A., "Mohammad's Ascension to Heaven" in K. Marti (ed.), *Studien zur semitischen Philologie und Religionsgeschichte, Julius Wellhausen zum siebzigten Geburtstag am 17. Mai 1914 gewidmet*, Giessen 1914 (Beihefte zur Zeitschrift fur die alttestamentliche Wissenschaft 27): 51–61.

33 Cf. for e.g. **BUḪ**[1]., vol. IV, bk. 54 (*Kitâb bad' al-ḫalq*), ch. 6, n. 429: 287–290, vol. IV, bk. 55 (*Kitâb aḥâdîṯ al-anbiyâ'*), ch. 5, (n.n.): 353–356, vol. V, bk. 58 (*Kitâb manâqib al-anṣâr*), ch. 41, n. 227: 143–148, **TIB**., vol. II, bk. 27 (*Kitâb al-fitan*), bb. 23: 1264–1274, **KṮR**[2]., vol. IV, *sûrat al-Isrâ'*: 239.

34 SCHRIEKE B., "Die Himmselsreise Muhammads" in *Der Islam* 6 (1916): 1–30.

35 HOROVITZ J., "Muhammeds Himmelfahrt" in *Der Islam* 9 (1919): 159–183 and HARTMANN R., "Die Himmselsreise Muhammads und ihre Bedeutung in der Religion des Islam" in F. Saxl (ed.), *Vorträge der Bibliothek Warburg*, Vorträge 1928–1929, Leipzig/Berlin 1930: 42–65.

36 KNAPPERT J., "Miʿradj" in H.A.R. Gibb et al. (eds.), *EI*[2], 1993, vol. VIIa: 97–99.

this night journey are contained in the books of *aḥâdîṯ*, with the story related in Q. 17: 1 being only one of them, and with these stories being adapted to the Qur'ânic version so as to present a unified picture. Three types of event are narrated in the *aḥâdîṯ*; an ascension (*mi*ʿ*râǧ*) by Muḥammad into heaven from a location in Mecca, a journey (*isrâ*ʾ) by Muḥammad from Mecca to a place called *al-masǧid al-aqṣâ*, and finally, a combination of the two events, found mostly in the older commentaries, with Mecca as the starting point of the *mi*ʿ*râǧ* and the temple in Jerusalem the starting point of the *isrâ*ʾ.

The oldest account of the *mi*ʿ*râǧ* is Ibn Saʿd's; he dates it as eighteen months before the *hiǧra*, with similar accounts (without the date) found in Ibn Ḥanbal (quoted by Ibn Kaṯîr), al-Buḫârî, Muslim and al-Nasâʾî.[37] The latter three (but not Ibn Saʿd) add the story of Muḥammad's breast being opened just before the ascension and his heart being purified. Busse insists that this story must be separated from the ascension and night journey material, since it already exists, standing on its own, as something that happened to Muḥammad when he was a boy.[38] The oldest account of the *isrâ*ʾ is found in Ibn Isḥâq, relayed by Ibn Hishâm and told in three versions. Almost the same details are given in later accounts, with Ibn Saʿd dating it as one year before the *hiǧra* (and thus obviously understanding these as two different events). It is also Ibn Isḥâq who provides the oldest evidence of the two stories being joined into one event (although he tells them separately), the one following immediately after the other and, as a natural consequence, the expression *al-masǧid al-aqṣâ* coming to be understood as the temple in Jerusalem.[39] Knappert suggests that the two interpretations became

---

[37] **SʿD.**, vol. 1, *Ḏikr al-mi*ʿ*râǧ*: 181, *Ḏikr laylat al-isrâ*ʾ: 182, **BUḪ[1].**, vol. V, bk. 57 (*Kitâb manâqib al-anṣâr*), n. 227: 143, n. 228: 148–149, **MSL.**, ch. 75, *Kitâb al-îmân*, n. 313: 103–106, **NSA[1].**, vol. I, *Kitâb al-ṣalât*, bb. 1 *farḍ al-ṣalât*: 217.

[38] BUSSE H., "Jerusalem in the Story of Muhammad's Night Journey and Ascension" in *Jerusalem Studies in Arabic and Islam*, 14 (1991): 25. Cf. **MSL.**, ch. 75, *Kitâb al-îmân*, n. 311: 103.

[39] Cf. **BUḪ[1].**, vol. IV, bk. 55 (*Kitâb aḥâdîṯ al-anbiyâ*ʾ), ch. 9, n. 585: 383 for a *ḥadîṯ* insisting that the first mosque to be constructed on earth

harmonized, with a 'night journey to Jerusalem' assigned to the term *isrâ'* and the ascension, having lost its original meaning, being altered in date and made to happen in a later period.[40]

Within the mass of acquiescence sounds a lone note of non-compliance. It is al-Ṭabarî, who places the event close to the beginning of Muḥammad's prophetic call, although this does not accord with most other Sunnî sources.[41] Al-Ṭabarî is following a much older tradition and elucidation of the 'night journey' not found in the later commentaries and is refusing the construal of *al-masǧid al-aqṣâ* as Jerusalem. Knappert concludes that the earlier tradition of Mecca as the starting point of the ascension has been ousted by later strands which made Jerusalem its starting point. Furthermore, some of the questions put to Muḥammad during the journey through the heavens indicate that the ascension originally belonged to a much early period, closer to his prophetic call than to the *hiǧra*. Considering their dating of Fâṭima's birth (and their insistence upon Muḥammad consuming heavenly fruit during his heavenly sojourn), one would at once conclude that the Shîʿa historians would, like al-Ṭabarî, insist on a much early date for the *isrâ' – miʿrâǧ*; in this way, their claim for a post-'night journey' birth date for Fâṭima would become substantially more plausible. But they do not; their historians are in basic agreement with their Sunnî counterparts, putting the date close to the *hiǧra*.[42] Their solution is not to insist on an early date, but to posit more than one night journey – not in the sense posited by Bevan, but as an entirely different event.

---

was the *masǧid al-ḥarâm* in Mecca, followed by the *masǧid al-aqṣâ* in Jerusalem.

[40] Cf. for e.g. **RWD¹**., vol. I, *al-Ǧuz al-awwal fî muʿǧizât nabî-nâ*, bb. 1 *faṣl min riwâyât al-ḫâṣa* (Fadak): 112. A Shîʿî transmitter, he discerns two events (*isrâ'* and *miʿrâǧ*) and places them three years after the prophetic call.

[41] **YṬB²**., vol. VII, n. 1156: 78.

[42] **YQB**., vol. II: 25, 34, 36, **MSD**., vol. III, bb. 72, n. 1476: 23, bb. 73, n. 1485: 27–28.

2.3. THE YEARS IN MEDINA

f) **c. 622**, the emigration (*hiğra*) to Medina. After the *hiğra*, Muḥammad moved his daughters Umm Kulṯûm and Fâṭima to Medina. One report holds that he dispatched his adopted son Zayd b. Ḥâriṯa to fetch them,[43] while another holds that Ibn al-ʿAbbâs undertook this mission, and that the journey had an inauspicious start when one al-Ḥuwayriṯ b. Nuqayḏ b. Wahb interfered with the camels, causing the girls to fall. In his history, al-Ṭabarî recounts that this man was killed by ʿAlî because he was one of those who annoyed Muḥammad in Mecca; this is confirmed by at least three Shîʿî transmitters, but nowhere is there any mention of the incident with the camels.[44]

g) **c. 2/624** or **3/625**, the marriage of ʿAlî and Fâṭima (according to the Sunnî scholars); Fâṭima would consequently have been nineteen or twenty at this time. The Sunnî historian al-Ṭabarî, in harmony with some other scholars, places their marriage just before the end of the month of Ṣafar in 1/623, before the battles of Badr and Uḥud (the latter was fought in 3/625).[45] Al-ʿIṣâmî transmits more

---

[43] **BLḎ[1]**., vol. I, n. 263: 269, n. 872: 414–415, **YṬB[2]**., vol. VII, n. 1263: 8 (Zayd b. Ḥâriṯa and Abû Râfiʿ were sent to fetch Muḥammad's wife Sawda as well as Umm Kulṯûm and Fâṭima).

[44] **YṬB[2]**., vol. VIII, n. 1640: 179, n. 1641: 181. Among the Shîʿa, cf. **MFD[1]**., vol. I: 136, **ṬBR[1]**.: 110, **ḤLL[1]**.: 250. Cf. AL-MÛSAWÎ M. B., *al-Kawṯar fî aḥwâl Fâṭima bt. al-nabî al-aṭhar*, 2002, vol. III, Part 3, bb. 2 (*Fâṭima wa-hiğratu-hâ ilâ Madîna*), n. 3/2118: 380–381, where the incident is mentioned (although the author misspells the name and offers no sources). Al-Ḥuwayriṯ is named as one of the horsemen sent by the Quraysh to expel ʿAlî and the women who were with him; he approaches the camel on which Fâṭima, already emaciated by the death of her mother and other events preceding her father's leaving for Medina, is riding, and she is thrown to the ground. Later, al-Ḥuwayriṯ is killed by ʿAlî.

[45] **YṬB[2]**., vol. VII, n. 1273: 18, vol. VII, n. 1367: 92, vol. VII, n. 1273: 18, vol. XXXIX, nn. 2434–2437: 166–169, **ḤNA**., vol. III, bk. 31 *(Kitâb maʿrifat al-ṣaḥâba), Manâqib Fâṭima bt. rasûl Allâh,* n. 4807: 185, **ĞWZ[2]**., vol. II, *Fâṭima bt. rasûl Allâh*: 2, **ḎHB[1]**., vol. I: 4, **SQL[4]**., vol. XII,

than one strand, suggesting that the marriage was either in the second or third year of the *hiğra*, some saying before the battle of Uḥud, others saying before Muḥammad married ʿÂʾisha, when Fâṭima was fifteen and ʿAlî twenty-one.[46] Ibn ʿAbd al-Barr agrees with the ages, but places the marriage after Uḥud.[47]

h) **c. 11/632**, the death of Muḥammad, aged about sixty-three,[48] followed by that of Fâṭima. Here, the discrepancies between the transmitters are narrowed down to a matter of months. While all agree that she died shortly after her father, the reports about the timing range between seventy-five days and six months, and her age at her death ranges among the Sunnî scholars between twenty-three and thirty-five.[49]

2.4. THE SHÎʿÎ VIEW

While the age of the sources and the shortage of source critical studies go some way in explaining the discrepancies and lack of precision among the Sunnî biographers, historians and transmitters, the counterviews of the Shîʿî scholars bring further uncertainty. The Shîʿa reject many of these Sunnî dates and calculations, insisting that Fâṭima was born five years after the first revelations, having been conceived after the 'night journey'; in this, they base

Kitâb al-nisâʾ, n. 4434: 441, **MTQ.**, vol. V: 99, **IṢM.**, vol. I, bb. 5: 425, **SHL.**, bb. *faḍl fî ḏikr manâqib ʿAlî b. Abî Ṭâlib*: 43

[46] **NSA².**: 5, **ATH².**, vol. V, bb. *ḥarf al-fâʾ*: 520, **IṢM.**, vol. I, bb. 5: 425.

[47] **BRR.**, vol. IV, *Kitâb al-nisâʾ*, n. 4057: 1893. Cf. also **ATH².**, vol. V, bb. *ḥarf al-fâʾ*: 520, **KṮR.**, vol. VI: 332.

[48] **BUḪ¹.**, vol. V, bk. 58 (*Kitâb manâqib al-anṣâr*), ch. 44, n. 243: 156, vol. V, bk. 59 (*Kitâb al-maġâzî*), ch. 83, n. 742: 528.

[49] **SʿD.**, vol. X, *Ḏikr banât rasûl Allâh*, n. 4927 (*Fâṭima*): 29, **BLḎ¹.**, vol. I, *Azwâğ rasûl Allâh*, n. 865: 402, **IṢH.**, vol. II, bb. 133 (*Fâṭima bt. rasûl Allâh*): 40, 42–43, **BRR.**, vol. IV, *Kitâb al-nisâʾ wa kunâ-hunna*, n. 4057: 1894, 1898–1899, **ḪWZ.**, Part 1, bb. *Faḍâʾil Fâṭima al-Zahrâʾ bt. rasûl Allâh*, n. 71: 128, **ĞWZ².**, vol. II, *Fâṭima bt. rasûl Allâh*: 5, **ATH¹.**, vol. II: 230–231, vol. V, bb. *ḥarf al-fâʾ*: 524, **ḎHB¹.**, vol. I: 13, **KṮR¹.**, vol. V: 250, 285, vol. VI: 332–334, **SQL⁴.**, vol. XII, *Kitâb al-nisâʾ*, n. 4434: 441.

themselves on a *ḥadîṯ* which will be examined more closely in a later chapter. According to the *ḥadîṯ*, transmitted by Shîʿî (and some Sunnî) scholars, Muḥammad, in the course of this 'night journey' was given heavenly fruit to eat by Ğibrîl, and upon his return had intercourse with Ḫadîğa, who conceived Fâṭima, ostensibly as a result of the heavenly fruit which had become sperm in Muḥammad's loins. Suffice it to say that some, but not all the Sunnî scholars[50] who transmit this *ḥadîṯ*, seem unconcerned by the problems it causes for dating Fâṭima's birth. Al-Ğawzî and al-Ḫawârizmî carry two versions of the *ḥadîṯ*, one of which places the eating of the heavenly fruit not during the 'night journey' but during a private visit to Muḥammad by Ğibrîl, a version which causes fewer difficulties in the process of dating events. The Shîʿî historians date the 'night journey' as do their Sunnî counterparts, close to the *hiğra*; going by the older reports, the Shîʿî idea (that she was born five years after the prophetic call and three years after the 'night journey') becomes quite credible. But failing to utilize this, the Shîʿa instead resort to introducing a second 'night journey'.

The Shîʿî scholar al-Mağlisî holds that Fâṭima was born in Mecca on 20TH Ğumâdâ al-âḫira, five years after the prophetic call and three years after the 'night journey', when the Quraysh were reconstructing the Kaʿba;[51] these details are in harmony with almost all the Shîʿî transmitters,[52] and with the Shîʿî historians, al-Yaʿqûbî and al-Masʿûdî. Al-Yaʿqûbî insists that Fâṭima was born

---

[50] **ḤNA.**, vol. III, bk. 31 (*Kitâb maʿrifat al-ṣaḥâba*), *Manâqib Fâṭima bt. rasûl Allâh*, n. 4801: 183–184 (with an annotation of rejection by al-Ḏahabî in the notes), **BĠD.**, vol. V, n. 2481: 87, **ḪWZ.**, Part 1, bb. *Faḍâʾil Fâṭima al-Zahrâʾ bt. rasûl Allâh*, n. 33: 105, n. 46: 110–111, **ĞWZ¹.**, vol. I, bb. *fî faḍl Fâṭima*: 411–413 (who condemns the *ḥadîṯ* as absolutely false), **RḤB.**: 36, 44–45, **SQL².**, vol. V, n. 541: 160 (with a warning note that Fâṭima's birth and Ḫadîğa's death were both pre-'night journey', rendering the *ḥadîṯ* impossible), **ṢFI.**, vol. II, bb. *manâqib Fâṭima al-Zahrâʾ*: 184, **SYṬ.**, vol. IV, *sûrat al-Isrâʾ*: 282, **HAY.**, vol. IX, bb. *manâqib Fâṭima bt. rasûl Allâh*: 202, **MTQ.**, vol. V: 97, **SHL.**, bb. *faḍl fî dikr manâqib ʿAlî b. Abî Ṭâlib*: 42.

[51] **MĞL.**, vol. XLIII, bb. 1, nn. 7, 8: 6–7.

[52] **KLY.**, vol. I, bk. 3 (*Kitâb al-ḥuğğa*), bb. *mawlid al-Zahrâʾ Fâṭima*: 458, **SHB.**, vol. III, bb. *manâqib Fâṭima al-Zahrâʾ*: 405.

after the start of the prophecy, while her siblings (al-Qâsim, Ruqayya, Zaynab, and Umm Kulṯûm) were all born before it.[53]

Going by the traditional dates, the Shîʿî position is untenable; in order to make their case, they would have either to change the date of Ḫadîğa's death (an unlikely option, since the event of a physical death, especially of one so prominent, is not hard to verify), or to change the date of the 'night journey' (an easier option, since it is more difficult to date precisely what is purportedly some sort of mystical experience). In fact, the Shîʿa do neither. In terms of the date of Fâṭima's birth, they claim that the Sunnî have falsified the date in order to play down the importance of Muḥammad's daughter (and thus the *ahl al-bayt* and their claims; the Sunnî portrayal of Fâṭima's relatively late marriage at the age of eighteen suggests that she was not as desirable as the Shîʿa claim) in favour of ʿÂʾisha, as well as to demystify her origins by discrediting the story of the heavenly fruit. This in itself is surprising, since a number of Sunnî transmitters carry the story and, while most of them reject the *ḥadîṯ*, they do so on account of the dating of Fâṭima's birth before the night journey rather than explicitly on account of the *motif* of the mystical fruit. The Shîʿa resolve their dilemma not by changing dates, but by positing that there was more than one journey by Muḥammad to heaven:

> Several of our companions, on the authority of Aḥmad b. Muḥammad, on the authority of al-Ḥusayn b. Saʿîd, on the authority of al-Qâsim b. Muḥammad al-Ğawharî, on the authority of ʿAlî b. Abî Ḥamza, who said Abû Baṣîr[54] asked Abû ʿAbd Allâh[55] (and I was present), saying: May I be made your ran-

---

[53] **YQB.**, vol. II: 19.

[54] Yaḥyâ b. al-Qâsim Abû Baṣîr b. al-Asadî (cf. **NĞA.**, n. 1187: 441, **MOD.**: 395). Modarressi notes that he was arguably the most prolific transmitter in the 2ND/8TH century, transmitting from the sixth and seventh Imâms.

[55] The sixth Imâm.

> som! How many times was the Messenger of God made to ascend? He replied: Twice.[56]

While in essence the more ancient theory of the 'night journey' being much closer to Muḥammad's prophetic calling would accord with the Shîʿî dating of Fâṭima's birth, al-Kulaynî and the others are referring to an entirely different mystical event. This added event is the only possible way of explaining how she could have been conceived when Muḥammad returned from the 'night journey' and the eating of mystical fruit, and yet only be born two years after that (that is, five years after Muḥammad's prophetic call).[57] Fâṭima is thus, according to the Shîʿa, born around 615, a whole ten years later than Sunnî reckonings, making her about seven or eight years of age when she was betrothed to ʿAlî (within the first year of the *hiğra*)[58] and seventeen or eighteen when she died.

2.5. An Outline of Fâṭima's Life

Hagiography notwithstanding, the life of Fâṭima would dishearten most biographers. Apart from the elaborate theology constructed around her life in the Shîʿî (and some Sunnî) books of *aḥâdîṯ*, we know practically nothing. That she lived close to her father, surviving him briefly and producing numerous descendents for him, and that she has a certain historical substance because of her husband and sons are all reasons for her prominence. So writes Veccia Vaglieri; and yet, she claims, Fâṭima remained on the fringes of early Islam's important events, receiving negligible attention in the earliest historical sources.[59] The sporadic attempts to unearth the authentic Fâṭima led to Lammens' depressing portrait of an unattrac-

---

[56] **KLY.**, vol. I, bk. 4 (Kitâb al-ḥuğğa), bb. mawlid al-nabî, n. 13: 442–443. Cf also **ṬSṬ¹**.: 550, **MĞL.**, vol. XVIII, bb. 3, n. 13: 356.

[57] **KFM¹**., Part 42: 511. He places her birth two years rather than five years after the prophetic call, in order to solve the problem of her conception when Muḥammad returned from the heavens.

[58] **YQB.**, vol. II: 42, **MSD.**, vol. III, bb. 72, n. 1485: 22–23, bb. 73, n. 1486: 27–28.

[59] VECCIA VAGLIERI L., "Fāṭima" in H.A.R. Gibb et al. (eds.), *EI²*, 1965, vol. IIb: 841.

tive, mediocre and ill-treated woman, gloomy and insignificant, and to Massignon's over-enthusiastic attempt to beatify her; neither really succeeds. Following circumspectly the Shîʿî dating system and the books of *aḥâdîṯ*, we can underscore a few recorded historical events in her life that shed some light on her personality and status.

She was born, by Shîʿî accounts, around 615, when her mother Ḫadîǧa was over fifty years of age, a factor which appears to present no real problem. A number of incidents have reached us from her childhood: one, prescient of things to come, was her extreme grief over the death of her mother,[60] although her grief over the death of Ḥamza, Muḥammad's uncle, at the battle of Uḥud, appears even more conspicuous.[61] Another is her comforting of her father and cleaning him when an opponent throws dirt over him while he is praying,[62] and weeping impotently over the Quraysh plots against Muḥammad.[63] In spite of Veccia Vaglieri's assertion that she remained on the fringes of early Islam's important events, the name of Fâṭima is associated with a number of occasions: one was her tending of her father's wounds and the washing of swords

---

[60] Among the Shîʿa, cf. **YQB**., vol. II: 35, **ṢDQ⁴**., vol. II, n. 116: 404, **RWD¹**., vol. II; 529, **MĞL**., vol. XVI, bb. 5, n. 6: 3, vol. XLIII, bb. 3, n. 31: 27–28.

[61] AL-MÛSAWÎ M. B., *al-Kawṯar fî aḥwâl Fâṭima bt. al-nabî al-aṭhar*, 2002, vol. V, Part 12, bb. 2 (*Bakkâʾ Fâṭima ʿalâ Ḥamza sayyid al-shuhadâʾ*), n. 1/3211: 158–159, AL-QAZWÎNÎ M., *Fâṭima al-Zahrâʾ min al-mahd ilâ al-laḥd*, Beirut 2002: 98–99. Fâṭima went every Saturday morning to the graves of the martyrs and at Ḥamza's grave would plead God's mercy and pardon for him. Cf. **MĞL**., vol. XLIII, bb. 4, n. 13: 90.

[62] **ḤNB**., vol. II, *Musnad ʿAbd Allâh b. Masʿûd*, n. 3722: 44, n. 3962: 95, **BUḪ¹**., vol. I, bk. 4 (*Kitâb al-wuḍûʾ*), ch. 73, n. 241: 151, vol. I, bk. 9 (*Kitâb sutra al-muṣallâ*), ch. 20, n. 449: 295, vol. IV, bk. 52 (*Kitâb al-ǧihâd*), ch. 98, n. 185: 113–114, vol. IV, bk. 53 (*Kitâb farḍ al-ḫums*), ch. 40, n. 409: 274, vol. V, bk. 58 (*Kitâb manâqib al-anṣâr*), ch. 28, n. 193: 122, **MSL**., vol. III, bk. 32 (*Kitâb al-ǧihâd*), bb. 39, nn. 107, 108: 1418–1419, **BLḎ¹**., vol. I, n. 251: 125.

[63] **ḤNB**., vol. I, *Musnad ʿAbd Allâh b. al-ʿAbbâs*, n. 2762: 649–650, n. 3485: 788.

after the battle of Uḥud and her subsequent habit of going to pray at graves of Ḥamza and others killed in the battle.[64] We also read of the imploration by Abû Sufyân of her and ʿAlî's intercession when Mecca was threatened with occupation; Abû Sufyân implores ʿAlî's intercession, which he refuses. Fâṭima is present with baby al-Ḥasan, and Abû Sufyân asks Fâṭima for her son's intercession, which she refuses. In the accounts of al-Ṭabarî, al-Balâḏûrî and Ibn Hishâm, Abû Sufyân does not actually ask Fâṭima's intercession, although Veccia Vaglieri intimates that he does:

> Abū Sufyān then turned to Fāṭimah and said, 'Daughter of Muḥammad, don't you want to command your little son here to make peace among the people, so that he will be lord of the Arabs forever?' 'By God,' she said, 'my little son is not old enough to make peace among the people, and no-one can do so against the will of the Messenger of God.'[65]

There is therefore no case here to ascribe to Fâṭima a presage of her later intercessory powers, as is imputed in Catholic theology to Mary when, at the Cana wedding, chronicled by the Gospel of St. John,[66] she intercedes with Jesus on behalf of an embarrassed bridegroom and brings about the first of his miraculous signs.

---

[64] **HSH.**, vol. II: 80 (which has ʿAlî bringing the water and Muḥammad washing his own face, omitting all reference to Fâṭima), **ḤNB.**, vol. VIII, *Ḥadîṯ Abî Malik Sahl b. Saʿd al-Shâʿadî*, n. 22863: 425, n. 22892: 432, **BUḪ**[1]., vol. I, bk. 4 (*Kitâb al-wuḍûʾ*), ch. 76, n. 224: 153, vol. IV, bk. 52 (*Kitâb al-ǧihâd*), ch. 80, n. 152: 98–99, ch. 85, n. 159: 102–103, ch. 163, n. 274: 170, vol. V, bk. 59 (*Kitâb al-maġâzî*), ch. 23, n. 402: 277–278, vol. VII, bk. 62 (*Kitâb al-nikâḥ*), ch. 124, n. 175: 126, vol. VII, bk. 71 (*Kitâb al-ṭibb*), ch. 27, n. 618: 415–416, **MSL.**, vol. III, bk. 32 (*Kitâb al-ǧihâd*), bb. 37, n. 101: 1416, **TRM.**, vol. VI, bk. 29 (*Kitâb al-ṭibb*), bb. 34, n. 2086: 271, **BLḎ**[1]., vol. I, n. 703: 324, **YṬB**[2]., vol. VII, n. 1426: 137. Among the Shîʿa, cf. **MĞL.**, vol. 43, bb. 4, n. 13: 90.

[65] **HSH.**, vol. II: 263, **BLḎ**[2]., n. 130: 42, **YṬB**[2]., vol. VIII, nn. 1623–1624: 164–165. Cf. VECCIA VAGLIERI L., "Fāṭima" in H.A.R. Gibb et al. (eds.), *EI*[2], 1965, vol. IIb: 841.

[66] Jn. 2: 1–11.

Her refusal of her son's intercession is an augury of things to come; her later position as intercessor is demarcated by some sources as pertaining only to the sinners of her father's community, although the Shîʿî transmitters, as we shall see, widen the scope of her mediation. However, it is an intercession that is at once positive and negative; for while she pleads on behalf of the aforementioned sinners, she also has the power not only to refuse to intercede for some, but also to ask that certain people be punished by God.

Her performance of the *ʿumra* around 10/632 is also recorded; it was almost certainly on this occasion that, upon leaving Mecca, the hysterical and now orphaned daughter of Ḥamza was placed into Fâṭima's care by ʿAlî, an act that would later lead him into a dispute with Zayd and Ǧaʿfar over who was ultimately responsible for the child.[67] Her role in the famous *mubâhala* incident, Muhammad's encounter with a group of visiting Christians, is also well documented by the Sunnî transmitters. The *ḥadîṯ al-mubâhala* recalls the visit, on a date that is widely disputed, of a delegation of Christians from Naǧrân (south of Mecca) to Muḥammad.[68] After lengthy discussions concerning the status of Jesus, when no agreement was reached, Muḥammad suggested the two sides engage in *mubâhala*, the invocation of a mutual imprecation or divine malediction for the side that was lying. Q. 3: 61 was held to have come down in

[67] **ḤNB.**, vol. I, *Musnad ʿAlî b. Abî Ṭâlib*, n. 770: 212, n. 931: 254, **BUḪ[1].**, vol. V, bk. 59 (*Kitâb al-maġâzî*), ch. 42, n. 553: 387–389, vol. III, bk. 49 (*Kitâb al-ṣulḥ*), ch. 6, n. 863: 536–538.

[68] **TRM.**, vol. VIII, bk. 48 (*Kitâb tafsîr al-qurʾân*), bb. 2, n. 3002: 182, vol. IX, bk. 50 (*Kitâb al-manâqib*), *Manâqib ʿAlî b Abî Ṭâlib*, bb. 67, n. 3726: 307–308. Cf. also **ḤNB.**, vol. I, *Musnad Abî Isḥâq Saʿd b. Abî Wiqâṣ*, n. 1608: 391, **MSL.**, vol. IV, bk. 44 (*Kitâb faḍâʾil al-ṣaḥâba*), bb. 4 (*Faḍâʾil ʿAlî b. Abî Ṭâlib*), n. 32: 1871, **BLḎ[1].**, n. 199: 77, **ḤNA.**, vol. III, Part 3, bk. 31 (*Kitâb maʿrifat al-ṣaḥâba*), *Manâqib ahl bayt al-nabî*, n. 4782: 176, **ZMR.**, vol. I, *sûrat Âl ʿImrân*, v. 61: 283, **QIḌ.**, vol. VII, bk. 44 (*Kitâb faḍâʾil al-ṣaḥâba*), bb. 4 (*Min faḍâʾil ʿAlî b. Abî Ṭâlib*), n. 42: 412–413, **AKR.**, vol. XLII: 16, 112, **RAZ.**, vol. VIII, *sûrat Âl ʿImrân*, v. 61: 85, 87–88, **QRṬ.**, vol. IV: 104, **BḌW.**, Part 3, *sûrat Âl ʿImrân*, v. 61: 76; **SHL.**, bb. 3 (*Fî ḏikr manâqib al-Ḥasan wa-l-Ḥusayn*): 100

this regard.[69] The Islamic accounts tell that Muḥammad ordered that in a field outside Medina, a thin black cloak be used as a shade between two trees. The Christians of Naǧrân stood on one side of the field, and on the other, Muḥammad, together with ʿAlî, Fâṭima, al-Ḥasan and al-Ḥusayn. Muḥammad recited Q. 33: 33 (*sûrat al-Aḥzâb*) and addressed the *ahl al-bayt* saying that he would invoke malediction for them and that they should say amen.[70]

2.6. THE MARRIAGE WITH ʿALÎ B. ABÎ ṬÂLIB

The Shîʿa insist that the marriage of ʿAlî and Fâṭima took place within the first year of the *hiǧra*.[71] A number of accounts show that both Abû Bakr and ʿUṯmân asked unsuccessfully for her hand,[72] refused by Muḥammad because he was waiting on God; the Shîʿa are adamant that he already had his instructions, and that God had ordered him to marry Fâṭima to ʿAlî, in a *ḥadîṯ* that occurs with diverse wording in both Sunnî and Shîʿa collections: "The Messenger of God said: O ʿAlî, God, may He be exalted, has married you to Fâṭima."[73]

---

[69] «And whoso disputeth with thee concerning him, after the knowledge which hath come unto thee, say (unto him): Come! We will summon our sons and your sons, and our women and your women, and ourselves and yourselves, then we will pray humbly (to our Lord) and (solemnly) invoke the curse of Allah upon those who lie».

[70] **QRṬ**., vol. IV: 104.

[71] **ATH²**., vol. V, bb. *ḥarf al-fâʾ*: 520. It is said to have been after the battle of Uḥud, although it is noted that others say it was before Muḥammad married ʿÂʾisha, and that Fâṭima was fifteen years of age at the time of the marriage. Among the Shîʿa, cf. **YQB**., vol. II: 42, **MSD**., vol. III, bb. 72, n. 1485: 22–23, bb. 73, n. 1486: 27–28.

[72] **SʿD**., vol. X, *Ḏikr banât rasûl Allâh*, n. 4927 (*Fâṭima*): 20, **ATH²**., vol. V, bb. *ḥarf al-fâʾ*: 520, **MTQ**., vol. V: 98–99, **BLḎ¹**., vol. I, *Azwâǧ rasûl Allâh*, n. 864: 402–403.

[73] Alternative versions read: "O ʿAlî, God has ordered me to marry you to Fâṭima." **ḤWZ**., Part 1, bb. *Faḍâʾil Fâṭima al-Zahrâʾ bt. rasûl Allâh*, n. 25: 101, n. 36: 106, n. 38: 107, n. 57: 120, n. 65: 125, **AKR**., vol. XLII: 126–131, **ǦWZ¹**., vol. I, bb. *fî ḏikr tazwîǧ Fâṭima bi-ʿAlî*: 415–416, 418–419, **ATH²**., vol. V, bb. *ḥarf al-fâʾ*: 520, **RḤB**.: 30–33; **ṢFI**., vol. II, bb. *manâqib*

Among the Shîʿî transmitters, Muḥammad receives this order during one of his two 'night journeys',[74] while among the Sunnî, al-Ğawzî rejects it as absolutely false (*mawḍûʿ*).[75] In his *Sunan*, al-Nasâʾî records a *ḥadîṯ* that Muḥammad's refusal of Abû Bakr and ʿUṯmân was by reason of Fâṭima's extreme youth,[76] but the Shîʿî transmitters, noting Muḥammad's own marriage to an exceedingly young ʿÂʾisha, reject this.[77]

The Shîʿî transmitters further stress the inevitability of the marriage through a *ḥadîṯ* worded, in terms of the Arabic grammar, in a manner suggesting that anything else would have been impossible:

> He said: Had it not been that God, may He be exalted, had created Fâṭima for ʿAlî, there would not have been anyone suitable for her on the face of the earth from Âdam and those after him.[78]

ʿAlî had vacillated in asking her hand (despite the encouragement of his family, who reminded him of his closeness to Muḥammad) because of his extreme poverty, and because two other suitors, im-

---

Fâṭima al-Zahrâʾ: 180, **HAY.**, vol. IX, bb. *manâqib Fâṭima bt. rasûl Allâh*: 204, **MTQ**., vol. V: 97, **SHL**., bb. *faḍl fî ḏikr manâqib ʿAlî b. Abî Ṭâlib*: 43.

74 Cf. AL-MÛSAWÎ M. B., *al-Kawṯar fî aḥwâl Fâṭima bt. al-nabî al-aṭhar*, 2002, vol. III, Part 3, bb. 4 (*Laylat al-miʿrâğ wa-l-waṣiyya ilâ rasûl Allâh fî tazwîğ ʿAlî min Fâṭima*), n. 1/2156: 405.

75 **ĞWZ**[1]., vol. I, bb. *fî ḏikr tazwîğ Fâṭima bi-ʿAlî*: 415–416, 418–419.

76 **NSA**[1]., vol. VI, bk. 26 (*Kitâb al-nikâḥ*), bb. *tazawwuğ al-marʾa*: 62, **NSA**[2].: 84–85.

77 Cf. AL-QAZWÎNÎ M., *Fâṭima al-Zahrâʾ min al-mahd ilâ al-laḥd*, 2002: 103.

78 Among the Shîʿa, cf. **RṬB**[1].: 10, **RṬB**[2].: 139, **ṢDQ**[1]., n. 18: 592, **ṢDQ**[3]., vol. III, bb. *al-akfâʾ*, n. 4383: 393, **ṢDQ**[4]., vol. II, n. 3: 414, **ṢDQ**[5]., vol. I, bb. 21, n. 3: 225, **FNR**., vol. I; 148, **ṬBR**[1]., vol. I, bb. 142, n. 3: 178, **IRB**., vol. I: 463, **ḤRR**[1]., vol. XX, bb. 27, n. 25067: 84, **MĞL**., vol. XLIII, bb. 2, n. 1: 10; bb. 5, n. 3: 92–93; bb. 5, n. 6: 97; bb. 5, n. 22; 107–108. Among the Sunnî, cf. **ḪWZ**., Part 1, bb. *Faḍâʾil Fâṭima al-Zahrâʾ bt. rasûl Allâh*, n. 38: 107.

portant men, had been refused.[79] He might have been disconcerted had he witnessed Fâṭima's response to her father's announcement that she would marry him; some *aḥâdîṯ* posit a stony silence (and thus a tacit agreement), while others portray a distraught Fâṭima protesting loudly and having to be calmed by her father with assurances that ʿAlî was his best man.[80]

---

[79] **SʿD.**, vol. X, *Ḏikr banât rasûl Allâh*, n. 4927 (*Fâṭima*): 20–22, **BLḎ[1].**, vol. I, *Azwâǧ rasûl Allâh*, n. 865: 402–403, **AKR.**, vol. XLII: 127, **ATH[2].**, vol. V, bb. *ḥarf al-fâʾ*: 520.

[80] **ḤNB.**, vol. VII, *Ḥadîṯ Maʿqil b. Yasâr*, n. 20329: 287–288, **ATH[2].**, vol. V, bb. *ḥarf al-fâʾ*: 520, **HAY.**, vol. IX: 102, **MTQ.**, vol. V: 98. Among the Shîʿa, a number of transmitters portray her weeping both at the proposal of the marriage, as well as after it. The latter is almost always qualified as a weeping over the poverty of her husband; the former is not always clarified. Ibn Shahrâshûb tells that, upon the announcement of the marriage, some of the local women told Fâṭima that some of the Quraysh women were saying her father was marrying her off to an indigent. When Fâṭima asks her father if this is true, Muḥammad insists that not only is this not true, but also that ʿAlî was the first to embrace Islam and is greater than all the rest in knowledge and discernment. Cf. **RṬB[2].**: 116, 174, **ṢDQ[1].**, n. 2: 439, **ṢDQ[4].**: 120, **MFD[1].**, vol. I: 36, **FNR.**, vol. I: 112, **SHB.**, vol. III, bb. *manâqib Fâṭima al-Zahrâʾ*: 392, **IRB.**, vol. I: 149, 350, 363, 368, 370, **ḤLL[2].**: 195, 316 (situated after the marriage: cf. also **ǦQM.**: 120), **MǦL.**, vol. XXXVIII, bb. 56, n. 36: 19, vol. XL, bb. 91, n. 34: 17, vol. XLIII, bb. 5, n. 33: 135, n. 36: 140, bb. 6, n. 6: 149. In this connection, al-Kulaynî transmits a curious *ḥadîṯ*, also found in other transmitters: "A number of our companions, on the authority of Aḥmad b. Muḥammad b. Ḫâlid, on the authority of ʿAlî b. Asbâṭ, on the authority of Dâwûd, on the authority of Yaʿqûb b. Shuʿayb, who said: When the Messenger of God married ʿAlî to Fâṭima, he came to her and she was crying. He said to her: What are these tears of yours? By God, if in my family there were one better than ʿAlî, I would not marry you to him. But as it is, it is not I who am marrying him to you; God is marrying you to him, and fixes for you the one-fifth as long as the heavens and the earth continue." Cf. **KLY.**, vol. V, bk. 18 (*Kitâb al-nikâḥ*), bb. *mâ tazawwaǧ ʿalay-hi amîr al-muʾminîn Fâṭima*, n. 6: 378, **ṬFA[2].**, bb. 2, n. 14–45: 40, **MǦL.**, vol. XLIII, bb. 5, n. 5: 94, n. 43: 144. The *ḥadîṯ*, while boosting the status of ʿAlî, never quite explains why Fâṭima should be crying over the planned marriage.

Numerous *aḥâdîṯ* tell of ʿAlî's dowry problems; some sources name an amount of money, while most speak of his dowry in terms of his meager possessions – some old armour (from the field of Badr, add some *aḥâdîṯ*, implying that the marriage was after the battle), a shield, a threadbare ram skin and the like.[81] While later Shîʿî *aḥâdîṯ* take up the theme of Fâṭima's own dower being, rather than a common and paltry sum of money, her position as intercessor for the sinners of her father's community, Ibn Ḥanbal records that her father gave her a dress of velvet, a skin pillow stuffed with palm fibers, two millstones, two earthenware jars and a waterskin.[82] The marriage itself could not, as some sources assert, have been consummated after the battle of Badr,[83] since their first child al-Ḥasan

---

The reference to the 'one-fifth' (the reference is to her bridal dower, and to the one-fifth tax, based on Q. 8: 41, which was orientated towards the needy and the orphans) suggests a serious worry over the finances of her husband-to-be. In Ibn Shaḥrâshûb's transmission, when she questions her father about whether he is marrying her to an indigent, Muḥammad, while praising ʿAlî's virtues, contradicts the charge that he is poor. In reality, the poverty of ʿAlî and therefore of Fâṭima's household is clearly demonstrated by a number of Shîʿî texts, which transmit *aḥâdîṯ* of Fâṭima weeping for hunger. Cf. for e.g. **SHB.**, vol. III, bb. *manâqib Fâṭima al-Zahrâʾ*: 319, **MĞL.**, vol. XXIV, bb. 36, n. 6: 99, vol. XLIII, bb. 5, n. 30: 120.

[81] **SʿD.**, vol. X, *Ḏikr banât rasûl Allâh*, n. 4927 (*Fâṭima*): 20–22, **BUḪ¹.**, vol. III, bk. 34 (*Kitâb al-buyûʿ*), ch. 29, n. 302: 171, vol. IV, bk. 53 (*Kitâb farḍ al-ḫums*), ch. 1, n. 324: 206, vol. V, bk. 59 (*Kitâb al-maġâzî*), ch. 11, n. 340: 226–227, **ADD.**, vol. I, bk. 12 (*Kitâb al-nikâḥ*), bb. 35: 490–491, vol. II, bk. 19 (*Kitâb al-ḫarâǧ*), bb. 20: 134, **BLḎ¹.**, vol. I, n. 865: 402, **SQL¹.**, vol. IV, bb. *ḥarf al-fâʾ*, n. 830: 366, **MTQ.**, vol. V: 98.

[82] **ḤNB.**, vol. I, *Musnad ʿAlî b. Abî Ṭâlib*, n. 643: 183, n. 715: 200, n. 819: 223, n. 838: 227–228, n. 853: 231.

[83] **SʿD.**, vol. X, *Ḏikr banât rasûl Allâh*, n. 4927 (*Fâṭima*): 23: it is posited here that the marriage took place five months after the *hiǧra* and was consummated when ʿAlî returned from the battle of Badr and when Fâṭima was eighteen years old.

was born in the second year of the *hiǧra*, followed, fifty days after his birth, by the conception of his brother al-Ḥusayn.[84]

The introductory notes of the English edition of ʿAlî's sermons and letters (*Nahǧ al-balâġa*), by Sayed Mohamed Askari Jafery, offer the following enthused description of their married life:

> He had been betrothed to her several days before the expedition to Bader. But the marriage was celebrated three months later, Hazrath Ali being in his 21ST year and Hazrath Fatima in 15TH year (*sic*) of her life (The Spirit of Islam). It was very happy marriage (*sic*). The transcendental distinctiveness of their individual characters blended so well with each other that they never quarreled and complained of one another and led a happy and contented life. Each one of them was rich in his own rights; Fatima was the only heir of one of the richest women of Arabia, Khadija, and had inherited many orchards and gardens in Mecca and Madina, besides that she was the daughter of the head of a rich clan and a king of a fast growing kingdom. Ali was a marshal who had very handsome shares from the spoils of war. Yet all that they owned went to the poor, cripples and orphans, and they themselves often starved. Their only luxury in life was prayers, and the company of each other and their children; and they willing shared the sorrows and suffering of poor (*sic*). They were given a slave girl, Fizza, but the Holy prophet (A.S.) had made arrangement that every alternate day was the off day of Fizza and her mistress would do all the household work. Even when Hazrath Fatima was ill on Fizza's off day, Fizza would not be allowed to tend to the duties, but Hazrath Ali would work…During the life time of Hazrath Fatima (A.S.) Hazrath Ali did not marry another woman.[85]

---

[84] **BLḎ**[1]., vol. I, *Azwâǧ rasûl Allâh*, n. 864: 404, **YṬB**[2]., vol. VII, n. 1431: 142 posits that al-Ḥasan was born in the third year of the *hiǧra* (thus c. 625), with al-Ḥusayn conceived fifty days later; but in the same volume, n. 1367: 91, he concedes that some hold al-Ḥasan to have been born in the second year of the *hiǧra*.

[85] REZA A., (trans.), *Peak of Eloquence. Nahjul Balagha*, Tahrike Tarsile Qur'an Inc., New York 1996: 15–16.

The final sentence of this adulatory passage calls for comment. While the Shîʿa and a number of the Sunnî transmitters (including al-Ṭabarî) insist that ʿAlî married no other woman until the death of Fâṭima,[86] a *ḥadîṯ* in Ibn Ḥanbal and al-Buḫârî[87] records that Muḥammad gives to ʿAlî a suit made of silk but grows inexplicably angry when ʿAlî subsequently wears it. ʿAlî decides to divide the suit up "among my women" (*bayna nisâʾî*). In terms of content, the *ḥadîṯ* is perplexing; why would Muḥammad make such a gift and then grow angry when it was used? Muslim reports Muḥammad as saying: "I did not send it to you to wear it, but to divide it among the women as a head covering."[88] Lammens', no less puzzlingly, translates the Arabic *nisâʾî* as 'my wives' and thinks that these words were spoken by ʿAlî in a moment when he "forgets himself",[89] insinuating that he had other wives whose existence was hidden from Fâṭima. This is untenable, considering not only the weight of evidence (that ʿAlî had no other wives while Fâṭima was alive), but also the fact that Lammens has been over rigorous in his translation of *nisâʾî*, which more generally means 'my women'. The greater possibility is that ʿAlî is speaking generically of the women in his life, referring to his wife Fâṭima, his daughters Zaynab and

---

86 Amongst the Sunnî, cf. for e.g. **NSA²**.: 5, **YṬB²**., vol XVII, n. 3470: 227, **BRR**., vol. IV, *Kitâb al-nisâʾ*, n. 4057: 1894, **KṮR¹**., vol. VI: 333, **SQL⁴**., vol. XII, *Kitâb al-nisâʾ*, n. 4434: 441. Among the Shîʿa, cf. **MSD**., vol. III, bb. 73, n. 1496: 31. The reason put forward by the Shîʿa for ʿAlî's monogamy is that Fâṭima was pure and did not menstruate (and was thus incomparable with other women). Even in Paradise, when other men can take the 'maidens of Paradise' as their brides, no such option will be open to ʿAlî. In Paradise, Fâṭima will be his only wife. Cf. **SHB**., vol. III, bb. *manâqib Fâṭima al-Zahrâʾ*: 372.

87 **ḤNB**., vol. I, *Musnad ʿAlî b. Abî Ṭâlib*, n. 963: 253 (where the intimation is that it is Muḥammad's and not ʿAlî's women being spoken of), n. 1185: 289–290 (where the women are qualified as Fâṭima and ʿAlî's aunts), **BUḪ¹**., vol. III, bk. 72 (*Kitâb al-libâs*), ch. 30, n. 731: 487–488.

88 **MSL**., vol. III, bk. 37 (*Kitâb al-libâs*), bb. 2, n. 17: 1644.

89 LAMMENS H., "Fatima and the Daughters of Muhammad" in Ibn Warraq (ed. and trans.), *The Quest for the Historical Muhammad*, 2000: 235.

Umm Kulṯûm, and his own mother Fâṭima. The first of the two texts offered by Ibn Ḥanbal intimates this, making a clear distinction between Fâṭima and the other women ("he sent one to Fâṭima and divided the other between his women'),[90] while the second qualifies that one of the women is Fâṭima and the other is definitely not another wife ("between Fâṭima and his aunt"). [91]

It is certain that, at least for the first few years of their marriage, and before the occupation of the Ḫaybar oasis, ʿAlî and Fâṭima lived in fairly severe poverty ("all we had" claimed ʿAlî, "was a sheep skin", which served both as a bed and a working mat)[92] that was by no means self-induced, so that sometimes there was nothing to eat and their children cried from hunger.[93] Lammens wonders why Muḥammad, who he claims was surely rich, did not assist them; but it is debatable whether Muḥammad was particularly rich before the occupation of Ḫaybar.[94] Ibn Ḥanbal records a report in which Fâṭima gives her father some bread – the first he has eaten in three days – which suggests he was not.[95]

---

[90] **ḤNB.**, vol. I, *Musnad ʿAlî b. Abî Ṭâlib*, n. 963: 253 (**فأمرني بنزعهما فأرسل بإحداهما إلى فاطمة و شقّ الأخرى بين نسائه**).

[91] Op. cit., vol. I, *Musnad ʿAlî b. Abî Ṭâlib*, n. 1185: 289–290 (**فأمرني فشققتها بين نسائي خمرًا بين فاطمة و عمته**).

[92] **BLḎ[1]**., vol. I, n. 865: 402.

[93] **SʿD.**, vol. X, *Ḏikr banât rasûl Allâh*, n. 4927 (*Fâṭima*): 22–24, **ḤNB.**, vol. IV, *Musnad Anas b. Mâlik*, n. 12526: 302, **ADD.**, vol. II, bk. 31 (*Kitâb al-libâs*), bb. 32, n. 383, bk. 10 (*Kitâb al-luqṭa*), bb. 16: 398, **ḪWZ.**, Part 1, bb. *Faḍâʾil Fâṭima al-Zahrâʾ bt. rasûl Allâh*, n. 19: 97–98, **ǦWZ[2]**., vol. II, *Fâṭima bt. rasûl*: 3, **MTQ.**, vol. V: 56.

[94] A rich oasis inhabited by Jewish tribes, conquered by Muḥammad in about 6/628, who then distributed some of his one-fifth share, a considerable yield of land and produce, among his wives and family. Cf. VECCIA VAGLIERI L., "Khaybar" in H.A.R. Gibb et al. (eds.), *EI²*, 1978, vol. IVb: 1137–1143.

[95] **ḤNB.**, vol. IV, *Musnad Anas b. Mâlik*, n. 13222: 425. Among the Shîʿa, cf. **ṢDQ[5]**., vol. II, bb. 31, n. 123: 40, **SHB.**, vol. III, bb. *manâqib Fâṭima al-Zahrâʾ*: 381, **ḤRR[1]**., vol. XXV, bb. 10, n. 31055: 25, **MǦL.**, vol. XVI, bb. 9, n. 28: 225, vol. XX, bb. 17, n. 10: 245, vol. XLIII, bb. 3, n. 41: 40.

Despite the claims of Sayed Mohamed Askari Jafery, there was apparently no servant, at least at the beginning, and Fâṭima was reduced to exhaustion through much menial work, as was, it seems, ʿAlî. Her request for a servant from her father, in most accounts at the suggestion of ʿAlî, was met with his teaching her and her husband a set of prayers to say at night ('God is the greatest' thirty-four times, 'praise be to God' and 'God be praised' thirty-three times).[96] At least one Sunnî transmitter records that Muḥammad did in fact give Fâṭima a servant[97] (while Ibn Ḥanbal has Muḥammad teaching the couple these prayers without them having asked for a servant).[98] The enigmatic refusal by Muḥammad of Fâṭima's ostensibly warranted request takes the form of a stylized and didactic genre; that Fâṭima needs a servant is not finally the point, for more important is the use of the event as an opportunity to teach the pre-eminence of prayer. Christian exegetes may find examples of a not dissimilar pedagogy in the Gospels; one of these is recorded in Lk. 11: 27–28 in which someone cries out to Jesus: "*Blessed is the womb that bore you and the breasts that suckled you!*" His disconcerting reply – "*More blessed is the one who hears the word of God and keeps it*" – is, classical exegesis insists, not finally a denigration

---

[96] **SʿD.**, vol. X, *Ḏikr banât rasûl Allâh*, n. 4927 (*Fâṭima*): 25–26, **ḤNB.**, vol. I, *Musnad ʿAlî b. Abî Ṭâlib*, n. 604: 174, n. 740: 206, n. 838: 227–228, n. 996: 260, n. 1141: 287, n. 1249: 309, vol. X, *Ḥadîṯ Umm Salama*, n. 26613: 187, vol. II, *Musnad ʿAlî b. Abî Ṭâlib*, n. 1228: 295, vol. X, *Musnad ʿAbd Allâh b. ʿAmr b. al-ʿÂṣ*, n. 6554: 82 which has Muḥammad teaching ʿAli and Fâṭima these bedtime prayers outside of the context of their asking for a servant, **BUḪ[1].**, vol. IV, bk. 53 (*Kitâb farḍ al-ḫums*), ch. 6, n. 344: 221–222, vol. VII, bk. 64 (*Kitâb al-nafaqât*), ch. 6, n. 274: 210, ch. 7, n. 275: 211, vol. VIII, bk. 75 (*Kitâb al-daʿwât*), ch. 11, n. 330: 222–223, vol. V, bk. 57 (*Kitâb faḍâʾil al-aṣḥâb*), ch. 10, n. 55: 46, **ADD.**, vol. II, bk. 19 (*Kitâb al-ḫarâǧ*), bb. 20: 135, bk. 40 (*Kitâb al-adab*), bb. 100: 609–610, **TRM.**, vol. IX, bk. 49 (*Kitâb al-daʿwât*), bb. 24, nn. 3405–3406: 112–113, **ḤNA.**, vol. III, bk. 31 (*Kitâb maʿrifat al-ṣaḥâba*), *Manâqib Fâṭima bt. rasûl Allâh*, n. 4787: 178, **IṢH.**, vol. II, bb. 133: 41, **KṮR[1].**, vol. VI: 332–333.

[97] **ADD.**, vol. II, bk. 31 (*Kitâb al-libâs*), bb. 32, n. 383.

[98] **ḤNB.**, vol. II, *Musnad ʿAbd Allâh b. ʿAmr b. al-ʿÂṣ*, n. 6565: 567–568.

of his mother, but the use of a particular occasion as an oblique allusion to the fact that it was not her motherhood, but her (and anybody else's) obedience to God's word that made her blessed.

Examples of a comparable pedagogy appear in events such as Muḥammad's proclamation: "Were Fâṭima the daughter of Muḥammad to steal, I would cut her hand off."[99] This suggests no disparagement of Fâṭima, but underscores that even one as exalted as the daughter of the Prophet is not exempt from faithful adherence to the Law. In the case of Fâṭima, this lack of disparagement is further underlined by the grammar employed in the expression of the *ḥadîṯ*, which implies that such a thing – Fâṭima's being a thief – is inconceivable. Lammens uses this *ḥadîṯ* as ammunition in his argument that Fâṭima had no special place or rank in the life of her father, but he has failed to understand the thrust behind the grammar, so that his contention is without merit.[100]

---

[99] **ḤNB.**, vol. V, *Musnad Ǧâbir b. ʿAbd Allâh*, n. 15151: 194, n. 15249: 210, vol. IX, *Musnad ʿÂʾisha*, n. 24193: 289, n. 25352: 510–511, **BUḪ[1].**, vol. IV, bk. 55 (*Kitâb aḥâdîṯ al-anbiyâʾ*), ch. 46, n. 681: 453, vol. V, bk. 57 (*Kitâb faḍâʾil al-aṣḥâb*), ch. 19, n. 79: 58–59, bk. 59 (*Kitâb al-maġâzî*), ch. 52, n. 597: 416, vol. VIII, bk. 81 (*Kitâb al-ḥudûd*), ch. 12, n. 778: 512 , ch. 13, n. 779: 512–513, **RAZ.**, vol. XII, Part 23, *sûrat al-Nûr*: 148. The Shîʿî transmitter Ibn Shaḥrâshûb adds a curious aside to this narrative; when Muḥammad spoke these words, Fâṭima overheard him and was distressed by them. Ǧibrîl then descended from heaven and revealed Q. 39: 65 («*And verily it hath been revealed unto thee as unto those before thee (saying): If thou ascribe a partner to Allah thy work will fail and thou indeed wilt be among the losers*». Muḥammad, in turn, was grieved by these words, and Ǧibrîl descended again, this time to reveal Q. 21: 22 («*If there were therein gods besides Allah, then verily both (the heavens and the earth) had been disordered. Glorified be Allah, the Lord of the Throne, from all that they ascribe (unto Him)*». Ǧibrîl explains that these verses were revealed to comfort Fâṭima. Cf. **SHB.**, vol. III, bb. *manâqib Fâṭima al-Zahrâʾ*: 372.

[100] LAMMENS H., "Fatima and the Daughters of Muhammad" in Ibn Warraq (ed. and trans.), *The Quest for the Historical Muhammad*, 2000: 266.

Eventually, both Fâṭima and her husband received shares in Ḫaybar.[101] ʿAlî built a house not far from Muḥammad's, but Fâṭima wanted to be nearer her father, so that finally a Medinan named Ḥâriṯa b. al-Nuʿmân gave them his.[102] This increase in prosperity may be aligned to a *ḥadîṯ* carried by a number of major Sunnî transmitters:

> On the authority of ʿÂʾisha, who said: When (the verse) «*And warn thy tribe of near kindred*» came down (*sûrat al-Shuʿarâʾ* [26] verse 214), the Messenger of God stood up and said: "O Fâṭima daughter of Muḥammad! O Ṣafiyya, daughter of ʿAbd al-Muṭṭalib! O children of ʿAbd al-Muṭṭalib! I have nothing which can avail you against God! You may ask me what you want of my worldly belongings."[103]

---

[101] **HSH.**, vol. II: 238–239, **SʿD.**, vol. X, *Ḏikr banât rasûl Allâh*, n. 4927 (*Fâṭima*): 28, **BLḎ².**, n. 83: 26–27, n. 99: 31.

[102] **SʿD.**, vol. X, *Ḏikr banât rasûl Allâh*, n. 4927 (*Fâṭima*): 23. According to this report: "When ʿAlî married Fâṭima, (Muḥammad) said to ʿAlî: Look for a house. ʿAlî looked for a house, and obtained one not far from the Prophet, in which the marriage was consummated. The Prophet came to (Fâṭima) and said to her: I want to move you closer to me. She said to the Messenger of God: Speak with Ḥâriṯa b. al-Nuʿmân about moving for me. The Messenger of God said: Ḥâriṯa has already moved for us, so that I would be embarrassed to face him! This came to the ears of Ḥâriṯa, who moved and came to the Prophet and said: O Messenger of God, it has come to my ears that you want to transfer Fâṭima closer to you. This is my house, and it is the nearest of the houses which the carpenter built for you. For I and my wealth are God's and His Messenger's, and by God, Messenger of God, the wealth which you take from me is more loved by me than that which you leave. The Messenger of God said: You have spoken sincerely, and may God bless you. Then the Messenger of God transferred (Fâṭima) to the house of Ḥâriṯa."

[103] **MSL.**, vol. I, bk. 1 (*Kitâb al-îmân*), bb. 89, n. 350: 192. Cf. also **ḤNB.**, vol. III, *Musnad Abî Hurayra*, n. 8609: 262, vol. IX, *Musnad ʿÂʾisha*, n. 25098: 462, n. 25592: 555. This *ḥadîṯ* appears in a number of variant forms: one of them reads: "O Fâṭima daughter of Muḥammad, save yourself from the Fire, for I have no power (to protect you) from God in anything except this, that I would sustain relationship with you." Cf. **ḤNB.**,

Of a certainty, there were four children born to ʿAlî and Fâṭima: al-Ḥasan, al-Ḥusayn, Zaynab and Umm Kulṯûm.[104] As to a fifth child, the boy named al-Muḥassin, there is some uncertainty, many of the Sunnî omitting any mention of him, or saying that he was born, but died in childhood; the Shîʿa remain adamant that Fâṭima miscarried as a result of physical violence perpetrated against her after Muḥammad's death; (the verb *saqaṭa*, observes Lane, indicates that the child was born abortively, but having a developed form).[105]

According to a handful of Sunnî reports, there appear to have been some disputes within the marriage; and so claim Lammens and Veccia Vaglieri, although neither offers any clear sources, and the minimal references in the books of *aḥâdîṯ* hardly permit us to arrive at these authors' conclusion that the marriage was miserable. Certainly, Ibn Saʿd records an incident in which "there were words" between ʿAlî and Fâṭima, causing Muḥammad to intervene and make peace (by lying down between them and holding their hands until reconciliation was achieved).[106] Lammens draws on another event recorded by Ibn Saʿd:

> ʿAlî was severe with Fâṭima, and she said: "By God, I will complain to the Messenger of God about you!" So, she set out, and ʿAlî set out after her. He (Muḥammad) stood listening to

---

vol. III, *Musnad Abî Hurayra*, n. 8409: 230, n. 8735: 284, **MSL**., vol. I, bk. 1 (*Kitâb al-îmân*), bb. 89, n. 348: 192.

[104] **SʿD**., vol. X, *Ḏikr banât rasûl Allâh*, n. 4927 (*Fâṭima*): 27, **NSA²**.: 5, **BRR**., vol. IV, *Kitâb al-nisâʾ wa-kunâ-hunna*, n. 4057: 1894. These authors mention only four children, omitting al-Muḥassin. Cf. also Ibn Mâlik., *al-Mawaṭṭaʾ*, bk. 26 (*Kitâb al-ʿaqîqa*), bb. 1, nn. 2–3: 501 for the record of Fâṭima shaving the hair of her four newborn children and giving in charity the weight in silver.

[105] Cf. LANE E.W., *An Arabic-English Lexicon*, Librairie du Liban, Beirut 1968, vol. IV: 1380. Among the Sunnî, al-Muḥassin is mentioned by: **ḤNB**., vol. I, *Musnad ʿAlî b. Abî Ṭâlib*, n. 769: 211–212, n. 953: 250–251, where his birth is recorded, n. 1370: 335 where it is omitted, **BLḎ¹**., vol. I, *Azwâǧ rasûl Allâh*, n. 865: 402, 404, **ḪWZ**., Part 1, bb. *Faḍâʾil Fâṭima al-Zahrâʾ bt. rasûl Allâh*, n. 73: 128, **ǦWZ²**., vol. II, *Fâṭima bt. rasûl Allâh*: 2, **RḤB**., 55.

[106] **SʿD**., vol. X, *Ḏikr banât rasûl Allâh*, n. 4927 (*Fâṭima*): 26–27.

> their words, and she complained to the Messenger of God about the harshness (*ġilaẓ*) of ʿAlî and his severity (*shidda*) against her. Then he said: "My daughter, listen closely and be reasonable. There is no authority for a woman who does not carry out the desire (*hawâ*) of her husband that he remain silent." ʿAlî said: "I refrained from what I was doing and I said: I will never again do something that you dislike."[107]

The Arabic *hawâ* could be translated as 'love', 'attachment', 'the inclination of the soul or mind to a thing', 'the object of love', 'desirous love' or even 'love and desire which is not praiseworthy'. It may, but does not necessarily, carry a sexual connotation.[108] As it stands, this text is puzzling and imprecise; the implication is that Fâṭima has not the authority to insist that ʿAlî not react should she not carry out his desire. Ibn Ḥağar al-ʿAsqalânî reports the words of Muḥammad slightly differently, in what may be a corrupted version of the *ḥadîṯ*: "There is no woman whose husband comes to her and remains silent."[109]

Lammens seizes upon the words 'severity' and 'harshness' and draws the conclusion that ʿAlî was 'violent' towards his wife,[110] further proving the disastrous nature of the marriage. Caetani examines the same text and decides that it refers to an occasion of violent scenes on the part of ʿAlî against his wife; on this alone, he concludes that the marriage was an unhappy one.[111] But an examination of the text itself necessarily leads us to very different conclusions; it remains puzzling that Lammens and Caetani should be so

---

107 **SʿD.**, vol. X, *Ḏikr banât rasûl Allâh*, n. 4927 (*Fâṭima*): 26.

108 Cf. LANE E W., *An Arabic-English Lexicon*, 1968, vol. VIII: 3046–3047.

109 **SQL[1]**., vol. IV, bb. *ḥarf al-fâ'*, n. 830: 368.

110 LAMMENS H., "Fatima and the Daughters of Muhammad" in Ibn Warraq (ed. and trans.), *The Quest for the Historical Muhammad*, 2000, nt. 275: 302.

111 "Abbiamo anche notizia che il matrimonio di Fāṯimah non fosse felice, e che fra 'Ali e lei avvenissero una volta scene violente, nelle quali 'Ali maltrattó la moglie: Fāṯimah corse per protezione presso il padre, e Maometto ristabili pace fra i coniugi." Cf. CAETANI L., *Annali dell'Islam*, vol. II, Tome I, Georg Olms Verlag, Hildesheim 1972: 690.

readily satisfied with a single incident as sufficient proof of their claims. It must be noted at once that this text is found only in Ibn Saʿd and Ibn Ḥağar (so that Lammens' contention that "the volumes of the Hadith mention violent scenes between the couple"[112] is untenable). We must question the nature of ʿAlî's 'violence'; the Arabic *shidda* has a whole range of meanings, including 'hardness', 'vehemence', 'severity', 'violence', 'strictness', 'intenseness' and 'stress'.[113] The term *ğilaẓ* also carries a variety of possible interpretations, among them 'churlish', 'uncompliant', 'surly', 'ill-natured', 'rude', 'uncivil' and 'unkind'.[114]

It seems improbable that it is physical violence that is meant here, for Muḥammad, who forbade ʿAlî a second marriage for fear of upsetting his daughter, and who insisted that whatever angered Fâṭima angered him (and that "O Fâṭima, verily God is angry when you are angry")[115] would hardly have permitted such a situation. Furthermore, physical violence on the part of ʿAlî towards his wife would almost certainly have found an echo in the other Sunnî accounts of their marriage. The insinuation of this passage is that ʿAlî is constantly severe with his wife (*kâna fî ʿAlî ʿalâ Fâṭima shidda*); were it violence, we would expect to find this state of affairs reported by other sources, especially earlier ones, just as we would expect Muḥammad to have reacted. However, it is not so; while other texts suggest momentary problems and marital disputes, this situation is reported upon only by Ibn Saʿd and Ibn Ḥağar, leading us to ponder its reliability.

---

112 LAMMENS H., "Fatima and the Daughters of Muhammad" in Ibn Warraq (ed. and trans.), *The Quest for the Historical Muhammad*, 2000: 248.

113 Cf. LANE E. W., *An Arabic-English Lexicon*, 1968, vol. IV: 1517–1519.

114 Op. cit., vol. VI: 2282–2283.

115 **ḤNA.**, vol. III, bk. 31 (*Kitâb maʿrifat al-ṣaḥâba*), *Manâqib Fâṭima bt. rasûl Allâh*, n. 4793: 181, **ḪWZ.**, Part 1, bb. *Faḍâʾil Fâṭima al-Zahrâʾ bt. rasûl Allâh*, n. 2: 90, **ATH²**., vol. V, bb. *ḥarf al-fâʾ*: 522, **ḎHB²**., vol. II, n. 4560: 492, **SQL¹**., vol. IV, bb. *ḥarf al-fâʾ*, n. 830: 366–367, **SQL⁴**., vol. XII, *Kitâb al-nisâʾ*, n. 4434: 441, **MTQ.**, vol. V: 97.

Nor can we easily believe that ʿAlî's 'violence' consisted of perpetual verbal abuse, since the picture of ʿAlî that emerges from the Sunnî records is one of a reticent and brooding character; this is the ʿAlî who says nothing when his attempts at taking other wives are thwarted (by Fâṭima) and forbidden (by Muḥammad), the ʿAlî who leaves the house and sleeps in the mosque when he and Fâṭima disagree, the ʿAlî who meekly accepts her rejection of the house he builds her, the ʿAlî who, after her death, pays to Abû Bakr the allegiance he had steadily refused while Fâṭima was alive, the ʿAlî who lives under the shadow of Muḥammad, not merely his cousin, but his Prophet and father-figure. Already, we have an indication of the nature of the *shidda* and *ġilaẓ* of which he stands accused, an indication that is confirmed by Muḥammad's words in the text (and in ʿAlî's subsequent reaction). Muḥammad's words are addressed primarily to Fâṭima, but contain an oblique rebuke of ʿAlî's conduct, which is unquestionably his failure to communicate in a civil manner with his wife, resulting in a churlish and sullen atmosphere in the house. Muḥammad admonishes a husband who remains silent when his wife fails to please him, but concomitantly points out to Fâṭima that all husbands grumble about the ministrations of their wives, and that she ought not to expect anything different, so that the reprimand is directed against both parties. As soon as Muḥammad has spoken, ʿAlî apologizes, promising never more to do what displeases Fâṭima. If, following Lammens, we accept this *ḥadîṯ* as authentic, we have no reason to disbelieve ʿAlî's change of heart.

There are other incidents extant; the most serious dispute is allegedly a suggestion made to 'Ali, and to which he was not unreceptive, that he marry a woman of the Banû Hishâm b. al-Muġîra of the Quraysh.[116] Muḥammad rejected the plan. At the same time, it is claimed that ʿAlî was contemplating taking as a second wife the daughter of Abû Ǧahl; according to al-Buḫârî and some others, he demanded her hand, causing Muḥammad to worry that Fâṭima

[116] **MSL.**, vol. IV, bk. 44 (*Kitâb faḍâʾil al-ṣaḥâba*), bb. 10 (*Faḍâʾil Fâṭima bt. al-nabî*), n. 93: 1902, n. 94: 1904, **TRM.**, vol. IX, bk. 50 (*Kitâb al-manâqib*), *Manâqib Fâṭima bt. Muḥammad*, bb. *fî faḍl Fâṭima*, n. 3866: 386, **BLḎ**[1]., vol. I, *Azwâǧ rasûl Allâh*, n. 865: 403–404

would be subjected to trials in her religion (because of jealousy).[117] Muḥammad, receiving complaints from Fâṭima, protested from the pulpit that the daughter of God's Prophet and the daughter of God's enemy could not live under the same roof, intimating that ʿAlî would have to divorce Fâṭima before going ahead with a second marriage.[118] Many transmitters make one or both of these marital disputes the context for Muḥammad's famous saying, recorded in these or similar words:

> Fâṭima is part of me. Whatever troubles her troubles me, and whatever injures her injures me."[119]

---

[117] **BUḪ¹**., vol. IV, bk. 53 (*Kitâb farḍ al-ḫums*), ch. 5, n. 342: 219–220, vol. V, bk. 57 (*Kitâb faḍâʾil al-aṣḥâb*), ch. 17, n. 75: 56–57, **MSL**., vol. IV, bk. 44 (*Kitâb faḍâʾil al-ṣaḥâba*), bb. 10 (*Faḍâʾil Fâṭima bt. al-nabî*), n. 95: 1903, **TRM**., vol. IX, bk. 50 (*Kitâb al-manâqib*), *Manâqib Fâṭima bt. Muḥammad*, bb. *fî faḍl Fâṭima*, n. 3868: 387.

[118] **MSL**., vol. IV, bk. 44 (*Kitâb faḍâʾil al-ṣaḥâba*), bb. 10 (*Faḍâʾil Fâṭima bt. al-nabî*), n. 96: 1903–1904.

[119] In the context of the marriage regarding a woman of the Banû Hishâm b. al-Muġîra of the Quraysh: **MSL**., vol. IV, bk. 44 (*Kitâb faḍâʾil al-ṣaḥâba*), bb. 10, n. 93: 1902, **TRM**., vol. IX, bk. 50 (*Kitâb al-manâqib*), bb. *fî faḍl Fâṭima bt. Muḥammad*, n. 3866: 386, **BLḎ¹**., vol. I, *Azwâğ rasûl Allâh*, n. 865: 402–403, **NSA²**.: 80–81, **QIḌ**., vol. VII, bk. 44 (*Kitâb faḍâʾil al-ṣaḥâba*), bb. 10 (*Faḍâʾil Fâṭima bt. al-nabî*), n. 93: 472, **ḪWZ**., Part 1, bb. *Faḍâʾil Fâṭima al-Zahrâʾ bt. rasûl Allâh*, n. 6: 91–92, **ĞWZ²**., vol. II, *Fâṭima bt. rasûl Allâh*: 4, **ATH²**., vol. V, bb. *ḥarf al-fâʾ*: 521, **MTQ**., vol. V: 96. In the context of the marriage regarding the daughter of Abû Ğahl: **ḤNB**., vol. VI, *Ḥadîṯ al-Masûr b. Maḫrama al-Zuhrî*, n. 18933: 492, n. 18935: 492–493, vol. V, *Ḥadîṯ ʿAbd Allâh b. Zubayr b. al-ʿAwwâm*, n. 16123: 453, **BUḪ¹**., vol. IV, bk. 53 (*Kitâb farḍ al-ḫums*), ch. 5, n. 342: 219–220, vol. V, bk. 57 (*Kitâb faḍâʾil al-aṣḥâb*), ch. 17, n. 75: 56–57, **MSL**., vol. IV, bk. 44 (*Kitâb faḍâʾil al-ṣaḥâba*), bb. 10, nn. 95, 96: 1903–1904, **ADD**., vol. I, bk. 12 (*Kitâb al-nikâḥ*), bb. 12: 478, **TRM**., vol. IX, bk. 50 (*Kitâb al-manâqib*), bb. *fî faḍl Fâṭima bt. Muḥammad*, n. 3868: 386–387, **ḤNA**., vol. III, bk. 31 (*Kitâb maʿrifat al-ṣaḥâba*), *Manâqib Fâṭima bt. rasûl Allâh*, nn. 4813, 4814, 4815: 187–188, **QIḌ**., vol. VII, bk. 44 (*Kitâb faḍâʾil al-ṣaḥâba*), bb. 10 (*Faḍâʾil Fâṭima bt. al-nabî*), nn. 95, 96: 472–474, **RAZ**., vol. XVI, Part 32, *sûrat al-Kâfirûn*: 141; 4, **KṮR¹**., vol. VI: 333, **MTQ**., vol. V: 97–98. The ostensibly

The Shî^ca record the *ḥadîṯ* but deny the context of ʿAlî attempting a second marriage while Fâṭima was still alive.[120] The designation of ʿAlî as *Abû Turâb* ('the father of dust')[121] is also given by some

---

Shîʿî Ibn al-Ḥadîd takes a decidedly Sunnî view: **ḤDI.**, vol. IV: 6. Outside of the context of marriage: **ḤNB.**, vol. VI, *Ḥadîṯ al-Masûr b. Maḫrama al-Zuhrî*, n. 18929: 486–487, n. 18952: 501–502, **BUḪ[1].**, vol. V, bk. 57 (*Kitâb faḍâʾil al-aṣḥâb*), ch. 13, n. 61: 50, vol. V, bk. 57 (*Kitâb faḍâʾil al-aṣḥâb*), ch. 29, n. 111: 75, **MSL.**, vol. IV, bk. 44 (*Kitâb faḍâʾil al-ṣaḥâba*), bb. 10, n. 94: 1903, **NSA[2].**: 81–82, **ḤNA.**, vol. III, bk. 31 (*Kitâb maʿrifat al-ṣaḥâba*), *Manâqib Fâṭima bt. rasûl Allâh*, n. 4797: 182, n. 4811: 186–187, **IṢH.**, vol. II, bb. 133: 40–41, **QIḌ.**, vol. VII, bk. 44 (*Kitâb faḍâʾil al-ṣaḥâba*), bb. 10 (*Faḍâʾil Fâṭima bt. al-nabî*), n. 94: 472, **ḪWZ.**, Part 1, bb. *Faḍâʾil Fâṭima al-Zahrâʾ bt. rasûl Allâh*, n. 29: 103, n. 49: 112, **RAZ.**, vol. XIV, Part 27, *sûrat al-Shûrâ*: 166, *sûrat al-Zuḫruf*: 200, vol. XV, Part 30, *sûrat al-Maʿâriǧ*: 126, **SQL[1].**, vol. IV, bb. *ḥarf al-fâʾ*, n. 830: 366, **SQL[4].**, vol. XII, *Kitâb al-nisâʾ*, n. 4434: 441, **KṮR[2].**, vol. V, *sûrat al-Muʾminûn*: 40, **MTQ.**, vol. V: 96–97; **IṢM.**, vol. I, bb. 4: 368. Here, Ibn al-Ḥadîd is in line with Shîʿî thought: **ḤDI.**, vol. XIII: 35, vol. XVI: 278.

120 Cf. for e.g.: **QḤL.**: 830, 868, **RṬB[1].**, bb. *ḫabar al-wafât wa-l-dafn*: 45, **RṬB[2].**, 70, 177, **KFI.**, bb. *faḍl al-ġayra*: 95, **RQM.**: 23, **ṢDQ[1].**, n. 3: 102, n. 18: 486, **ṢDQ[8].**, vol. I, n. 2: 185, 187, **MFD[5].**, n. 2: 259, **FNR.**, vol. I: 149, **RWD[2].**: 14, **SHB.**, vol. III, bb. *manâqib Fâṭima al-Zahrâʾ*: 378, **BṬQ.**, nn. 757, 758: 384, n. 767: 385, n. 769: 388, **IRB.**, vol. I: 363, 466, **DAY.**, vol. II: 231, 430, **ḤLL[1].**: 351, 362, **AḤS.**, vol. IV, n. 131: 93, **ÂML.**, vol. I: 170, vol. II: 118, 282, 289, vol. III: 12, **SHT.**: 140, 147, **ḤRR[1].**, vol. XX, bb. 24, n. 25054: 67, vol. XX, bb. 129, n. 25510: 232, **MĞL.**, vol. XXI, bb. 32: 279, vol. XXIII, bb. 7, n. 97: 143, bb. 13: 234, vol. XXVII, bb. 1: 62, **NṬR.**, vol. XIV, bb. 61, n. 16450: 182.

121 **BUḪ[1].**, vol. I, bk. 8 (*Kitâb al-ṣalât*), ch. 58, n. 432: 288, vol. VIII, bk. 72 (*Kitâb al-adab*), ch. 113, n. 223: 143, vol. VIII, bk. 74 (*Kitâb al-istiʾḏân*), ch. 40, n. 297: 197–198, vol. V, bk. 57 (*Kitâb faḍâʾil al-aṣḥâb*), ch. 10, n. 53: 44–45 (outside of the context of a marriage dispute), **MSL.**, vol. IV, bk. 44 (*Kitâb faḍâʾil al-ṣaḥâba*), bb. 4 (*Faḍâʾil ʿAlî b. Abî Ṭâlib*), n. 38: 1874–1875 (in the context of a marriage dispute), **NSA[2].**: 24 (outside of the context of a marriage dispute), **YṬB[2].**, vol. VII, nn. 1272–1273: 16–17 (he offers two accounts, neither of which is in the context of a marriage dispute, but which occur before the marriage), **QIḌ.**, vol. VII, bk. 44 (*Kitâb faḍâʾil al-ṣaḥâba*), bb. 4 (*Min faḍâʾil ʿAlî b. Abî Ṭâlib*), n. 38: 1874–

transmitters within the context of a marital dispute, with ʿAlî, rather than speaking angrily to his wife, leaving the house and sleeping in the mosque. This apparent desire to circumvent conflict brings into question his purportedly harsh treatment of his wife. It is also a curious reaction on the part of ʿAlî, who declares about women:

> O ye peoples! Women are deficient in Faith, deficient in shares and deficient in intelligence. As regards the deficiency in their Faith, it is their abstention from prayers and fasting during their menstrual period. As regards deficiency in their intelligence it is because the evidence of two women is equal to that of one man. As for the deficiency of their shares that is because of their share of inheritance being half of men. So beware of the evils of women. Be on your guard even from those of them who are (reportedly) good. Do not obey them even in good things so that they may not attract you to evil.[122]

In the light of these words, we must conclude that certain actions on the part of ʿAlî – his leaving the house after a quarrel with her (either through incontrollable anger or extraordinary submissiveness and the desire not to speak angrily with her), his acceptance of the thwarting of his alleged marriage plans through Fâṭima's complaints to her father, his powerlessness to marry a second wife while Fâṭima was still alive, his apparently meek acquiescence to her rejection of the house he built, and, as carefully noted by a number of Sunnî scholars, his capitulation in paying allegiance to Abû Bakr only after Fâṭima's death as he begins to notice, subsequent to her death, a decline in peoples' respect for him[123] – all of this intimates that treated his wife in a way different from all oth-

---

1875, **AKR**., vol. 42: 17–19 (in the context of a marriage dispute), **ṢBB**.: 144. There is no mention in Ibn al-Ḥadîd's account of a marriage dispute, even in a footnote which mentions Fâṭima: cf. **ḤDI**., vol. I: 2).

[122] REZA A., (trans.), *Peak of Eloquence. Nahjul Balagha*, 1996: 204.

[123] **BUḪ**[1]., vol. V, bk. 59 (*Kitâb al-maġâzî*), ch. 37, n. 545: 381–384, **MSL**., vol. III, bk. 32 (*Kitâb al-ǧihâd*), bb. 16, n. 52: 1380–1381, **YṬB**[2]., vol. IX, nn. 1825, 1826: 196–197, **BRR**., vol. III, n. 1633: 973, **ḤDI**., vol. II: 22, vol. VI: 11, 46, **KṮR**[1]., vol. V: 249, 286.

ers. The picture that emerges from the Sunnî corpus of *aḥâdîṯ* is not of a Fâṭima palely loitering in the shadow of her husband's constant severity, but rather of an ʿAlî who consistently backs down before the strong will of his wife.

2.7. RELATIONS WITH HER FATHER

It is Lammens' contention that Fâṭima was a source of irritation to her father and her husband.[124] An examination of the books of *aḥâdîṯ* certainly reveals some incidents, besides the three marriage disputes already mentioned. On one occasion, Muḥammad meets Fâṭima out walking, and in response to his query about what has brought her from her house, she replies that she has come to give comfort to a grieving family. Muḥammad then interrogates her about whether she had accompanied the family to the graveyard, something he had apparently forbidden to women. She had not. But he speaks some harsh words to her; and while Abû Dâwûd does not record them, al-Nasâʾî does. She is told that had she gone to the graveyard, she would not have seen Paradise until the grandfather of her father had seen it, and since he would never enter Paradise, nor would she.[125] This is an inexplicable incident, considering Fâṭima's regular visits to the grave of her uncle Ḥamza, killed at Uḥud[126] (on one occasion, Muḥammad sits next to his weeping daughter at the grave of Ruqayya, and wipes away her tears with his robe).[127] One author claims that Muḥammad had given her special

[124] Lammens characterizes Muḥammad as "bored and worn out" by Fâṭima's incessant complaining, suggesting that Muḥammad rejected her and was indifferent to her. Cf. LAMMENS H., "Fatima and the Daughters of Muhammad" in Ibn Warraq (ed. and trans.), *The Quest for the Historical Muhammad*, 2000: 228, 245.

[125] **ḤNB.**, vol. II, *Musnad ʿAbd Allâh b. ʿAmr b. al-ʿÂṣ*, n. 6585: 573, n. 7104: 690, **ADD.**, vol. II, bk. XX (*Kitâb al-ǧanâʾiz*), bb. 22: 171, **NSA**[1]., vol. IV, bk. 21 (*Kitâb al-ǧanâʾiz*): 26–27.

[126] Cf. HOWARD I.K.A. (trans.), *The Revolution of al-Husayn. Its Impact on the Consciousness of Muslim Society*, The Muhammadi Trust, London 1985: 27.

[127] **ḤNB.**, vol. I, *Musnad ʿAbd Allâh b. al-ʿAbbâs b. ʿAbd al-Muṭṭalib*, n. 3103: 717–718.

dispensation for graveyard visits, but he offers no sources for this claim.[128]

On another occasion, Muḥammad came to Fâṭima just as she was removing from her neck a gold chain given her by ʿAlî. "Does it please you," asks Muḥammad, "that the people are saying that Fâṭima, the daughter of Muḥammad, has a chain of fire in her hand?" Fâṭima disposes of the chain and purchases the freedom of a slave.[129] In a similar narrative, Muḥammad arrived at Fâṭima's house to find that she had hung a colourful curtain over the door. He was annoyed, and refused to enter, reducing his daughter to puzzled tears until her husband explained the problem and she removed the curtain.[130] ʿAlî was no less irritated on the occasion of the Pilgrimage one year to discover that his wife had removed her *iḥrâm*, the pilgrim's robes, and had put on colourful clothing and perfume. He complained to Muḥammad, only to discover that he himself had ordered it.[131]

A final incident concerns both ʿAlî and Fâṭima; Muḥammad came to their house, exhorting them to rise from sleep and to pray

---

[128] NEVILL A., (trans.), *Shiʾite Islam*, 1995: 25.

[129] **ḤNA**., vol. III, bk. 31 (*Kitâb maʿrifat al-ṣaḥâba*), *Manâqib Fâṭima bt. rasûl Allâh*, n. 4788: 178–179. This is an inexplicable incident, coming from the same Muḥammad who mused that, had Usâma, son of Zayd b. Ḥâriṯa been a girl, he would have bedecked and attired her until she was provided for (the sense being that he would have covered her in jewels and fine clothing until a husband was found: cf. **ḤNB**., vol. X, *Musnad ʿÂʾisha*, n. 25919: 49–50); and who gave to his grandaughter Umâma, daughter of Zaynab and Usâma b. Zayd, a magnificent necklace of onyx (**ḤNB**., vol. IX, *Musnad ʿÂʾisha*, n. 24758: 399, vol. X, *Musnad ʿÂʾisha*, n. 26309: 121–122).

[130] **ḤNB**., vol. II, *Musnad ʿAbd Allâh b. ʿUmar b. al-Ḫaṭṭâb*, n. 4727: 244–245, vol. VIII, *Ḥadîṯ Abî ʿAbd al-Raḥmân al-Safîna*, n. 21981: 214, vol. VIII, *Ḥadîṯ Ṯawbân*, n. 22426: 320, **BUḪ[1]**., vol. III, bk. 47 (*Kitâb al-hibba*), ch. 27, n. 783: 474, **ADD**., vol. II, bk. 26 (*Kitâb al-aṭʿima*), bb. 8, n. 309, bk. 31 (*Kitâb al-libâs*), bb. 32: 283, bk. 32 (*Kitâb al-taraǧǧul*), bb. 21: 404–405.

[131] **ḤNB**., vol. V, *Musnad Ǧâbir b. ʿAbd Allâh*, n. 14447: 62–64, **ADD**., vol. I, bk. 11 (*Kitâb manâsik wa-l-ḥaǧǧ*), bb. 24: 417, bb. 56: 441, **YṬB[2]**., vol. IX, n. 1752: 110.

the *taḥağğud* – the optional prayers offered from the middle to the last part of the night. The response from ʿAlî – that their lives were in the hands of God and that if He wanted them to pray He Himself would rouse them – is also put into Fâṭima's mouth by Ibn Ḥanbal and Ibn Kaṯîr; but whoever spoke it, it caused Muḥammad no little distress, and he left the scene grumbling about human stubbornness.[132]

But these are, in the wider scheme, trivial incidents, and hardly serve as a credible foundation for the claims of Lammens. Of no less significance is Muḥammad's statement, already seen, that whatever angers Fâṭima angers him, as well as a *ḥadîṯ*, on the authority of ʿÂʾisha and carried by a number of Sunnî transmitters, in which Muḥammad's tender care for Fâṭima is described:

> On the authority of the Mother of the believers ʿÂʾisha, may God be pleased with her, that she said: "I never saw anyone more similar to the Messenger of God, God bless and save him and his family, in respect of talk and speech, than Fâṭima. Whenever she came to visit him, he welcomed her, and stood and took her by her hand, kissed her and made her sit where he was sitting."[133]

Considering the prominence of ʿÂʾisha's name in the chain of transmitters, this is a startlingly positive description of Fâṭima. The

---

[132] **ḤNB.**, vol. I, *Musnad ʿAlî b. Abî Ṭâlib*, n. 571: 167, n. 575: 168, n. 715: 200, n. 900: 239, **BUḪ¹.**, vol. II, bk. 21 (*Kitâb al-taḥağğud*), ch. 4, n. 227: 127, vol. IX, bk. 93 (*Kitâb al-tawḥîd*), ch. 31, n. 557: 418, **KṮR².**, vol. IV, *sûrat al-Kahf*: 400. Ibn Kaṯîr places the last part of Q. 18: 54 («*...but man is more than anything contentious*») on the lips of Muḥammad as his complaint.

[133] **SʿD.**, vol. X, *Ḏikr banât rasûl Allâh*, n. 4927 (*Fâṭima*): 27, **BUḪ².**: 137, **MSL.**, vol. IV, bk. 44 (*Kitâb faḍâʾil al-ṣaḥâba*), bb. 10, n. 97: 1904–1905, **ADD.**, vol. II, bk. 40 (*Kitâb al-adab*), bb. 144: 645, **ḤNA.**, vol. III, bk. 31 (*Kitâb maʿrifat al-ṣaḥâba*), *Manâqib Fâṭima bt. rasûl Allâh*, n. 4795: 181, **IṢH.**, vol. II, bb. 133 (*Fâṭima bt. rasûl Allâh*): 42, **BRR.**, vol. IV, *Kitâb al-nisâʾ*, n. 4057: 1896, **ḪWZ.**, Part 1, bb. *Faḍâʾil Fâṭima al-Zahrâʾ bt. rasûl Allâh*, n. 7: 93, **ATH².**, vol. V, bb. *ḥarf al-fâʾ*: 522, **SQL¹.**, vol. IV, bb. *ḥarf al-fâʾ*, n. 830: 367, **SQL³.**, vol. VIII, bb. 84, n. 4434: 171.

two women had no love for each other, and their internecine strife continued even after Muḥammad's death. Ibn Ḥanbal and Ibn Kaṯîr record an incident in which ʿAlî sent Fâṭima to her father to complain about ʿÂʾisha's alleged slander and 'scoring hits' against them; Muḥammad's reply to his daughter – "She is the beloved of your father and of the Lord of the Kaʿba" – is all the answer she gets.[134] On this occasion, ʿAlî takes the part of Fâṭima to the point of rebuking Muḥammad: "Wasn't it enough for you," he asks "that ʿÂʾisha should insult us? Did you have to then tell Fâṭima that ʿÂʾisha is 'the beloved of your father and of the Lord of the Kaʿba'?"[135]

ʿÂʾisha was quick to deny that Muḥammad had designated ʿAlî as his successor,[136] and found herself banned from Fâṭima's deathbed (or, others claim, simply refused to be present).[137] Muḥammad's wives, led by Umm Salama (who herself had tried and failed) used Fâṭima as a spokeswoman to express their mutual resentment against his apparent preference for ʿÂʾisha. Fâṭima rarely succeeded in these demands upon her father; his reply, "Do you not love those whom I love" brought this particular mission to an end and she refused to try a second time.[138] One Shîʿî author, developing the theme that the Sunnî authorities deliberately downplay Fâṭima in order to highlight ʿÂʾisha, and writing of ʿÂʾisha's malice towards ʿAlî,[139] notes:

---

[134] **ḤNB.**, vol. IX, *Musnad ʿÂʾisha*, n. 25040: 451–452, **KṮR²**., vol. VI, *sûrat al-Shûrâ*: 210.

[135] Ibid.

[136] **BUḪ¹**., vol. V, bk. 59 (*Kitâb al-maġâzî*), ch. 81, n. 736: 525.

[137] Once again, the ostensibly Shîʿî Ibn al-Ḥadîd takes a Sunnî view of this matter. Cf. **ḤDI.**, vol. IX: 198.

[138] **ḤNB.**, vol. IX, *Musnad ʿÂʾisha*, n. 24629: 375, n. 25229: 488–489, **BUḪ¹**., vol. III, bk. 47 (*Kitâb al-hibba*), ch. 8, n. 775: 454–456, **MSL.**, vol. IV, bk. 44 (*Kitâb faḍâʾil al-ṣaḥâba*), bb. 13, n. 83: 1891–1892, **ADD.**, vol. II, bk. 40 (*Kitâb al-adab*), bb. 41: 572–573, **BLḎ¹**., vol. I, n. 873: 415.

[139] Abbott maintains that ʿÂʾisha's hostility towards ʿAlî had its genesis in his refusal to take her part in the so-called 'incident of the necklace', when rumours were spread about her fidelity to Muḥammad. Cf. ABBOTT N., *Aishah the Beloved of Mohammed*, 1988: 37–38.

> One cause for this hatred and malice was the presence of Ḥaḍrat Fāṭimah (p.b.u.h.) whose wholesome dignity and esteem pricked her heart like a thorn. Her jealousy towards the other wives (of the Prophet) did not allow her to let the Prophet love the daughter of his other wife to such a degree that he should stand on her approach, seat her in his own place, declare her most honourable of all the women of the world and bear such love towards her children as to call them his own sons…in short, all these things created the passion of hatred in her heart, as a result of which she off and on complained to the Prophet against Ḥaḍrat Fāṭimah but could not succeed in diverting the Prophet's attention from her.[140]

This attitude is more subtly expressed in another *ḥadîṯ* carried, with diverse wording, by some Sunnî transmitters:

> On the authority of ʿÂʾisha, who said: I said: Messenger of God, why is it that whenever Fâṭima comes, you kiss her as far as putting the whole of your tongue into her mouth, as if you wanted to lick her like honey?[141]

This *ḥadîṯ* continues with a description of the mystical fruit eaten by Muḥammad in Paradise, and is thus rejected by al-ʿAsqalânî and al-Hayṯamî, not on the grounds of the theology but on the basis of the impossibility of Fâṭima having been born after the night journey.

"The most beloved of my family to me is Fâṭima," declares Muḥammad in a *ḥadîṯ* carried by a number of the Sunnî transmitters[142] and, also by the Sunnî, "The most loved of women to the

---

[140] REZA A., (trans.), *Peak of Eloquence. Nahjul Balagha*, New York 1996: 318.

[141] Cf. **BĠD.**, vol. V, n. 2481: 87, **SQL²**., vol. V, n. 541: 160, **HAY.**, vol. IX, *Manâqib Fâṭima bt. rasûl Allâh*: 202, **SHL.**, bb. *faḍl fî ḏikr manâqib ʿAlî b. Abî Ṭâlib*: 42.

[142] Cf. for e.g. **ḤNB.**, vol. VIII, *Ḥadîṯ Usâma b. Zayd*, n. 21836: 181–182, **TRM.**, vol. IX, bk. 50 (*Kitâb al-manâqib*), bb. *manâqib Usâma b. Zayd*, n. 3821: 359 and bb. *fî faḍl Fâṭima bt. Muḥammad*, n. 3867: 386, **ḤNA.**, vol. III, bk. 31 (*Kitâb maʿrifat al-ṣaḥâba*), *Manâqib Fâṭima bt. rasûl Allâh*, nn. 4798,

Prophet of God is Fâṭima and the most loved of men is ʿAlî."[143] It is also related that when Muḥammad travelled, the last person he greeted upon leaving and first he greeted upon arriving back was Fâṭima.[144]

2.8. MISTRESS OF THE WOMEN

Much lamentation and weeping marks the life of Fâṭima during the final illness and death of her father[145] and her own last months. "Among the women believers," Ğibrîl tells her when her father dies, "there is no greater grief than yours",[146] while Ibn Kaṯîr, among others, reports that she never once laughed after her father's death.[147] Even the act of burying her father's body distresses her, with her words, as reported by a number of Sunnî transmitters,

---

4799: 182–183, n. 4808: 186, **BRR.**, vol. IV, *Kitâb al-nisâʾ*, n. 4057: 1897, **ḪWZ.**, Part 1, bb. *Faḍâʾil Fâṭima al-Zahrâʾ bt. rasûl Allâh*, nn. 12, 13: 95, **ATH².**, vol. V, bb. *ḥarf al-fâʾ*: 520, 552.

[143] **TRM.**, vol. IX, bk. 50 (*Kitâb al-manâqib*), bb. *fî faḍl Fâṭima bt. Muḥammad*, n. 3867: 386, n. 3873: 390, **ḤNA.**, vol. III, bk. 31 (*Kitâb maʿrifat al-ṣaḥâba*), *Manâqib Fâṭima bt. rasûl Allâh*, n. 4799: 183, n. 4808: 186, **ḪWZ.**, Part 1, bb. *Faḍâʾil Fâṭima al-Zahrâʾ bt. rasûl Allâh*, n. 12: 95, n. 17: 96–97, n. 18: 97. Cf. also **ATH².**, vol. V, bb. *ḥarf al-fâʾ*: 522. In spite of this *ḥadîṯ*, the Sunnî transmitters also carry a report in which the names 'Fâṭima' and 'ʿAlî' (or 'her husband') are replaced with 'ʿÂʾisha' and 'her father'.

[144] **ḤNB.**, vol. VIII, *Ḥadîṯ Ṯawbân*, n. 22426: 320, **ADD.**, vol. II, bk. 32 (*Kitâb al-taraǧǧul*), bb. 21: 404, **ḤNA.**, vol. I, bk. 16 (*Kitâb al-munâsik*), n. 1849: 669, vol. III, bk. 31 (*Kitâb maʿrifat al-ṣaḥâba*), *Manâqib Fâṭima bt. rasûl Allâh*, n. 4802: 184 (al-Ḏahabî claims that al-Nîsâbûrî's chain of transmission is weak), **RḤB.**: 37.

[145] **SʿD.**, vol. II, *Ḏikr al-ḥuzn ʿalâ rasûl Allâh*: 720, **ḤNB.**, vol. IV, *Musnad Anas b. Mâlik*, n. 13030: 392, **BUḪ¹.**, vol. V, bk. 59 (*Kitâb al-maġâzî*), n. 739: 526–527, **MĞA.**, vol. I, bk. 6 (*Kitâb al-ğanâʾiz*), bb. 65, n. 1630: 522, **NSA¹.**, vol. IV, *Kitâb al-ğanâʾiz*, bb. *fî al-bukâʾ ʿalâ al-mayyit*: 12–13, **ḤNA.**, vol. I, bk. 13 (*Kitâb al-ğanâʾiz*), n. 1409: 532–533, vol. III, bk. 30 (*Kitâb al-maġâzî*), n. 4457: 65, **BĠD.**, vol. VI, n. 3292: 261–262.

[146] **SQL³.**, vol. VIII, bk. 6 (*Kitâb al-maġâzî*), bb. 84, n. 4434: 171.

[147] **IṢH.**, vol. II, bb. 133: 42–43, **KṮR¹.**, vol. VI: 333.

taking on a note of hysteria: "Anas! Does it please you to throw earth over God's Messenger?"[148] But while this grief is disparaged as weakness by Lammens, it is a noble characteristic within the context of Shîʿî spirituality and piety. It is during this time that we are offered another *ḥadîṯ* directly relating to Fâṭima, containing a twofold prediction and transmitted in many forms by the Sunnî, on the authority of ʿÂʾisha:

> On the authority of ʿÂʾisha, who said: "I met Fâṭima, peace be upon her, and her walk was like the walk of the Messenger of God, God bless and save him. He said: Welcome, my daughter! Then he made her sit on his left side, and he whispered a saying to her and she wept. I said: The Messenger of God, God bless and save him, favours you with his saying and you weep! Then he whispered a saying to her and she laughed. I said: I never, as today, saw happiness so close to sadness! I asked her about what he had said, and she said: I would never disclose the secret of the Messenger of God, God bless and save him. When he died, God bless and save him, I asked, and she said: he whispered to me and said that every year Ǧibrîl used to review the Qurʾân with me once, but this year he has compared it with me twice. I cannot see it except that the time of my death is present, and you will be the first of my family to follow me. So I wept for that. Then he said: Does it not please you to be the mistress of the women of this community or the mistress of the women of the believers? She said: So I laughed for that."[149]

---

[148] **SʿD.**, vol. II, *Ḏikr al-ḥuzn ʿalâ rasûl Allâh*: 720, **ḤNB.**, vol. IV, *Musnad Anas b. Mâlik*, n. 13115: 406–407, **BUḪ¹.**, vol. V, bk. 59 (*Kitâb al-maġâzî*), n. 739: 526–527, **MǦA.**, vol. I, bk. 6 (*Kitâb al-ǧanâʾiz*), bb. 65, n. 1630: 522, **ḤNA.**, vol. I, bk. 13 (*Kitâb al-ǧanâʾiz*), n. 1409: 532–533, **BĠD.**, vol. VI, n. 3292: 261–262.

[149] **SʿD.**, vol. X, *Ḏikr banât rasûl Allâh*, n. 4927 (*Fâṭima*): 27, **ḤNB.**, vol. X, *Aḥâdîṯ Fâṭima*, n. 26475: 157–158, **BUḪ¹.**, vol. IV, bk. 56 (*Kitâb al-manâqib*), ch. 24, n. 819: 526–527, vol. VI, bk. 61 (*Kitâb faḍâʾil al-qurʾân*), ch. 7: 485, vol. VIII, bk. 74 (*Kitâb al-istiʾḏân*), ch. 43, n. 301: 201–202, **MSL.**, vol. IV, bk. 44 (*Kitâb faḍâʾil al-ṣaḥâba*), bb. 10 (*Faḍâʾil Fâṭima bt. al-*

The first part of the prediction, in which Fâṭima is told that she will be the first to follow her father, is not always related in the context of this *ḥadîṯ*.[150] Both of these predictions have been underscored

---

nabî), n. 98, 99: 1904–1906, **NSA²**.: 77–80, **ḤNA**., vol. III, bk. 31 (*Kitâb maʿrifat al-ṣaḥâba*), *Manâqib Fâṭima bt. rasûl Allâh*, n. 4804: 184, **SHL**., bb. *faḍl fî ḏikr manâqib ʿAlî b. Abî Ṭâlib*: 43, **IṢH**., vol. II, bb. 133: 39–40 recounts the whole *ḥadîṯ*, but substitutes 'of paradise' with 'of the worlds', **BRR**., vol. IV, *Kitâb al-nisâʾ wa-kunâ-hunna*, bb. *al-fâʾ*, n. 4057: 1894–1895, **QIḌ**., vol. VII, bk. 44 (*Kitâb faḍâʾil al-ṣaḥâba*), bb. 10 (*Faḍâʾil Fâṭima bt. al-nabî*), nn. 98, 99: 475, **ḪWZ**., Part 1, bb. *Faḍâʾil Fâṭima al-Zahrâʾ bt. rasûl Allâh*, n. 7: 92–93, and, outside the context of this *ḥadîṯ*, n. 19: 97–98, n. 77: 131, **AKR**., vol. XLII: 134 (not in the traditional context), **ĞWZ²**., vol. II, *Fâṭima bt. rasûl Allâh*: 4, **ATH²**., vol. V, bb. *ḥarf al-fâʾ*: 522 recounts the whole Tradition, but substitutes 'of paradise' with 'of the worlds', **MTQ**., vol. V: 98, **SQL³**., vol. VIII, bb. 84, n. 4434: 171. Among the Shîʿa, cf. **ṢDQ¹**., n. 2: 595, **MFD¹**., vol. I: 181, **ĞQM**.: 112, **FNR**., vol. I: 150, **ṬBR¹**.: 133, **RWD³**., bb. 13, n. 433: 357, **SHB**., vol. III, bb. *manâqib Fâṭima al-Zahrâʾ*: 410, **BṬQ**., n. 764: 386, **IRB**., vol. I: 453, **DAY**., vol. I: 33, **MĞL**., vol. XXII, bb. 1, n. 19: 466, n. 20: 472, vol. XXXI: 214, vol. XXXV, bb. 5: 230, vol. XXXVII, bb. 50, n. 30: 67, vol. XLIII, bb. 3, n. 48: 51, bb. 7, n. 12: 171.

150 Cf. **SʿD**., vol. X, *Ḏikr banât rasûl Allâh*, n. 4927 (*Fâṭima*): 27, **ḤNB**., vol. X, *Musnad ʿÂʾisha*, n. 26091: 82, n. 26476: 158, n. 26482: 159, **DRM**., vol. I, *al-Muqaddima*, bb. *fî wafât al-nabî*, n. 77: 37, **BUḪ¹**., vol. IV, bk. 56 (*Kitâb al-manâqib*), ch. 24, n. 819: 526–527, vol. VI, bk. 61 (*Kitâb faḍâʾil al-qurʾân*), ch. 7: 485, vol. VIII, bk. 74 (*Kitâb al-istiʾḏân*), ch. 43, n. 301: 201–202, vol. V, bk. 57 (*Kitâb faḍâʾil al-aṣḥâb*), ch. 13, n. 62: 50–51, vol. V, bk. 59 (*Kitâb al-maġâzî*), ch. 81, n. 718: 513, **MSL**., vol. IV, bk. 44 (*Kitâb faḍâʾil al-ṣaḥâba*), bb. 10 (*Faḍâʾil Fâṭima bt. al-nabî*), n. 97: 1904, n. 99: 1905–1906, **NSA²**.: 79–80, **ḤNA**., vol. III, bk. 31 (*Kitâb maʿrifat al-ṣaḥâba*), *Manâqib Fâṭima bt. rasûl Allâh*, n. 4786: 177–178 (Fâṭima, al-Ḥasan and al-Ḥusayn will be the first to enter paradise with Muḥammad), **IṢH**., vol. II, bb. 133: 40, **BRR**., vol. IV, *Kitâb al-nisâʾ wa-kunâ-hunna*, bb. *al-fâʾ*, n. 4057: 1894, **QIḌ**., vol. VII, bk. 44 (*Kitâb faḍâʾil al-ṣaḥâba*), bb. 10 (*Faḍâʾil Fâṭima bt. al-nabî*), nn. 97, 99: 474–476, **ḪWZ**., Part 1, bb. *Fuḍâʾil Fâṭima al-Zahrâʾ bt. rasûl Allâh*, n. 56: 120 (recorded outside of the usual context), **ĞWZ²**., vol. II, *Fâṭima bt. rasûl Allâh*: 4, **KṮR¹**., vol. II, *Qiṣṣat ʿÎsâ b. Maryam*: 60, vol. VI: 332, **MTQ**., vol. V: 98, **SHL**., bb. *faḍl fî ḏikr manâqib ʿAlî b. Abî*

and developed by the Shîʿî transmitters. But they are transmitted in various forms by the Sunnî authorities, who are not in complete agreement over the wording or the theology:

a) **Fâṭima is the mistress of the women of this community and of the women of the believers**: Ibn Ḥanbal, al-Buḫârî, Muslim, Qâḍî ʿIyâḍ and al-Ǧawzî. All of these are transmitted on the authority of ʿÂʾisha.[151]

b) **Fâṭima is the mistress of the women of this community and of the women of the believers and of the women of the worlds**: al-Nîsâbûrî (on the authority of ʿÂʾisha) and Ibn al-Aṯîr.[152]

c) **Fâṭima is the mistress of the women of this community and of the women of the worlds**: Ibn Saʿd, al-Nasâʾî, al-Iṣbahânî, Ibn

Ṭâlib: 43. The Shîʿî transmitters of this *ḥadîṯ* include: **QḤL.**: 565, **RṬB¹.**: 43, **RṬB².**: 177, 199, 271, **RQM.**: 62, 124, **ṢDQ¹.**, n. 2: 112, n. 18: 486, n. 2: 595, **ṢDQ².**, vol. I, bb. 24, n. 10: 262, **ṬFA².**, bb. 7, n. 18–316: 188, bb. 14, n. 40–892: 400, **FNR.**, vol. I: 149–150, **SHB.**, vol. III, bb. *manâqib Fâṭima al-Zahrâʾ*: 410, **BṬQ.**, n. 763: 385, n. 765: 386, **ṬSṬ².**, vol. I: 247, **IRB.**, vol. I: 17, 453, 497, vol. II: 468, **ḤLL¹.**: 432, **ḤLL².**, bb. 195: 487, **MǦL.**, vol. XXII, bb. 2, nn. 36–38: 532–536, vol. XXVII, bb. 2, n. 4: 31, n. 21: 52, vol. XXIX, bb. 11: 112, vol. XXXV, bb. 5: 230, vol. XXXVI, bb. 41, n. 85: 264, n. 110: 288, n. 146: 307, n. 184: 328, vol. XXXVII, bb. 50, n. 38: 68, 71, n. 52: 84, vol. XLIII, bb. 3, n. 20: 20, n. 22: 25, n. 48: 51, bb. 7, n. 2: 156, n. 13: 172, n. 16: 180, n. 30: 201, n. 36: 207, bb. 8, n. 13: 227, vol. LI, bb. 1, n. 37: 78, vol. LXXVIII, bb. 7, n. 40: 282, **NṬR.**, vol. II, bb. 43, n. 1–2187: 358, n. 5–2191: 361, vol. X, bb. 33, n. 28–12007: 275.

[151] **ḤNB.**, vol. X, *Aḥâdîṯ Fâṭima*, n. 26475: 157–158, **BUḪ¹.**, vol. VIII, bk. 74 (*Kitâb al-istiʾḏân*), ch. 43, n. 301: 201–202, **MSL.**, vol. IV, bk. 44 (*Kitâb faḍâʾil al-ṣaḥâba*), bb. 10 (*Faḍâʾil Fâṭima bt. al-nabî*), n. 98, 99: 1904–1906, **QIḌ.**, vol. VII, bk. 44 (*Kitâb faḍâʾil al-ṣaḥâba*), bb. 10 (*Faḍâʾil Fâṭima bt. al-nabî*), nn. 98, 99: 475, **ǦWZ².**, vol. II, *Fâṭima bt. rasûl Allâh*: 4.

[152] **ḤNA.**, vol. III, bk. 31 (*Kitâb maʿrifat al-ṣaḥâba*), *Manâqib Fâṭima bt. rasûl Allâh*, n. 4804: 184, **ATH².**, vol. V, bb. *ḥarf al-fâʾ*: 522.

ʿAbd al-Barr (all on the authority of ʿÂʾisha), al-ʿAsqalânî and al-Shablanǧî (on the authority of ʿÂʾisha).[153]

d) **Fâṭima is the mistress of the women of the people of Paradise**: Ibn Ḥanbal (on the authority of Ḥuḏayfa), al-Buḫârî (on the authority of ʿÂʾisha), al-Nîsâbûrî (on the authority of Ḥuḏayfa), Ibn al-Aṯîr (on the authority of Umm Salama), Ibn Kaṯîr (on the authority of ʿÂʾisha), al-ʿAsqalânî (on the authority of ʿÂʾisha), al-

[153] **SʿD**., vol. X, *Ḏikr banât rasûl Allâh*, n. 4927 (*Fâṭima*): 27, **NSA²**.: 78–80, **IṢH**., vol. II, bb. 133: 39–40, **BRR**., vol. IV, *Kitâb al-nisâʾ*, bb. *al-fâʾ*, n. 4057: 1894–1895, **SQL¹**., vol. IV, bb. *ḥarf al-fâʾ*, n. 830: 367, **SHL**.: 43. The Shîʿî transmitters of this *ḥadîṯ* ("Fâṭima is the mistress of the women of the worlds") include: **QḤL**.: 780, **RṬB¹**.: 10, 47, 54, **RṬB²**.: 12, 16, 23–24, 69, 115, 155, 177, 197, **KLY**., vol. I, bk. 4 (*Kitâb al-ḥuǧǧa*), bb. *mawlid al-Zahrâʾ Fâṭima*, n. 3: 458–459, **NUM**., bb. 4, n. 1: 57, **QQM**., n. 8: 174, n. 17: 230, n. 2: 309, **RQM**.: 36, 98, **ṢDQ¹**., n. 2: 25, n. 9: 26, n. 10: 57, n. 2: 112, n. 8: 125, n. 8: 178, n. 12: 298, n. 10: 467, n. 6: 473, n. 18: 486, **ṢDQ²**., vol. I, n. 1: 256, n. 26: 260, n. 27: 305, **ṢDQ³**., vol. II: 572, vol. IV: 179, 420, **ṢDQ⁴**., vol. I: 1, **ṢDQ⁵**., vol. I, n. 67: 306, vol. II: 269, **ṢDQ⁶**., n. 9: 58, n. 1: 107, n. 1: 164, **ṢDQ⁷**., n. 84: 98, **AYY**., vol. I, bb. 3, n. 48: 173, **MFD¹**., vol. I: 5, 354, vol. III: 5, **MFD²**.: 14, 37, 90, **MFD³**.: 132, **MFD⁴**.: 167, **ṬFA¹**., vol. III: 110, vol. VI, bb. 3: 10, bb. 11: 39, bb. 10: 41, bb. 18: 56, **ṬFA²**., bb. 22, n. 1/1175: 568, **ṬFA³**.: 210, 213, **ǦQM**.: 8, 10, 85, 118, 169, **FNR**., vol. I: 100, 102, 111, 125, 149, 254–255, **ṬBR¹**.: 150, 154, 156, 203; **ṬBR²**., vol. I: 134, 314, **RWD¹**., vol. II: 907, **SHB**., vol. III, bb. *manâqib Fâṭima al-Zahrâʾ*: 369–370, **BṬQ**., n. 764: 386, n. 767: 387, **ṬSṬ²**., vol. I, n. 129: 91, n. 162: 110: 178, 218, 250, 258, 266, 268, 272, 275, **ṬSṬ³**.: 60, 296, 332, 335, 466, 565, 589, 591, 623–624, 712, **ṬSṬ⁴**., bb. 72: 236, bb. 154: 414, **ṬSṬ⁵**.: 173, 286, **IRB**., vol. I: 80, 348, 360, 366, 440, 444, 452, 514, vol. II: 120, **DAY**., vol. II: 221, 231, 295, 314, 323, **ḤLL¹**.: 254, 362, **ḤLL²**.: 194–195, 456, **KFM¹**.: 47, 476, 482, 491, 581, 739, **KFM²**.: 34, 158, 194, 269, 278, 281, 287, 291, 356; **ABḎ**.: 200, **NṬR**., vol. I, bb. 1, n. 17: 75, vol. II, bb. 22, n. 9/6897: 316, vol. X, bb. 6, n. 8/11830: 194, bb. 14, n. 3/11904: 210, bb. 23, n. 3/11905: 226, bb. 86, n. 16/12273: 412. Al-Maǧlisî imputes this title to her more than one-hundred-and-fifty times. Cf. for e.g. **MǦL**., vol. XLIII, bb. 3, n. 13: 22, n. 20: 24, n. 25: 26, n. 41: 37, n. 46: 49, n. 63: 76, bb. 5, n. 22: 107, n. 32: 130, bb. 6, n. 2: 147, bb. 7, n. 13: 172, n. 21: 193.

Hayṯamî (who notes that the chain of transmission is weak) and al-Muttaqî al-Hindî (on the authority of ʿÂʾisha).[154]

e) **Fâṭima is the mistress of the women of the people of Paradise with the exception of (or 'after') Maryam the daughter of ʿImrân**: Ibn Ḥanbal (on the authority of Abû Saʿîd al-Ḫudrî), al-Tirmiḏî (on the authority of Umm Salama), al-Nasâʾî (on the authority of Umm Salama and Abû Saʿîd al-Ḫudrî), al-Ṭabarî (with a chain that does not include ʿÂʾisha), al-Nîsâbûrî (on the authority of Abû Saʿîd al-Ḫudrî), Ibn ʿAbd al-Barr (on the authority of Abû Saʿîd al-Ḫudrî and on the authority of Ibn ʿAbbâs: the mistresses of the women of the people of Paradise after Maryam are Fâṭima, Ḫadîǧa and Âsiya), Ibn Kaṯîr (on the authority of ʿÂʾisha and on the authority of Abû Saʿîd al-Ḫudrî), al-ʿAsqalânî (on the authority of Abû Saʿîd al-Ḫudrî and ʿÂʾisha), al-Suyûṭî (on the authority of Ibn Abî Shayba), al-Hayṯamî (on the authority of Abû Saʿîd al-

[154] **ḤNB.**, vol. IX, *Ḥadîṯ Ḥuḏayfa*, n. 23389: 91, **BUḪ[1].**, vol. IV, bk. 56 (*Kitâb al-manâqib*), ch. 24, n. 819: 526–527, vol. VI, bk. 61 (*Kitâb faḍâʾil al-qurʾân*), ch. 7, n.n.: 485, vol. VIII, bk. 74 (*Kitâb al-istiʾḏân*), ch. 43, n. 301: 201–202, vol. V, bk. 57 (*Kitâb faḍâʾil al-aṣḥâb*), ch. 29: 74, **ḤNA.**, vol. III, bk. 31 (*Kitâb maʿrifat al-ṣaḥâba*), *Manâqib Fâṭima bt. rasûl Allâh*, nn. 4784, 4785: 177, n. 4796: 182, **ATH[2].**, vol. V, bb. *ḥarf al-fâʾ*: 523, **KṮR[1].**, vol. VI: 332, **SQL[3].**, vol. VIII, bb. 84, n. 4434: 171, **HAY.**, vol. IX, bb. *manâqib Fâṭima bt. rasûl Allâh*: 201, **MTQ.**, vol. V: 98–99. The Shîʿî transmitters of this *ḥadîṯ* include: **QIIL.**: 565, 643, 675, 686, 790, 839, 907, 909, **RṬB[2].**: 243, 253, 276, **QQM.**, n. 2: 309, **RQM.**: 98, 124, **ṢDQ[1].**, n. 7: 125, **ṢDQ[2].**, vol. I, bb. 24, n. 10: 262, **ṢDQ[3].**, vol. II, n. 3210: 602, **ṢDQ[4].**, vol. II, n. 31: 553, n. 1: 572, **ṢDQ[5].**, vol. II, n. 1: 267, **MFD[1].**, vol. I: 23, 352, **MFD[2].**: 183, **MFD[5].**, n. 4: 22, **ǦQM.**: 118, 135, **ṬFA[1].**, vol. VI, bb. 35: 86, **ṬFA[2].**, bb. 3, n. 36/127: 84, bb. 9, n. 28/436: 248, bb. 13, n. 7/667: 232, bb. 20, n. 4/1168: 545, bb. 31, n. 7/1305: 633, **FNR.**, vol. I, n. 128: 148, **ṬBR[1].**: 159, **ṬBR[2].**, vol. I: 278, **ṬBR[3].**: 93, **RWD[1].**, vol. I: 209, **SHB.**, vol. III, bb. *manâqib Fâṭima al-Zahrâʾ*: 370–371, bb. *maʿâlî umûrihimâ*: 445, **BṬQ.**, n. 756: 384, n. 768: 388, **ṬSṬ[2].**, vol. I, n. 129: 91, n. 348: 247, nn. 364, 366: 262–263, n. 705: 275, **IRB.**, vol. I: 32, 255, 284, 495, vol. II: 10, **DAY.**, vol. II: 259, 428, **ḤLL[1].**: 389, 391, **ḤLL[2].**: 111, 313, 352, 421, **MǦL.**, vol. XXI, bb. 32: 279, vol. XXII, bb. 1, n. 31: 404, bb. 2, n. 38: 536.

Ḫudrî) and al-Muttaqî al-Hindî ('with the exception of Maryam' on the authority of ʿÂʾisha and 'after' Maryam on the authority of Umm Salama).[155]

f) **The mistresses (or 'the best') of the women of the people of Paradise are four**: Ibn Ḥanbal (on the authority of Ibn ʿAbbâs: Ḫadîǧa, Fâṭima, Maryam, Âsiya: in the last one, Maryam, Ḫadîǧa, Fâṭima, Âsiya), al-Nîsâbûrî (on the authority of Ibn ʿAbbâs – but he mentions only Ḫadîǧa and Fâṭima), Ibn ʿAbd al-Barr (on the authority of Ibn ʿAbbâs: Ḫadîǧa, Fâṭima, Maryam, Âsiya), al-Ḫawârizmî (quoting Ibn Ḥanbal: Maryam, Fâṭima, Ḫadîǧa, Âsiya), al-Qurṭubî (on the authority of Ibn ʿAbbâs: Ḫadîǧa, Fâṭima, Maryam, Âsiya), Ibn Kaṯîr (Ḫadîǧa, Fâṭima, Maryam, Âsiya), al-ʿAsqalânî (on the authority of Ibn ʿAbbâs: Ḫadîǧa, then Fâṭima, then Maryam, then Âsiya), al-ʿIṣâmî (Ḫadîǧa, Fâṭima, Maryam, Âsiya) and al-Shablanǧî (on the authority of ʿÂʾisha: Maryam, Fâṭima, Ḫadîǧa, Âsiya).[156]

g) **The mistresses (or 'the best') of the women of the people of the worlds are four**: Ibn Ḥanbal (on the authority of Anas b. Mâlik: Maryam, Ḫadîǧa, Fâṭima, Âsiya), al-Tirmiḏî (on the authority of

---

[155] **ḤNB.**, vol. IV, *Musnad Abî Saʿîd al-Ḫudrî*, n. 11756: 159, **TRM.**, vol. IX, bk. 50 (*Kitâb al-manâqib*), bb. *fî faḍl Fâṭima bt. Muḥammad*, n. 3872: 389–390, **NSA².**: 77–78, **YṬB¹.**, vol. III, *sûrat âl ʿImrân*, n. 7032: 398–399, **ḤNA.**, vol. III, bk. 31 (*Kitâb maʿrifat al-ṣaḥâba*), *Manâqib Fâṭima bt. rasûl Allâh*, n. 4796: 182, **BRR.**, vol. IV, *Kitâb al-nisâʾ*, bb. *al-fâʾ*, n. 4057: 1823, 1894–1895, **KṮR¹.**, vol. II, *Qiṣṣat ʿÎsâ b. Maryam*: 60, **SQL¹.**, vol. IV, bb. *ḥarf al-fâʾ*, n. 830: 366–367, **SQL⁴.**, vol. XII, *Kitâb al-nisâʾ*, n. 4434: 441, **SYṬ.**, vol. II, *sûrat âl ʿImrân*: 42, **HAY.**, vol. IX, bb. *manâqib Fâṭima bt. rasûl Allâh*: 201, **MTQ.**, vol. V: 98–9.

[156] **ḤNB.**, vol. I, *Musnad ʿAbd Allâh b. al-ʿAbbâs b. ʿAbd al-Muṭṭalib*, n. 2668: 627–628, n. 2903: 278, n. 2960: 689, **ḤNA.**, vol. III, bk. 31 (*Kitâb maʿrifat al-ṣaḥâba*), *Manâqib Fâṭima bt. rasûl Allâh*, n. 4818: 189, **BRR.**, vol. IV, *Kitâb al-nisâʾ*, bb. *al-fâʾ*, n. 4057: 1821–1822, **ḪWZ.**, Part 1, bb. *Faḍâʾil Ḫadîǧa*, n. 6: 48, **QRṬ.**, vol. IV, *sûrat âl ʿImrân*: 83, **KṮR².**, vol. VII, *sûrat al-Taḥrîm*: 25, **SQL¹.**, vol. IV, bb. *ḥarf al-fâʾ*, n. 830: 366, **SQL⁴.**, vol. XII, *Kitâb al-nisâʾ*, n. 4434: 441, **IṢM.**, vol. I, bb. 4: 368, **SHL.**, bb. *faḍl fî ḏikr manâqib ʿAlî b. Abî Ṭâlib*: 42–43.

Anas b. Mâlik: Maryam, Ḫadîǧa, Fâṭima, Âsiya), al-Ṭabarî (on the authority of Abû Saʿîd al-Ḫudrî: Maryam, the wife of Pharoah, Ḫadîǧa, Fâṭima, and on the authority of Anas b. Mâlik: Maryam, Âsiya, Ḫadîǧa, Fâṭima), al-Nîsâbûrî (on the authority of Anas b. Mâlik: Maryam, Âsiya, Ḫadîǧa, Fâṭima), al-Ṯaʿlabî (on the authority of Abû Hurayra: Maryam, Âsiya, Ḫadîǧa, Fâṭima), Ibn ʿAbd al-Barr (on the authority of Abû Hurayra: Maryam, the daughter of Muzâḥim and wife of Pharoah, Ḫadîǧa, Fâṭima), al-Qurṭubî (on the authority of Abû Hurayra: Maryam, Âsiya, Ḫadîǧa, Fâṭima, and on the authority of Anas b. Mâlik: Maryam, Ḫadîǧa, Fâṭima, Âsiya), Ibn Kaṯîr (on the authority of Anas b. Mâlik: Maryam, Âsiya, Ḫadîǧa, Fâṭima and, on the authority of Ǧâbir b. ʿAbd Allâh: Fâṭima, Ḫadîǧa, Âsiya, Maryam, on the authority of Anas b. Mâlik: Maryam, Ḫadîǧa, Fâṭima, Âsiya), al-ʿAsqalânî (on the authority of Abû Hurayra: Maryam, Âsiya, Ḫadîǧa, Fâṭima and on the authority of Ibn ʿAbbâs: Maryam, Âsiya, Ḫadîǧa, Fâṭima or, also on the authority of Ibn ʿAbbâs: Ḫadîǧa, then Fâṭima, then Maryam, then Âsiya), al-Suyûṭî (on the authority of Anas b. Mâlik and Ibn ʿAbbâs: Maryam, Âsiya, Ḫadîǧa, Fâṭima, with the addition that Fâṭima is the best of them) and al-ʿIṣâmî (Maryam, Ḫadîǧa, Fâṭima, Âsiya).[157]

h) **Maryam the daughter of ʿImrân is the mistress of the women of her world and Fâṭima the daughter of Muḥammad the mistress of the women of hers**: al-Iṣbahânî, Ibn ʿAbd al-Barr and Ibn ʿAsâkir.[158]

---

[157] **ḤNB.**, vol. IV, *Musnad Anas b. Mâlik*, n. 12394: 273, **TRM.**, vol. IX, bk. 50 (*Kitâb al-manâqib*), bb. *fî faḍl Ḫadîǧa*, n. 3888: 396–397, **YṬB¹.**, vol. III, *sûrat âl ʿImrân*, n. 7028: 395, n. 7030: 397, **ḤNA.**, vol. III, bk. 31 (*Kitâb maʿrifat al-ṣaḥâba*), *Manâqib Fâṭima bt. rasûl Allâh*, nn. 4809, 4810: 186, **ṮLB.**: 372, **BRR.**, vol. IV, *Kitâb al-nisâʾ* , bb. *al-fâʾ*, n. 3311: 1821, n. 3311: 1822, **QRṬ.**, vol. IV, *sûrat âl ʿImrân*: 83, vol. XVIII, *sûrat al-Taḥrîm*: 204, **KṮR¹.**, vol. II, *Qiṣṣat ʿÎsâ b. Maryam*: 59–60, **KṮR².**, vol. II, *sûrat âl ʿImrân*, vv. 42–44: 36–37, **SQL¹.**, vol. IV, bb. *ḥarf al-fâʾ*, n. 830: 366, **SQL⁴.**, vol. XII, *Kitâb al-nisâʾ*, n. 4434: 141, **SYṬ.**, vol. II, *sûrat âl ʿImrân*: 42, **IṢM.**, vol. I, bb. 4: 368.

[158] **IṢH.**, vol. II, bb. 133: 40, **BRR.**, vol. IV, *Kitâb al-nisâʾ*, bb. *al-fâʾ*, n. 4057: 1894–1895, **AKR.**, vol. 42: 134.

i) **Only four women have reached perfection**: al-Ṭabarî (on the authority of Abû Mûsâ al-Ashʿarî: Maryam, Âsiya, Ḫadîǧa, Fâṭima) and al-Shablanǧî (on the authority of al-Buḫârî, Muslim and al-Tirmiḏî: Maryam, Âsiya, Ḫadîǧa, Fâṭima).[159]

According to the Shîʿa, the words "Fâṭima is the mistress of the women of the worlds" spoken by Muḥammad, are already predated, since Âdam has already seen them written in light on the leg of God's throne.[160] The inconsistency concerning the mistress or 'the best' of the women of Paradise (Fâṭima, or Fâṭima with the exception of Maryam, or Fâṭima as one among four) is found throughout the Sunnî exegetes. Al-Qurṭubî suggests the excellence of Maryam over all other women, from Ḥawwâʾ until the last, because she, like the prophets, received revelation from God; but after her in excellence is Fâṭima, then Ḫadîǧa, and then Âsiya. In support of this he quotes a *ḥadîṯ*, found also in Ibn ʿAbd al-Barr and Ibn Kaṯîr, on the authority of Ibn ʿAbbâs: "The mistress of the women of the worlds is Maryam, then Fâṭima, then Ḫadîǧa, and then Âsiya."[161] Ibn Kaṯîr, al-Ṭabarî, al-Tirmiḏî, Ibn Ḥanbal, al-Buḫârî and Muslim carry a *ḥadîṯ*, on the authority of ʿAlî b. Abî Ṭâlib or ʿAbd Allâh b. Ǧaʿfar, that "Maryam is the best of her women and Ḫadîǧa is the best of hers" (suggesting a chronological interpretation).[162] Fâṭima's name is also missing from a *ḥadîṯ* carried

[159] **YṬB¹**., vol. III, *sûrat âl ʿImrân*, n. 7031: 397–398, **SHL**., 42–43.

[160] **ṢDQ⁵**., vol. I, bb. 28, n. 67: 306, **ṢDQ⁶**., n. 1: 124, **MǦL**., vol. II, bb. 3, n. 9: 164–165; vol. XI, bb. 3, n 9: 164–165; vol. XVI, bb. 11, n. 62: 362; vol. XXVI, bb. 6, n. 15: 273.

[161] **BRR**., vol. IV, *Kitâb al-nisâʾ*, bb. *al-fâʾ*, n. 3311: 1822–1823, n. 4057: 1823, **QRṬ**., vol. IV, *sûrat âl ʿImrân*: 83, **SQL⁴**., vol. XII, *Kitâb al-nisâʾ*, n. 4434: 441, **KṮR¹**., vol. II, *Qiṣṣat ʿÎsâ b. Maryam*: 61, **SYṬ**., vol. II, *sûrat âl ʿImrân*: 42.

[162] **ḤNB**., vol. I, *Musnad ʿAlî b. Abî Ṭâlib*, n. 640: 182, n. 1211: 302, **BUḪ¹**., vol. IV, bk. 55 (*Kitâb aḥâdîṯ al-anbiyâʾ*), ch. 40, n. 642: 427, vol. V, bk. 58 (*Kitâb manâqib al-anṣâr*), ch. 21, n. 163: 103, **MSL**., vol. IV, bk. 44 (*Kitâb faḍâʾil al-ṣaḥâba*), bb. 12, n. 69: 1886, **YṬB¹**., vol. III, *sûrat âl ʿImrân*, nn. 7026–7027: 394, **TRM**., vol. IX, bk. 50 (*Kitâb al-manâqib*), bb. *fî faḍl Ḫadîǧa*, n. 3887: 396, **YṬB¹**., vol. VI, *sûrat âl ʿImrân*, n. 7026: 394, **BRR**.,

by Ibn Kaṯîr and al-Qurṭubî on the authority of Abû Mûsâ al-Ashʿarî, stating that the only women to have reached perfection are Maryam, Ḫadîǧa, and Âsiya,[163] as well as one of numerous *aḥâdîṯ* extolling ʿÂʾisha above all other women, which runs: "The superiority of ʿÂʾisha over the women is like the superiority of *ṯarîd* (a traditional dish) over other foods."[164]

Some of these texts have been examined by Jane Dammen McAuliffe,[165] who uses as her starting point Q. 3: 42 and its exegesis by four Sunnî scholars (al-Zamaḫsharî, al-Ṭabarî, al-Râzî and Muḥammad Rashîd Riḍâ) and three Shîʿî scholars (Abû al-Futûḥ Râzî, Kâshânî and Ṭabâṭabâʾî).

Al-Ṭabarî prefers the chronological interpretation, positing that Maryam is chosen above the women of her time only, while quoting a *ḥadîṯ* which seems to suggest the opposite, in which Muḥammad says: "Ḫadîǧa excels over the women of my community as Maryam excels over the women of the worlds" (whom al-Ṭabarî interprets as the women of Paradise).[166] Al-Zamaḫsharî[167]

---

vol. IV, *Kitâb al-nisâʾ*, bb. *al-fâʾ*, n. 3311: 1823, **KṮR²**., vol. II, *sûrat âl ʿImrân*: 36, **SYṬ**., vol. II, *sûrat âl ʿImrân*: 42, **SHL**.: 406.

163 **BUḪ¹**., vol. IV, bk. 55 (*Kitâb aḥâdîṯ al-anbiyâʾ*), ch. 28, n. 623: 411, ch. 41, n. 643: 428, vol. V, bk. 57 (*Kitâb faḍâʾil al-aṣḥâb*), ch. 30, nn. 113–114: 75–76, who omits Ḫadîǧa from his list, **QRṬ**., vol. IV, *sûrat âl ʿImrân*: 82–83, **KṮR²**., vol. II, *sûrat âl ʿImrân*: 36, *sûrat al-Taḥrîm*: 25, **SYṬ**., vol. II, *sûrat âl ʿImrân*: 42 (and who omits Ḫadîǧa).

164 **BUḪ¹**., vol. IV, bk. 55 (*Kitâb aḥâdîṯ al-anbiyâʾ*), ch. 28, n. 623: 411, ch. 41, n. 643: 428, vol. V, bk. 57 (*Kitâb faḍâʾil al-aṣḥâb*), ch. 30, nn. 113–114: 75–76, **MSL**., vol. IV, bk. 44 (*Faḍâʾil al-ṣaḥâba*), bb. 12, n. 70: 1886–1887, bb. 13, n. 89: 1895, **QRṬ**., vol. IV, *sûrat âl ʿImrân*: 82–83, **KṮR²**., vol. II, *sûrat âl ʿImrân*: 36–37, *sûrat al-Taḥrîm*: 25, **SYṬ**., vol. II, *sûrat âl ʿImrân*: 42.

165 McAULIFFE J. D., "Chosen of all women: Mary and Fāṭima in Qur'anic Exegesis" in *Islamochristiana* 7 (1981): 19–28.

166 **YṬB¹**., vol. III, *sûrat âl ʿImrân*, n. 7033: 393, 399–340. Cf. also **ḤWZ**., Part 1, bb. *Faḍâʾil Ḫadîǧa*, n. 5: 48, n. 17: 56, **SYṬ**., vol. II, *sûrat âl ʿImrân*: 42.

167 **ZMR**., vol. I: 429.

and al-Râzî[168] reject the chronological approach, the latter quoting the *ḥadîṯ* in which Maryam, Âsiya, Ḫadîğa and Fâṭima are declared to be the most excellent of all women and positing that while this *ḥadîṯ* may suggest that these four are superior to all other women, the Qur'ân makes it clear that Maryam is superior to them. Al-Zamaḫsharî holds that Maryam's preference over all other women depended upon the exalted mark of esteem (*karâma*) for which God selected her and in the birth of a child without male intervention, not given to any other woman. Rashîd Riḍâ (d. 1354/1935)[169] offers no opinion in terms of the chronological interpretation, but quotes the same *ḥadîṯ* as al-Zamaḫsharî, suggesting that all four are of equal (eternal) importance. These four are fairly representative of their own tradition; al-Qurṭubî, for example, insists upon Maryam's superiority, based on the Qur'ânic text and the corpus of *aḥâdîṯ*, because she is a receiver of revelation.

The Shîʿa, represented by al-Futûḥ Râzî (d. c. 1087/1131),[170] diverge sharply from the various Sunnî exegetes, insisting upon the absolute pre-eminence of Fâṭima over all women of all time because she is part of the body of Muḥammad and what is part of Muḥammad is greater than what is part of ʿImrân (the father of Maryam). He quotes some *aḥâdîṯ* to support this view of her superiority, including the one in which Muḥammad says that Fâṭima is the mistress of the women of the worlds. Fatḥ Allâh Kâshânî[171] (d. 988/1580–1), a Shîʿî exegete writing in Persian, is, like al-Futûḥ Râzî, at pains to assert that Fâṭima is absolutely superior to all women of all time. However, like some other scholars (not just of the Shîʿa), he opts for the position that Maryam was chosen above all other women of her time (thus a chronological choice), and this by reason of her being given a child without a husband. In his turn, Muḥammad Ṭabâṭabâ'î[172] rejects the chronological interpretation,

---

[168] **RAZ.**, vol. VIII, *sûrat âl ʿImrân*: 45–46.

[169] *Tafsîr al-qur'ân al-ḥakîm al-shâhir bi-tafsîr al-manâr*, vol. III: 300.

[170] *Tafsîr rawḍ al-ğinân wa-rûḥ al-ğanân*, vol. III: 36.

[171] *Tafsîr al-kabîr al-manhağ al-ṣâdiqîn fî ilzâm al-muḫâlifîn*, vol. II: 223.

[172] **ṬBṬ.**, vol. III: 203–205. Cf. also AYOUB M., *The Qur'an and Its Interpreters*, vol. II, *The House of ʿImrān*, State University of New York Press, Albany 1992: 122–130.

but, unlike other Shîʿî scholars, draws no comparison between Maryam and Fâṭima. Maryam's choice implies an excellence and precedence over other women in something given specifically to her and not to others, that is, the virginal conception of her son. It is precisely in this aspect of her life, to the exclusion of all other women, that she enjoys a special precedence.

The Shîʿî translation of the Qurʾân, with its commentary by Mir Aḥmed ʿAlî, opts for the solution that Maryam is above all women of her own time, appealing to the authority of Muḥammad, who said that Maryam was the most blessed woman of her age, but that Fâṭima is the most blessed woman of all ages. To support this, Mir Aḥmed ʿAlî appeals to Q. 33: 33, which establishes the purity of the *ahl al-bayt*; Fâṭima is the only woman of the five, and therefore the most blessed of all women. The objection is raised that Maryam is mentioned by name in the Qurʾân, while Fâṭima is mentioned only by implication, suggesting that Maryam is superior. He answers that Maryam is mentioned because it is necessary to defend her chastity, whereas Fâṭima's chastity is incontestable, and her physical and spiritual purity is recognized by all. Fâṭima is, furthermore, the seed of Ibrâhîm and the daughter of Muḥammad, the seal (*ḫâtim*) of the prophets. She is the wife of an Imâm who is next only to Muḥammad in all respects as of one and the same divine light. She is the mother of eleven holy Imâms of the same grade and the same divine light, with the last one being the one through whom the divine will and justice shall prevail on the earth.

Faced with apparent contradictions and inconsistencies, it may be noted that those *aḥâdîṯ*, carried by Sunnî transmitters, and which place Fâṭima in some degree of exaltation (either as mistress of the women of the worlds or of the women of the people of paradise, or as mistress of the people of paradise except for Maryam, or even as one of four) far outweigh those *aḥâdîṯ* that omit her name altogether, or raise someone else (like Ḫadîǧa) to this status. The position of Âsiya, daughter of Muzâḥim and wife of Pharaoh, remains incongruous; in the Qurʾân, in contrast with the unfaithful wives of the prophets Nûḥ and Lûṭ, she is offered as a model of faith:

> «*And Allah citeth an example for those who believe: the wife of Pharaoh when she said: My Lord! Build for me a home with Thee in the Garden, and deliver me from Pharaoh and his work, and deliver me from evil-doing folk*» (Q. 66: 11).

But this is not the only time that the name Âsiya will be connected to that of Fâṭima, as we shall see when we examine the narratives of Fâṭima's birth.

2.9. THE *SAQÎFA* EVENT

After the death of Muḥammad two serious events thrust Fâṭima abruptly into prominence. The first was the alleged attempt to force ʿAlî's allegiance (*bayʿa*) to Abû Bakr, an event that is recorded by a number of Sunnî transmitters and is underscored by the Shîʿa. It appears that the intention of ʿUmar, Abû Bakr and some others, angered by ʿAlî's refusal to pay allegiance, was to take him by force to the mosque and compel him to do so. An armed group went to the house of ʿAlî and Fâṭima, threatening to set fire to it. They forced their way in, seriously injuring Fâṭima in the process, causing her to miscarry her unborn child, and wielding their swords in the house. There are countless reports of this incident, all of them fragmented and omitting one or more details.[173] The report of al-Ṭabarî reads:

> 'Umar b. al-Khaṭṭāb came to the house of 'Alī. Ṭalḥah and al-Zubayr and some of the Muhājirūn were [also] in the house [with 'Alī]. 'Umar cried out, "By God, either you come out to render the oath of allegiance [to Abū Bakr], or I will set the house on fire."[174]

Admittedly, al-Ṭabarî makes no mention of violence against Fâṭima; the translator of the text, in a footnote, merely mentions that, "The scene grew violent and Fāṭimah was furious."[175]

The Sunnî transmitters who carry this story are cautious in its telling; for the most part, the threat by ʿUmar to burn everyone (including Fâṭima) alive is the only actual violence mentioned. Ibn

---

[173] For Sunnî accounts, cf. **BLḎ**[1]., vol. I, nn. 1184, 1186: 586, **YṬB**[2]., vol. IX, n. 1818: 186–187, **ḤDI**., vol. II: 23, vol. VI: 11, 47–49. For Shîʿî accounts, cf **YQB**., vol. II: 141.

[174] **YṬB**[2]., vol. IX, n. 1818: 186–187.

[175] **YṬB**[2]., vol. IX, n. 1818, p 187, nt. 1291.

al-Ḥadîd includes in his account, besides the storming of the house, the wielding of swords and the beating of Zubayr, a screaming and angry Fâṭima who adjures God and vows never again to speak to ʿUmar.[176] Among the Sunnî sects, claims al-Shahrastânî, the al-Naẓẓâmiyya believe that ʿUmar, besides threatening to burn the house, struck Fâṭima and caused her to miscarry.[177]

Muḥammad Faḍlallâh, a contemporary Lebanese Shîʿî reformist, refuses to allow himself to be influenced by the *aḥâdîṯ* about the physical violence perpetrated against her, claiming that the stories are weakly documented or contradictory and that there are too many legends that are exaggerated and hard to prove. He does not, however, deny some sort of attack.[178] In point of fact, a number of Sunnî sources record that ʿAlî only pledged his allegiance after the death of Fâṭima; this allegiance is hard to fathom, not solely in terms of waiting for his wife to die, but also in terms of ʿAlî ever making such a pledge in the light of the alleged violence perpetrated at his house and the death of his unborn child. One of the reasons given in some Sunnî sources is that he noticed a decline in his popularity after his wife's death.[179]

2.10. FADAK

The second event was the denial of Fâṭima's claim to Fadak.[180] The small town of Fadak had been allocated to Muḥammad after the

---

[176] Ibn al-Ḥadîd takes a view held by some other Shîʿî transmitters: cf. **ḤDI.**, vol. VI: 11, 47–49.

[177] **SHR.**, vol. I: 57.

[178] ROSINY S., "The Tragedy of Fāṭima al-Zahrā' in the Debate of Two Shiite Theologians in Lebanon" in BRUNNER R and ENDE W (eds.), *The Twelver Shia in Modern Times*, Brill, Leiden 2001: 207–219.

[179] **BUḪ[1]**., vol. V, bk. 59 (*Kitâb al-maġâzî*), ch. 37, n. 545: 381–384, **MSL.**, vol. III, bk. 32 (*Kitâb al-ğihâd*), bb. 16, n. 52: 1380–1381, **YṬB[2]**., vol. IX, nn. 1825, 1826: 196–197, **BRR.**, vol. III, n. 1633: 973, **ḤDI.**, vol. II: 22; **KṮR[1]**., vol. V: 249, 286.

[180] **SʿD.**, vol. II: 273–275, vol. X: 28–29, **BUḪ[1]**., vol. V, bk. 62 (*Kitâb faḍâʾil aṣḥâb al-nabî*), ch. 13, n. 60: 49–50, **BLḎ[2]**., n. 119: 37–38, **RAZ.**, vol. XV, Part 30, *sûrat al-Ḥashr*: 284, **KṮR[1]**., vol. V: 249. Among the Shîʿa, cf. **YQB.**, vol. II: 142.

conquest of Ḫaybar; he dedicated its not inconsiderable revenues to the needs of the poor (travellers and members of the Banû Hishâm). After Muḥammad's death Fâṭima asked Abû Bakr to hand over the possessions of her father he was still holding. Over the land of Fadak and over the share of Ḫaybar, Abû Bakr refused, insisting that he had heard Muḥammad say that everything he left would be a public property for benevolent purposes (*ṣadaqa*).

This is somewhat contradicted by a *ḥadîṯ* in which Muḥammad told Fâṭima that she could ask anything from his wealth, but that he could not save her from the fire (or, in other accounts, he could obtain nothing, either good or bad, for her from God).[181] The *aḥâdîṯ* narrating the event suggest two or more attempts to regain Fadak, one with Fâṭima and Ibn ʿAbbâs working in concert,[182] another with Fâṭima sending some unnamed agent (possibly ʿAlî, for al-Buḫârî notes in his account that when Abû Bakr refused, ʿAlî acknowledged his superiority)[183] and still another involving Fâṭima alone: "Who will inherit from you when you die?" she demands of Abû Bakr, and when he replies, "My children and my family," she

---

[181] **SʿD.**, vol. II: 273–275, **ḤNB.**, vol. III, *Musnad Abî Hurayra*, n. 8609: 262, nn. 8734, 8735: 284, n. 9800: 460, n. 10730: 604, **BUḪ[1].**, vol. IV, bk. 51 (*Kitâb al-waṣâyâ*), ch. 11, n. 16: 12–13, vol. IV, bk. 56 (*Kitâb al-manâqib*), ch. 12, n. 728: 479.

[182] **ḤNB.**, vol. I, *Musnad Abî Bakr al-Ṣiddîq*, n. 9: 19, n. 58: 32–33, **BUḪ[1].**, vol. V, bk. 59 (*Kitâb al-maġâzî*), ch. 13, n. 368: 247–248, vol. VIII, bk. 80 (*Kitâb al-farâʾiḍ*), ch. 3, n. 718: 471–472 (al-Buḫârî and Ibn Ḥanbal, among others, transmit that they went to claim 'their' share, suggesting that Ibn ʿAbbâs was not merely being altruistic. In Ibn Ḥanbal's transmission Fâṭima appears to retain no anger against Abû Bakr), **YṬB[2].**, vol. IX, n. 1825: 196, **ḤDI.**, vol. VI: 46, **KṮR[1].**, vol. V: 285. Among the Shîʿa, cf. for e.g. **MǦL.**, vol. XXVIII, bb. 4: 353.

[183] **ḤNB.**, vol. I, *Musnad Abî Bakr al-Ṣiddîq*, n. 14: 20, n. 55: 31–32, **BUḪ[1].**, vol. V, bk. 57 (*Kitâb faḍâʾil al-aṣḥâb*), ch. 13, n. 60: 49–50, vol. V, bk. 59 (*Kitâb al-maġâzî*), ch. 37, n. 545: 381–384, **MSL.**, vol. III, bk. 32 (*Kitâb al-ǧihâd*), bb. 16, n. 52: 1380–1381, **ADD.**, vol. II, bk. 19 (*Kitâb al-ḫarâǧ*), bb. 19: 128–130.

retorts, "Then why can we not inherit from the Prophet?"[184] In fact, there is also a recorded transmission of ʿAlî going to ʿUmar in an attempt to gain for Fâṭima what Abû Bakr had previously refused,[185] as well as one of Fâṭima approaching Abû Bakr and ʿUmar together.[186] Nor was Fâṭima the only one to attempt this; the wives of Muḥammad, risking the wrath of ʿÂʾisha, themselves sent ʿUṯmân to see Abû Bakr to claim their share of Muḥammad's inheritance. He refused them on the same grounds that Fâṭima had been refused.[187] It must be admitted that this latter report helps to highlight his apparent impartiality and lack of bias for or against Fâṭima and might have been introduced precisely for that purpose.

Scholars from both sides, including al-Suyûṭî (on the authority of Abû Saʿîd al-Ḫudrî), in their commentary on the verse, «*give the kinsman his due*» (Q. 17: 26), hold that when this verse was revealed, Muḥammad gave Fâṭima the village of Fadak, which he saw as part of the peace treaty between him and the Jews[188] (al-Maǧlisî disa-

---

184 **ḤNB.**, vol. I, *Musnad Abî Bakr al-Ṣiddîq*, n. 25: 25, n. 60: 33, n. 79: 39, vol. III, *Musnad Abî Hurayra*, n. 8644: 269 (in these last two instances she approaches Abû Bakr and ʿUmar together, and they both claim to have heard the interdiction of Muḥammad against a prophet leaving inheritance), **BUḪ¹.**, vol. IV, bk. 53 (*Kitâb farḍ al-ḫums*), ch. 1, n. 325: 208–209, **ADD.**, vol. II, bk. 19 (*Kitâb al-ḫarâǧ*), bb. 19: 128–130, **TRM.**, vol. V, bk. 22 (*Kitâb al-sayr*), bb. 44, nn. 1608, 1609: 331–332, **BLḎ¹.**, vol. I, n. 1044: 552, **BLḎ².**, n. 115: 35 36, **KṮR¹**, vol. V: 285, vol. VI: 333. Among the Shîʿa, cf. for e.g. **MǦL.**, vol. XXIX, n. 41: 128–129.

185 **BUḪ¹.**, vol. IV, bk. 53 (*Kitâb farḍ al-ḫums*), ch. 1, n. 326: 209–213.

186 **ḤNB.**, vol. I, *Musnad Abî Bakr al-Ṣiddîq*, n. 79: 39; vol. III, *Musnad Abî Hurayra*, n. 8644: 269.

187 **BUḪ¹.**, vol. V, bk. 59 (*Kitâb al-maġâzî*), ch. 13, n. 367: 243–247. In some accounts the wives are reprimanded by ʿÂʾisha for wanting to do this. Cf. **MSL.**, vol. III, bk. 32 (*Kitâb al-ǧihâd*), bb. 16, n. 51: 1379, **ADD.**, vol. II, bk. 19 (*Kitâb al-ḫarâǧ*), bb. 19: 130, **BLḎ².**, n. 110: 34, **KṮR¹.**, vol. V: 285.

188 **BLḎ².**, n. 119: 37–38, **ḎHB².**, vol. II, n. 4560: 492, **KṮR².**, vol. IV, *sûrat al-Isrâʾ*: 302 (he denies the possibility, insisting that the verse was revealed long before Muḥammad gave Fadak to Fâṭima), **SYṬ.**, vol. IV, *sûrat al-Isrâʾ*: 320, **HAY.**, vol. VII, *sûrat al-Isrâʾ*: 49, who declares the *ḥadîṯ*

grees, recording that it was with the sending down of the same words, but recorded in Q. 30: 38).[189] Abû Bakr demanded that Fâṭima produce witnesses that Muḥammad had given Fadak to her, but she could only produce her husband and a woman named Umm Ayman.[190] Abû Bakr, insisting that she would need two male (or one male and two female) witnesses, maintained his position, based on what he claimed to have heard from Muḥammad, that Fadak was to remain a matter of public charity.[191] There follow accounts of her anger with Abû Bakr; some say she refused to see him, remaining angry with him until she died,[192] while others, such as Ibn Saʿd, transmit that she saw him with great reluctance, and only because this pleased ʿAlî. While some record that she turned her face to the wall, or reduced Abû Bakr to tears with a stern lecture, Ibn Saʿd reports merely that "she was satisfied with him."[193]

While a detailed analysis of the Fadak controversy lies beyond the scope of this work, it does raise a number of immediate questions. If, as maintained by Shîʿî and some Sunnî scholars, Fadak was a gift of Muḥammad to Fâṭima while he was still alive, then it could hardly be counted as part of the deceased Muḥammad's estate. A pre-mortem gift is not an inheritance. Concomitantly, if it were indeed in the nature of a gift, why would Fâṭima need to go to

---

is 'weak' (*ḍaʿîf*) and 'abandoned' (*matrûk*). Among the Shîʿa, cf. **BḤR.**, vol. II, Part 15, *sûrat al-Isrâʾ*, n. 1: 414–415 (insisting that Muḥammad was ordered by God to give Fadak to Fâṭima); also, al-Ṭûsî., *al-Tibyân fî tafsîr al-qurʾân*, vol. VI, *sûrat al-Isrâʾ*: 468.

189 **MĞL.**, vol. XXIX, n. 41: 127.

190 **BLḎ².**, nn. 113, 114: 35.

191 VECCIA VAGLIERI L., "Fadak" in H.A.R. Gibb et al. (eds.), *EI²*, 1965, vol. IIb: 725–727.

192 **ḤNB.**, vol. I, *Musnad Abî Bakr al-Ṣiddîq*, n. 25: 25, n. 60: 33, **BUḪ¹.**, vol. V, bk. 59 (*Kitâb al-maġâzî*), ch. 37, n. 545: 381–384, vol. VIII, bk. 80 (*Kitâb al-farâʾiḍ*), ch. 3, n. 718: 471–472, **MSL.**, vol. III, bk. 32 (*Kitâb al-ğihâd*), bb. 16, n. 52: 1380–1381, **YṬB².**, vol. IX, n. 1825: 196, **ḤDI.**, vol. VI: 46, **KṮR¹.**, vol. V: 249–250, 285.

193 **SʿD.**, vol. X, *Ḏikr banât rasûl Allâh*, n. 4927 (*Fâṭima*): 28. Cf. also **KṮR¹.**, vol. VI: 333, who claims that Abû Bakr came to her on her deathbed, asked forgiveness and was reconciled with her.

Abû Bakr to claim it after her father's death, unless he were holding it illegally? Wilferd Madelung offers a slightly different perspective to the whole debate, positing that, as it stands, the report placed in the mouth of Abû Bakr when he refused Fadak to Fâṭima was "manifestly in conflict with the letter and the spirit of the Qur'ân."[194] He quotes the *ḥadîṯ* from Ibn Saʿd's *Kitâb al-ṭabaqât al-kabîr*:

> We were informed by Muḥammad b. ʿUmar; I was informed by Hishâm b. Saʿd on the authority of ʿAbbâs b. ʿAbd Allâh b. Maʿbad, on the authority of Abû Ǧaʿfar, who said: Fâṭima went to Abû Bakr to ask for her inheritance, and al-ʿAbbâs b. ʿAbd al-Muṭṭalib went asking for his, and ʿAlî went with them. Abû Bakr said: "The Messenger of God said: We do not have heirs; whatever we leave is alms. Whatever sustenance the Prophet provided, it is now my responsibility." ʿAlî responded: "«*And Solomon was David's heir*» and Zakariyyâ' said «*who shall inherit of me and inherit (also) of the house of Jacob*»." Abû Bakr replied: "It is like this, and you know it as well as I!" ʿAlî said: "This is the Book of God speaking!" And they were silent and went away.[195]

Among Ibn Saʿd's transmissions of the event, this one stands alone by virtue of ʿAlî retorting to Abû Bakr with two quotes from the Qur'ân, the first from Q. 27: 16 and the second from Q. 19: 6. The issue, Madelung points out, revolves around what Muḥammad had meant by 'we'; himself only, or the prophets in general? In some variants of the *ḥadîṯ*, the latter meaning is underscored, while in others it is the former. Ibn Kaṯîr in his *al-Bidâya wa-l-nihâya* maintains that the two Qur'ânic verses placed into the mouth of ʿAlî referred to kingship (in the case of Dâwûd) and spiritual leadership (in the case of Zakariyyâ', the poor carpenter), and not to the inheritance of goods. Madelung also examines the contention of Caetani that Abû Bakr was following Muḥammad's express will; in

---

[194] Cf. MADELUNG W., *The Succession to Muḥammad. A study of the early Caliphate*, Cambridge University Press, Cambridge 1997: 360ff.

[195] **SʿD.**, vol. II: 273–275, vol. X: 28–29. Among the Shîʿa, cf. **RṬB¹**.: 35, **ṬBR²**., vol. I: 104.

other words, Fadak had not been his personal property to begin with, but belonged to the common good of the community. However, the Qur'ân on at least one occasion directs that land taken by Muḥammad in conquest belongs not to the common good of the community but to Muḥammad himself (Q. 59: 6). Furthermore, as noted earlier, a number of Sunnî scholars posit that Muḥammad did in fact give Fadak to Fâṭima.[196] With *aḥâdîṯ* on both sides, the issue remains unresolved between the Shîʿa and the Sunnî.

At the very end of her life, compounding all her other sorrows, Fâṭima was involved, together with her husband, in an ugly slanging match with Abû Bakr. ʿAlî, challenging Abû Bakr about his treatment of Fâṭima, and specifically his refusal to accept the testimony of the daughter of the Prophet of God, declares: "You stave off the witness of God that she is pure, and assent to the testimony of the people about her, just as you stave off the judgment of God and the judgment of His Messenger that he granted Fadak to her and that she took possession of it in his lifetime, and then you assent to the testimony about her of a Bedouin who urinates on his own ankle!"[197] Addressing a gathering of women in the mosque, Fâṭima preaches a lengthy sermon, and ends with a stinging reproach, telling the menfolk what they ought to do with the leadership of Abû Bakr: "Beware of it! Bag it, put it on the back of a sick, thin-humped she-camel, branded by the disgrace of eternity, bound for the «*fire of Allah, kindled, which leapeth up over the hearts (of men)*» (Q. 104: 7–8). By God's witness of what you do, «*those who do wrong will come to know by what a (great) reverse they will be overturned*» (Q. 26: 227).[198]

Abû Bakr then mounts the pulpit and launches an attack on Fâṭima's husband and his supporters:

---

[196] **BLḎ²**., n. 119: 37–38, **ḎHB²**., vol. II, n. 4560: 492, **SYṬ**., vol. IV, *sûrat al-Isrâ'*: 320.

[197] **ṬBR²**., vol. I: 90, **MĞL**., vol. XXIX, bb. 11, n. 26: 82.

[198] Cf. **RṬB¹**.: 37, **ṬBR²**., vol. I: 104, **SHB**., vol. II, bb. *faṣl fî ẓulâmat ahl al-bayt*: 236, **ḤDI**., vol. XVI: 212, **IRB**., vol. I: 489, **MĞL**., vol. XXIX: 192.

> In the course of reporting about Fadak, Ibn Abî al-Ḥadîd related, on the authority of Aḥmad b. ʿAbd al-ʿAzîz al-Ǧawharî, that when Abû Bakr heard the sermon of Fâṭima, peace be upon her, concerning Fadak, he was troubled by her talk. He ascended the pulpit and said: "People, what is this respect for every speech? Where were these in the lifetime of the Messenger of God, may God bless and save him and his family? If someone heard something, let him say so! If someone witnessed something, let him speak. But he is a fox, whose witness is his own tail, who cleaves to every dissension. He it is who says: make her young again after she has become old! You ask help from the weak and you ask assistance from women, like Umm Ṭiḥâl, whose people liked to fornicate with her"[199]

ʿAlî himself suffers a bout of his wife's sorrow and frustration. Coming in from arguing with Abû Bakr, she finds ʿAlî sitting in the house:

> She said to the Commander of the Faithful, peace be upon him: "Ibn Abî Ṭâlib, peace be upon you. You have enclosed yourself like a placenta of the womb and remained in the room of the suspicious! Having demolished the arrival of the falcon, you are hoodwinked by the feathers of the defenseless! This son of Abû Quḥḥâfa has gone to great lengths to harm me, and by God he has angrily disputed my claim, so that even the leading woman has refused me her help and the emigrant woman her support, and the community casts down its look before me. There is neither supporter nor protector. I went out, by God, suppressing my anger, and have returned coerced. Would that there were no option for me! Would that I

---

[199] **RṬB¹**.: 38, **ḤDI**., vol. XVI: 214, **MǦL**., vol. XXIX: 208. Al-Maǧlisî transmits incorrectly from Ibn al-Ḥadîd; the latter reads: "they ask help from the weak and they ask assistance from women", while the former reads 'you' (pl.) instead of 'they'). The sense is that ʿAlî is accused of rekindling trouble after it has died down.

had died before this, died before my humiliation, died before my fate…"[200]

In terms of the text, there are a number of discrepancies between the transmitters; one of al-Maglisî's transmissions for instance, contains Fâṭima's accusation that ʿAlî has "grown weak since you laid down your sword", but other transmissions omit this phrase. Some texts read "the cloak of the womb" while others are rendered as "placenta of the womb." A slightly freer translation of this text might run: "You are hiding like a fetus in the womb…you have run home like those guilty of being untrustworthy…and having destroyed the strongest, you have been overcome by these weaklings." The mental anguish of Fâṭima ought to be considered when reading this outburst.

2.11. THE DEATH OF FÂṬIMA

Sunnî and Shîʿa scholars agree that Fâṭima died in the same year as her father, their deaths separated by an indeterminate number of weeks or months. Some say she died reconciled to Abû Bakr, others not. Some say she faced death calmly; washing herself, anointing herself with balm, dressing in coarse garments and insisting (to ʿAlî or to her sister-in-law Asmâʾ bt. ʿUmays) that she should not be uncovered after death.[201] This fear that her wasted form might be seen extended to having Asmâʾ create a special bier for her.[202]

---

[200] **ṬBR²**., vol. I: 107, **SHB**., vol. II, bb. *faṣl fî ẓulâmat ahl al-bayt*: 236–237, **MĞL**., vol. XXIX: 206. Almost exactly the same sentiments are expressed by Maryam: «*She said: Oh, would that I had died ere this and become a thing of naught, forgotten*» (Q. 19: 23).

[201] **SʿD**., vol. X, *Ḏikr banât rasûl Allâh*, n. 4927 (*Fâṭima*): 28, **BLḎ¹**., vol. I, n. 865: 402, **IṢH**., vol. II, bb. 133: 42–43, **RḤB**.: 53, **KṮR¹**., vol. VI: 333; **SQL¹**., vol. IV, bb. *ḥarf al-fâʾ*, n. 830: 367.

[202] According to a number of Shîʿî transmitters, Fâṭima was the first for whom a bier was created: cf. **KLY**., vol. III, bk. 11 (*Kitâb al-ğanâʾiz*), bb. *al-nawâdir*, n. 6: 251, **ṢDQ³**., vol. I, bb. *al-nawâdir*, n. 597: 194, **ṬFA¹**., vol. I, bb. 23, nn. 184–185: 469, **ṬBR¹**.: 141, **ḤRR¹**., vol. III, bb. 52, nn. 3454–3455, 3457–3458: 219–220, **MĞL**., vol. XXII, bb. 2: 202, vol.

But others relate a different story; that she severely rebuked Muḥammad's wives and the Quraysh women who came to visit her, and that ʿÂʾisha was prevented from entering.[203]

While Lammens posits that ʿAlî came late for her death, the sources recount that ʿAlî and Asmâʾ bt. ʿUmays washed her,[204] buried her by night and performed the prayers; other accounts say that these were done by Abû Bakr (although still other accounts claim he did not know of her death, kept deliberately uninformed by ʿAlî),[205] and that she was buried by night almost certainly in the Baqîʿ cemetery (where a number of others assisted ʿAlî).[206]

XLIII, bb. 7, nn. 42–43: 212, vol. LXXVIII, bb. 6, n. 7: 249, n. 9: 250, **NṬR**., vol. II, bb. 43, n. 1–2187: 358, n. 5–2191: 361.

[203] **RḤB**.: 53, **ATH²**., vol. V, bb. *ḥarf al-fâʾ*: 524. Among the Shîʿa, cf. **YQB**., vol. II: 128–129.

[204] **SʿD**., vol. X, *Ḏikr banât rasûl Allâh*, n. 4927 (*Fâṭima*): 28. Certainly, Ibn Saʿd insinuates that ʿAlî was not present at the moment of her death; he offers contradictory reports, positing that ʿAlî ordered someone else to wash her, but also transmitting a *ḥadîṯ* which has ʿAlî doing the washing himself. However, **BLḎ¹**., vol. I, n. 865: 402 suggests strongly that ʿAlî was present when Fâṭima died, and that he washed her when she was on the point of death. Cf. also **YṬB²**., vol. X, n. 1869: 39, **ATH¹**., vol. II: 230–231, **ḤDI**., vol. VI: 46, **KṮR¹**., vol. V: 286, vol. VI: 333 (ʿAlî, Asmâʾ bt. ʿUmays and Salamâ Umm Râfiʿ washed her), **SQL¹**., vol. IV, bb. *ḥarf al-fâʾ*, n. 830: 367, **SQL⁴**., vol. XII, *Kitâb al-nisâʾ*, n. 4434: 441. Among the Shîʿa, cf. **YQB**., vol. II: 128.

[205] **BUḪ¹**., vol. V, bk. 59 (*Kitâb al-maġâzî*), ch. 37, n. 545: 381–384, **BLḎ¹**., vol. I, n. 865: 402 (who adds that ʿUmar was equally uninformed), **ḤDI**., vol. VI: 46, **KṮR¹**., vol. V: 286, **SQL¹**., vol. IV, bb. *ḥarf al-fâʾ*, n. 830: 367 (who says the *ḥadîṯ* about Abû Bakr saying the prayers is weak).

[206] **SʿD**., vol. X, *Ḏikr banât rasûl Allâh*, n. 4927 (*Fâṭima*): 29–30 transmits a number of strands claiming, alternatively, that ʿAlî performed the prayers and buried her at night, or that ʿAbbâs ʿAbd al-Muṭṭalib prayed over her and that ʿAlî, ʿAbbâs ʿAbd al-Muṭṭalib and Faḍl b. ʿAbbâs buried her. Another *ḥadîṯ* says that Abû Bakr performed the prayers, and that four people helped to bury her. Cf. also **YṬB²**., vol. X, n. 1869: 39, **IṢH**., vol. II, bb. 133: 42–43, **ATH¹**., vol. II: 230–231, **ATH²**., vol. V, bb. *ḥarf al-fâʾ*: 524, **KṮR¹**., vol. VI: 333, **SQL¹**., vol. IV, bb. *ḥarf al-fâʾ*, n. 830: 367, **SQL⁴**., vol. XII, *Kitâb al-nisâʾ*, n. 4434: 441.

As for her *kunya* (pl. *kunâ*)[207] Umm Abî-hâ ('the mother of her father'), it is possibly of Shîʿî origin, and is found in later sources.[208] The Shîʿa claim that she had learned that the last of her descendants would be named Muḥammad. Considering the lateness of the sources, Veccia Vaglieri ponders a connection with Mary's title 'Mother of God'. In view of the similarity of the theologies constructed around the two women by their adherents, this is a distinct possibility, but hard to prove.

While the sources exult in the beauty of her sister Ruqayya, they pass in silence over Fâṭima. One well-known *ḥadîṯ*, on the authority of ʿÂʾisha and transmitted by numerous Sunnî authorities, tells of how her walk resembled that of Muḥammad;[209] but it also highlights the love and gentleness with which Muḥammad ostensibly treated her, bringing into question some of Lammens' opinions.

---

[207] A *kunya* is patronymic, comprising two parts: 'Abû' or 'Umm' in connection with a second term. It comes from the root meaning 'to speak of someone or something in an allusive way'. If the name is of a person, the *kunya* indicates the relationship of parent to child. It is possible to distinguish between this, the 'real' *kunya*, and a metaphorical, figurative *kunya*, in which this bond of kinship is impossible. For a succinct explanation of the components of Arabic names, cf. PIERCE M., *Twelve Infallible Men. The Imams and the Making of Shiʿism*, Harvard University Press, Cambridge Mass., 2016: 155.

[208] **BRR.**, vol. IV, *Kitâb al-nisâʾ*, bb. *al-fâʾ*, n. 4057: 1899, **ATH²**., vol. V, bb. *ḥarf al-fâʾ*: 520, **KṮR¹**., vol. VI: 332, **SQL¹**., vol. IV, bb. *ḥarf al-fâʾ*, n. 830: 365, **SQL⁴**., vol. XII, *Kitâb al-nisâʾ*, n. 4434: 440.

[209] **SʿD.**, vol. X, *Ḏikr banât rasûl Allâh*, n. 4927 (*Fâṭima*): 27, **ḤNB.**, vol. X, *Aḥâdîṯ Fâṭima*, n. 26475: 157–158, **BUḪ¹**., vol. IV, bk. 56 (*Kitâb al-manâqib*), ch. 24, n. 819: 526–527, vol. VI, bk. 61 (*Kitâb faḍâʾil al-qurʾân*), ch. 7: 485, vol. VIII, bk. 74 (*Kitâb al-istiʾḏân*), ch. 43, n. 301: 201–202, **MSL.**, vol. IV, bk. 44 (*Kitâb faḍâʾil al-ṣaḥâba*), bb. 10 (*Faḍâʾil Fâṭima bt. al-nabî*), nn. 98, 99: 1904–1905, **NSA²**.: 78–80, **ḤNA.**, vol. III, bk. 31 (*Kitâb maʿrifat al-ṣaḥâba*), *Manâqib Fâṭima bt. rasûl Allâh*, n. 4795: 181, **IṢH.**, vol. II, bb. 133: 39–40, **BRR.**, vol. IV, *Kitâb al-nisâʾ wa-kunâ-hunna*, n. 4057: 1896, **SQL³**., vol. VIII, bb. 84, n. 4434: 171, **ATH²**., vol. V, bb. *ḥarf al-fâʾ*: 522, **SHL.**, bb. *faḍl fî ḏikr manâqib ʿAlî b. Abî Ṭâlib*: 43. Among the Shîʿa cf. **ṢDQ¹**.: 595.

Lammens is also inaccurate in his claim about her perpetual sickliness and weakness, and we must ponder his sources; she bore four (or possibly five) children, was actively present during at least one major battle, ran the household almost single handedly, made no fewer than two journeys to Mecca and campaigned energetically on behalf of her husband's claim for the Caliphate.

The Shîʿî transmitters and hagiographers highlight many of her moral attributes, making her a perfect model for all women ("the woman that Islam wants a woman to be" insists Shariati).[210] In fact, in his famous work *Fatima is Fatima*, Shariati, while stressing her humanity above all the supernatural qualities attached to her, imputes to her innumerable virtues, but without ever providing his reader with a single source;[211] another hagiographer, the Jordanian Abû Muḥammad Ordoni, faithfully offers primary and secondary Arabic and Persian sources for the incidents of her life, drawing from these incidents the virtues which he weaves carefully into the pattern of her life.[212]

Hardworking and diligent, she enjoyed helping others. It seems certain too that she was not as diffident as is claimed; it was she who prevented ʿAlî from taking a second wife, but noteworthy too are her reaction against Abû Bakr concerning Fadak, her behaviour during the forcing of ʿAlî's allegiance and her house to house campaigns to win support for her husband's candidacy. Ibn al-Ḥadîd describes her on a donkey, accompanying ʿAlî to the houses of the *anṣâr* (the Medinan supporters of Muḥammad who gave him refuge after the *hiğra*) to ask their backing, with Fâṭima asking specifically that they would side with ʿAlî. Their response is recorded in the texts; the people have already given their allegiance to Abû Bakr, but if only ʿAlî had come earlier they would not have turned from him. "Should I have left the Messenger of God, lifeless in his house and not prepared him, in order to come to the

---

210 SHARIATI A., *Red Shiʾism*, The Shariati Foundation, Tehran 1979: 5.

211 SHARIATI A., *Fatima is Fatima*, The Shariati Foundation, Tehran (n.d.).

212 ORDONI A. M., *Fatima the Gracious*, Ansariyan Publications, Qum (n.d.).

people and contest with them about his power?" protests ʿAlî. Fâṭima's response is laconic: "The father of al-Ḥusayn has done nothing except what he ought." [213] In that pithy sentence, she encapsulates all the great Shîʿî claim and underscores their overriding conviction that justice was ever on their side.

---

[213] **ḤDI.**, vol. VI: 13.

CHAPTER TWO.
PART ONE: THE SUPERNATURAL QUALITIES IN THE ANNUNCIATION AND BIRTH OF FÂṬIMA IN SHÎʿÎ TRADITION, TEACHING AND PIETY

This chapter changes the focus from Sunnî to Shîʿî tradition, examining the expressly Shîʿî conception of Fâṭima in her pre-existence, conception and birth. It presents a bulk of material that is, with some rare exceptions, absent in the vast majority of Sunnî texts, leading to a theology constructed around the life of Fâṭima which is unique to Shîʿî theology and piety.

2.1. THE CONCEPTION AND BIRTH OF FÂṬIMA IN SHÎʿÎ MUSLIM TRADITION

> Fâṭima is not like the women of the children of Adam: she is not defective, as they are defective.[1]

This *ḥadîṯ*, which has as its context the report of Fâṭima's conception as a result her father eating mystical fruit, is declared impossible by the Sunnî transmitters al-Ǧawzî and al-Hayṯamî (but not by al-Ḫawârizmî); in fact, although they are not alone among the Sunnî in carrying the *ḥadîṯ* of the fruit, they are almost the only ones who record this particular part of it. They reject not simply

[1] **ḪWZ.**, Part 1, bb. *Faḍâʾil Fâṭima al-Zahrâʾ bt. rasûl Allâh*, n. 33: 105, **ǦWZ**[1]., vol. I, bb. *fî faḍl Fâṭima*: 413, **HAY.**, vol. IX, bb. *manâqib Fâṭima bt. rasûl Allâh*: 202. Among the Shîʿa, cf. **ṬSṬ**[2]., vol. I, n. 163: 111, **MǦL.**, vol. XXXVII, bb. 50, n. 36: 64, vol. XLIII, bb. 2, n. 14: 16.

this specific element of the *ḥadîṯ*, but the *ḥadîṯ* as a whole, primarily because they cannot accept the dating of Fâṭima's birth after the 'night journey'. The eighth-form verb *iʿtalla-yaʿtallu* carries the sense of being 'weak' or 'defective', and in spite of its rejection by al-Hayṯamî, the *ḥadîṯ* offers an intimation of the level to which Fâṭima has been elevated. The Shîʿî transmitters Ibn Ṭâ'ûs and al-Mağlisî qualify this *ḥadîṯ*, in the sense that the lack of defectiveness concerns the absence of menstruation. However, it is clear that in front of the vigorous theology constructed around her in the *aḥâdîṯ* of the Shîʿa, the almost grey figure of Fâṭima in the Sunnî corpus seems to fade and vanish away; for the Shîʿa employ language, concepts and a mystical vision about Fâṭima that is so wholly different from their Sunnî counterparts that at times it is scarcely credible that one is treating of the same woman. She is certainly not without substance in the Sunnî corpus of *aḥâdîṯ*; but Lammens contends that she is an altogether dull and lackluster creature, a contention which is inaccurate even if, like him, one discards the whole Shîʿî corpus and follows the Sunnî alone. If the most radical notion found about her among the Sunnî scholars (besides the minority who carry the *ḥadîṯ* of Muḥammad eating heavenly fruit) is that she is, ostensibly, the mistress of the women of Paradise (or at least, of the women of the Muslim community and of the worlds) – and even this is not entirely settled among the transmitters – the Shîʿa move considerably further than this, transmitting *aḥâdîṯ* about her creation from light and her concomitant pre-existence, and the altogether miraculous nature of her conception and birth.

There is no 'immaculate conception' in the theology of Fâṭima, although, as one of the five primary members of the *ahl al-bayt*, she is regarded as infallible and sinless (*maʿṣûma*). The technical nature of this sinless state is not clearly articulated in terms of its precise timing and how God achieved such a favoured state in His creature, although the *aḥâdîṯ* surrounding her being named Fâṭima suggest that her purification from sin took place before her birth.[2]

---

[2] As regards her son al-Ḥusayn, the texts attempt to articulate the technical nature and timing of his sinless state by maintaining that he was born already cleansed and purified by God. Cf. for example **ṢDQ**[1]., n. 5: 136, **FNR**., vol. I: 155, **MĞL**., vol. XLIII, bb. 11, n. 16: 243, n. 24: 256.

There are three conspicuous strands of theology which merit appraisal. The first is the notion of Fâṭima's creation from light and her pre-existence, for this stands at the heart of the Shîʿî mystical vision of her personhood. The second is her conception by Ḫadîğa, miraculous not only by reason of divine intervention (such as a form of 'annunciation' to Muḥammad by an angel), but also by reason of Muḥammad eating miraculous fruit in heaven; it is ostensibly as a result of this that Fâṭima was conceived, making her, in Muḥammad's words, a "maiden of Paradise in human form" (*ḥawrâʾ insiyya*)[3] and causing him to say, in a *ḥadîṯ* carried with diverse wording even by some Sunnî transmitters, that "Whenever I long for the fragrance of Paradise I smell the neck of Fâṭima."[4]

A third theological component concerns the supernatural events surrounding the pregnancy of Ḫadîğa and the parturition of Fâṭima.

2.1.1. The Pre-Existence of Fâṭima

At the very core of Shîʿî mystical theology and its understanding of the *ahl al-bayt* stands the so-called *ashbâḥ ḥadîṯ* in which Adam, and

---

[3] Among the Sunnî, cf. **BĠD.**, vol. V, n. 2481: 87, vol. XII, n. 6772: 331, **ḪWZ.**, Part 1, bb. *Faḍâʾil Fâṭima al-Zahrâʾ bt. rasûl Allâh*, n. 33: 105, **ǦWZ[1].**, vol. I, bb. *fî faḍl Fâṭima*: 411–413, bb. *fî ḏikr tazwîğ Fâṭima bi-ʿAlî*: 421, **ṢFI.**, vol. II, bb. *manâqib Fâṭima al-Zahrâʾ*: 184, **MTQ.**, vol. V: 97. Among the Shîʿa, cf. **ṢDQ[1].**, n. 7: 460, **ṢDQ[5].**, vol. I, bb. 11, n. 3: 115, **ṢDQ[6].**, n. 53: 396, **FNR.**, vol. I: 149, **ṬBR[2].**, vol. II: 408, **SHB.**, vol. III, bb. *manâqib Fâṭima al-Zahrâʾ*: 383, **ABḎ.**: 240, **MĞL.**, vol. IV, bb. 1, n. 4: 3, vol. VIII, bb. 23, n. 6: 119, n. 160: 188, vol. XLIII, bb. 1, nn. 2–3: 4, bb. 2, n. 17: 18, bb. 3, n. 42: 43, vol. XLIV, bb. 30, n. 33: 240.

[4] Some alternative versions read 'kiss' instead of 'smell' and 'fragrance' instead of 'neck'. Among the Sunnî, cf. **ḤNA.**, vol. III, bk. 31 (*Kitâb maʿrifat al-ṣaḥâba*), *Manâqib Fâṭima bt. rasûl Allâh*, n. 4801: 183–184 (with an annotation of rejection by al-Ḏahabî in the notes), **BĠD.**, vol. V, n. 2481: 87, **ḪWZ.**, Part 1, bb. *Faḍâʾil Fâṭima al-Zahrâʾ bt. rasûl Allâh*, n. 33: 105, **ǦWZ[1].**, vol. I, bb. *fî faḍl Fâṭima*: 410–411, 413, who condemns it as absolutely false, **RḤB.**: 36, **ṢFI.**, vol. II, bb. *manâqib Fâṭima al-Zahrâʾ*: 184, **SYṬ.**, vol. IV, *sûrat al-Isrâʾ*: 282, **HAY.**, vol. IX, bb. *manâqib Fâṭima bt. rasûl Allâh*: 202, **SHL.**, bb. *faḍl fî ḏikr manâqib ʿAlî b. Abî Ṭâlib*: 42.

sometimes Ḥawwâʾ (Eve) with him, sees five figures of light in his own shape and form prostrating before God; thinking himself to be alone, he asks after their identity:

> When God created Adam and Ḥawwâʾ, they strutted through Paradise and said: "Who are better than we?" At that moment they noticed an image of a girl never seen before; from this girl came an illuminating light so bright that it almost blinded the eyes. They said: "Lord, what is this?" He answered: "This is the image of Fâṭima, the mistress of the women of your descendants." Adam asked: "What is the crown on her head?" God said: "Her husband ʿAlî." Adam then asked: "What are the two earrings?" God replied: "Her two sons. This existed hidden in my knowledge two thousand years before I created you."[5]

This *ashbâḥ ḥadîṯ*, most often addressed to Adam (wherein his question is always: "Did You create someone before me?") and with its application of a pre-existent state to Muḥammad, ʿAlî, Fâṭima, al-Ḥasan and al-Ḥusayn (but not the ostensibly miscarried Muḥassin or the daughters of Fâṭima), is found in this or comparable wording throughout the corpus of Shîʿî *aḥâdîṯ*. One would hardly expect the Sunnî to carry it; in fact, it is transmitted by al-Ḫawârizmî, who makes no comment on it, by al-Ğawzî[6] and by Ibn Ḥağar al-ʿAsqalânî, who includes the eleventh Imâm Abû Muḥammad al-Ḥasan b. ʿAlî al-ʿAskarî in his chain of transmission. Al-ʿAsqalânî condemns the *ḥadîṯ* as absolutely false (*mawḍûʿ*) as does al-Ğawzî before him. Another Sunnî scholar, al-Ṣaffûrî, transmits the *ḥadîṯ* in a particularly detailed narrative; in his *Nuzhat al-mağâlis wa-muntaḫab al-nafâʾis*, Fâṭima is envisaged as a brilliant girl from whom light pours forth, and crowned with a gold and diamond crown, the likes of which Adam has never seen. Her husband ʿAlî is a young man,

---

[5] **ḪWZ.**, Part 1, bb. *faḍâʾil Fâṭima al-Zahrâʾ bt. rasûl Allâh*, n. 37: 106–107, **SQL**[2]., vol. III, n. 1409: 346–347.

[6] Cf. **ĞWZ**[1]., vol. I, bb. *fî faḍl Fâṭima*: 414, **SQL**[2]., vol. III, n. 1409: 347.

as beautiful as the Qurʾânic Yûsuf, reclining on a golden bed in a ruby palace.[7]

The Shîʿî al-Mağlisî records an account more diverse and detailed than his Sunnî counterparts:

> On the authority of Abû Hurayra, who said: "The Messenger of God said that when God created Adam and blew into him of His spirit, Adam looked at the right side of the Throne, and there were five figures, and he said: Lord, have You created any of mankind before me? He replied: No. He said: Then who are these whose names I see? He answered: These five are of your descendants. Were it not for them, I would not have created you, nor would I have created Paradise, or the Throne, or the Seat, or the heavens, or the earth, or the angels, or the *ğinn*, or mankind. For these five I cleft a name from my names. I am the Praised (*al-Maḥmûd*) and this is Muḥammad. I am the Most High (*al-ʿAlî*) and this is ʿAlî. I am the Creator (*al-Fâṭir*) and this is Fâṭima. I am the Master of beneficence (*ḏû al-iḥsân*) and this is al-Ḥasan. I am the Beneficent (*al-Muḥsin*) and this is al-Ḥusayn. I have sworn by myself that no-one shall come to me with love for any of them in his heart the weight of a mustard seed, except that I shall make him enter my Paradise. I have sworn by my might that no-one shall come to me with hatred for any of them in his heart the weight of a mustard seed, except that I shall make him enter my Fire. Adam, these are the best of my creation, by whom I save whom I save and by whom I destroy whom I destroy."[8]

In another, very similar version of this *ḥadîṯ*, al-Mağlisî offers an alternative derivation of the names:

> God said: "Âdam, these figures are the best of my creatures and of my creation. This is Muḥammad, and I am the Praise-

[7] **ṢFI.**, vol. II, bb. *manâqib Fâṭima al-Zahrâʾ*: 185.

[8] **MĞL.**, vol. XXVII, bb. 10, n. 10: 5. Cf. also **RWD³.**, bb. 3, n. 10: 39, **ABḎ.**, 52, **MĞL.**, vol. XVI, bb. 11, nn. 61, 62: 361–362, vol. XXV, bb. 1, n. 8: 5–6, vol. XXVI, bb. 6, n. 15: 273, vol. XXVII, bb. 7, n. 67: 199–200, vol. XXXVI, bb. 40, n. 18: 216–217, n. 21: 222.

> worthy (*al-Ḥamîd*), the Praised (*al-Maḥmûd*) in my works. I have cleft for him a name from my names. This is ʿAlî, and I am the Most High (*al-ʿAlî*), the Great (*al-ʿAẓîm*). I have cleft for him a name from my names. This is Fâṭima, and I am the Creator (*al-Fâṭir*) of the heavens and the earth, the Weaner (*al-Fâṭim*) of my enemies from my mercy on the day of my final judgment, the Weaner of my friends from what afflicts and dishonours them. I have cleft for her a name from my names. This is al-Ḥasan and this is al-Ḥusayn, and I am the Beneficent (*al-Muḥsin*), the Embellisher (*al-Muǧmil*). I have cleft for them a name from my names. These are the best of my creatures, the distinguished of my creation. Through them I choose, through them I give, through them I punish and through them I reward. Gain access to me through them, Adam, and whenever calamity befalls you, I will make them your intercessors to me. I have sworn by myself a true oath: I will not delude one who hopes through them and I will not refuse one who asks through them. Consequently, when sin brought him down, God, powerful and lofty, called him through them and he repented and He pardoned him." [9]

These two *aḥâdîṯ* articulate some of the most crucial Shîʿî theology pertaining to Fâṭima and concomitantly to the *ahl al-bayt*. They are the best of all God's creatures[10] and of the whole of His creation; God accomplishes everything, including the whole of creation, through them. They are the *raison d'être* for everything that God does, and the very salvation of humankind depends upon love for them. Each of them bears a name cleft from a divine name,[11] and they are intercessors for humankind with God.

---

[9] **MǦL.**, vol. XI, bb. 2, n. 25: 150–151, vol. XXVI, bb. 7, n. 10: 326–327.

[10] **ABḎ.**, 803, **MǦL.**, vol. II, bb. 3, n. 9: 164–165, **NṬR.**, vol. VIII, bb. 15, n. 9229–3: 138, vol. XXVI, bb. 6, n. 15: 273.

[11] **MǦL.**, vol. XVI, bb. 11, n. 61: 361–362, vol. XXVII, bb. 7, n. 67: 199–200, vol. XXXVI, bb. 40, n. 21: 222, vol. XXXVI, bb. 41, nn. 82, 83: 261, vol. XXXVII, bb. 50, n. 32: 62.

However, these same *aḥâdîṯ* lead to an unusual and more arcane strand, a *ḥadîṯ qudsî*,[12] recorded by al-Mûsawî in his seven-volume *al-Kawṯar fî aḥwâl Fâṭima bt. al-nabî al-aṭhar*. He names only two sources for the *ḥadîṯ* but fails to give adequate details. The first, which he names as *al-ʿAwâlim* is ostensibly the work entitled *ʿAwâlim al-ʿulûm*, by al-Baḥrânî,[13] a pupil of al-Mağlisî. The second, which he names as *Mustadrak safînat al-biḥâr* is possibly *Safînat al-biḥâr wa-madînat al-ḥikam wa-l-âṯâr* (or a supplement to it), an index of al-Mağlisî's *Biḥâr al-anwâr* compiled by ʿAbbâs al-Qummî.[14] The *ḥadîṯ* itself is carried neither by any of the books of *aḥâdîṯ* regarded as canonical by the Shîʿa, nor in the major works of the well-known transmitters named in the chain of transmission (Ğamâl al-Dîn b. Fahd al-Ḥillî[15] and *Shayḫ* al-Ṣadûq).[16] It must therefore be treated with great caution. In essence, the *ḥadîṯ* claims that God created Muḥammad and ʿAlî for the sake of Fâṭima, so that she becomes God's underlying principle for all His creative activity:

> *Shayḫ* Ibrâhîm b. al-Ḥasan al-Ḏirâq, on the authority of *Shayḫ* ʿAlî b. Hilâl al-Ğazâʾirî, on the authority of *Shayḫ* Aḥmad b. Fahd al-Ḥillî, on the authority of *Shayḫ* Zayn al-Dîn ʿAlî b. al-Ḥasan al-Ḫâzin al-Ḥâʾirî, on the authority of *Shayḫ* Abû ʿAbd Allâh Muḥammad b. Makkî al-Shahîd in his continuous paths (of transmission) to Abû Ğaʿfar Muḥammad b. ʿAlî b. Mûsâ b. Bâbawayh al-Qummî in his path (of transmission) to Ğâbir b.

---

[12] A specific category of *aḥâdîṯ* attributed to God Himself and communicated to Muḥammad, through the mediation of Ğibrîl, in a number of different ways (such as inspiration or dreams).

[13] ʿAbd Allâh b. Nûr Allâh al-Baḥrânî (d. 1110/1698: cf. GAL S. II: 504).

[14] ʿAbbâs al-Qummî (d. 1359/1940: cf. GAS II: 573). Besides noting that his work is based on al-Mağlisî's, Brockelmann provides no further information. Cf. KOHLBERG E., "Shīʿī *Ḥadīth*" in A.F.L. Beeston et al., (eds.), *Arabic Literature to the End of the Umayyad Period*, 1983: 307.

[15] Aḥmad b. Muḥammad b. Fahd al-Asadî al-Ḥillî (d. 841/1438). Cf. **MOD.**: 416.

[16] The *ḥadîṯ* is found, sometimes with diverse wording and not always relating to Fâṭima, in a number of works: cf. for e.g. **ĞQM.**: 128, **FNR.**, vol. I, 84, **BḤR.**, vol. II: 443, **MĞL.**, vol. XXXV, bb. 1, n. 15: 23.

> Yazîd al-Ǧuʿfî,[17] on the authority of Ǧâbir b. ʿAbd Allâh al-Anṣârî, on the authority of the Messenger of God, on the authority of God, may He be blessed and exalted, Who said: "Aḥmad! Were it not for you, I would not have created the celestial spheres, and were it not for ʿAlî I would not have created you, and were it not for Fâṭima I would not have created either of you."[18]

The implication of the *ḥadîṯ* is that the status of Fâṭima is more exalted than that of her father, reminding one of the extremist position of a group like the Nuṣayrî, for whom Fâṭima is the feminine manifestation of the masculine deity. While the Shîʿî corpus has no lack of *aḥâdîṯ* insisting that God would not have created Adam or any other part of creation were it not for the *ahl al-bayt*,[19] we do not find any hint that Fâṭima alone is the divine incentive for creation.

In itself, the notion of pre-existence is certainly not foreign to Sunnî Islam. This is confirmed by the mystical theology of the 'Muḥammadan Light' (*nûr muḥammadî*), a name given to Muḥammad's pre-existent entity ('entity', for there was much disagreement over whether this pre-existence was in body or in soul). Not all the scholars or theologians are agreed upon the nature of this pre-existence, or about what was created immediately after the *nûr muḥammadî*. In a general way, the theological tradition, which

[17] Cf. **ṬFA⁴**., n. 6–1316: 129, **MOD**.: 86–103.

[18] al-MŪSAWÎ M., *al-Kawṯar fî aḥwâl Fâṭima bt. al-nabî al-aṭhar*, 2000, vol. I: 111. The same author, in Part 3, ch. 2 of his first volume, claims a *ḥadîṯ* in which God claims that had it not been for Fâṭima, He would have created neither the heavens, nor the earth, nor the Throne, nor Paradise, nor hell, nor even Adam. This is misleading, for a closer examination of the text reveals that it forms part of the *ashbâḥ* tradition; in fact, the text does not anywhere suggest that God created all these things for the sake of Fâṭima alone, but rather that He created them all for the sake of the five 'figures' seen by Adam (Muḥammad, ʿAlî, Fâṭima, al-Ḥasan and al-Ḥusayn). This is more consistent with the classical Shîʿî renditions of the *ashbâḥ ḥadîṯ*. Cf. **BAḤ**., vol. XI, bb. 4, n. 1: 43–44.

[19] **ǦQM**.: 128, **ṢDQ⁵**., vol. I, bb. 28, n. 67: 306, **RWD³**., bb. 3, n. 10: 39, **DAY**., vol. II: 145, **MǦL**., vol. II, bb. 3, n. 9: 164–165, vol. XVI, bb. 11, n. 62: 362, vol. XXVI, bb. 6, n. 15: 273, vol. XXVII, bb. 10, n. 10: 5.

has a number of variations, posits that Muḥammad was the first and most exalted of God's creation. For example:

> ...before everything else God created from His light the light of your Prophet. He made this light turn by His power where He wanted it to turn. In that time, the Well-Guarded Tablet did not exist, nor did the Pen, nor Paradise, nor the Infernal Fire, nor angels, nor sky, nor earth, nor sun, nor moon, nor demon, nor man. When God the Most High wanted to create creatures, He divided this light into four parts. From the first part He created the Pen, from the second the Tablet, from the third the Throne, and then He divided the fourth part into another four parts. From the first He created the skies, from the second the earth, from the third Paradise and Hell, and then He divided the fourth part into four parts. From the first He created the vision of the believers, from the second the light of their hearts, which is in fact the knowledge of the Most High, from the third He created the lights of their affability, which is the faith in the One God...[20]

For scholars like al-Ġazâlî and Ibn Taymiyya,[21] the primordial creation of the Prophet did not imply pre-existence, but only predestination. However, al-Subkî[22] opposed them, supporting the dogma of pre-existence. Rubin[23] points out that while the early corpus of *aḥâdîṯ* holds that Muḥammad was the first of all the prophets to be created (and thus posits his pre-existence), the same corpus identified the *nûr muḥammadî* with the spermatic substance in the loins of his Arab ancestors. Bearing in their loins the divine 'Muḥammadan substance', his Arab ancestors are designated as true Muslims, and even as prophets. Through the process of procreation, this light reaches the physical Prophet. God is conceived of as light, which

---

[20] Cf. BANNERTH E., "La Khalwatiyya en Egypte", *MIDEO* 8, Dar al-Maaref, 1964–1966: 15.

[21] Taqî al-Dîn Aḥmad b. al-Ḥalîm b. Taymiyya al-Ḥanbalî (d. 728/1328), a theologian and jurist of the rigorous Ḥanbalî School.

[22] Taqî al-Dîn al-Subkî (d. 756/1355).

[23] For an in-depth treatment, cf. RUBIN U., "Nūr Muḥammadī" in H.A.R. Gibb et al. (eds.), *EI²*, 1995, vol. VIIIa: 125.

emanates in its luminosity and 'personifies' (or 'individualizes') itself as the primordial *nûr muḥammadî*. This issue of divine light comprises Muḥammad in his light nature; a translucent shaft of light, a primeval man who is, concomitantly, the prototype of mankind. His primordial adoration of God throughout a measureless epoch of time (some *aḥâdîṯ* say ten-thousand years, during which time God looked at it seventy-thousand times a day, while others claim Muḥammad as a light fourteen-thousand years before the creation of Adam) represents the original idea and image of the human being, the believing, obedient creature fashioned in divine light. This concept of the primeval *nûr muḥammadî* is inherently connected with the 'Verse of the Light' (Q. 24: 35):

> «*Allah is the Light of the heavens and the earth. The similitude of His light is as a niche wherein is a lamp. The lamp is in a glass. The glass is as it were a shine star. (This lamp is) kindled from a blessed tree, an olive neither of the East nor of the West, whose oil would almost glow forth (of itself) though no fire touched it. Light upon light. Allah guideth to His light whom He will. And Allah speaketh to mankind in allegories, for Allah is Knower of all things*».

A number of the Ṣûfî masters (notably al-Tustarî)[24] developed their theory of the *nûr muḥammadî* from the idea of "*the similitude of His light*". God, the inaccessible mystery of divine light articulates Himself in the likeness of the light of Muḥammad. The origin of the *nûr muḥammadî* is depicted as a luminous mass of primordial adoration, which takes the shape of a transparent column of divine light and constitutes Muḥammad as the primal articulation of God. In his exegesis, al-Tustarî explains:

> When God willed to create Muḥammad, He made appear a light from His light. When it reached the veil of the majesty, it bowed in prostration before God. God created from its pros-

---

[24] Sahl b. ʿAbd Allâh al-Tustarî (d. 283/896), a Ṣûfî master and teacher of, among others, al-Ḥallâǧ and al-Makkî, and author of an important Qur'ânic commentary.

> tration a mighty column like crystal glass of light that is outwardly and inwardly translucent.[25]

This *nûr muḥammadî* is, accordingly, a kind of 'primal matter', shaped by God from His own light and from which issues all existence. Muḥammad is therefore the primal cosmic origin of mankind, the first creation in pre-existence, enshrining the archetype of all created beings; God caused all the rest of creation to proceed from the *nûr muḥammadî*, so that were it not for Muḥammad, God would not have created.

However, the Ṣûfî masters were not alone in developing these themes. The Shî'î scholars took up the texts, reworking and reinterpreting them so that, for example, the sixth Imâm, Abû 'Abd Allâh Ǧa'far b. Muḥammad al-Ṣâdiq, in an exegesis of the 'Verse of the Light', envisages Fâṭima as the niche and as the shining star (since she is like the radiant star among the women of the world):

> Abû 'Abd Allâh[26] said, in the words of God, may He be exalted, God is the Light of the heavens and the earth. The similitude of His light is like a niche, Fâṭima, in whom is a lamp, al-Ḥasan. The lamp is in a glass, al-Ḥusayn. The glass is as a shining star, Fâṭima, a shining star among the women of the people of the world, kindled from a blessed tree, Ibrâhîm, an olive neither of the East nor of the West, nor Jewish, nor Christian, whose oil all but glows forth – knowledge all but overflowing from it – though no fire touched it. Light upon light; from it, Imâm after Imâm. God guides to His light those whom He will; God guides to the Imâms those whom He will. God imparts words of wisdom to humankind.[27]

Fâṭima's pre-existence does not therefore imply eternity; she herself is, like her husband, sons and the Imâms who will come after them, created from Muḥammad's own light. They are, in varied *aḥâdîṯ*,

---

[25] Cf. BÖWERING G., *The Mystical Vision of Existence in Classical Islam*, Walter de Gruyter, Berlin 1980: 149.

[26] The sixth Imâm.

[27] **KLY**., vol. I, bk. 4 (*Kitâb al-ḥuǧǧa*), bb. *al-a'imma nûr Allâh*, n. 5: 595.

created by God as "figures of light from my Light" (*ashbâḥ nûr min nûrî*),[28] or "from an origin of light" (*sinḫ*),[29] or from "one light" (*nûr wâḥid*).[30] The mystery of this creation is expressed by a *ḥadîṯ* carried by, among others, al-Kulaynî:

> On the authority of Abû ʿAbd Allâh,[31] who said: "God, may He be blessed and exalted, said: Muḥammad, I created you and ʿAlî a light, that is, a spirit without a body, before I created my heavens, my earth, my Throne and my sea. You did not fail to proclaim me unique[32] and to glorify me. Then I combined your two lights and made them one, which was praising, hallowing and exulting me. Then I divided it into two, and divided the two into two, and they became four: one Muḥammad, one ʿAlî, and two al-Ḥasan and al-Ḥusayn. Then God created Fâṭima from light, beginning as a spirit without a body. Then He anointed us with His right hand and made His light arrive in us."[33]

Al-Maǧlisî records a number of analogous *aḥâdîṯ*, some very close to al-Kulaynî's much earlier one and others somewhat more comprehensive.

2.2. The Conception and Birth of Fâṭima

Aside from the disputes over the date of her birth, the actual details of Ḫadîǧa's pregnancy and Fâṭima's parturition are, with some Sunnî exceptions (notably, al-Ṭabarî and al-Ṣaffûrî) transmitted almost wholly by Shîʿî transmitters. Three basic strands of *ḥadîṯ* predominate; firstly, that Muḥammad consumed heavenly fruit,

---

[28] **ṬSṬ²**., vol. I, n. 270: 172, **MǦL**., vol. XVI, bb. 11, n. 61: 361–362, vol. XXXVI, bb. 41, nn. 82, 83: 261, vol. XXXVII, bb. 50, n. 32: 62.

[29] **MǦL**., vol. XXVII, bb. 7, n. 67: 199–200, vol. XXXVI, bb. 40, n. 18: 216–217.

[30] **ṬFA³**., bb. 4, n. 24: 93, **ÂML**., vol. II: 141, **MǦL**., vol. XXXVI, bb. 40, n. 21: 222, bb. 41, n. 100: 280.

[31] The sixth Imâm.

[32] The Arabic verb *hallala – yuhallilu* literally means 'to proclaim the words: There is no god but God' (*lâ ilâha illâ llâh*).

[33] **KLY**., vol. I, bk. 4 (*Kitâb al-ḥuǧǧa*), bb. *mawlid al-nabî*, n. 3: 440.

secondly, that Fâṭima communicated with her mother whilst in the womb and thirdly, that Ḫadîğa was attended by a number of heavenly midwives.

2.2.1. The Heavenly Fruit

> On the authority of ʿÂʾisha, that the Prophet, God bless and save him, was often kissing the neck of Fâṭima, and I said: "Messenger of God, I saw you doing something you never do!" He said: "Did you not know, Ḥumayrâʾ[34] that God, powerful and lofty, when He caused me to journey to heaven, ordered Ğibrîl who brought me into Paradise and made me stop at a tree. I have never seen one with a better fragrance, or with better fruit. Ğibrîl drew near, rubbed it and made me eat, and God, powerful and lofty, created from it sperm in my loins. When I came back to the world I had intercourse with Ḫadîğa and she became pregnant with Fâṭima."[35]

According to this *ḥadîṯ*, transmitted by only a handful of Shîʿî and Sunnî scholars, Muḥammad, in the course of his 'night journey' (*isrâʾ*) was given heavenly fruit to eat by Ğibrîl, and upon his return had intercourse with Ḫadîğa, who conceived Fâṭima ostensibly as a result of the heavenly fruit which had become sperm in Muḥammad's loins. The Sunnî scholars who transmit this *ḥadîṯ* are not unconcerned by the problems it causes for dating Fâṭima's birth. Both al-ʿAsqalânî and al-Hayṯamî, as we have noted, reject the *ḥadîṯ*, calling it absolutely false and adding that its impossibility

---

[34] A pet name used by Muḥammad for ʿÂʾisha.

[35] **ḤNA.**, vol. III, bk. 31 (*Kitâb maʿrifat al-ṣaḥâba*), *Manâqib Fâṭima bt. rasûl Allâh*, n. 4801: 183–184 (with an annotation of rejection by al-Ḏahabî in the notes), **BĠD.**, vol. V, n. 2481: 87, **ḪWZ.**, Part 1, bb. *Faḍâʾil Fâṭima al-Zahrâʾ bt. rasûl Allâh*, n. 33: 104–105, n. 46: 110–111, **ĞWZ¹.**, vol. I, bb. *fî faḍl Fâṭima*: 412–413, **RḤB.**: 36, 44–45, **SQL².**, vol. V, n. 541: 160, **ṢFI.**, vol. II, bb. *manâqib Fâṭima al-Zahrâʾ*: 180; **SYṬ.**, vol. IV, *sûrat al-Isrâʾ*: 282, **HAY.**, vol. IX, bb. *manâqib Fâṭima bt. rasûl Allâh*: 202, **MTQ.**, vol. V: 97, **SHL.**, bb. *faḍl fî ḏikr manâqib ʿAlî b. Abî Ṭâlib*: 42. Among the Shîʿa, cf. **YQB.**, vol. II: 128, **MSD.**, vol. III, bb. 72, n. 1485: 22–23 and bb. 73, n. 1496: 31.

lies in the fact that Fâṭima was born before the 'night journey'. Curiously, their rejection touches only implicitly upon the actual subject of the fruit. Al-Shablanǧî notes that not all accept this *ḥadîṯ*, again because of the dating of the 'night journey'. Al-Ǧawzî and al-Ḫawârizmî also carry an alternative version of the *ḥadîṯ*, which place the eating of the heavenly fruit not during the 'night journey' but during a private visit to Muḥammad by Ǧibrîl: "Ǧibrîl the Faithful Spirit[36] descended to me with a cluster of fruit picked from Paradise, and I ate and had intercourse with Ḫadîǧa and Fâṭima was born."[37]

The Sunnî transmitter al-Ṭabarî begins with the episode of the heavenly fruit, which he appears to situate outside of the context of the 'night journey', and develops his theme to include all the other major strands:

> Al-Malâ transmitted in his biography that the Prophet said: "Ǧibrîl brought me an apple from Paradise, and I ate it and I had intercourse with Ḫadîǧa and she became pregnant with Fâṭima."[38]

The concept of the mystical fruit is intimately bound with the notion of Fâṭima's pre-existent light and with the concept that she is a 'maiden of Paradise in human form'. This threefold correlation is clearly seen in a lengthy *ḥadîṯ* relayed by *Shayḫ* al-Ṣadûq, which comprises in one text various elements that we have already seen or will see concerning Fâṭima's origins and status:

> The Messenger of God said: "The light of Fâṭima was created before the earth and the heaven were shaped." Some of the people queried: "Prophet of God, so she is not human?" He replied: "Fâṭima is a maiden of Paradise in human form." Someone said: "Prophet of God, how is she a maiden of Paradise in human form?" He said: "God, powerful and lofty, created her from His light before He created Adam or there were

---

[36] Cf. Q. 26: 193.

[37] **ḪWZ.**, Part 1, bb. *Faḍâ'il Fâṭima al-Zahrâ' bt. rasûl Allâh*, n. 46: 110–111, **ǦWZ[1].**, vol. I, bb. *fî faḍl Fâṭima*: 412. Cf. also **RḤB.**: 44.

[38] **RḤB.**: 44–45.

> spirits. When God, powerful and lofty, created Adam, she was displayed to Adam." Someone said: "Prophet of God, where was Fâṭima?" He said: "She was in a hollow under the leg of the Throne." They said: "Prophet of God, what was her food?" He said: "The glorification, acclamation and praise of God. When God, powerful and lofty, created Adam and drew me from his loins, it pleased God, powerful and lofty, to draw her from my loins. He placed her in an apple in Paradise, and Ğibra'îl came to me bearing it, and said to me: Peace be upon you, and the mercy of God and His blessings, Muḥammad. I said: And peace be upon you, and the mercy of God, my beloved Ğibra'îl. He said: Muḥammad, your Lord greets you with peace. I said: Peace comes from Him and peace returns to Him. He said: Muḥammad, this is an apple. God, powerful and lofty, gives it to you as a present from Paradise. I took it and pressed it to my breast. He said: Muḥammad, God, lofty His splendour, says: Eat it. I split it open, and saw a brilliant light, and was frightened by it. He said: Muḥammad, why are you not eating it entirely? Do not fear! That light is *al-Manṣûra* in heaven, and on earth she is Fâṭima. I said: My beloved Ğibra'îl, why is she called *al-Manṣûra* in heaven and Fâṭima on earth? He said: She is called Fâṭima on earth because she has separated her adherents (*shîʿa*) from the Fire, and she has separated her enemies from her love, and in heaven she is called *al-Manṣûra*, for this is the speech of God, powerful and lofty, «*and in that day believers will rejoice in Allah's help to victory. He helpeth to victory whom He will*»,[39] that is, the help of Fâṭima for her loved ones." [40]

This *ḥadîṯ* not only places the eating of the mystical fruit outside of the 'night journey', but it also encapsulates in one text numerous strands spread throughout the Shîʿî corpus. The concept of a pregnancy resulting from the eating of fruit is foreign to the Christian and Jewish texts, in which fruit, and specifically the fruit of the 'tree

[39] Cf. Q. 30: 4–5.

[40] **ṢDQ**[6]., n. 53: 396. Cf. also **MĞL.**, vol. XLIII, bb. 1, n. 3: 4; bb. 2, n. 17: 18.

of knowledge' recorded in the book of Genesis,[41] is principally to be understood in an analogical sense; the only parallel that might be drawn is that, just as Fâṭima's conception by means of a fruit from Paradise made her otherworldly, a 'maiden of Paradise in human form', so too the temptation proffered by Satan to Adam and Eve in the garden was that eating the obviously distinct fruit of the tree of knowledge would make them godlike, raising them above the status of ordinary humanity. However, such stories of pregnancy resulting from mystical fruit are not unknown in the realm of mythology. In Incan mythology, the virgin goddess Cavillaca (or Cavillace) ate fruit which was in fact the sperm of the moon-god Coniraya, and thereby became pregnant (without sexual intercourse). Phrygian (Anatolian) mythology tells that Nana, daughter of the god of the river Sangarius, fell pregnant with Attis after placing in her lap (or on her breast) the fruit of an almond tree, generated by the blood of the androgynous Agdistis, the Phrygian mother-goddess.[42] What differentiates the case of Fâṭima's birth from the myths is that it was primarily Muḥammad, the father of the child, rather than Ḫadîǧa, the mother, who ate the mystical fruit (although some of the *aḥâdîṯ* insist that both of them ate of the fruit offered by Ǧibrîl); nor is there any refutation of normative sexual intercourse taking place, a factor precisely missing from the texts of mythology.

2.2.2. Fâṭima Speaks From the Womb

The *ḥadîṯ* of Fâṭima talking to her mother from within the womb is carried by surprisingly few Shîʿî transmitters. Al-Ṭabarî takes up the theme in a continuation of the *ḥadîṯ* quoted above, with Ḫadîǧa speaking: "She said: I had a light pregnancy, and whenever I went out the one in my womb spoke with me."[43]

The version offered by al-Maǧlisî is more detailed but, like al-Ṭabarî, he binds together in one report all the major themes:

[41] Gen. 2: 16–17, 3: 2–7.

[42] PRICE S. and KEARNS E., (eds.), *The Oxford Dictionary of Classical Mythology*, Oxford University Press, Oxford 2004: 12, 75.

[43] **RḤB.**: 44–45. Cf. also **RṬB¹.**: 8, **ṢDQ¹.**, n. 1: 593, **FNR.**, vol. I: 143, **RWD¹.**, vol. II: 524, vol. III: 1051; **MǦL.**, vol. XLIII, bb. 1, n. 1: 2.

> On the authority of al-Mufaḍḍal b. ʿUmar,[44] who said: "I said to Abû ʿAbd Allâh Ǧaʿfar b. Muḥammad:[45] How was the birth of Fâṭima? He said: Yes, when the Messenger of God married Ḫadîǧa, may God be pleased with her, the women of Mecca disassociated from her, and did not visit her or greet her, and did not let a woman visit her. Ḫadîǧa felt lonely on account of this, and when she was pregnant with Fâṭima, Fâṭima began to talk with her from her womb, and to make her patient. Ḫadîǧa was hiding this from the Messenger of God and one day he visited and heard Ḫadîǧa talking to Fâṭima, and he said to her: Ḫadîǧa, who is talking to you? She said: The fetus which is in my womb is talking to me and keeping me company. He said to her: This Ǧibraʾîl announced to me, that she is a female, and that she is a pure and auspicious person, and that God, may He be blessed and exalted will bring about my progeny from her, and He will bring about from her progeny Imâms in the community, whom He will make leaders on His earth after the termination of His revelation."[46]

The declaration of a form of annunciation of a child to Muḥammad is almost secreted within this *ḥadîṯ*, obscured by the emphasis upon the fetus which speaks from the womb. The annunciation by Ǧibrîl, which follows some of the strands of the Biblical pattern, thus highlighting especially the noble character and future of the child to be born, is starkly different in one major element; it is an annunciation not made to the mother of the child, but to the child's father (and closer then, on one level, to the angel-

[44] According to Modarressi, al-Mufaḍḍal b. ʿUmar transmitted from the sixth and seventh Imâms, but was inclined towards Shîʿî extremist tendencies, especially the Nuṣayrî sect. A number of his works have been deemed spurious by the Shîʿî scholar al-Naǧâshî. Cf. **NĞA.**, n. 1112: 416, **ṬFA⁴.**, n. 23–5166: 343, **MOD.**: 333–334.

[45] The sixth Imâm.

[46] **RṬB¹.**: 8, **ṢDQ¹.**, n. 1: 593, **FNR.**, vol. I: 143, **RWD¹.**, vol. II: 524, **SHB.**, vol. III, bb. *manâqib Fâṭima al-Zahrâʾ*: 388, **MĞL.**, vol. XII, bb. 5: 80, vol. XVI, bb. 5: 80–81.

ic announcement to Joseph in St. Matthew's gospel).[47] The curiosity of this particular *ḥadîṯ* is that while Ḫadîğa attempts to hide from her husband that her unborn child is communicating to her, Muḥammad for his part seems not to have relayed to her the news of this annunciation at the moment it occurred; its occurrence arises almost secondarily in the course of a dialogue between husband and wife.

2.2.3. Midwives from Heaven

Al-Ṭabarî then introduces a third strand into his report:

> When she wanted to give birth, she sent to the women of the Quraysh to come to her and take charge over her in the way women take charge over those are giving birth. They would not do it and said: "We will not help you, since you became the husband of Muḥammad." While she was in this situation, four women came to her, arrayed in beauty and light which cannot be described. One of them said to her: "I am your mother Ḥawwâʾ." Another said: "I am Âsiya, daughter of Muzâḥim." Another said: "I am Kulṯûm, sister of Mûsâ." And another said: "I am Maryam, daughter of ʿImrân, mother of ʿÎsâ. We have come to take charge over you in your need in the way women take charge."[48]

Al-Mağlisî takes up the same theme, but with a change in the names of the visitors:

> Ḫadîğa, may God be pleased with her, continued in this way until her delivery came. She sent to the women of the Quraysh and the women of the Banû Hâshim to come and take charge over her in the way women take charge over women. They sent to her: "You have defied us and did not hear our words, and you married Muḥammad, the poor and penniless orphan of Abû Ṭâlib. We will not come and we will not take charge

[47] Cf. Matthew 1: 18–25.

[48] **RḤB**.: 45. Cf. also **RṬB¹**.: 8, **ṢDQ¹**., n. 1: 593, **FNR**., vol. I: 143, **RWD¹**., vol. II: 524, vol. III: 1051, **SHB**., vol. III, bb. *manâqib Fâṭima al-Zahrâʾ*: 388.

> over your situation whatsoever." Ḫadîǧa was greatly distressed by this. While this was happening, there came to her four women, tall, as though they were of the women of the Banû Hâshim, and she was afraid of them. One of them said to her: "Ḫadîǧa, do not be sad. We are messengers of your Lord to you, and we are your sisters. I am Sâra, and this is Âsiya, daughter of Muzâḥim, and she is your slave in Paradise; and this is Maryam, daughter of ʿImrân, and this is Ṣafrâʾ, daughter of Shuʿayb. God, may He be exalted, sent us to you to take charge over your need, in the way women help women."[49]

In another version of the same *ḥadîṯ*, al-Maǧlisî names the four heavenly midwives as Sâra, Âsiya, Maryam, and Kulṯûm, sister of Mûsâ.[50]

These *aḥâdîṯ* raise a number of noteworthy points and questions. While Âsiya is described, as are the others, as a 'sister' to Ḫadîǧa, her status in Paradise is more specifically defined as being that of Ḫadîǧa's slave (*raqîqa*), suggesting that she is not, together with Ḫadîǧa, Maryam and Fâṭima, one of the mistresses of the women of that place. Maryam's status too in the *ḥadîṯ* is quite obviously one of subservience, for she comes as a messenger and a helper. This deference to Fâṭima, even while she is still in the womb, will be repeated at the end of her life when, in Fâṭima's final illness, Maryam comes to nurse her.[51]

The band of heavenly visitors is noteworthy; all of them, although unnamed in the text of the Qurʾân (with the exception of Maryam), are intimately connected with personalities found there. Sâra is the wife of Ibrâhîm who, insists Q. 2: 135, was neither Jew nor Christian, but an upright man (*ḥanîf*). Kulṯûm is named as the sister of Mûsâ, while Ṣafrâʾ is the daughter of Shuʿayb, the messenger to the people of Midian named in Q. 7: 85, Q. 11: 84, Q. 26:

[49] **MǦL.**, vol. XVI, bb. 5: 80–81.

[50] **MǦL.**, vol. XLIII, bb. 1, n. 1: 2.

[51] "Then her ailment started and she grew ill, and God, powerful and lofty, sent to her Maryam bt. ʿImrân, to nurse her and keep her company in her illness…" Cf. **RṬB²**.: 199, **ṢDQ¹**., n. 2: 112, **MǦL.**, vol. XIV, bb. 16, n. 22: 205, vol. XXVIII, bb. 2: 39, vol. XLIII, bb. 7, n. 13: 172.

177 and Q. 29: 36, and who is sometimes identified with Jethro of the Old Testament.[52] We have already come across Âsiya the daughter of Muzâḥim and wife of Pharaoh (Q. 66: 11). While al-Ṭabarî clearly names Maryam both as the daughter of ʿImrân and as the mother of ʿÎsâ, in al-Mağlisî the reference to ʿÎsâ is omitted.

Fâṭima's speaking in the womb and, as we shall see, her making the testimony of faith at the moment of her birth, do not present clear-cut equivalents in other traditions or texts (unless one conjectures a parallel with John the Baptist leaping for joy in his mother's womb).[53] Of ʿÎsâ, the Qurʾân proclaims that «*He will speak unto mankind in his cradle…*» (Q. 3: 46), which he does, despite a protest from Maryam's relations that such a thing could not happen (Q. 19: 29–30). Quite possibly, although the text is not clear, it is also the newborn ʿÎsâ who speaks to console his mother in the pangs of childbirth; if it is him, then he speaks to her either from the womb or immediately after his birth (Q. 19: 23–24). However, Fâṭima's case supersedes all of these occurrences, since she speaks as an unborn fetus in the womb of Ḫadîğa.

2.2.4. The Parturition of Fâṭima

Finally, al-Ṭabarî notes a detail of the actual moment of birth: "And she said: Fâṭima was born, and when she fell to the earth she fell prostrating, extending her finger."[54] Al-Mağlisî offers a little more detail:

> One of them sat on her right and the other on her left, and the third in front of her and the fourth behind her, and Ḫadîğa gave birth to Fâṭima, pure, immaculate; and when she fell to the earth, a light radiated from her, so that it entered the houses of Mecca, and there did not remain a place in the east of the world or in its west in which that light did not shine. The woman who was in front of her received her and washed her with the water of *al-Kawṯar*, brought out two cloths, whiter than milk and more fragrant than musk and ambergris, and

[52] Jethro, father-in-law of Moses: cf. Exodus 3: 1, 4: 18.

[53] Lk. 1: 41, 44.

[54] **RḤB.**: 45.

> wrapped her with the one and veiled her with the other. Then she questioned her, and Fâṭima uttered the *shahâda*, 'that there is no god but God and that my father is the Messenger of God, master of the prophets, and that ʿAlî is the master of those entrusted, and that my first offspring is master of the tribes.[55] Then she greeted them and addressed each one of them by her name and they smiled at her. The maidens of Paradise rejoiced, and the people of Paradise spread the good news to one another about the birth of Fâṭima.[56]

Texts such as these, with all their symbolic gestures and rites, must be read for the religious significance they impart to the adherents of a particular faith. Fâṭima the newborn infant is washed in water from Paradise and clothed in its fragrant garments by its residents, who are patently subservient to her. In a sense, the *ḥadîṯ* serves to highlight certain theological points – that she is born pure and sinless, with a nature (*fiṭra*) that is wholly Islamic as intended by God for all humanity, and that ʿAlî's claims are justified by heaven – as well as a portent of the future, when Fâṭima will be clothed in the glory of Paradise, gathered at the pool of *al-Kawṯar* where her husband ʿAlî will stand as judge. The stylistic language serves a didactic purpose, and for this the *ḥadîṯ* must be accepted.

2.3. THE NAMING OF FÂṬIMA

> Abû ʿAbd Allâh[57] said: "Fâṭima has nine names with God, powerful and lofty: Fâṭima, *al-Ṣiddîqa* ('the Righteous'), *al-Mubâraka* ('the Blessed'), *al-Ṭâhira* ('the Pure'), *al-Zakiyya* ('the Chaste'), *al-Râḍiyya* ('the Satisfied'), *al-Murḍiyya* ('she who satis-

[55] The grammar here suggests that only one son is being spoken off. In another version of this *ḥadîṯ* carried by al-Mağlisî, 'sons' is in the plural form, suggesting more than the customary two (al-Ḥasan and al-Ḥusayn).

[56] **RṬB¹**.: 8, **ṢDQ¹**., n. 1: 598, **FNR**., vol. I: 143, **RWD¹**., vol. II: 524, **MĞL**., vol. XVI, bb. 5: 80–81, vol. XLIII, bb. 1, n. 1: 3.

[57] The sixth Imâm.

fies God'), *al-Muḥaddaṯa* ('the one to whom the angels spoke') and *al-Zahrâ'* ('the Radiant').[58]

Three things are at once striking about this catalogue of names. The first is that two crucial names are missing; those of *al-Batûl* and *al-ʿAḏrâ'* (both rendered as 'the Virgin'), a title ascribed to Fâṭima in numerous *aḥâdîṯ*. The second is that al-Maǧlisî carries another *ḥadîṯ*, from Abû Ǧaʿfar al-Qummî, in which no less than twenty-three names are attributed to Fâṭima, although these are not qualified as her names 'with God'. A third point of note is that throughout the texts of *aḥâdîṯ*, there are numerous other names attributed to Fâṭima, not all of which are found in al-Maǧlisî's ostensibly official lists. Al-Mûsawî in the first volume of his *al-Kawṯar fî aḥwâl Fâṭima bt. al-nabî al-aṭhar* provides a long list of Fâṭima's names, some of which he categorizes as her *kunâ* (sing. *kunya*) and others as her *alqâb* (pl. *laqab*).[59] He is transmitting primarily from four works: al-Maǧlisî in his *Biḥâr al-anwâr*, al-Baḥrânî in his *ʿAwâlim al-ʿulûm*, al-Muḥallâtî[60] in his *Rayâḥîn al-sharîʿa* and al-Fayrûzâbâdî in his *Faḍâ'il al-ḫamsa min al-ṣiḥâḥ al-sitta*. These lists comprise the best-known names, and many others hardly known – al-Fayrûzâbâdî claims that there are close to one-hundred-and-forty-five names among her *alqâb* alone. Each of the names tells something of her history, or of her status, or of the mystical *motifs* that surround her. Sometimes, confusingly, the same name is found listed as a *kunya* and as a *laqab*, while others lose much of their succinctness in translation.

Each of her names encapsulates a distinct theology and tradition, delineating specific virtues and a precise status for Fâṭima.

---

58 **MǦL**., vol. XLIII, bb. 2, n. 1: 10–11. Cf. also: **RṬB**[1].: 10, **ṢDQ**[1]., n. 18: 592, **ṢDQ**[4]., vol. II, n. 3: 414, **FNR**., vol. I: 148, **ṬBR**[1].: 148, **IRB**., vol. I: 463.

59 A nickname conveying a certain esteem, of which one might be the bearer of several. The *laqab* might signal some moral quality or distinct merit, might accentuate a physical peculiarity or simply underscore one's belonging to a particular sect or group.

60 *Shayḫ* Ḏabîḥ Allâh al-Muḥallâtî. Neither his name nor his works are recorded by Brockelmann.

Noteworthy too in all the *aḥâdîṯ* about the names of Fâṭima is the prominence given to physical purity and chastity:

> Her names are Mother of al-Ḥasan, Mother of al-Ḥusayn, Mother of al-Muḥassin and Mother of her father. Her names, as cited by Abû Ǧaʿfar al-Qummî, are: Fâṭima, *al-Batûl* ('the Virgin'), *al-Ḥaṣân* ('the Inviolable'), *al-Ḥurra* ('the Free'), *al-Sayyida* ('the Mistress'), *al-ʿAḏrâʾ* ('the Virgin'), *al-Zahrâʾ* ('the Radiant'), *al-Ḥawrâʾ* ('the Maiden of Paradise'),[61] *al-Mubâraka* ('the Blessed'), *al-Ṭâhira* ('the Pure'), *al-Zakiyya* ('the Chaste'), *al-Râḍiyya* ('the Satisfied'), *al-Marḍiyya* ('she who satisfies God'), *al-Muḥaddaṯa* ('the one to whom the angels spoke'), *Maryam al-Kubrâ* ('Maryam the Greater'), *al-Ṣiddîqa al-Kubrâ* ('the Greater righteous one'); and it is said in heaven, *al-Nûriyya al-samâwiyya* ('the heavenly luminary') and *al-Ḥâniyya* ('the Affectionate')."[62]

2.3.1. Fâṭima

Transmitting from the *Tafsîr Furât b. Ibrâhîm al-Kûfî* and from *Shayḫ* al-Ṣadûq's *Maʿânî al-aḫbâr*, al-Maǧlisî reports that 'Fâṭima' is the earthly name of Muḥammad's daughter, while in heaven, she is known as *al-Manṣûra* ('the one aided by God'):

> I said: "My beloved Ǧibraʾîl, why is she called *al-Manṣûra* in heaven and Fâṭima on earth?" He said: "She is called Fâṭima on earth because she has separated her adherents (*shîʿa*) from the Fire, and her enemies have been separated from her love, and in heaven she is called *al-Manṣûra*, for this is the word of God, powerful and lofty, «*and in that day believers will rejoice in Allah's help to victory. He helpeth to victory whom He will*»,[63] that is, the help of Fâṭima for her loved ones."[64]

---

[61] Literally, one possessing eyes that have a marked contrast between black and white.

[62] **MĞL.**, vol. XLIII, bb. 2, n. 15: 16–17.

[63] Cf. Q. 30: 4–5.

[64] **MĞL.**, vol. XLIII, bb. 1, n. 3: 4, bb. 2, n. 17: 18. Cf. **ṢDQ**^{6}., n. 53: 396.

The name 'Fâṭima' is, accordingly, a wordplay on the Arabic root *f-ṭ-m*, with its primary meaning 'to wean'.[65] The concept of Muḥammad's daughter as one who has been weaned by God and as one by whom God weans others, is expressed by numerous *aḥâdîṯ*, and although most of these have diverse wording, the word-play constituting the central element remains the same. Al-Mağlisî records this *ḥadîṯ* from *Shayḫ* al-Ṣadûq's *ʿUyûn aḫbâr al-Riḍâ*: "The Messenger of God said: I called my daughter Fâṭima because God, powerful and lofty, has separated her and separated those who love her from the Fire."[66]

Transmitting from *Shayḫ* al-Ṣadûq's *ʿIlal al-sharâʾiʿ*, al-Mağlisî notes that the concept of being weaned means 'to be separated'.[67] In this sense, the texts delineate a four-fold separation for Fâṭima by God; she is separated from the Fire,[68] from evil[69] (suggesting that her purification, at the very least, took place in the womb), from polytheism (*shirk*)[70] and from menstruation.[71] In addition, the

---

[65] The import is to 'cut' or to 'sever', weaning someone away from someone or something in the sense of disengagement. Cf. LANE E W., *An Arabic-English Lexicon*, Beyrouth 1968, vol. VI: 2418.

[66] **MĞL.**, vol. XLIII, bb. 2, n. 4: 12. Cf. **ṢDQ[5].**, vol. II, bb. 31, n. 174: 46. Among the Sunnî, cf. **ḤNA.**, vol. III, bk. 31 (*Kitâb maʿrifat al-ṣaḥâba*), *Manâqib Fâṭima bt. rasûl Allâh*, nn. 4788, 4789: 178–179, n. 4792: 180, **ḪWZ.**, Part 1, bb. *Faḍâʾil Fâṭima al-Zahrâʾ bt. rasûl Allâh*, n. 2: 90, **ĞWZ[1].**, vol. I, bb. *fî ḏikr tazwîğ Fâṭima bi-ʿAlî*,: 421, **RḤB.**: 26, **ṢFI.**, vol. II, bb. *manâqib Fâṭima al-Zahrâʾ*: 179, **MTQ.**, vol. V: 97, **IṢM.**, vol. 1, bb. 5: 425, **SHL.**, bb. *faḍl fî ḏikr manâqib ʿAlî b. Abî Ṭâlib*,: 43.

[67] **MĞL.**, vol. XLIII, bb. 2, n. 7: 13. Cf. **ṢDQ[8].**, vol. I, bb. 142, n. 2: 178.

[68] **RṬB[1].**: 15, **ṢDQ[5].**, vol. II, bb. 31, n. 336: 72, **ṢDQ[8].**, vol. I, bb. 142, nn. 5–6: 179, **ṬFA[2].**, bb. 22, n. 5–1179: 570, **SHB.**, vol. III, bb. *manâqib Fâṭima al-Zahrâʾ*: 377, **IRB.**, vol. I: 463, **MĞL.**, vol. XLIII, bb. 2, nn. 3–4: 12, n. 10: 14, nn. 12, 14: 15, nn. 17–18: 18–19.

[69] **ṢDQ[1].**, n. 18: 592, **ṢDQ[4].**, vol. II, n. 3: 414, **ṢDQ[8].**, vol. I, bb. 142, n. 3: 178, **FNR.**, vol. I: 148, **SHB.**, vol. III, bb. *manâqib Fâṭima al-Zahrâʾ*: 377–378, **IRB.**, vol. I: 463, **MĞL.**, vol. XLIII, bb. 2, n. 1: 10, n. 14: 15–16.

[70] **RṬB[1].**: 10.

texts use the root *f-ṭ-m* in the sense of 'to wean' as one would wean a child, in that God has 'reared' Fâṭima with knowledge:

> I weaned you with knowledge, that is, I suckled you with knowledge until you had no more need and were weaned; and I weaned you from ignorance by means of knowledge; and I brought about your weaning with milk combined with knowledge…[72]

The texts also demarcate four recipients of this separation from the Fire: her followers (*shîʿa*),[73] those who love her,[74] her offspring[75] and those who support her and her offspring.[76]

The separation of Fâṭima's offspring from the Fire is intimately connected to a *ḥadîṯ* that is more profuse both in Sunnî and Shîʿî sources; that Fâṭima has guarded her chastity, and because of this, God has saved her offspring from the Fire. Although the question of Fâṭima's chastity will be examined in a later chapter, this *ḥadîṯ*

---

[71] **KLY**., vol. I, bk. 4 (*Kitâb al-ḥuǧǧa*), bb. *mawlid al-Zahrâʾ Fâṭima*, n. 6: 460, **ṢDQ⁸**., vol. I, bb. 142, n. 4: 179, **SHB**., vol. III, bb. *manâqib Fâṭima al-Zahrâʾ*: 378, **IRB**., vol. I: 463, **MǦL**., vol. XLIII, bb. 2, n. 9: 14–15, n. 14: 15–16.

[72] **MǦL**., vol. XLIII, bb. 2, n. 9: 13.

[73] **RṬB¹**.: 53, **ṢDQ⁵**., vol. II, bb. 31, n. 336: 72, **ṢDQ⁶**., n. 53: 396, **ṢDQ⁸**., vol. I, bb. 142, n. 5: 179, **FUR**., n. 435: 321, **SHB**., vol. III, bb. *fî manzilati-hâ*: 377–378, **IRB**., vol. I: 463, **MǦL**., vol. XLIII, bb. 1, n. 3: 4, bb. 2, n. 3: 12, n. 10: 14, n. 14: 15, n. 17: 18, vol. LXV, bb. 15, n. 135: 76.

[74] **RṬB²**.: 123, 131, 184, **ṢDQ⁵**., vol. II, bb. 31, n. 174: 46, **ṢDQ⁶**., n. 14: 64, **ṢDQ⁸**., vol. I, bb. 142, n. 1: 178, **ṬFA¹**., vol. III: 98, **ṬFA²**., bb. 11, n. 18–571: 294, **ṬBR¹**.: 148, **SHB**., vol. III, bb. *manâqib Fâṭima al-Zahrâʾ*: 377, **ṬSṬ³**.: 182, **IRB**., vol. I: 463, **ḤLL²**.: 352, **DAY**., vol. II: 232, **MǦL**., vol. XLIII, bb. 2, n. 4: 12, n. 8: 13, n. 12: 15, n. 14: 16, vol. LXV, bb. 18, n. 66: 133, vol. XCV, bb. 7: 139.

[75] **RṬB¹**.: 53, **ṬFA²**., bb. 22, n. 5–1179: 570, **MǦL**., vol. XLIII, bb. 2, n. 18: 18–19.

[76] **ṢDQ⁸**., vol. I, bb. 142, n. 6: 179, **IRB**., vol. I: 463, **MǦL**., vol. VIII, bb. 21, n. 57: 50, vol. XLIII, bb. 2, n. 11: 14.

merits a place here: "Fâṭima has guarded her chastity and God has forbidden her offspring to the Fire."[77]

Thus, while her name indicates the fact of the weaning or separation, it is her chaste lifestyle that becomes the *raison d'être* for the salvation of her progeny. A number of texts identify these offspring as al-Ḥasan, al-Ḥusayn, Zaynab and Umm Kulṯûm.[78] There are two more recipients of the act of weaning or separation and connected to the name of Fâṭima; her offspring have been separated from greed[79] and her enemies have been separated from her love with a separation that will be most clearly seen in Fâṭima's actions on the Day of Judgment.[80]

The name 'Fâṭima' is written on the gate of Paradise and on the leg of the Throne and is seen there by Adam[81] as well as by

---

[77] **ṢDQ⁵**., vol. II, bb. 31, n. 264: 63, bb. 58, n. 1: 232, **ṢDQ⁶**., nn. 1–6: 105–106, **RWD¹**., vol. I: 281, **SHB**., vol. III, bb. *manâqib Fâṭima al-Zahrâʾ*: 373, **IRB**., vol. I: 468, vol. II: 144, 310, 346, **ḤLL²**.: 351, **MĞL**., vol. XLIII, bb. 3, n. 6: 20, bb. 9, n. 2: 230, nn. 3–6: 231, n. 7: 232, vol. XLVI, bb. 11, n. 51: 185, vol. XLVIII: 315, vol. XLIX, bb. 16, nn. 2–3: 217, vol. LXXV, bb. 16, n. 52: 78, vol. XCIII, bb. 27, nn. 14–18: 221–223. Among the Sunnî, cf. **ḤNA**., vol. III, bk. 31 (*Kitâb maʿrifat al-ṣaḥâba*), *Manâqib Fâṭima bt. rasûl Allâh*, n. 4789: 179, **IṢH**., vol. IV, bb. 268, n. 5277: 209, **ḤWZ**., Part 1, bb. *Faḍâʾil Fâṭima al-Zahrâʾ bt. rasûl Allâh*, n. 9: 94, **RḤB**.: 48, **HAY**., vol. IX, bb. *manâqib Fâṭima bt. rasûl Allâh*: 202, **MTQ**., vol. V: 97.

[78] **IRB**., vol. I: 468 (inexplicably, this text mentions al-Ḥasan, al-Ḥusayn and Umm Kulṯûm, but omits Zaynab), **MĞL**., vol. XLIII, bb. 9, n. 4: 231, vol. XLIX, bb. 16, n. 3: 218, vol. XCIII, bb. 27, n. 16: 223.

[79] **ṢDQ⁸**., vol. I, bb. 142, n. 2: 178, **MĞL**., vol. XLIII, bb. 2, n. 7: 13.

[80] **ṢDQ⁶**., n. 53: 396, **FUR**., n. 435: 321, **MĞL**., vol. XLIII, bb. 1, n. 3: 4, bb. 2, n. 17: 18.

[81] **ĞQM**.: 128, **ṢDQ⁵**., vol. I, bb. 28, 67: 62, **ṢDQ⁶**., n. 1: 124, **RWD³**., bb. 3, n. 11: 45, **ABḎ**.: 49, **MĞL**., vol. XI, bb. 3: 157, n. 9: 164, vol. XVI, bb. 11, n. 62: 362, vol. XXVI, bb. 7, n. 6: 324, vol. XXVII, bb. 10, n. 11: 6. It must be admitted that the Shîʿa transmit a number of *aḥâdîṯ* in which Adam sees written only the names of Muḥammad and ʿAlî. Cf. **RWD³**., bb. 4, n. 26: 51, **ḤLL²**., bb. 42: 190, b. 74: 234, **MĞL**., vol. XI, bb. 3, n. 34: 181, vol. XXVI, bb. 7, n. 6: 324, vol. XXVII, bb. 10, n. 15: 7, **NṬR**., vol. V, bb. 35, n. 14–5770: 237.

Muḥammad during his 'night journey'.[82] In a further, well-attested transmission, it is reported that 'Fâṭima' is among the words which Adam received from his Lord, based upon Q. 2: 37 – «*Then Adam received from His Lord words (of revelation) and He relented toward him*» – and by which he repents.[83] It is also noted that 'Fâṭima' is among the words with which Ibrâhîm was tested by his Lord, based upon Q. 2: 124 – «*And (remember) when his Lord tried Abraham with (His) command…*».[84] Finally, a handful of *aḥâdîṯ* posit that the name of Fâṭima is written in the *Tawrât*, in a narrative that is worth examining. Al-Mağlisî is transmitting from *Shayḫ* al-Ṣadûq:

---

[82] **ĞQM.**: **ṬFA**^{2}., bb. 12, n. 77–737: 355, 83, **FNR.**, vol. I: 83, **ṬSṬ**^{2}., vol. I, n. 65: 64, **IRB.**, vol. I: 94, 526, **ḤLL**^{2}.: 459, **DAY.**, vol. II: 234, **MĞL.**, vol. VIII, bb. 23, n. 167: 191, vol. XXVII, bb. 10, nn. 6, 8: 3–4, n. 30: 228, vol. XXXVI, bb. 41, n. 191: 331, vol. XXXVII, bb. 50, n. 41: 76, n. 59: 95, n. 64: 97, vol. XLIII, bb. 12: 303.

[83] **ṢDQ**^{1}., n. 2: 75, n. 7: 250, **ṢDQ**^{2}., vol. II, bb. 33, n. 57: 358, **ṢDQ**^{4}., vol. I, n. 8: 270, n. 84: 304, **ṢDQ**^{6}., nn. 1–2: 125, **AYY.**, vol. I, bb. 2, n. 27: 41, **FNR.**, vol. I: 157, **RWD**^{3}., bb. 4, n. 26: 51, bb. 5, n. 31: 54, **SHB.**, vol. I, bb. *fî al-âyât al-munzala*: 345, **BṬQ.**, n. 745: 379, **ṬSṬ**^{2}., vol. I, n. 166: 112, **IRB.**, vol. I: 465, **ḤLL**^{1}.: 179; **ḤLL**^{2}.: 14, **DAY.**, vol. II: 210, 421, **ABḎ.**: 76, 82, **ḤRR**^{1}., vol. VII, bb. 37, nn. 8843–8845: 98–99, n. 8847: 100, **MĞL.**, vol. XI, bb. 3, n. 20: 175, n. 22–24: 176–177, n. 34: 181, vol. XII, bb. 3, n. 12: 66, bb. 9, n. 23: 260, vol. XVIII, bb. 9, n. 1: 83, vol. XXIV, bb. 50, n. 21: 183, vol. XXVI, bb. 7, nn. 3–6, 9: 323–324, n. 15: 333, vol. XXVII, bb. 11, n. 1: 13, vol. XXXII, bb. 34, n. 3: 56, vol. XXXVII, bb. 50, n. 36: 65, vol. XLIV, bb. 30, n. 44: 245, vol. LX, bb. 2, n. 36: 80, vol. XCI, bb. 28, n. 15: 20; **NṬR.**, vol. V, bb. 35, nn. 8–5764, 9–5765: 232, nn. 14–5770, 15–5771: 237–238.

[84] In Q. 2: 37, Pickthall renders the Arabic *kalimât* as 'words'; in Q. 2: 124 he translates the same word as 'commands'. The thrust of these *aḥâdîṯ* is that Adam and Ibrâhîm received the same words from God. Cf. **ṢDQ**^{2}., vol. II, bb. 33, n. 57: 358, **ṢDQ**^{4}., vol. I, n. 84: 304, **ṢDQ**^{6}., n. 1: 126, **SHB.**, vol. I, bb. *fî al-âyât al-munzala*: 345, **DAY.**, vol. II: 421, **ABḎ.**: 82, **ḤRR**^{1}., vol. VII, bb. 37, n. 8844: 99, **MĞL.**, vol. XI, bb. 3, n. 24: 177, vol. XII, bb. 3, n. 12: 66, vol. XXIV, bb. 50, n. 8: 177, vol. XXVI, bb. 7, n. 3: 323.

> A person of the Jews came to the Messenger of God…and the Jew said: Inform me of five things written in the *Tawrât*…the Prophet replied: The first thing written in the *Tawrât* is 'Muḥammad is the Messenger of God'…then the Messenger of God recited this verse: «*whom they will find described in the Torah and the Gospel (which are) with them…and bringeth good tidings of a messenger who cometh after me, whose name is the Praised One*». In the second line is the name of my entrusted, ʿAlî b. Abî Ṭâlib, in the third and fourth my grandsons al-Ḥasan and al-Ḥusayn, and in the fifth line their mother, Fâṭima, mistress of the women of the worlds. In the *Tawrât*, the name of my entrusted is Iliyyâ,[85] the names of my grandsons are Shabbar and Shabbîr,[86] and they are the lights of Fâṭima. The Jew said: You have spoken the truth, Muḥammad."[87]

Two things are conspicuous in this narrative. The first is that the *ḥadîṯ* mixes two different Qur'ânic verses, the first part of Q. 7: 157 and most of Q. 61: 6, so that someone unfamiliar with the Qur'ân would think them to be one verse.[88] The second is that, of the 'holy five', only Fâṭima does not receive another name; instead, she is qualified by her epithet 'mistress of the women of the worlds'.

2.3.2. al-Zahrâ'

In the case of Fâṭima, the appellation *al-Zahrâ'* ('the Radiant') is directly connected with the themes of light that are suffused throughout her story. Some descriptions of her conception aug-

---

[85] In some texts written Îliyyâ, and in Old Testament usage used for the prophet Elijah.

[86] In Islamic tradition, the names of the sons of Hârûn.

[87] **ṢDQ¹**.: 191, **MFD²**.: 37, **MĞL**., vol. IX, bb. 2: 298, vol. XIII, bb. 11, n. 11: 331, vol. XXXVII, bb. 50, n. 4: 36.

[88] The first part of Q. 7: 157 reads: «*Those who follow the messenger, the Prophet who can neither read nor write, whom they will find described in the Torah and the Gospel (which are) with them…*». Q. 61: 6 reads: «*And when Jesus son of Mary said: O Children of Israel! Lo! I am the messenger of Allah unto you, confirming that which was (revealed) before me in the Torah, and bringing good tidings of a messenger who cometh after me, whose name is the Praised One…*».

ment the accounts, with depictions of light emanating from God to Muḥammad and then to Fâṭima and ʿAlî. Al-Mağlisî in *Biḥâr al-anwâr* portrays the light that flowed daily from Fâṭima as she stood in prayer; white at dawn, yellow at noon, red in the evening. This light passed from her to her sons, and subsequently to the other Imâms.

In a lengthy *ḥadîṯ*, which he transmits from *Shayḫ* al-Ṣadûq's *ʿIlal al-sharâʾiʿ*, al-Mağlisî offers an explanation for this appellation, so routinely attached to the name of Fâṭima:

> I said to Abû ʿAbd Allâh:[89] "Son of the Messenger of God, why was *al-Zahrâʾ* named 'radiant' (*ẓahrâʾ*)?" He said: "Because three times in the day she shone with light on the Commander of the Faithful. The light of her face was shining in the morning prayer and on the people in their beds; the whiteness of that light entered their rooms in Medina and whitened their walls. They were astonished at this, and they came to the Prophet and asked him about what they had seen. He sent them to the house of Fâṭima. They came to her house, and saw her sitting in her prayer niche, praying. They light of her face spread from her prayer niche, and they understood that what they had seen was from the light of Fâṭima. When the day reached its zenith and she lined up for the prayer, the light of her face shone with a yellow colour, and the yellowness entered the rooms of the people and yellowed their walls and their complexion. They came to the Prophet and asked him about what they had seen, and he sent them to the house of Fâṭima. They saw her standing in her prayer niche, and the light of her face – the blessings of God be upon her, and upon her father and husband and children – was shining with yellow. They understood that what they had seen was from the light of her face. At the end of the day, when the sun had set, the face of Fâṭima took on a reddish colour, and her face radiated with the redness, joyfully and thankfully to God, powerful and lofty. The redness of her face entered the rooms of the people and reddened their walls. They were astonished at this, and they

[89] The sixth Imâm.

> came to the Prophet and asked him about what they had seen, and he sent them to the house of Fâṭima. They saw her sitting, praising God and glorifying Him, and they understood that what they had seen was from the light of Fâṭima's face. This light did not cease on her face until al-Ḥusayn was born."[90]

While only *Shayḫ* al-Ṣadûq and al-Mağlisî record such detail about the various colours of the light, almost all the *aḥâdîṯ* detailing the name *al-Zahrâʾ* follow the essential *leitmotif* of light, already an important part of the narratives of Fâṭima's pre-existent state. From al-Ṣadûq's *ʿIlal al-sharâʾiʿ* and from *Miṣbâḥ al-anwâr*, al-Mağlisî transmits the following:

> On the authority of Abû ʿAbd Allâh,[91] who said: I said: Why was Fâṭima *al-Zahrâʾ* named 'radiant' (*zahrâʾ*)? He said: "Because God, powerful and lofty, created her from the light of His majesty, and when she radiated she illuminated the heavens and the earth with her light. The vision of the angels was overwhelmed, and the angels fell down before God, prostrating and saying: Our God and our Master, what is this light? God revealed to them: This is light from my light. I have lodged it in my heavens and created it from my majesty. I brought it forth from the loins of the Prophet of my prophets, and I have preferred him over all the prophets. I have brought forth from that light Imâms to accomplish my command and guide to my truth, and I have made them my Caliphs in my earth after the termination of my revelation."[92]

Fâṭima is designated with the title *al-Zahrâʾ* because, creating her from the light of His majesty,[93] God placed her before the

---

[90] **ṢDQ⁸**., vol. I, bb. 143, n. 2: 180, **MĞL**., vol. XLIII, bb. 2, n. 2: 11–12.

[91] The sixth Imâm.

[92] **ṢDQ⁸**., vol. I, bb. 143, nn. 1–3: 179, **IRB**., vol. I: 464, **MĞL**., vol. XLIII, bb. 2, n. 5: 12.

[93] **RṬB¹**.: 54, **ṢDQ⁶**., n. 16: 64, **SHB**., vol. III, bb. *manâqib Fâṭima al-Zahrâʾ*: 378.

Throne[94] so that she shone over the whole world,[95] making the heavens and the earth manifest by her light.[96] On the day of her birth, a light shone in the heavens, such as the angels had never witnessed prior to that day.[97] From her light, God brought forth lamps which He suspended like pendants on the Throne; these shone upon the heavens and the earth, which then radiated with the light of Fâṭima.[98] When she stood in her prayer niche, the light of Fâṭima's face shone on the people of the heavens in the same way that the light of the stars shine on the people of the earth. This same light shone on ʿAlî at the beginning of the day like the fore-noon sun, and at the end of the day like the luminous moon and the glittering star.[99] In heaven, Fâṭima is possessor of a dome made of ruby; its height in the air stretches for the distance of a year, and it is suspended by the power of the Omnipotent. It has neither strap above it to suspend it nor prop below it to hold it up. It contains 100 000 doors, each attended by 1000 angels. The people of Paradise see Fâṭima as clearly as each sees the glittering star, gleaming in the horizon of heaven, and they proclaim that she is *al-Zahrâʾ*, the radiant one.

2.3.3. Other Titles Given to Fâṭima

The name Fâṭima and the appellation *al-Zahrâʾ* are the chief names given to the daughter of Muḥammad, and receive much attention in the books of *aḥâdîṯ*; her other titles, at least twenty-seven in al-Mağlisî's 'official' litanies,[100] although used consistently throughout the *aḥâdîṯ*, are accorded less elucidation. Many of them focus upon

---

[94] **ĞQM**.: 128, **ABḎ**.: 591, **MĞL**., vol. XXXVI, bb. 37, n. 24: 73.

[95] **ĞQM**.: 128, **DAY**., vol. II: 403, **ABḎ**.: 143, 591, **MĞL**., vol. XXXVII, bb. 50, n. 51: 82, vol. XL, bb. 91, n. 81: 43.

[96] **MĞL**., vol. XXV, bb. 1, n. 30: 16.

[97] **MĞL**., vol. XVI, bb. 5: 80.

[98] **DAY**., vol. II: 143, **ABḎ**.: 143, **MĞL**., vol. XLIII, bb. 2, n. 16: 17, vol. XXXVII, bb. 50, n. 51: 82.

[99] **RṬB¹**.: 54, **ṢDQ⁶**., n. 15: 64, **ṢDQ⁸**., vol. I, bb. 143, n. 3: 181, **SHB**., vol. III, bb. *manâqib Fâṭima al-Zahrâʾ*: 378, **MĞL**., vol. XLIII, bb. 2, n. 6: 11–12, n. 14: 15–16.

[100] **MĞL**., vol. XLIII, bb. 2, n. 1: 10–11, n. 15: 16–17.

the issue of physical and spiritual purity, with a brief clarification offered for *al-Ṭâhira* ('the Pure'); Fâṭima is called *al-Ṭâhira* on account of her purity from every uncleanness (*danas*) and obscenity (*rafaṯ*).[101] The text then goes on to insist that she neither menstruated nor shed blood in childbirth, a phenomenon that will be examined later in terms of her virginity. To the title *al-Ṭâhira*, which Shîʿî scholars connect with the so-called *Taṭhîr* verse (Q. 33: 33), a verse that they hold to be addressed exclusively to Muḥammad, ʿAlî, Fâṭima, al-Ḥasan and al-Ḥusayn, some authors add the derivatives *al-Ṭuhra* ('the Clean') and *al-Muṭahhara* ('the Immaculate'), as well as the name *al-Naqiyya* ('the Unstained').[102] Her purity is further stressed by the use of the titles *al-Zakiyya* ('the Chaste'),[103] *al-Ḥaṣân* ('the Inviolable')[104] and *al-ʿAḏrâʾ* ('the Virgin'),[105] a designation expressed more frequently by the use of the term *al-Batûl*, which will be examined in more detail later in this work.

It is not Fâṭima alone who is given the epithet *al-Muḥaddaṯa*; a reference to one with whom the angels converse, it is also used of Maryam (cf. for example Q. 3: 42–43, 45–46), who converses not

---

[101] **MĞL.**, vol. XLIII, bb. 2, n. 20: 19.

[102] **QQM.**, n. 2: 309, **ṢDQ³.**, vol. II, n. 3210: 602, **ṢDQ⁵.**, vol. II, bb. 68, n. 1: 267.

[103] For examples of this title, cf. **RṬB¹.**: 10, **RṬB².**: 12, **QQM.**, n. 17: 230, n. 2: 309, **ṢDQ¹.**, n. 18: 592, **ṢDQ³.**, vol. II: 572, n. 3210: 602, **ṢDQ⁴.**, vol. II, n. 3: 414, **ṢDQ⁵.**, vol. II, bb. 68, n. I: 267, **ṢDQ⁶.**, n. 9: 58, **ṢDQ⁸.**, vol. I, bb. 142, n. 3: 178, **ĞQM.**: 82, **ṬFA¹.**, vol. VI, bb. 3, n. 12: 10, **FNR.**, vol. I: 148, **ṬBR¹.**: 148, **RWD¹.**, vol. II: 542; **SHB.**, vol. III, bb. *manâqib Fâṭima al-Zahrâʾ*: 406, **IRB.**, vol. I: 30, 463, **ḤLL².**, bb. 121: 318, **ÂML.**, vol. I: 172, vol. III: 77, **KFM².**: 303, **MĞL.**, vol. XXXIII, bb. 14, n. 392: 47, bb. 20, n. 547: 282, vol. XXXV, bb. 2, n. 1: 45, vol. XLIII, bb. 2, n. 1: 10, n. 15: 16, vol. XLV, bb. 44: 276, vol. XCVI, bb. 30, n. 1: 74, vol. XCVII, bb. 5, n. 12: 195, n. 15: 197, n. 20: 199, vol. XCVIII, bb. 18: 179, vol. XCIX, bb. 5, n. 1: 44, bb. 8: 198.

[104] **SHB.**, vol. III, bb. *manâqib Fâṭima al-Zahrâʾ*: 406, **MĞL.**, vol. XLIII, bb. 2, n. 15: 16.

[105] **SHB.**, vol. III, bb. *manâqib Fâṭima al-Zahrâʾ*: 406, **KFM².**: 335, **MĞL.**, vol. XLIII, bb. 2, n. 15: 16, vol. XLVI, bb. 5: 259, vol. XCVII, bb. 129: 383.

merely with angels, but also with Ğibrîl himself (Q. 19: 18–22), of Sâra, wife of Ibrâhîm (Q. 11: 71–73) and by some scholars of the mother of Mûsâ (Q. 28: 7). Fâṭima is declared to be *muḥaddaṯa*;[106] she is given this title, writes al-Mağlisî, because the angels descended from heaven and proclaimed to her, as they had proclaimed to Maryam daughter of ʿImrân: "And when the angels said: Fâṭima! «*Lo! Allah hath chosen thee and made thee pure, and hath preferred thee above (all) the women of creation*»."[107] This is a remarkable *ḥadîṯ*, which takes a direct quotation from Q. 3: 42 but removes the name Maryam and replaces it with Fâṭima; an unavoidable necessity if the transmitters are to maintain their argument that at the very least, Fâṭima is equal to Maryam. Other texts are then used to demonstrate that Fâṭima is in fact superior. Part of the Shîʿî reasoning would be that Fâṭima would have to have been a *muḥaddaṯa*, for if not, Maryam, Sâra and the wife of Mûsâ would rank above her. In fact, the texts surrounding Fâṭima's birth, with the appearance of the heavenly women whose number includes Sâra and Maryam in a position subservient to Fâṭima, serve to illustrate her superiority.

The title *al-Marḍiyya* ('she who satisfies God') is also linked by the transmitters to a Qur'ânic verse: «*But ah! thou soul at peace! Return unto thy Lord, content in His good pleasure!*» (Q. 89: 27–28). The *aḥâdîṯ* posit that this verse, like Q. 33: 33, was addressed to Muḥammad and the *ahl al-bayt*, making Fâṭima both *al-Marḍiyya* and *al-Râḍiyya* ('she who is satisfied').[108]

In answer to a question about who washed Fâṭima after her death, the transmitters record a *ḥadîṯ* which gives ʿAlî as the answer,

---

[106] **QḤL.**: 821, **MFD²**.: 329, **SHB.**, vol. III, bb. *manâqib Fâṭima al-Zahrâʾ*: 384, **IRB.**, vol. I: 468, **MĞL.**, vol. XXX, bb. 19: 132, vol. XLIII, bb. 3, n. 48: 55, n. 66: 79.

[107] **RṬB¹**.: 10, 56, **ṢDQ⁸**., vol. I, bb. 146, nn. 1–2: 182, **MĞL.**, vol. XIV, bb. 16, n. 23: 206, vol. XLIII, bb. 3, n. 65: 78.

[108] Cf. **KLY.**, vol. III, bk. 2 (*Kitâb al-ğanâʾiz*), bb. *al-muʾmin lâ yakrah ʿalâ qabḍ rûḥi-hi*, n. 2: 128, **MĞL.**, vol. VI, bb. 6, n. 31: 162, bb. 7, n. 49: 196, vol. XXIV, bb. 34, n. 7: 94, vol. LVIII, bb. 42, n. 24: 48.

with the justification that she was *al-Ṣiddîqa* ('the Righteous') and could only be washed by one who was also righteous (*ṣiddîq*).[109]

2.4. THE MIRACULOUS FOOD

An incident taken up in the Qur'ânic text in a narrative concerning the childhood of Maryam, reads:

> «*And her Lord accepted her with full acceptance and vouchsafed to her a goodly growth; and made Zechariah her guardian. Whenever Zechariah went into the sanctuary where she was, he found that she had food. He said: O Mary! Whence cometh unto thee this (food)? She answered: It is from Allah. Allah giveth without stint to whom He will*» (Q. 3: 37).

Unsurprisingly, Fâṭima too is fed by angels; this forms part of a particular genre by which almost everything posited about Maryam – from her conversation with angels to her virginity – is posited equally about Fâṭima, so as not to diminish her superiority. In Fâṭima's case, two elements are of note. The first concerns her 'food' during the period of her pre-existence, reported by al-Mağlisî transmitting from *Shayḫ* al-Ṣadûq:

> Someone said: "Prophet of God, where was Fâṭima?" He said: "She was in a hollow under the leg of the Throne." They said:

[109] **KLY.**, vol. I, bk. 4 (*Kitâb al-ḥuğğa*), bb. *mawlid al-Zahrâ' Fâṭima*, n. 2: 458, n. 4: 499, vol. III, bk. 2 (*Kitâb al-ğanâ'iz*), bb. *al-rağul yağsil al-mar'a*, n. 13: 159, **ṢDQ[3]**., vol. I, n. 399: 142, **ṢDQ[8]**., vol. I, bb. 148, n. 1: 184, **ṬFA[1]**., vol. I, bb. 23, n. 67: 440, **SHB.**, vol. III, bb. *manâqib Fâṭima al-Zahrâ'*: 413, **ḤRR[1]**., vol. II, bb. 24, n. 2825: 530, n. 2834: 533, **MĞL.**, vol. XIV, bb. 16, n. 3: 197, vol. XXVII, bb. 2, n. 7: 291, vol. XLIII, bb. 7, n. 16: 184, n. 32: 206, vol. LXXVIII, bb. 8, n. 16: 299, **NṬR.**, vol. II, bb. 21, n. 6–1758: 185. Some of the transmitters link Fâṭima in this to Maryam, positing that just as Maryam, when she died, could only have been washed by ʿÎsâ, so Fâṭima could only have been washed by ʿAlî. Cf. **KLY.**, vol. I, bk. 4 (*Kitâb al-ḥuğğa*), bb. *mawlid al-Zahrâ' Fâṭima*, n. 4: 459, **ṢDQ[8]**., vol. I, bb. 148, n. 1: 184, **ḤRR[1]**., vol. II, bb. 24, n. 2825: 530, n. 2834: 533, **MĞL.**, vol. XXVII, bb. 2, n. 7: 251, vol. XLIII, bb. 7, n. 32: 299, vol. LXXVIII, bb. 8, n. 16: 299.

> "Prophet of God, what was her food?" He said: "The glorification, hallowing, acclamation and praise of God..."[110]

A second strand denotes a miraculous feeding after her birth and takes up as its theme the story of Maryam's miraculous feeding during her childhood under the guardianship of Zakariyyâʾ: in the case of Fâṭima, the story is told in various contexts and with diverse wording. In the account related below, the context is of ʿAlî awaking one morning and finding that she has nothing with which to feed him. He goes out to beg money in order to buy provisions – a confirmation of the great poverty in which the couple lived – and, having prayed with Muḥammad in the mosque, they return home to Fâṭima:

> Then the Prophet took ʿAlî by the hand, and they hurried to Fâṭima. She was in her prayer niche, and in front of her was a simmering bowl. When she heard the words of the Messenger of God she went and greeted him; she was the most beloved of people to him. He returned her greetings of peace and rubbed her head with his hand...she took the bowl and placed it in front of the Messenger of God. He said: "Fâṭima, where did you get this food? I have never seen a colour like it, or smelt fragrance like it, or eaten anything as good!" Then he put his hands on my shoulders and said: "This is given in exchange for your dinars! «*Allah giveth without stint to whom He will*»."[111]

Like Maryam, Fâṭima received this heavenly food while in her place of prayer, immediately situating the story in a religious framework.

---

[110] **ṢDQ**[6]., n. 53: 396, **MĞL**., vol. XLIII, bb. 1, n. 3: 4.

[111] **RṬB**[1]., 51, **AYY**., vol I, bb. 3, n. 41: 171, **ṬFA**[2]., bb. 69, n. 7–1271: 214–217, **RWD**[1]., vol. II: 528, 532, **SHB**., vol. III, bb. *manâqib Fâṭima al-Zahrâʾ*: 387, 409, **ṬSṬ**[3].: 529, **IRB**., vol. I: 469, **ÂML**., vol. I: 171, **ABḎ**.: 114, 359, **MĞL**., vol. XIII, bb. 16, n. 4: 197, vol. XXI, bb. 22, n. 14: 21, vol. XXXV, bb. 6: 251, n. 14: 255, vol. XXXVII, bb. 51, n. 7: 103, n. 8: 105, vol. XLI, bb. 102: 30, vol. XLIII, bb. 3, n. 30: 27, n. 35: 29, n. 38: 31, n. 51: 59, n. 60: 68, n. 63: 76, bb. 12, n. 73: 310, vol. XCIII, bb. 15, n. 25: 147. Among the Sunnî, cf. **RḤB**.: 45–46. The quote is that of Q. 3: 37

In all the accounts, the relevant verse of the Qur'ân concerning Maryam in the temple is quoted; sometimes it is Fâṭima herself who declares the origin of the food by quoting the verse, while other accounts place the words on the lips of Muḥammad. The story further serves the purpose of underscoring both the extreme poverty of ʿAlî and Fâṭima, at least in the early part of their marriage, as well as their unqualified dependence on God and His providence towards the *ahl al-bayt*. In his commentary on the *ḥadîṯ*, al-Mağlisî notes that it is carried by the Sunnî exegete al-Zamaḫsharî; Ibn Kaṯîr and al-Suyûṭî also carry it.[112] Their Shîʿî counterpart, al-Baḥrânî, transmits it too, but curiously, the more pro-Fâṭima Sunnî transmitters like al-Nîsâbûrî remain silent.

---

112 **MĞL.**, vol. XLIII, bb. 3: 29. Cf. **ZMR.**, vol. I, *sûrat âl ʿImrân*: 427. Cf. also **KṮR²**., vol. II, *sûrat âl ʿImrân*, v. 37: 33, **SYṬ.**, vol. II, *sûrat âl ʿImrân*: 36.

Chapter Two. Part Two: Fâṭima the Virgin: Traditions, Teaching and Piety Surrounding the Conception and Birth of al-Ḥusayn

Remaining with the Shîʿî texts and sources, we now examine the Shîʿî avowal that Fâṭima is concurrently virgin and mother. This is not, as we shall see, a unique notion, since parallels are effortlessly found in the literature of paganism as well as in the texts of other major religious traditions. What is of particular note for our purposes is the curious stress which the Shîʿî theologians lay on virginity, in a religion which, while it insists upon and honours virginity before marriage, nevertheless elevates marriage high beyond the virgin state.

2.1. Virginity in Pagan and Classical Traditions

In the pre-Christian Roman Empire, the notion of 'virgin birth' was a coded language, used as a way of denoting a man's divinity. In reality, classical and pagan mythologies are suffused with accounts of 'virgin' births, most often expressed through impregnation by a god in human form, or an animal, or even an inanimate object, but almost always without sexual intercourse. In one sense, miraculous conceptions and extraordinary circumstances for births enable humanity to believe in innocence and rectitude, and serve as an example of how cultures maintain a 'saviour's' character pure and unsullied. The societal aspiration is that by not permitting its saviour to be born through the carnal, sexual act, his or her essence or soul will be without sin. The belief that purity is necessary in all mythological leaders is a universal value (and not, as some hold, an innovation of Christianity), easily traceable in stories from most cultures; the wide diffusion of such stories throughout diverse cultures seems to confirm the so-called 'Parallelist School' of Carl Jung (d. 1961), which proposes that the concepts of mythology/religion evolved out of the popularity of evolutionary thought. Human beings react correspondingly to analogous stimuli because they are human, genetically patterned to respond in that way. After a prolonged period of reacting in a particular way, humans pass on (that is, draw from the collective consciousness) acquired traits: the stories of mythology and religion develop because reactivity is part of the collective consciousness. Themes common in mythological stories create a subconscious bond between mankind. The use of unusual or mystical circumstances around mythological births allows people to see a correlation between one culture and another. In this, Jung is diametrically opposed, for example, to the so-called 'Ritualistic School' or 'Diffusionist School' of Sir James Frazier (d. 1941) and others, which holds that all humans had their origin in one place and spread worldwide, carrying their cultures (stories) with them, so that if separate peoples have the same stories or gods, there must have been contact in which the more sophisticated group passed on its ideas to the more primitive.[1]

---

[1] Jung held that certain ostensibly universal symbols or images are innate and encoded in humanity, archetypes that reside so deep in the collective unconscious that they can never be articulated consciously. He employed this concept of inherent symbols present in all human psyches to explain the cross-cultural appearance of specific images and narrative prototypes. Jung was struck by the fact that his patients in therapy often 'spontaneously' told stories or had dreams that included imagery reminiscent of classical mythology and ethnographic reports from around the world. Faced with this, he eventually hypothesized that these were innate symbols that all humans have and can access and use. Thus, he implicitly assumed a strong parallelism between individual psychic processes and (group) cultural processes. Much like Freud, Jung felt that myths were group expressions of an innately human psychic phenomenon. Drawing upon a variety of literature, Jung assembled a list of what he saw as common archetypes. He posited that these assisted human beings in processing and dealing with the empirical experiences they went through in their lives, providing a lens by which to make sense of different people,

The Hellenistic world alone has a plethora of virgin birth narratives (among them, Pythagoras, Plato and Alexander). Zeus achieved notoriety for having fathered numerous children by human mothers, impregnating Semele by means of a thunderbolt[2] and Danaë in a shower of gold.[3] In the Greek and Roman pantheon of gods and goddesses, the goddesses themselves could be said to be virgin mothers. Athena and Artemis were regarded as virgins, for having given birth, they dipped themselves into the rivers so that their virginity was renewed. A Greek myth held the same of Juno, who habitually renewed her virginity by bathing in a magical fountain; there are also accounts of a goddess who restored her virginity after sexual intercourse by bathing in a fountain located between the upper Tigris and Euphrates in the territory in which contemporary Zoroastrians[4] located some of their holy places. This renewable virginity would eventually find a resonance in the Islamic Traditions concerning the maidens of Paradise, but strands of it may well be significant in understanding Fâṭima as 'Virgin and Mother'.

The ancient Egyptian queens were believed to have been impregnated by the gods, a *leitmotif* that extends even to the mother of the first Japanese Emperor and the mother of Buddha, who gave birth through divine favour. Even the Chinese had a mother-goddess and virgin with child in her arms, as did the ancient Etruscans. Devaki, the radiant virgin of the Hindu mythology, became the wife of the god Vishnu and bore Krishna, the beloved hero, by Vishnu's hair being placed in her womb. The old Teutonic goddess Hertha (the Earth) was a virgin, but was impregnated by the heav-

---

events, etc., and providing the unconscious with a language to express psychological needs or aspects that were underdeveloped or needing attention. According to Jung, the myths are filled with archetypes, which is why he felt that myths usually resonate with people

[2] PRICE S. and KEARNS E., (eds.), *The Oxford Dictionary of Classical Mythology*, 2004: 504.

[3] Op. cit.: 145.

[4] The major, ancient, monotheistic and pre-Islamic religion of Persia, with its founder, Zoroaster, active in the 6TH century B.C. or even earlier. The supreme god was Ahura Mazdâ. Zoroastrianism gradually became contaminated with strands of older religious systems.

enly Spirit (the Sky), and her image with a child in her arms was to be seen in the sacred groves of Germany. In Norse mythology, Frigga conceived and bore a son, Balder, healer and saviour of mankind, through the embrace of Odin, the All-Father. In the Aztec story of Chimalman and Quetzalcoatl, the culture has the virgin Chimalman impregnated by the highest of the gods. There is no mention in the story of the traditional sexual act; instead Chimalman is 'breathed' upon by the Aztec God and becomes pregnant. The child or hero born from Chimalman is considered the 'Son of the Lord of the High Heavens'.[5] Other cultures too have utilized the concept of virgin conceptions to describe the births of their legendary heroes. Campbell writes of 'modified' virgin births, citing Sargon of Argade, a ruler of Mesopotamia (c. 2350 BC) and Moses, drawn from the bulrushes.[6] He also names Mithra,[7] the Persian saviour who was born under a sacred tree beside a hallowed stream, and is depicted as 'emerging' from a 'mother' or 'generative' rock, perceived as the earth giving birth to the archetypal man.[8] Campbell is adamant that Jesus' virgin birth "must be interpreted as a mystic motif from the Persian or Greek, not Hebrew side of the Christian heritage."[9]

By tradition Zoroaster, who began to disseminate his religion in Persia around the 6TH century B.C., was born of a virgin impreg-

---

[5] Cf. KINGSBOROUGH E. K., *Mexican Antiquities*, A Aglio, London 1830–48, vol. VI: 176.

[6] CAMPBELL J., *The Masks of God: Occidental Mythology*, Souvenir Press, London 2001: 73, 133.

[7] Prior to the advent of Zoroastrianism, Persia had a polytheistic religious system, of whom Mithra was the most important in the pantheon of gods.

[8] CAMPBELL J., *The Masks of God: Occidental Mythology*, 2001: 260–261. The precise relationship between Ahura Mazdâ to his virginal consort Anahita is unclear: it is not implausible that she was regarded as the virgin mother of Mithra, having conceived miraculously, and having, like Mary in Catholic theology, given birth to a child miraculously, without rupture of her hymen. Alternatively, the traditions relate her giving birth and having the power to renew her virginity by bathing in magical water.

[9] Op. cit.: 336.

nated by a supreme god who sent an emanation of himself to accomplish this task. Zoroaster's unabashedly supernatural parturition was preceded, accompanied, and followed by miracles similar to those recounted in the birth of others touched in a singular way the hand of the gods.[10] But celibacy, so extolled by Mani,[11] was abhorred by the virgin-born Zoroaster. Manichaeism extols celibacy as the greatest virtue, advocating it for those initiated in the higher orders; when all other desires are dispelled by a fervent longing for the love of God, and when that love becomes the controlling factor of the devout, he is instructed to take a vow of chastity, not entering into marriage if he desires to serve God unequivocally. Marriage is declared incompatible with sanctity and is envisaged as impure and defiling. Mani posits sexual intercourse as the worst type of uncleanliness, with virginity as the highest form of life. All this is conflicts radically with the teachings of Zoroaster. In no period of the history of his religion was celibacy ever deemed a virtue. Those practicing it were not considered more holy or held in higher reverence, as among the Manichaeans; in contrast, their chosen lifestyle was strongly reprehended. Even the priests were not to be celibates, for it was a cardinal point of the faith of every true Zoroastrian that he should marry and rear a family. It is improbable that in the variegated strands of Persian Zoroastrian thought we might discover theological the roots of Fâṭima's virginity.

Illustrated here is not merely the wide dispersion of the concept of the virgin-mother, but also its great antiquity. The vision of the 'Perfect Man' has ever hovered over the mind of humanity; and a perfectly instinctive supposition with regard to such a being was

---

[10] Zoroaster distinguished himself from all others whose birth contained supernatural elements: for while Fâṭima, for example, fell to the ground and proclaimed the oneness of God, as soon as Zoroaster emerged from his mother's womb, having dazzled bystanders with the alluring light of his divine ancestry, he laughed stridently, signifying that life is good and ought to be enjoyed.

[11] Mani or Manes was born around A.D. 216 and propagated a dualistic religion, Manichaeism, which spread throughout Persia and met with severe persecution during the ʿAbbâsid period.

that he would be born from a 'Perfect Woman', who according to early ideas would necessarily be the Virgin Earth itself, mother of all things.

2.2. FÂṬIMA AS VIRGIN AND MOTHER

Of all the theological and spiritual titles given to Fâṭima, the designation 'virgin', expressed by the Arabic *al-ʿaḏrâʾ* and more frequently by *al-batûl* remains the most enigmatic. It is at once obvious that the Islamic understanding of her virginity is vastly different from the Catholic conception of Mary's virginity. Why would Islam insist so unwaveringly upon the designation 'virgin' for Fâṭima, even though it had to devise an innovative definition of virginity in order to do so, and is quite unmistakably speaking of a virginity that is not the same physical virginity of Mary (or of the Qurʾanic Maryam)? Shîʿî Islam presents Fâṭima as married with (at least) four children, and there is no suggestion that any of her children were not the result of sexual intercourse or that her marriage with ʿAlî was devoid of sexual relations. It is patently clear that Fâṭima must be declared a virgin if she is not to become secondary to Maryam, whose virginity is underscored both in the Qurʾânic text and in the books of *aḥâdîṯ*. However, the texts never overcome the ongoing problem that while Maryam's virginity is quite clearly physical, Fâṭima's is not. As a way of solving this problem, the books of Shîʿî *aḥâdîṯ* propose a very specific definition of virginity.

> «*And when the angels said: O Maryam! Lo! Allah hath chosen thee and made thee pure, and hath preferred thee above (all) the women of creation*» (Q. 3: 42).

The Qurʾânic conception of Maryam's virginity is almost entirely physical. While the verse that declares that God has made her pure is not necessarily a reference to physical virginity, the Qurʾân does insist that Maryam's son ʿÎsâ is unfathered (Q. 3: 47, 19: 18–20). It is this unfathered conception and deliverance of a child that clearly defines her virgin state. Even so, these verses, in contradistinction to Catholic Tradition, do not essentially suggest that Maryam's virginity is perpetual, continuing after the birth of ʿÎsâ. Nor does the

Qur'ânic text in any way insinuate that God has removed from the life of Maryam the natural but, in Islamic eyes, reprehensible pain and bleeding of the menstrual cycle, although this is the interpretation proposed by some exegetes, like al-Râzî.[12]

Fâṭima's virginity is presented in dissimilar and varied ways; at least one of these consists of a reinterpretation of the verse of Maryam being purified (Q. 3: 42) by substituting the name of Fâṭima. This, however, does not automatically suggest perpetual virginity, any more than it does in the case of Maryam. Nonetheless, the explanation of Fâṭima's virginity, unlike that of Maryam, is not of something physical, but of something esoteric. At no time is there a hint that any of her children are parallel to ʿÎsâ in that they are unfathered. Hers is a singularity that is expressed in multifaceted theology.

To begin with, number of texts speak of Fâṭima guarding her chastity: "Fâṭima has guarded her chastity and God has forbidden her offspring to the Fire."[13]

---

[12] The Sunnî exegete al-Râzî, in his treatment of Q. 3: 42, posits that freedom from menstruation was one of five elements in the purification of Maryam by God (*ṭahhara-hâ ʿan al-ḥayḍ*). Cf. **RAZ.**, vol. VIII, *sûrat âl ʿImrân*, v. 42: 43. Cf. also **QRṬ.**, vol. IV, *sûrat âl ʿImrân*, v. 42: 82–83. The contemporary Shîʿî scholar al-Ṭabâṭabâ'î raises the issue in his examination of the same verse, writing that "it has also been said that her purification means that she was a virgin who did not menstruate." Cf. **ṬBṬ.**, vol. VI, *sûrat âl ʿImrân*, v. 42: 6–7. Cf. also AYOUB M., *The Qur'an and Its Interpreters*, vol. II, *The House of ʿImrān*, 1992: 126, 128.

[13] **ṢDQ[5]**., vol. II, bb. 31, n. 264: 63, bb. 58, n. 1: 232, **ṢDQ[6]**., nn. 1–6: 105–106, **RWD[1]**., vol. I: 281, **SHB.**, vol. III, bb. *manâqib Fâṭima al-Zahrâ'*: 373, **IRB.**, vol. I: 468, vol. II: 144, 310, 346, **ḤLL[2]**.: 351, **MǦL.**, vol. XLIII, bb. 3, n. 6: 20, bb. 9, n. 2: 230, nn. 3–6: 231, n. 7: 232, vol. XLVI, bb. 11, n. 51: 185, vol. XLVIII: 315, vol. XLIX, bb. 16, nn. 2–3: 217, vol. LXXV, bb. 16, n. 52: 78, vol. XCIII, bb. 27, nn. 14–18: 221–223. Among the Sunnî, cf. **ḤNA.**, vol. III, bk. 31 (*Kitâb maʿrifat al-ṣaḥâba*), *Manâqib Fâṭima bt. rasûl Allâh*, n. 4789: 179, **IṢH.**, vol. IV, bb. 268, n. 5277: 209, **ḪWZ.**, Part I, bb. *Faḍâ'il Fâṭima al-Zahrâ' bt. rasûl Allâh*, n. 9: 94, **RḤB.**: 48, **HAY.**, vol. IX, bb. *manâqib Fâṭima bt. rasûl Allâh*: 202, **MTQ.**, vol. V: 97.

This verse, literally translated as 'fortified' or 'made inaccessible her private parts' (the same words used of Maryam in Q. 21: 91) certainly confirms her temporary virginity, that is, prior to her marriage with ʿAlî. The texts then offer two diverse explanations of virginity, with a tentative definition of Maryam and Fâṭima together, that at once raise a number of difficulties:

> On the authority of ʿAlî, the Prophet was asked: "What is the 'virgin'? Because, Messenger of God, we heard you say: Maryam is a virgin and Fâṭima is a virgin." He said: "The virgin is she who does not secrete blood ('redness'), that is, does not menstruate, because menstruation is reprehensible in the daughters of the prophets."[14]

Virginity in this text is carefully redefined, for nothing can be posited about Maryam that cannot also be posited about Fâṭima; if Maryam is declared a virgin, Fâṭima must be a virgin too. However, nowhere in the Qur'ânic texts is Maryam's virginity ever explicitly defined as anything else but that she conceived and gave birth to ʿÎsâ without sexual intercourse. This *ḥadîṯ*, in antithesis, specifies Fâṭima's virginity in an innovative and peculiar way, making the lack of menstruation the basis of her maidenhood. Even more troublesome is that freedom from menstruation is nowhere posited of other daughters of the prophets: certainly, there are no texts that make a similar claim for Muḥammad's other daughters, Zaynab, Ruqayya and Umm Kulṯûm. In this, Lammens is quite correct in his claim that, at the approach of Fâṭima, her three sisters vanish and fade unaccountably into history.[15]

Ibn Ḥanbal proposes a *ḥadîṯ* that seems, at first glance, to contradict this interpretation of Fâṭima's virginity. In it, Fâṭima comes

---

[14] **RṬB**[1].: 54, **ṢDQ**[6] ., n. 17: 64, **ṢDQ**[8]., vol. I, bb. 144, n. 1: 181, **FNR**., vol. I: 149, **SHB**., vol. III, bb. *manâqib Fâṭima al-Zahrâ'*: 378, **IRB**., vol. I: 464, **NṬR**., vol. II, n. 3–1344, bb. 37: 37, **MĞL**., vol. XLIII, bb. 2, nn. 13–14: 15–16, vol. LXXVIII, bb. 4, n. 36: 112, vol. XCII, bb. 129: 383.

[15] LAMMENS H., "Fatima and the Daughters of Muhammad" in Ibn Warraq (ed. and trans.), *The Quest for the Historical Muhammad*, 2000: 221.

to Muḥammad to say that she is menstruating; he tells her that the blood she is shedding is not menstrual, but merely a vein, and directs her to cease with her prayer, wait a few days until it is settled, then to wash, change garments and pray. The woman involved is identified merely as 'Fâṭima', leading one to believe that it could be Muḥammad's daughter.[16] Nevertheless, all the other major transmitters who carry this report identify the woman involved either as Fâṭima bt. Abî Ǧaysh, or as Fâṭima bt. Abî Ḥubaysh, or as Fâṭima bt. Qays (or otherwise as Umm Ḥabîba bt. Ǧahsh, or merely as 'a woman'). In most, but not all cases, Ibn Ḥanbal, when writing of Muḥammad's daughter, clearly identifies her either as 'daughter of Muḥammad' or 'daughter of the Messenger of God', or by the customary 'peace be upon her' or 'may God be pleased with her'. In the *ḥadîṯ* of the menstruating woman, he does not; and the strong sense is that he speaking of Muḥammad's daughter. Nevertheless, the weight of evidence lies with the majority of transmitters.[17]

A curious reference to this state of affairs in the life of Fâṭima is found in a *ḥadîṯ*, carried with a slight variation in the wording, by some Sunnî and Shîʿî transmitters: "Between the bearing of al-

---

[16] **ḤNB.**, vol. X, *Ḥadîṯ Umm Salama*, n. 26655: 196, n. 26802: 227. But cf. also **ḤNB.**, vol. IX, *Ḥadîṯ ʿÂʾisha*, n. 24592: 367 (in which the bleeding woman is identified as Umm Ḥabîba), n. 25679: 569 and vol. X, *Ḥadîṯ ʿÂʾisha*, n. 25739: 15, n. 26315: 122–123 (in which the woman in question is named as Fâṭima bt. Abî Ḥubaysh).

[17] Cf. **DRM.**, vol. I, bk. 1 (*Kitâb al-ṣalât wa-l-ṭahâra*), bb. 80, n. 114: 196, n. 120: 198, nn. 124, 125: 199, n. 128: 200, **BUḪ[1].**, vol. I, bk. 4 (*Kitâb al-wuḍûʾ*), ch. 67, n. 228: 146, bk. 6 (*Kitâb al-ḥayḍ*), ch. 10, n. 303: 183, n. 317: 190–191, n. 322: 194, **MSL.**, vol. I, bk. 3 (*Kitâb al-ḥayḍ*), ch. 131, nn. 652, 653, 654, 655, 656: 189, nn. 657, 658: 190, **MǦA.**, vol. I, bk. 1 (*Kitâb al-ṭahâra wa-sunani-hâ*), bb. 115, nn. 620, 621: 203, n. 624: 204, bb. 116, n. 626: 205, **ADD.**, vol. I, bk. 1 (*Kitâb al-ṭahâra*), bb. 107: 63–64, bb. 108: 65, **NSA[1].**, vol. I, bk. 1 (*Kitâb al-ṭahâra*), bb. *ḏikr al-iġtisâl min al-ḥayḍ*: 116–119, bb. *al-aqrâʾ*: 120–122, bk. 3 (*Kitâb al-ḥayḍ wa-l-istiḥâḍa*), bb. *ḏikr al-istiḥâḍa wa-iqbâl al-dam*: 181–182, bb. *ḏikr al-aqrâʾ*: 183–184.

Ḥusayn and the birth of al-Ḥasan there was (one period of) purity" (*kâna bayna al-Ḥasan and al-Ḥusayn ṭuhr wâḥid*).[18]

Unquestionably, going by its content and its context, this *ḥadîṯ* does not refer to whether Fâṭima menstruated or not, but points rather to the time period between the births of her two sons. It certainly cannot mean, by its use of the concept of 'purity', that Fâṭima had no sexual relations with her husband during the period between the boys' births; for one thing, Shîʿî tradition holds the conception of al-Ḥusayn to be in the time period denoted elsewhere in the *ḥadîṯ* quoted above (fifty days after the birth of al-Ḥasan), and for another, this would mean that al-Ḥusayn's was a virginal conception, and there is no hint of this in Sunnî or Shîʿî Islam. It can only refer to Fâṭima's lack of menstruation; the concept of *ṭuhr* denotes the period of purity between menstrual cycles so that, between the birth of her first child and the conception of her second, Fâṭima did not return to the cycle of menstruation normal to a woman. This particular had does not clarify that God removed menstruation from her entirely: for that, we have to search the texts more deeply.

The solitary Qurʾânic reference to menstruation is found in Q. 2: 222, in which the male believer is instructed:

> «*They question thee (O Muhammad) concerning menstruation. Say: it is an illness, so let women alone at such times and go not in unto them till they are cleansed. And when they have purified themselves, then go in unto them as Allah hath enjoined upon you. Truly Allah loveth those who turn unto him, and loveth those who have a care for cleanness*».

---

[18] Among the Sunnî, cf. **BĠD.**, vol. I: 142; **BRR.**, vol. I: 393, **ATH².**, vol. II: 18, **RḤB.**: 118, **SQL¹.**, vol. I, n. 1724: 331, **HAY.**, vol. IX, bb. *manâqib al-Ḥusayn*: 185, **SHL.**, n. 875: 404. Among the Shîʿa, cf. **KLY.**, vol. I, bk. 4 (*Kitâb al-ḥuǧǧa*), bb. *mawlid al-Ḥusayn*, n. 2: 463–464, **SHB.**, vol. III, bb. *fî maʿâlî umûri-hâ*: 449, **ḤRR¹.**, vol. XXI, bb. 17, n. 23355: 381, **MĞL.**, vol. XLIII, bb. 11, n. 21: 257, n. 46: 258, **NṬR.**, vol. XV, bb. 12, n. 3–17732: 124, bb. 50, n. 2–17838: 158. Some transmitters add the word 'perfect' to denote the purity, while others omit the words 'bearing' and 'birth', so that it reads literally: "There was (a/one period of) purity between al-Ḥasan and al-Ḥusayn."

The Arabic *adan*, which Pickthall renders as 'illness', carries the sense of 'damage' or 'harm' or 'injury', but is diversely rendered by English translators who, without diminishing its negativity, give it a broad range of meanings.[19] The Muslim commentators attempt to clarify the precise meaning: for al-Ṭabarî, menstruation is called *adan* by reason of the stench of its odour and the uncleanness or filth (*qadar*) of its impurity (*nağâsa*).[20] Al-Zamaḫšarî designates it as something unclean or filthy (*qadir*), which leads to antipathy and revulsion in those who encounter it.[21] Al-Qurṭubî renders *adan* slightly less censoriously, as something which hurts, or offends, or wrongs women, but then concurs with al-Ṭabarî that it is an allegory for *qadar*, and applies to it the term *makrûh* (reprehensible). He refers his reader to further Qur'ânic texts: Q. 2: 264 (in both 2: 263 and 2: 264 Pickthall renders the word *adan* as 'injury') and Q. 33: 48 (in which Pickthall translates the same word as 'noxious talk').[22] Al-Râzî too, designates *adan* as the manifestation of an illness or weakness, stressing the necessity of isolation for a woman who is in her menses, not only for its disagreeable odour and foul colour, but also because of the powerful impetuosity it produces in its victim.[23]

Certainly, the Islamic restrictions against menstruating women, as reflected in the corpus of *aḥâdît*, are less harsh than those of the Jewish, permitting almost everything (including association) except for sexual intercourse.[24] There are a number of *aḥâdît* forbidding women to fast and pray during the 'temporary illness' of their menses,[25] but the prayers, unlike the fasting, need not be

---

[19] While Rodwell, Sale and Yusuf Ali prefer 'pollution', Palmer renders it as 'hurt' and Irving, more blandly, as 'nuisance'. Shakir and Assad, like Irving, reduce the negativity somewhat by translating it as 'discomfort' and 'vulnerable condition' respectively.

[20] **YṬB**[1]., vol. IV, *sûrat al-Baqara*, v. 222, nn. 4234–4237: 394–375.

[21] **ZMR**., vol. I, *sûrat al-Baqara*, v. 222: 201.

[22] **QRṬ**., vol. III, *sûrat al-Baqara*, v. 222: 85–86.

[23] **RAZ**., vol. VI, *sûrat al-Baqara*, v. 222: 66.

[24] Cf. for e.g. **TIB**., vol. I, bk. 27 (*Kitâb al-fitan*), bb. 12, n. 545: 171.

[25] **BUḪ**[1]., vol. I, bk. 6 (*Kitâb al-ḥayḍ*), ch. 8, n. 301: 181–182, ch. 10, n. 303: 183, ch. 26, n. 322: 194, ch. 30, n. 327: 196.

made up afterwards.[26] Nor is circambulation (*ṭawâf*) of the *Kaᶜba* permitted,[27] but there appears to be no prohibition of reading or reciting the Qur'ân.[28] This notwithstanding, ultimately menstruation militates against a woman; for although forbidden to pray and fast during menstruation, this is nonetheless regarded as a defect in their religion.[29]

But Fâṭima is spared all of this, by a unique divine favour, for not even of Maryam is it explicitly claimed that her purification by God entailed a suspension or removal of menses; indeed, the texts insist that this lack of menstruation makes Fâṭima unlike all other women.[30] The miracle granted to Fâṭima echoes in a sense Mary's Immaculate Conception in Catholic dogma; a God who steps in and bends the laws of nature by removing something that is inevitable but odious.

> On the authority of Abû Ǧaᶜfar,[31] who said: "When Fâṭima, peace be upon her, was born, God, powerful and lofty, inspired an angel, by whom He loosened the tongue of Muḥammad, who called her Fâṭima. Then He said: I have weaned you with knowledge and I have weaned you from menstruation. Then Abû Ǧaᶜfar said: By God! God, may He be blessed and exalted, has weaned her with knowledge and from menstruation by the covenant."[32]

Nor does this matter go unnoticed by Fâṭima's peers: "On the authority of Anas b. Mâlik, on the authority of his mother, who said: I never saw Fâṭima bleed, either in menstruation or in parturi-

---

[26] Op. cit.: ch. 22, n. 318: 191.

[27] Op. cit.: ch. 3, n. 293: 177–178, ch. 9, n. 302: 182–183.

[28] **BUḪ[1]**., vol. I, bk. 6 (*Kitâb al-ḥayḍ*), ch. 9: 182.

[29] Op. cit.: ch. 8, n. 301: 181–182.

[30] **ṬSṬ[2]**., vol. I, n. 163: 111, **MǦL**., vol. XXXVII, bb. 2, n. 9: 43.

[31] The fifth Imâm.

[32] **KLY**., vol. I, bk. 4 (*Kitâb al-ḥuǧǧa*), bb. *mawlid al-Zahrâ' Fâṭima*, n. 6: 460, **ṢDQ[8]**., vol. I, bb. 142, n. 4: 179, **IRB**., vol. I: 463, **MǦL**., vol. XLIII bb. 2, n. 9: 7, n. 14: 16.

tion."[33] The Shîʿî texts then offer a second specification of virginity. In al-Mağlisî it is elucidated in a note attached to one of the *aḥâdîṯ* about menstruation being reprehensible for a prophet's daughter:

> The virgin is separated; that is, she is separated from the women of her time by the lack of seeing blood. He said, at the end: A woman virgin is separated from men, who have no lust for her. Maryam the mother of ʿÎsâ was named in this way, and Fâṭima was named 'the Virgin' to separate her from the women of her time, in superiority, religion and nobility. It was also said to separate her from the world for the service of God Most High. Al-Fayrûzâbâdî said something similar to this."[34]

The theme of separation in this *ḥadîṯ*, already extant in the definition of the name Fâṭima, is highlighted by a number of similar *aḥâdîṯ*. Al-Mağlisî transmits that:

> Abû ʿAbd Allâh[35] said: God forbade ʿAlî women while Fâṭima was still alive because she was pure and did not menstruate. ʿUbayd al-Harawî[36] said in *al-Ġarîbayn* that Maryam was called a virgin because she was cut off from men, and Fâṭima was called a virgin because she was cut off from an equal.[37]

The declaration that Fâṭima is a 'maiden of Paradise in human form' (*ḥawrâʾ insiyya*)[38] means, in a sense, virginity, for this is the

---

[33] **ṢDQ¹**., n. 9: 182, **ṢDQ³**., vol. I, n. 193: 89, **ṬBR¹**.: 148, **MĞL**., vol. XXXVII, bb. 50, n. 36: 64, vol. XLIII bb. 3, n. 9: 21. Among the Sunnî, cf. **RḤB**.: 44.

[34] **MĞL**., vol. XLIII, bb. 2, n. 13: 15.

[35] The sixth Imâm.

[36] Abû ʿUbayd Aḥmad b. Muḥammad b. Muḥammad b. ʿAbd al-Raḥmân al-Harawî al-Bashânî (d. 401/1010: Cf. GAL S. 1: 200) in his *Kitâb al-ġarîbayn fî al-qurʾân wa-l-ḥadîṯ*.

[37] **MĞL**., vol. XLIII, bb. 2, n. 14: 16. Cf. also **IRB**., vol. III: 330.

[38] **ṢDQ¹**., n. 7: 460, **ṢDQ⁵**., vol. I, bb. 11, n. 3: 115, **ṢDQ⁶**., n. 53: 396, **FNR**., vol. I: 149, **ṬBR²**., vol. II: 408, **SHB**., vol. III, bb. *manâqib Fâṭima al-Zahrâʾ*: 383, **ABḎ**.: 240, **MĞL**., vol. IV, bb. 1, n. 4: 3, vol. VIII, bb. 23, n. 6: 119, n. 160: 188, vol. XLIII, bb. 1, nn. 2–3: 4, bb. 2, n. 17: 18,

perpetually renewable status of these creatures. The Arabic singular *ḥawrâʾ* (with its plural *ḥûr*) has come to mean the 'maidens of Paradise', the large black pupils of whose eyes are in sharp and beautiful contrast to the whiteness of the irises (and the paleness of their skin). Most pertinent in terms of Fâṭima are the Qurʾânic verses which describe these *ḥûr* as 'virgins', designated by the Arabic plural *abkâr* (Q. 56: 36), untouched by man or *ǧinn* (Q. 55: 56, 74) and 'pure wives', which Pickthall inexplicably renders as 'companions' (Q. 2: 25, 4: 57). This last virtue is, according to the commentators, that they are free from bodily impurity and defects of character. To the brief Qurʾânic statements are added the *aḥâdîṯ* and traditional exegesis; what must be underlined here is that their virginity is consistently renewable, a theme already encountered in pagan mythology. Having been purified, they suffer neither the distress of menstruation, nor any human craving, nor the pain of childbirth, for they bear none.

In which of these characteristics precisely is Fâṭima a human *ḥawrâʾ*? Is her virginity understood in like manner to theirs, as something renewable? Of itself, the designation serves to render Fâṭima ethereal and not quite human, giving her a slightly indefinable status, by which physical, human virginity cannot be effectively judged. While some Sunnî transmitters hold that she is a human *ḥawrâʾ* because, like them, she does not suffer menses,[39] it is clear, as we have seen, that her status of human *ḥawrâʾ* is most intimately bound up with the notion of her pre-existent light and of her conception in the womb of her mother Ḫadîǧa by means of heavenly fruit.

---

bb. 3, n. 42: 43, vol. XLIV, bb. 30, n. 33: 240. Among the Sunnî, cf. **BĠD.**, vol. V, n. 2481: 87, vol. XII, n. 6772: 331, **ḪWZ.**, Part I, bb. *Faḍâʾil Fâṭima al-Zahrâʾ bt. rasûl Allâh*, n. 33: 105, **ǦWZ¹.**, vol. I, bb. *fî faḍl Fâṭima*: 411–413, bb. *fî ḏikr tazwîǧ Fâṭima bi-ʿAlî*: 421, **ṢFI.**, vol. II, bb. *manâqib Fâṭima al-Zahrâʾ*: 184, **MTQ.**, vol. V: 97.

39 Cf. for e.g. **ǦWZ¹.**, vol. I, bb. *fî ḏikr tazwîǧ Fâṭima bi-ʿAlî*: 421, **MTQ.**, vol. V: 97.

2.3. THE NARRATIVES OF AL-ḤUSAYN'S CONCEPTION AND BIRTH

The conception and birth of al-Ḥusayn, in tandem with that of Fâṭima his mother, is not only meticulously encased in accounts of heavenly intervention, but also contains elements upon which the transmitters are not wholly agreed. One of these more pragmatic features is the dating of his birth, although this factor is not as crucial as it is in Fâṭima's life. The Sunnî historian al-Ṭabarî notes that al-Ḥasan was born about halfway through Ramaḍân of the 3RD year of the *hiğra* (i.e. 3/625) and that Fâṭima became pregnant with al-Ḥusayn in the same year, some saying within fifty days of al-Ḥasan's birth.[40] Later in his work, he posits that al-Ḥusayn was born in Shaʿbân of the 4TH year of the *hiğra* (i.e. January 4/626),[41] adding that there are some who claim that al-Ḥasan was in fact born in the 2ND year of the *hiğra* (and, concomitantly, al-Ḥusayn in the 3RD), but that if Fâṭima and ʿAlî were married in the 2ND year of the *hiğra*, such reports about al-Ḥasan are erroneous.[42] Few other Sunnî transmitters are much occupied with the dating of his birth; al-Nîsâbûrî, for example, merely mentions that he was born one year and ten months after his brother al-Ḥasan, while al-Ḫawârizmî, noting the discrepancies among the transmitters, posits the 3RD year of the *hiğra* for al-Ḥasan and the 4TH year for al-Ḥusayn, as does al-Shablanğî.[43]

It is the Shîʿî transmitters who cannot agree; with rare exceptions (positing the months of Rabîʿ al-awwal or Ğumâdâ al-ûlâ), most agree that he was born in the month of Shaʿbân. The major

---

[40] **YṬB**[2]., vol. VII, n. 1431: 142. Among the Sunnî transmitters, cf. for e.g. **SQL**[1]., vol. I: 393, **SHL.**: 113.

[41] **YṬB**[2]., vol. VII., n. 1453: 161.

[42] Op. cit., n. 1367: 91–92.

[43] **ḤNA.**, vol. III, Part 3, bk. 31 (*Kitâb maʿrifat al-ṣaḥâba*), *Manâqib ahl bayt rasûl Allâh*, n. 4885: 210, **ḪWZ.**, Part I, bb. *Faḍâʾil al-Ḥasan wa-l-Ḥusayn,* n. 1: 135, ch. 7, *Faḍâʾil al-Ḥusayn wa-l-ḫâṣṣat bi-hi*, n. 1: 209, **SHL.**: 113.

discrepancy lies in which year of the *hiğra* the birth occurred; some posit the 3RD,[44] others the 4TH.[45]

The miraculous stories that encase the annunciation of his birth, his conception and his parturition are a fusion of the emblematic genre of story that is constructed around the birth of any saviour or a hero. Among these, what follows are the most significant.

2.3.1. The Pre-Existence of al-Ḥusayn

We have already examined some of the texts dealing with the pre-existence of Fâṭima and her creation from light; most prominent among these are the *ashbâḥ* reports, which almost inevitably contain reference to al-Ḥusayn and his older brother al-Ḥasan (but not their sisters Zaynab and Umm Kulṯûm) as constituent members of a pre-existent family deriving from the light of God. These texts, with variant wording, are found throughout the corpus of Shîʿî *aḥâdîṯ*, as well as in some Sunnî books, and sufficient examples are given earlier in this work.

2.3.2. The Period of Gestation

Attendant upon the date of al-Ḥusayn's birth is a well-attested *ḥadîṯ*, carried by many of the foremost Shîʿî transmitters, that Fâṭima carried him in her womb for a period of only six months. Most of them correlate this miraculous gestation with ʿÎsâ son of Maryam, who is held by pious tradition to have had a gestation of the same period of time: "She gave birth to him in six months: the birth of a child in six months is unheard of, except for al-Ḥusayn and ʿÎsâ son of Maryam."[46]

---

[44] **RṬB¹**.: 71, **KLY**., vol. I, *Kitâb al-ḥuğğa*, bb. *mawlid al-Ḥusayn b. ʿAlî*, n. 3: 464, **ṬFA¹**:, vol. II, bb. 15: 41.

[45] **ṬSṬ⁶**.: 12, **IRB**., vol. II: 40, 53, **MĞL**., vol. XIX, bb. 8: 192, vol. XX, bb. 16, n. 2: 182, vol. XLIII, bb. 11, n. 1: 237, vol. XLIV, bb. 26 n. 15: 198, bb. 26: 201.

[46] **RṬB¹**.: 71–72, **KLY**., vol. I, *Kitâb al-ḥuğğa*, bb. *mawlid al-Ḥusayn b. ʿAlî*, n. 4: 464, **QQM**., bb. 16, n. 6: 125, **ṢDQ⁸**., vol. I, bb. 156: 205, **SHB**., vol. III, bb. *fî musâwâti-hi*: 300, vol. IV, bb. *fî muʿğizâti-hi*: 57, **IRB**., vol. I: 583, **ḤRR¹**., vol. II, bb. 12, n. 2756: 502, **MĞL**., vol. XIV, bb. 17,

Curiously, a few transmitters omit the name of ʿÎsâ, ascribing a six month gestation instead to Yaḥyâ, son of Zakariyyâʾ,[47] leading the Shîʿî scholar al-Ḥillî to offer a laconic note in his *Muṯîr al-aḥzân* that "some say ʿÎsâ and some Yaḥyâ."[48] The Sunnî historian al-Ṭabarî mentions that the Christians claimed that Yaḥyâ (understood as John the Baptist) was born six months before ʿÎsâ.[49] So in fact do some Muslims, like al-Ṯaʿlabî in his *Qiṣaṣ al-anbiyâʾ*.[50] However, although the *ḥadîṯ* of Yaḥyâ (or ʿÎsâ) being only six months in the womb abounds among the Shîʿa, it is scarcely found among their Sunnî counterparts, suggesting that the six months' gestation could be a interpolation of the six month period between the births of Yaḥyâ and ʿÎsâ. Nevertheless, the *ḥadîṯ* achieves its primary aim; to elevate al-Ḥusayn, while still in the womb, to the distinctive status of Yaḥyâ or ʿÎsâ, thereby separating him from other men, and suggesting something very special about him even from the time of his conception.

This elevation is complemented by a second *ḥadîṯ*, which will be examined later in this work, and which claims that the heavens and the earth have only ever wept for two men, Yaḥyâ and al-Ḥusayn, as well as a third *ḥadîṯ*, based on Q. 19: 7 carried by very few transmitters, which posits that, as in the case of Yaḥyâ, so too in the case of al-Ḥusayn, no-one had ever been named thus before:

> On the authority of ʿAbd al-Ḫâliq b. ʿAbd Rabbih,[51] who said: "I heard Abû ʿAbd Allâh[52] saying: «*We have given the same name*

---

nn. 2–3: 207, vol. XXV, bb. 9, n. 15: 254, vol. XXXIX: 71, vol. XLIII, bb. 11, n. 31: 253, n. 44: 258, vol. XLIV, bb. 22: 162, bb. 26, n. 14: 198, bb. 30, n. 17: 232, vol. LXVI, bb 37: 266. Among the Sunnî, cf. **RḤB**.: 118.

[47] **ABḎ**.: 292, 294, 562–563, 565, **MĞL**., vol. XXIII, bb. 15, n. 23: 272, vol. XXXVI, bb. 39, n. 137: 158, vol. XLIII, bb. 11, n. 20: 245, n. 31: 253, nn. 44–45: 208.

[48] Nağm al-Dîn Ğaʿfar b. Muḥammad b. Ğaʿfar b. Hibat Allâh b. Namâ al-Ḥillî (d. 680/1281). Neither his name nor his work is recorded by Brockelmann. Cf. *Muṯîr al-aḥzân*: 12.

[49] **YṬB**²., vol. IV, nn. 711–712: 102.

[50] **ṮLB**.: 12.

[51] ʿAbd al-Ḫâliq b. ʿAbd Rabbih. Cf. **ṬFA**⁴., n. 722–3813: 366.

[52] The sixth Imâm.

> *to none before (him)*». Al-Ḥusayn b. ʿAlî; no-one before him had this name, and Yaḥyâ b. Zakariyyâʾ; no-one before him had this name…"[53]

2.3.3. Protection in the Womb From Iblîs

The detachment of al-Ḥusayn from other men and his elevation to a higher status is articulated in another arcane *ḥadîṯ*, transmitted by al-Mağlisî from al-Astarâbâḏî and from al-Karâğakî's[54] *Kanz ğâmiʿ al-fawâʾid*: "She became pregnant with al-Ḥusayn, and God guarded her and the one in her womb from Iblîs."[55]

This report is carried by none of the major Shîʿî sources, but is closely related to the Qurʾânic verse in which the wife of ʿImrân and mother of Maryam, having consecrated to God the child in her womb, dedicates her to God at the moment of her birth:

> «*And when she was delivered she said: My Lord! Lo! I am delivered of a female – Allah knew best of what she was delivered – the male is not as the female; and lo! I have named her Mary, and lo! I crave Thy protection for her and for her offspring from Satan the outcast*» (Q. 3: 36).

This verse is expanded by Muḥammad in a *ḥadîṯ* we have already seen: "There is none born of the children of Adam whom Satan does not touch as soon as he is born, and who does not raise his voice in a cry from the touch of Satan, except for Maryam and her son."[56] To Maryam and her son is now added al-Ḥusayn, enriching his status in a careful re-reading of the Qurʾânic verse and adaptation of this *ḥadîṯ*, first carried by al-Buḫârî.

---

[53] **QMM.**, bb. 28, n. 10: 182–183, **AYY.**: 295, **MĞL.**, vol. XLV, bb. 40, n. 22: 211.

[54] Abû al-Fatḥ Muḥammad b. ʿAbd al-Raḥmân b. ʿUṯmân al-Karâğakî (d. 499/1057: cf. GAL S. 1: 602, 969 and GAS 1: 551).

[55] **ABḎ.**: 562, **MĞL.**, vol. XXIII, bb. 15, n. 23: 272, vol. XXXVI, bb. 39, n. 137: 108.

[56] **BUḪ¹.**, vol. IV, bk. 55 (*Kitâb aḥâdîṯ al-anbiyâʾ*), ch. 39, n. 641: 426–427.

2.3.4. Annunciation of his Birth and Forewarnings of his Death

> On the authority of Abû ʿAbd Allâh,[57] who said: "When Fâṭima became pregnant with al-Ḥusayn, Ǧibraʾîl went to the Messenger of God and said: Fâṭima will give birth to a boy, whom your community after you will kill. When Fâṭima became pregnant with al-Ḥusayn she was reluctant in carrying him and at the time of her giving birth to him, she was reluctant at his birth. Then Abû ʿAbd Allâh said: Never in the world has a mother been seen to give birth to a boy with such reluctance, but she was reluctant after having learned that he will be killed. He said: And this verse came down about her: «*And We have commended unto man kindness toward parents. His mother beareth him with reluctance, and bringeth him forth with reluctance, and the bearing of him and the weaning of him is thirty months*»."[58]

The insertion in this *ḥadîṯ* by al-Kulaynî and others of the Qurʾânic verse (Q. 46: 15) to underscore the parturition of al-Ḥusayn by Fâṭima 'in tears' heralds a whole series of harrowing forewarnings of his future martyrdom even before his birth; the major part of this series is expressed through angelic visitation, but the warnings also come through Muḥammad in some sort of vision, or by individuals in their dreams. Three examples will suffice to illustrate this genre:

> On the authority of Abû ʿAbd Allâh,[59] who said: "Ǧibraʾîl came down to Muḥammad and said to him: Muḥammad, God announces to you a child who will be born of Fâṭima, and

---

[57] The sixth Imâm.

[58] **KLY.**, vol. I, *Kitâb al-ḥuǧǧa*, bb. *mawlid al-Ḥusayn b. ʿAlî*, n. 3: 464, **QQM.**, bb. 16, n. 4: 122, **SHB.**, vol. IV, bb. *fî imâmat Abî ʿAbd Allâh al-Ḥusayn*: 57, **ABḎ.**: 563, **MǦL.**, vol. XLIII, bb. 11, n. 21: 246, n. 31: 253, vol. XLIV, bb. 30, n. 16: 231, vol. LIII, bb. 29, n. 126: 102, vol. LXVI, bb. 37: 266. Cf. Q. 46: 15. I have followed Pickthall in rendering the verb *karaha-yakrahu* as 'reluctance' although in reality it carries a much stronger sense of 'to loathe', 'to hate' or 'to feel disgust'.

[59] The sixth Imâm.

> whom your community after you will kill. He said: Ǧibra'îl, peace to my Lord, I have no need of a child who will be born of Fâṭima, and whom my community after me will kill. He ascended, and then came down and said the same thing to him. Muḥammad said: Ǧibra'îl, peace to my Lord, I have no need of a child who will be born of Fâṭima, and whom my community after me will kill. Ǧibra'îl ascended to heaven, and then came down and said: Muḥammad, your Lord greets you and announces to you that He is the One who sets in his descendants the Imamate (*al-imâma*), the authority (*al-wilâya*) and the testament (*al-waṣiyya*). He said: I am content. Then he sent to Fâṭima: God has announced to me a child who will born of you, and whom my community after me will kill. Fâṭima sent to him: I have no need of a child from me, whom your community after you will kill. He sent to her: God has already placed in his descendants the Imamate, the authority and the testament. She sent to him: I am content. And "*she bore him with reluctance and brought him forth with reluctance…*"."[60]

This story is archetypical in the narratives of al-Ḥusayn's conception and birth, and is recounted in various ways and in different settings. One of the most prominent, for example, is a visit by God to Muḥammad as he sits in the house of Fâṭima with al-Ḥusayn in his lap. Inexplicably, Muḥammad begins to weep, and in response to Fâṭima's puzzlement, says that he has, in that very hour, seen the Most High in a most beautiful form (*fî aḥsan ṣûra*).[61] God questions

---

[60] **KLY.**, vol. I, *Kitâb al-ḥuǧǧa*, bb. *mawlid al-Ḥusayn b. ʿAlî*, n. 4: 464, **QQM.**, bb. 16, n. 6: 123–124, **ṢDQ⁸.**, vol. I, bb. 156, n. 3: 205, **SHB.**, vol. IV, bb. *fî imâmat Abî ʿAbd Allâh al-Ḥusayn*: 62–63, **ABḎ.**: 562–563, **MǦL.**, vol. XXIII, bb. 15, n. 23: 272, vol. XXV, bb. 9, n. 15: 254, vol. XLIII, bb. 11, n. 20: 245, vol. XLIV, bb. 30, n. 17: 232.

[61] Only on rare occasions in the Old and New Testaments is God Himself said to appear in a dream (Gen. 20: 3, 28: 13, 1 Kgs. 3: 5): otherwise, He communicates through an angel. For a Sunnî discussion of Muḥammad seeing God in 'a most beautiful form' (*fî aḥsan ṣûra*) during his 'night journey', cf. **KṮR².**, vol. VI, *sûrat Ṣâd*, vv. 65–70: 84, *sûrat al-Naǧm*, vv. 5–18: 448–449, **SYṬ.**, vol. V, *sûrat Ṣâd*, vv. 67–70: 596–597, vol. VI, *sûrat al-Naǧm*, vv. 5–18: 159.

Muḥammad about his love for al-Ḥusayn. "He is the delight of my eye," replies Muḥammad, "my sweet basil, the fruit of my heart and the skin between my eyes." God then places His hand on al-Ḥusayn's head, saying that His blessings, prayers, mercy and favour are upon the boy, but announcing that he is the master of the martyrs from first to last.[62] In some of the accounts, Muḥammad is given red soil from Karbalâʾ, the place of al-Ḥusayn's death. In others, it is either Ǧibrîl or God who makes the announcement. Still others omit any reference to divine or angelic visitation, and articulate the announcement of death through a vision given to Muḥammad.[63]

A further exemplar of this category of narrative is found in the stories of angels, sometimes alone and sometimes in large numbers, often in curious shapes and forms, visiting Muḥammad in various places – frequently in the house of Umm Salama – to console him over al-Ḥusayn's future martyrdom. An example is recorded by Ibn Ṭâʾûs:

> The transmitter of the *ḥadîṯ* said: "A full year after the birth of al-Ḥusayn, twelve angels came down to the Messenger of God; one of them was in the form of a lion, the second in the form of a bull, the third in the form of a sea monster (dragon) and the fourth in the form of a child of Adam, and the remaining eight in various forms. Their faces were red, their eyes wet with tears, and having spread their wings they said: Muḥammad, what befell Hâbîl (Abel) through Qâbîl (Cain) will befall your child al-Ḥusayn, son of Fâṭima; he will receive the same recompense as Hâbîl, and his killers will bear the same

---

62 Cf. **QQM.**, bb. 21, n. 1: 140, n. 2: 70, **MĞL.**, vol. XLIV, bb. 30, n. 29: 238.

63 Among the Sunnî transmitters of this genre, cf. **TRM.**, vol. IX, bk. 50 (*Kitâb al-manâqib*), bb. *manâqib al-Ḥasan wa-l-Ḥusyan*, n. 3774: 333, **ḤNA.**, vol. III, Part 3, bk. 31 (*Kitâb maʿrifat al-ṣaḥâba*), bb. *awwal faḍâʾil Abî ʿAbd Allâh al Ḥusayn b. ʿAlî*, n. 4884: 210, n. 4888: 211–212, nn. 4890, 4892: 213, **RḤB.**: 146–147, **TIB.**, vol. III, bk. 30 (*Kitâb al-manâqib*), bb. 10 (*Manâqib ahl bayt al-nabî*), n. 6136: 1733, n. 6157: 1737–1738, **SQL⁴.**, vol. II: 347, **HAY.**, vol. IX, bb. *manâqib al-Ḥusayn*: 187–189, **SHL.**: 114.

> responsibility as Qâbîl. There was not in the heavens an angel 'drawn near'[64] who did not come down to the Prophet, each of them greeting him and consoling him about al-Ḥusayn. They informed him about the reward he would receive and showed him his tomb, and the Prophet said: God, forsake those who forsake him and kill those who kill him…"[65]

The symbolism of the angelic forms is resonant of the sort of apocryphal language used in the Old Testament Book of Daniel, as well as in some of the prophets like Isaiah and Ezekiel and in the New Testament Book of Revelation.[66]

The books of *aḥâdîṯ* abound with these stories, related with an assortment of details. The Sunnî transmitter al-Ḫawârizmî, for example, dedicates a whole chapter of his *Maqtal al-Ḥusayn* to relating them from various sources, while a number of his Sunnî colleagues, including Ibn Ḥanbal in his *Musnad*, al-Nîsâbûrî in his *Kitâb al-mustadrak ʿalâ al-ṣaḥîḥayn* and al-Ṭabarî in his *Ḏaḫâʾir al-ʿuqbâ*, relate the story in various settings, sometimes in an angelic visitation, sometimes in a vision, always containing the same strand of a tragic augury.[67]

---

[64] The 'angels drawn near' are named in the Qurʾân as the *muqarrabûn*. Cf. Q. 4: 172, where Pickthall renders the word as 'favoured'.

[65] **ṬSṬ⁶**.: 13–14, **MǦL**., vol. XLIV, bb. 30, n. 46: 246. Among the Sunnî, cf. **ḪWZ**., Part I, bb. *Aḫbâr rasûl Allâh ʿan al-Ḥusayn wa-aḥwâli-hi*, n. 12: 237.

[66] For example, the four heavenly creatures described by John in the Book of Revelation; the first like a lion, the second like an ox, the third with a face like a man and the fourth like an eagle (Rev. 4: 7). Ezekiel's four creatures all have the shape of a man, but each has four faces; of a man, of a lion, of an ox and of an eagle (Ez. 1: 5–11). Cf. also Muḥammad's vision during his 'night journey' of the four angels bearing the Throne (Q. 40: 7); the first in the form of a man, the second in the form of a bull, the third in the form of an eagle and the fourth in the form of a lion. Cf. **SYṬ**., vol. VI, *sûrat al-Naǧm*, vv. 5–18: 159.

[67] **ḤNB**., vol. I, *Musnad ʿAlî b. Abî Ṭâlib*, n. 648: 184–185; vol. IV, *Musnad Anas b. Mâlik*, n. 13539: 482, n. 13796: 527, **TRM**., vol. IX, bk. 50 (*Kitâb al-manâqib*), bb. *al-Ḥasan wa-l-Ḥusayn*, n. 3774:333, **ḤNA**., vol. III, bk. 31 (*Kitâb maʿrifat al-ṣaḥâba*), bb. *awwal faḍâʾil Abî ʿAbd Allâh al-Ḥusayn b.*

A final example of such accounts is expressed in the dreams of people. One of these dreams, that of Umm al-Faḍl, is recorded both by Sunnî and Shîʿî transmitters, and although it has ominous overtones, Muḥammad interprets it in a positive manner:

> On the authority of Umm al-Faḍl, daughter of al-Ḥâriṯ, that she went to the Messenger of God and said: "Messenger of God, tonight I had a shocking dream!" He replied: "What was it?" She said: "It was ominous!" He said: "What was it?" She answered: "I saw what seemed to be a piece of your body, which was cut off and placed in my lap." He said: "You saw something good. Fâṭima will give birth to a boy, and he will be in your lap." Fâṭima gave birth to al-Ḥusayn and Umm al-Faḍl said: "He was in my lap, just as the Messenger of God had said."[68]

Ultimately, the dream which Umm al-Faḍl thought so ominous, and which Muḥammad interprets so encouragingly, is portentous after all, for the same *ḥadîṯ* continues with a forewarning from Ǧibrîl and Muḥammad in tears. However, this is not finally the point of the report; primarily, as Ayoub notes, it serves to elucidate the close relationship between the Imâm and the Prophet.[69] A number of Sunnî scholars record a slightly different dream, this time of Ibn ʿAbbâs, in which he sees Muḥammad collecting al-

---

ʿAlî, n. 4890: 213, vol. IV, bk. 31 (*Kitâb maʿrifat al-ṣaḥâba*), *Ḏikr Umm Salama*, nn. 6843, 6844: 101, vol. IV, bk. 47 (*Taʿbîr al-ruʾyâ*), n. 8282: 553–554, **ḤWZ.**, Part I, bb. *Faḍâʾil Fâṭima al-Zahrâʾ bt. rasûl Allâh*, **ATH¹.**, vol. III: 169, **RḤB.**: 147–148, **SQL⁴.**, vol. II, bb. *al-ḥâʾ*: 347, **HAY.**, vol. IX, bb. *manâqib al-Ḥusayn*: 189–190, 193.

[68] **RṬB¹.**: 72, **MFD¹.**, vol. II: 129, **ṬBR¹.**: 218, **ṬSṬ⁶.**: 12–13, **IRB.**, vol. II: 7, **MǦL.**, vol. XLIV, bb. 30, n. 30: 238, n. 46: 246. Among the Sunnî, cf. **ḤNA.**, vol. III, Part 3, bk. 31 (*Kitâb maʿrifat al-ṣaḥâba*), bb. *awwal faḍâʾil Abî ʿAbd Allâh al-Ḥusayn b. ʿAlî*, n. 4884: 210, **TIB.**, vol. III, bk. 30 (*Kitâb al-manâqib*), bb. 10 (*Manâqib ahl bayt al-nabî*), n. 6171: 1741, **SHL.**: 114.

[69] AYOUB M., *Redemptive Suffering in Islam. A Study of the Devotional Aspects of ʿAshura in Twelver Shiʿism*, 1978: 74.

Ḥusayn's blood in a container,[70] as well as a similar dream by Umm Salama, in which she sees Muḥammad, weeping and with dust on his head, after he has been forewarned.[71] A handful of the Sunnî transmitters also carry accounts of such predictions of the killing of al-Ḥusayn, sometimes by Ǧibrîl, to his father ʿAlî.[72]

The Shîʿa scholar al-Maǧlisî, transmitting from al-Ṣadûq, records another ominous dream, of one Umm Ayman, so distressing that she is hardly able to relate it to Muḥammad. She dreams that some of his limbs are discarded in her home. Once more, an ill-omened dream is given a positive interpretation by Muḥammad; that Fâṭima is about to give birth to al-Ḥusayn (already named thus before his birth, although other Shîʿî texts clarify this as being by divine command),[73] and that Umm Ayman will assist in raising him

---

[70] **ḤNB.**, vol. I, *Musnad ʿAbd Allâh b. al-ʿAbbâs*, n. 2165: 521, n. 2553: 606, **ḤNA.**, vol. IV, bk. 47 (*Taʿbîr al-ruʾyâ*), n. 8281: 553, **BĠD.**, vol. I: 142, **BRR.**, vol. I: 395–396, **ATH¹.**, vol. II: 22, **RḤB.**: 148, **TIB.**, vol. III, bk. 30 (*Kitâb al-manâqib*), bb. 10, *Manâqib ahl bayt al-nabî*, n. 6172: 1741–1742, **SQL¹.**, vol. I, n. 1724: 331, **HAY.**, vol. IX, bb. *manâqib al-Ḥusayn*: 93–94.

[71] **TRM.**, vol. IX, bk. 50 (*Kitâb al-manâqib*), bb. *manâqib al-Ḥasan wa-l-Ḥusayn*, n. 3774: 333, **ḤNA.**, vol. IV, bk. 31 (*Kitâb maʿrifat al-ṣaḥâba*), *Ḏikr Umm Salama*, n. 6843: 101, **ATH².**, vol. II: 22, **RḤB.**: 148, **SQL⁴.**, vol. II, bb. *al-ḥâʾ*: 356. Among the Shîʿa, cf. for e.g. **SHB.**, vol. IV, bb. *fî imâmat Abî ʿAbd Allâh al-Ḥusayn*: 63.

[72] **SQL⁴.**, vol. II: 347, **HAY.**, vol. IX, bb. *manâqib al-Ḥusayn*: 187.

[73] A discussion of the naming of al-Ḥusayn falls outside of the contours of this work and would be a digression. Suffice it to say that there are two major strands among the transmitters; the first is that Muḥammad names him al-Ḥusayn at the command of God given through Ǧibrîl (cf. **ṢDQ¹.**: 134, **ṢDQ⁵.**, vol. II, bb. 31, n. 5: 25, **ṢDQ⁶.**, n. 6: 57, **ṢDQ⁸.**, vol. I, bb. 112, n. 7: 138; **FNR.**, vol. I: 153, **ṬBR¹.**: 205, 218, **SHB.**, vol. III, bb. *maʿâlî umûri-himâ*: 448, **MĞL.**, vol. XLIII, bb. 11, n. 3: 238, n. 4: 238–239, n. 8: 240–241, n. 10: 241, n. 26: 250–251, vol. XLIII, bb. 22, n. 3: 134, bb. 11, nn. 3–4: 238–239, n. 8: 240–241, n. 10: 241, n. 40: 257, vol. CI, bb. 4, n. 18: 110). The second strand, commonly carried by the Sunnî (although almost always without reference to an angelic visitation) has Muḥammad questioning ʿAlî about the name he has given to his son and, upon discovering that ʿAlî has named him 'Ḥarb', changes it to al-Ḥusayn (among

and caring for him. Thus, concludes Muḥammad positively, some of his limbs will indeed be found in the house of Umm Ayman. At al-Ḥusayn's birth, the text continues, Umm Ayman prepares the child and swaddles him in his father's garment;[74] for al-Ḥusayn, unlike Fâṭima, there are no heavenly midwives, no washing in the water of *al-Kawṯar* and no garments of Paradise in which he is enveloped.

---

the Shîʿa, cf. **ṢDQ**[5]., vol. II, bb. 31, n. 5: 25, **FNR**., vol. I: 153, **ṬBR**[1].: 218, **SHB**., vol. III, bb. *maʿâlî umûri-himâ*: 448, **MĞL**., vol. XXXIX: 62, vol. XLIII, bb. 11, n. 4: 238, n. 28: 251, n. 33: 254. Among the Sunnî, cf. for e.g. **ḤNB**., vol. I, *Musnad ʿAlî b. Abî Ṭâlib*, n. 569: 211–212, n. 953: 251). There are also a number of curious *aḥâdîṯ* found in the Shîʿî texts; one insists that al-Ḥusayn is given a derivative of his brother al-Ḥasan's name because he is 'better' than al-Ḥasan (cf. **RṬB**[1].: 20, **ṢDQ**[6]., n. 7: 57, **ṢDQ**[8]., vol. I, bb. 112, n. 10: 138, **SHB**., vol. III, bb. *maʿâlî umûri-himâ*: 448, **MĞL**., vol. LXIII, bb. 11, n. 12: 242, n. 28: 251). Another holds that al-Ḥusayn's name is 'cleft' from that of al-Ḥasan (cf. **MĞL**., vol. LXIII, bb. 11, n. 11: 241–242), although this contradicts a *ḥadîṯ* we have already examined in which God claims to have cleft for al-Ḥusayn a name from the divine names. A further strand, in which ʿAlî's relation to Muḥammad is compared with Hârûn's relation to Mûsâ, Ğibrîl commands that ʿAlî's two children be named after the children of Hârûn – Shabbar and Shabbîr. "My tongue is Arabic," complains Muḥammad, not understanding the names, and Ğibrîl translates them as al-Ḥasan and al-Ḥusayn. Cf. **QḤL**.: 705, **RṬB**[2].: 174, **ṢDQ**[1]., n. 3: 134, 191, 439, **ṢDQ**[5]., vol. II, bb. 31, n. 5: 25, **ṢDQ**[6]., n. 6: 57, **ṢDQ**[8]., vol. I, bb. 116, n. 6: 138, **FNR**., vol. I: 123, 153, **ṬBR**[1].: 160, 218, **SHB**., vol. III, bb. *maʿâlî umûri-himâ*: 448, **RWD**[1]., vol. I: 345, **ṬSṬ**[3].: 382, **MĞL**., vol. IX, bb. 2: 298, vol. XIII, bb. 11, n. 11: 331, vol. XXXVI, bb. 50, n. 4: 36, vol. XXXVII, bb. 50: 37, 92, vol. XXXVIII, bb. 63: 190, vol. XXXIX, bb. 72: 33, 62, vol. XLIII, bb. 11, n. 1: 237, nn. 3–4: 238, n. 10: 241, n. 29: 245, vol. XLIX, bb. 4: 77, vol. XCIX, bb. 8: 191, vol. CI, bb. 4, n. 18: 110, **NṬR**., vol. I, bb. 8, n. 7–1163: 461, vol. XV, bb. 32, n. 7–17805: 144. Al-Mağlisî carries yet another strand, in which ʿAlî names his sons Ḥamza (al-Ḥasan) and Ğaʿfar (al-Ḥusayn), but changes them at Muḥammad's order (**MĞL**., vol. LXIII, bb. 11, n. 28: 251, n. 33: 254–255.

[74] **ṢDQ**[1]., n. 1: 82, **FNR**., vol. I: 154, **MĞL**., vol. XLIII, bb. 11, n. 15: 242–243.

2.3.5. The Legend of Fuṭrus

In the midst of all these *aḥâdîṯ* of Fâṭima conceiving and giving birth to al-Ḥusayn, some transmitters insert an arcane report, worth examining for its novelty. It concerns a banished angel, by name of Fuṭrus,[75] who yearns to accompany Ğibrîl, *en route* to Muḥammad, and who has recourse to Muḥammad's intercessory powers to realize his desire:

> When al-Ḥusayn was born God ordered Ğibra'îl to descend with a crowd of angels to congratulate Muḥammad. He descended and passed an island on which was an angel called Fuṭrus. God had sent him to do something, but he had delayed, and God broke his wings and cast him on that island, where he had served God for seven hundred years. He said: Ğibra'îl, where are you going? He replied: To Muḥammad. Fuṭrus said: Carry me with you to Muḥammad; perhaps he would pray for me. When Ğibra'îl came to the Prophet and informed him of the situation of Fuṭrus, the Prophet said to him: Tell him to rub his wings against this child. Fuṭrus rubbed against the cradle of al-Ḥusayn, and at once God restored his wings. Then he ascended with Ğibra'îl to heaven and was named the liberated slave of al-Ḥusayn.[76]

---

[75] Al-Mağlisî carries one account of this same *ḥadîṯ* in which the angel is named Ṣalṣâ'îl (**MĞL.**, vol. XLIII, bb. 11, n. 47: 258–259). Al-Qazwînî in his *ʿAğâ'ib al-muḫlûqât* records a tradition on the authority of Ibn ʿAbbâs, in which the angels in the seven heavens are in a number of forms, including cattle, hawks, eagles, green birds, 'maidens of Paradise' and humans. The angels assigned to these groups include Ṣalṣâ'îl (fourth heaven, in charge of angels who are in form of a horse). The name Fuṭrus might be a corruption of Buṭrus (Peter).

[76] **RṬB¹**.: 79; **RṬB²**.: 219; **QQM**., bb. 20, n. 1: 140–141; **ṢDQ¹**., n. 8: 137; **FNR**., vol. I: 155; **RWD¹**., vol. I: 252; **SHB**., vol. IV, bb. *fî âyâti-hi baʿda wafâti-hi*: 63; **ṬSṬ³**.: 698; **ÂML**., vol. II, n. 5: 179 (not in the context of al-Ḥusayn's birth); **KFM¹**.: 543; **KFM²**.: 185; **MĞL**., vol. XXVI, bb. 8, n. 10: 340, vol. XLIII, bb. 11, n. 18: 243, n. 27: 250, vol. XLIV, bb. 25, n. 7: 182, L, bb. 3, n. 47: 66, vol. XCVIII, bb. 32, n. 9: 367; **NṬR**., vol. X, bb. 86, n. 14–12271: 410.

The story serves to underscore the miraculous power of the baby al-Ḥusayn, although he is very much the passive agent in this power, thus distinguishing him, for example, from the child Jesus of the Apocryphal Gospels, who performs miracles himself.

2.3.6. Angelic Activity Surrounding his Birth

A further strand in this genre of angelic activity, found in a particularly rare *ḥadîṯ*, recounts the orders given by God to the angels in heaven suitably to celebrate the birth of a child for Muḥammad:

> When al-Ḥusayn b. ʿAlî was born, his birth the late evening of Thursday or the night of Friday, God, powerful and lofty, inspired Mâlik,[77] keeper of the Fire, to subdue the fires for its people in honour of the child born to Muḥammad; and He inspired Riḍwân,[78] keeper of the Gardens, to adorn the Gardens and to perfume them in honour of a child born to Muḥammad on the earth. And God, may He be blessed and exalted, inspired the maidens of Paradise to dress up and to visit each other in honour of a child born to Muḥammad on the earth; and God, powerful and lofty, inspired the angels to perform in ranks the glorification of God (*al-tasbîḥ*), the praise of God (*al-taḥmîd*), the exaltation of God (*al-tamǧîd*) and the proclamation that God is the greatest (*al-takbîr*) in honour of a child born to Muḥammad on the earth…[79]

The whole cosmological effect of al-Ḥusayn's birth is articulated here; in the Christian reading of the birth of Jesus, the angels rejoice, but their glorification is entirely centered upon God, while

---

[77] Traditionally, the keeper of Hell, named in Q. 43: 77. Pickthall translates this as 'master', but by all accounts, it is a proper name. Cf. MURATA S., "The Angels" in S.H. Nasr (ed.), *Islamic Spirituality. Foundations*, vol. XIX of *World Spirituality: An Encyclopedic History of the Religious Quest*, The Crossroad Publishing Company, New York 1997: 325.

[78] The angel who looks after Paradise, possibly alluded to in Q. 9: 21 and 57: 20. Cf. MURATA S., "The Angels" in S.H. Nasr (ed.), *Islamic Spirituality. Foundations*, 1997: 325.

[79] **ṢDQ**[2]., vol. I, bb. 24, n. 36: 282, **MĞL**., vol. XLIII, bb. 11, n. 24: 248.

the cosmological effects of the Incarnation still lie in the future. Conversely, the birth of al-Ḥusayn has an immediate consequence for those in Heaven and Hell, a portent of his martyrdom, which the Shîʿa envisage as a 'cosmic' event, touching all of human history, of nature and of the universe. Ayoub offers a longer, more detailed transmission of this *ḥadîṯ* from Darbandî,[80] in which the mystical tree of Paradise, Ṭûbâ, is ordered freely to disperse its fruits of precious stones and life-giving, healing leaves (an image that resonates strongly with the life-giving and medicinal trees prophesied in Ez. 47: 12). The angels, youths (of whom al-Ḥasan and al-Ḥusayn will be declared the masters by Muḥammad) and maidens of Paradise are permitted to gather these in celebration.[81]

Numerous other accounts of angelic intervention are widely diffused throughout the books of *aḥâdîṯ*.[82] A final, and rare report is quoted by Ayoub,[83] who takes it from al-Baḥrânî, although it is also extant in al-Râwandî and al-Mağlisî. This *ḥadîṯ* is markedly different from all the others precisely in that in all the others, it is Muḥammad who receives the angelic announcements of the birth and forewarning of the death; he then passes this information on to Fâṭima (in itself a paradox, for at other moments of her life, such as in her grief at her father's death, angels do speak to her). In the *ḥadîṯ* that follows, it is Fâṭima who is the recipient of an angelic visitation, although no words are actually spoken to her by the angels, and it is for Muḥammad to interpret the meaning for her. "I see a light shining on your face," he says to his daughter, in a *leitmotif* of light we have examined at length, *à propos* her pre-existence, her purity and the future Imâms who spring from her, "you shall

---

[80] Mullâ Âkhund Darbandî, in his *Iksîr al-ʿibâdât fî asrâr al-shahâdât*, Dâr al-Ṭibâʿah, Tehran n.d.: 94ff.

[81] AYOUB M., *Redemptive Suffering in Islam. A Study of the Devotional Aspects of ʿAshura in Twelver Shiʿism*, 1978: 74.

[82] Cf. for e.g. **RṬB**[2].: 189, **ṢDQ**[2]., vol. I, bb. 24, n. 36: 282, **ṢDQ**[6]., n. 6: 57, **ṢDQ**[8]., vol. I, bb. 116, n. 7: 138, **ṬSṬ**[6].: 13, **MĞL**., vol. XLIII, bb. 11, n. 3: 238, n. 8: 240, n. 24: 248, vol. L, bb. 3, n. 43: 66.

[83] Cf. AYOUB M., *Redemptive Suffering in Islam. A Study of the Devotional Aspects of ʿAshura in Twelver Shiʿism*, 1978: 71–72.

give birth to a proof (*ḥuǧǧa*) of God over this creation." The following *ḥadîṯ* is narrated by Fâṭima herself:

> At the end of the first month of my pregnancy, I felt a fever in my womb, and told my father. He called for a pitcher of water, spoke over it, spat into it, and said: Drink! So, I drank it, and God banished what I was feeling. I reached the fortieth day and I felt a crawling on my back, like the crawling of ants between the skin and the garment, which did not cease until the completion of the second month, when I felt a restiveness and movement and, by God, the child had already started to move in my womb. I had no need for food and drink; God preserved me from them, as though I had drunk a largess of milk, until the completion of the third month, when I felt bounty and increase in my house. When I reached the fourth month, God caused him to keep me company in my loneliness; I stayed in the mosque, not leaving it except when I need to purify myself. I was increasing and nimble, exteriorly and interiorly, until I completed the fifth month. When I entered the six month, I did not need a lamp on the darkest night; and when I was by myself in my prayer niche, I could hear the glorification (*tasbîḥ*) and sanctification of God (*taqdîs*) in my womb. At the conclusion of nine days in the sixth month, I increased in strength but was lacking in joy, and I mentioned this to Umm Salama, and through her, God fortified my strength. At the completion of the tenth day of the sixth month I was sleeping, and there came to me in my sleep one who rubbed his wings against my back; I was alarmed, and arose, performed the ritual washing and prayed two prostrations. Then I slept again, and there came to me in my sleep one garbed in white, who sat at my head and blew in my face and on my neck. I arose, fearful, performed the ritual washing and prayed four prostrations. Then I slept again, and there came to me in my sleep one who made me sit up and made incantations over me and prayed God's protection over me. In the morning I awoke; it was the day of blessed Umm Salama. A dove entered (my) robes. I came to Umm Salama, and the Prophet looked at my face, and I saw

joy on his. All that I had experienced lifted from me and I recounted it to the Prophet. He said: Rejoice! As regards the first, he is my friend ʿIzrâʾîl,[84] guardian and opener of the wombs of women; as regards the second, he is my friend Mîkâʾîl,[85] guardian of the wombs of the people of my house. Did he blow on you? I said, yes! (Fâṭima then said): Then he held me to himself and said: Regarding the third, he is my brother Ǧibraʾîl, to whom God has given care of your child. I returned and delivered him at the completion of the sixth month."[86]

Once more we have before us a narrative that is so suffused with symbolic details that one might easily miss crucial elements; one of the more important here is that al-Ḥusayn praised God while still in his mother's womb.[87] This ties him to his mother, who ad-

---

[84] The angel of death and sometimes angel of the last trumpet. He is alluded to but unnamed in Q. 32: 11 and, by tradition, is so overcome by grief when he looks into Hell, that the earth risks being flooded by his tears. Cf. WENSINCK A.J., "Izrāʾīl" in H.A.R Gibb et al., (eds.), *SEI*, E.J. Brill, Leiden 1995: 190.

[85] The angel named in Q. 2: 98. By tradition, he has never laughed since the creation of Hell, and weeps for pity over sinners, imploring God's mercy for them. Cf. WENSINCK A.J., "Mīkāl" in *SEI*, H.A.R Gibb et al., (eds.), 1995: 378–379.

[86] **RWD**[1]., vol. II: 841, **MǦL**., vol. XLIII, bb. 12, n. 39: 272–273, **BAḤ**., vol. XII, bb. 69: 899, vol. XVI, bb. 6: 12.

[87] The element of al-Ḥusayn speaking in the womb ties him at once to a Qur'ânic theme (ʿÎsâ speaking as an infant) as well as to his mother Fâṭima, who spoke in the womb of Ḫadîǧa. Speaking while still in the womb is posited both of Fâṭima and of al-Ḥusayn but is not so clearly of ʿÎsâ. Q. 19: 24–26 contains a dialogue that bears some investigation. The verses read: «*Then (one) cried unto her from below her, saying: Grieve not! Thy Lord hath placed a rivulet beneath thee, And shake the trunk of the palm-tree toward thee, thou wilt cause ripe dates to fall upon thee, So eat and drink and be consoled. And if thou meetest any mortal, say: Lo! I have vowed a fast unto the Beneficent, and may not speak this day to any mortal*». This is Pickthall's interpretation of the verses: he adds the word 'one' in brackets, although not only is this not in the Arabic; but the Arabic (*fa-nâdâ-hâ*) in essence reads: «*Then he cried out to*

her…». This 'he' is hard to identify, and other English translations exhibit the difficulty of rendering the Arabic into English. «*But (a voice) cried unto her from beneath the (palm tree)…*» is Ali's attempt, although 'a voice' and 'palm tree' are not in the Arabic. Arberry tries «*But the one that was below her called to her…*» (the second 'her' in the Arabic could refer either to Maryam or to the palm tree, i.e. the call was from below Maryam or from below the palm tree); Palmer renders it «*he called to her from beneath her…*», which is a precise translation of the Arabic as it stands. Palmer adds a footnote that the 'he' refers either to the infant himself or to Gabriel. ʿAbd al-Haleem translates «*a voice cried to her from below…*» and Bell as «*Then he called to her from beneath her…*», adding a footnote that posits the 'he' is probably the child. If, as Palmer and Bell note, the voice could be the voice of the child, the question is whether he is speaking from the womb or from a place at the foot of the tree, where he lies, newly born. In their most literal reading, the context of the verses suggests from the womb, since they are describing the labour of Maryam. Conversely, many scholars regard the voice to be that of the infant newly-born, who will speak again as an infant a few verses later (Q. 19: 30), while others hold it to be the voice of Ǧibrîl, still guiding Maryam. The Muslim exegetes do not bring clarity; al-Ṭabarî quotes many *aḥâdîṯ* in which the 'he' is said to be Ǧibrîl (or another angel), but states also that it could be ʿÎsâ, presumably, after his birth, although the reports he quotes in this regard do not always make this clear (**YṬB**[1]., vol. XVI, *sûrat Maryam*, v. 24: 67–70). Al-Zamaḫsharî suggests Ǧibrîl (in the role of midwife), acknowledging that some hold it to be ʿÎsâ (**ZMR**., vol. III, *sûrat Maryam*, v. 24: 9–10). Al-Qurṭubî and Ibn Kaṯîr both quote Ibn ʿAbbâs, saying that the speaker was Ǧibrîl, since ʿÎsâ did not speak until Maryam took him to her people; but they also quote *aḥâdîṯ* holding the speaker to be ʿÎsâ (**QRṬ**., vol. XI, *sûrat Maryam*, v. 24: 93–94, **KṮR**[2]., vol. IV, *sûrat Maryam*, v. 24: 449–450). The Shîʿî exegete al-Baḥrânî maintains that it was ʿÎsâ (**BḤR**., vol. III, *sûrat Maryam*, v. 24: 8). In the final analysis, whether it was from the womb, immediately after his birth or a little after that from the cradle, ʿÎsâ spoke in a miraculous fashion. In his exegesis, al-Râzî examines the grammar of the sentence, explaining that the *min* (designating the direction from which the voice came) could also be read as *man* (designating the presence of a speaker), although the former is the more widespread reading. He offers the same three possibilities as the other exegetes; it could be ʿÎsâ, it could be Ǧibrîl (whom al-Râzî designates as a sort of 'midwife'), or it could be dressed words to her mother whilst still a fetus, as well as to the Christian reading of John the Baptist's gestation, during which he recognized the presence of Jesus (in the womb of Mary) and leapt for joy in his mother's womb[88] with a precocious spiritual awareness that in this *ḥadîṯ* is predicated of al-Ḥusayn. The mention of the dove in the text is somewhat problematic; neither al-Râwandî nor al-Mağlisî are clear in their transmission concerning whose robe it was the dove entered (*fa-daḫalat fî ṯawbi ḥamâmat*). It may be, as al-Baḥrânî suggests, a mistake, and ought to read *ṯawbî* ('my robe'). Ayoub clarifies that the dove entered the robe of Fâṭima while she was at the house of Umm Salama.[89]

This is al-Ḥusayn, born, already cleaned and purified by God,[90] of the virgin Fâṭima and touched, as a newborn child, by the wings of Ğibrîl.[91] Her immeasurable grief begins already in her pregnancy, goaded by the knowledge that her son will be murdered. In his conception and birth al-Ḥusayn brings distress and heartbreak, a reality encapsulated in a peculiar story, transmitted by the Sunnî historian al-Baġdâdî and by a few of the later Shîʿî transmitters:

> It was related in his chains on the authority of Abû al-ʿAbbâs who said: "I was with the Prophet; on his left thigh he had his son Ibrâhîm and on his right thigh al-Ḥusayn b. ʿAlî. He was kissing, now the one, now the other, when Ğibrîl descended to him with revelation from the Lord of the worlds. When he had gone from him, he said: Ğibrîl came to me from my Lord and

---

the angel (if read as *min*) or ʿÎsâ (if read as *man*) (**RAZ**., vol. XXI, *sûrat Maryam*, v. 24: 204–206). None of the exegetes appear to support the idea that, if it is ʿÎsâ speaking, he is doing so from the womb. Nevertheless, he does speak as an infant, possibly here, and most certainly a few verses on (Q. 19: 30), and this must be regarded as miraculous.

[88] Lk. 1: 41, 44.

[89] Cf. AYOUB M., *Redemptive Suffering in Islam. A Study of the Devotional Aspects of ʿAshura in Twelver Shiʿism*, 1978: 72.

[90] *Allâhu qad naẓẓafa-hu wa-ṭahhara-hu*. **ṢDQ**[1]., n. 5: 136, **FNR**., vol. I: 155, **MĞL**., vol. XLIII, bb. 11, n. 16: 243, n. 24: 256.

[91] **MĞL**., vol. XLIII, bb. 11, n. 27: 250.

> said: Muḥammad, your Lord greets you with peace, and says to you that you cannot have both of them. Ransom one of them for his companion. The Prophet looked at Ibrâhîm and wept and looked at al-Ḥusayn and wept. Then he said: the mother of Ibrâhîm is a slave, and when he dies, no one will grieve for him except me. But the mother of al-Ḥusayn is Fâṭima and his father is ʿAlî, son of my uncle, my flesh and blood, and when he dies my daughter will grieve, and so will ʿAlî and so will I. I prefer my grief to theirs. Ǧibrîl, take Ibrâhîm: and he ransomed (al-Ḥusayn) with Ibrâhîm. He said: he died after three days, and whenever the Prophet saw al-Ḥusayn coming, he kissed him, and hugged to him to his chest, and sucked his teeth and said: I have ransomed the one I have ransomed with my son Ibrâhîm."[92]

Fâṭima will grieve for him throughout her life, and persist in her sorrow after death, where her tears, on the Day of Resurrection, become an anguished plea that God should punish her son's murderers and all who in any way injure the 'people of the house'. It is to this sorrow and these tears, so characteristic of the piety of Shîʿî Islam, that we must now turn.

---

[92] Among the Sunnî, cf. **BĠD.**, vol. II, n. 635: 254. Among the Shîʿa, cf. **SHB.**, vol. IV, bb. *fî al-mufradât min manâqibi-hi*: 88–89, **ṬSṬ²**., vol. I, n. 289: 202, **ḤLL¹**.: 256, **ḤLL²**., 321, **AḤS.**, vol. IV, n. 127: 92, **MĞL.**, vol. XXII, bb. 1, n. 5: 153, vol. XLIII, bb. 12, n. 2: 261.

Chapter Three.
Part One: The Motif of Grief and Suffering in the Life of Fâṭima Among the 'People of the House'

Having examined the miracles surrounding the birth of Fâṭima and of her son al-Ḥusayn, this chapter moves to consider a third key aspect of her life; that of grief and mourning. It offers as a context the themes of weakness, suffering and tears, not only prominent in Shîʿî piety, but also intrinsic to their theology of the Imamate, and then appraises some of the texts which underscore the sorrow of Fâṭima on earth, and her unremitting weeping until the Day of Resurrection.

3.1. On the Grief of the Shîʿa

Throughout the Shîʿî corpus, and particular in texts like *Shayḫ* al-Ṣadûq's *Ṣifât al-shîʿa* and *Faḍâʾil al-shîʿa*, the Shîʿa are singled out by and portrayed in terms of precise characteristics and marks, all of which indicate a life that is grim and sorrowful. Their faces are wane and pale from prolonged vigils of prayer at night; their stomachs are empty as a result of fasting and the remembrance of God; their mouths are dry from unremitting prayer. They are a people covered with the dust of the submissive, emaciated, slender and wasted; their backs bent from standing in prayer, their faces ashen and their eyes unfocused from their fear of God and from incessant weeping. Worship has disquieted their faces, long nights of prayer have worn them down and the heat of the midday sun has taken its toll on their bodies.[1] They grieve, while all around them people are happy:

> Their eyes are tear-filled, many their tears, many their prayers, many their supplications. They recite the Book of God, and when people are happy, they are grieving.[2]

The whole fabric of Shîʿî piety is coloured by an intense and harrowing grief and lamentation, open and unabashed, for "God loves every grieving heart."[3] It is a sorrow compounded by a number of factors; the usurpation of their power at the very beginning, the unwavering refusal to accord ʿAlî and the Imâms their rightful place, the ill-treatment of Fâṭima and the members of her family, and the persecution of those faithful to the *ahl al-bayt* as a constant through Islamic history. Notwithstanding all of these factors, the grief of the Shîʿa finds its culmination and summit in the death of al-Ḥusayn on the field of Karbalâʾ – the very name means 'land of sorrow and calamity' – and it is the Karbalâʾ event by which the

---

[1] **KLY**., vol. II, Book 5 (*Kitâb al-îmân wa-l-kufr*), bb. *al-muʾmin wa ʿalâmâti-hi*, nn. 7, 10: 233, **ṢDQ⁴**., vol. II, n. 40: 444, **ṢDQ⁹**., bb. 18: 279, bb. 19: 280, bb. 20: 282, bb. 24: 286, bb. 33: 292–293, bb. 40: 310, **ṢDQ¹⁰**., bb. 20: 417, **MFD¹**., vol. I: 237, **ṬFA²**., bb. 8, n. 27–377: 216, bb. 23, n. 3–1189: 576, **FNR**., vol. II: 294, **SHB**., vol. II, bb. *al-musâbaqa bi-l-yaqîn wa-l-ṣabr*: 138, **ḤDI**., vol. V: 120, vol. VII, bb. 120: 291, **ṬSṬ¹**., bb. 9, n. 156: 66, **IRB**., vol. I: 100, **KFM²**.: 333, **DAY**., vol. I: 107, 144, **ḤRR¹**., vol. I, bb. 20, n. 203: 86, n. 205: 87, n. 214: 90, n. 218: 96, vol. II, bb. 11, n. 7700: 191, vol. V, bb. 5, n. 8997: 157, vol. XV, bb. 4, n. 20242: 189, **MĞL**., vol. XXVII, bb. 4, n. 155: 144, vol. XXXIII, bb. 23, n. 597: 362, vol. XLI, bb. 99, n. 4: 4, vol. LIII: 222, vol. LXIV, bb. 12: 248, vol. LXV, bb. 19, n. 2: 149, nn. 4–5: 150–151, n. 30: 169, n. 32: 176, n. 34: 177, n. 40: 186, n. 43: 188, vol. LXVI, bb. 37, n. 30: 308, vol. LXXIV, bb. 15, n. 30: 404, vol. LXXV, bb. 15, n. 91: 26, vol. XCII, bb. 129, n. 27: 379, 381.

[2] **ṢDQ⁴**., vol. II, n. 40: 444, **ṢDQ⁹**., bb. 19: 281, bb. 40: 310, **FNR**., vol. II: 294, **MĞL**., vol. LXV, bb. 19, n. 30: 169.

[3] **KLY**., vol. II, Book 5 (*Kitâb al-îmân wa-l-kufr*), bb. *al-shukr*, n. 30: 99, **ḤDI**., vol. II: 193, **DAY**., vol. I: 154, **ḤRR¹**., vol. VII, bb. 29, n. 8771: 76, vol. XVI, bb. 8, n. 21626: 310, **MĞL**., vol. LXVIII, bb. 61, n. 25: 38, vol. LXX, bb. 125, n. 3: 157.

grief is articulated and finds physical interpretation. All the suffering and grief of the *ahl al-bayt* converges in the solitary figure of al-Ḥusayn, and all subsequent pain and sorrow is nothing more than a way of participating in his own grief. This shared, communal grief is not solely an internal sadness, but is expressed in rites and ritual actions by which the Karbalâʾ event is revisited and made present. Karbalâʾ is an event that slips beyond the sentries of time and space, giving it a timelessness that allows Shîʿî communities to gauge themselves against the example of al-Ḥusayn in the fight against any injustice.[4] Concurrently, these rites are a physical manifestation which incorporate a far more comprehensive grief.

The suffering of al-Ḥusayn, writes Ayoub, "has been taken by the Shīʿa community to be a source of salvation through the interiorization and emulation of that suffering by the community..."[5]

A chief ingredient of this process of assimilation and imitation, according to the corpus of Shîʿî *aḥâdît*, is weeping for his sufferings. This is a lament

> ...more concentrated and more extreme than any to be found elsewhere. No faith has ever laid greater emphasis on lament.

---

[4] Most particularly, participating each year (during the first ten days of the sacred month of Muḥarram and culminating on the tenth day, ʿÂshûrâ), in the rites and rituals that commemorate al-Ḥusayn's martyrdom is motivated by the belief that such an activity will serve as succour to salvation on the Last Day. Al-Ḥusayn represents atonement, and his redemptive martyrdom gives the possibility of salvation to all. The community expresses this notion of the vicarious suffering of the innocent al-Ḥusayn (and all the *ahl al-bayt*) through the ceremonies of mourning. The foundation of the argument is that al-Ḥusayn and the other Imâms sacrificed themselves for the Shîʿî community, for Islam and for all of mankind. Such sacrificial deaths have redemptive powers, which are rendered efficacious when the believers themselves take an active part in the suffering. Their suffering (particularly the grief that they express in varied ways and often in self inflicted pain) becomes, in a sort of anamnesis, the suffering of Karbalâʾ, for and with al-Ḥusayn.

[5] AYOUB M., *Redemptive Suffering in Islam. A Study of the Devotional Aspects of ʿAshura in Twelver Shiʿism*, 1978: 15.

> It is the highest religious duty, and many times more meritorious than any other good work.[6]

The high reward for this weeping, the salvific or redemptive[7] quality in the chagrin of their devotees, is a recurrent theme running through all the pertinent *aḥâdîṯ*. This is expressed, for example, in a narrative coming from the sixth Imâm Ǧaʿfar al-Ṣâdiq:

> On the authority of ʿÎsâ b. Abî Manṣûr, who said: "I heard Abû ʿAbd Allâh[8] saying that the sighs of the sorrowful for us, distress for the wrong done us, is glorification of God, his sorrow for our affair is worship, and his concealment of our secret is a striving in the path of God." Muḥammad b. Saʿîd said to me: "Write this in gold! You won't write anything better than it!"[9]

---

[6] CHELKOWSKI P., "ʿAshura" in J Esposito (ed.), *The Oxford Encyclopedia of the Modern Islamic World*, Oxford University Press, Oxford 1995, vol. I: 141–142.

[7] Ayoub insists that there is no doctrine of redemption in Islam *per se*, although redemption plays a forceful role in the life of the community. At the same time, he does admit that, while the theologically loaded Christian concept of 'redemption' remains Christian, and the Shîʿî one remains Shîʿî, there are common elements. In order to avoid confusion with the technical Christian conception, I have followed Ayoub's definition of redemption as 'fulfillment through suffering' or 'the healing of existence'. In these terms, he sees redemption as a vital force through the acceptance and understanding of suffering. Nor would he be alone in suggesting that all suffering can be redemptive. Perhaps the crucial point is that those who share, through weeping and in various ways, in the suffering of the *ahl al-bayt* will benefit by their intercessory prerogatives. Cf. AYOUB M., *Redemptive Suffering in Islam. A Study of the Devotional Aspects of ʿAshura in Twelver Shiʿism*, 1978: 15.

[8] The sixth Imâm.

[9] **RṬB**[2].: 105, 257, **KLY**., vol. II, Book 5 (*Kitâb al-îmân wa-l-kufr*), bb. *al-kitmân*, n. 16: 226, **ṢDQ**[1]., bb. 4, n. 32–178: 115, **MFD**[5]., n. 3: 338; **ḤRR**[1]., vol. XVI, bb. 34, n. 21485: 249, **MǦL**., vol. II, bb. 13, n. 1: 64, bb. 19, n. 16: 147, vol. XLIV, bb. 34, n. 4: 278, vol. LXXII, bb. 45, n. 33: 83.

Al-Ḥusayn himself, third Imâm and 'chief of martyrs', articulates this phenomenon: "I am the martyr of tears," he proclaims, "and no believer will remember me except that he will weep."[10] For those who do remember and weep, is held out the promise of Paradise:

> On the authority of al-Ḥusayn b. ʿAlî, who said: "There is no servant whose eyes flow with tears for our sake, and whose eyes are wet with frequent weeping for our sake, except that by them, God will bring him to Paradise for an age."[11]

A comparable *ḥadîṯ* comes from ʿAlî b. al-Ḥusayn, the fourth Imâm and son of al-Ḥusayn, who survived Karbalâʾ only because he was too ill to fight. He was to become a model for all who would have fought with al-Ḥusayn had they been able[12] and a paragon of weeping and lament – the *aḥâdîṯ* tell us that he wept for between twenty and forty years, and never was food placed before him but the tears flowed.[13] More than anyone, it was the fourth Imâm who set the

---

[10] **QQM.**, bb. 36, nn. 3, 6: 215–216, **ṢDQ[1].**, n. 7: 137, **FNR.**, vol. I: 170, **SHB.**, vol. IV, bb. *fî maqtali-hi*: 95, **MĞL.**, vol. XLIV, bb. 34, n. 5: 279, n. 19: 284, vol. XCVIII, bb. 30, n. 1: 355; **NṬR.**, vol. X, bb. 49, n. 1–12072: 311.

[11] **RṬB[2].**: 62, **MFD[5].**, n. 2: 340, **ṬFA[2].**, bb. 4, n. 35–181: 116, **ḤRR[1].**, vol. XIV, bb. 66, n. 19704: 507, **MĞL.**, vol. XLIV, bb. 34, n. 8: 279.

[12] ʿAlî b. al-Ḥusayn was too ill to take part in the fighting and was thus among the survivors captured after the battle. While some reports would offer us a picture of the youngster having to be restrained from staggering sickly onto the battlefield to fight with his father, his non-participation is a more important model for the contemporary community. Given the opportunity, the boy would have fought. Thus do the members of the faithful community participate in the sufferings of al-Ḥusayn, believing that they too would have fought alongside him had the opportunity been given them.

[13] **QQM.**, bb. 35, n. 1: 213, **ṢDQ[1].**, n. 5: 140, **ṢDQ[4].**, vol. I, n. 15: 272, vol. II, n. 4: 517, **FNR.**, vol. I: 170, vol. II: 450, **ṬBR[3].**: 315, **SHB.**, vol. IV, bb. *fî karami-hi wa-ṣabri-hi*: 179, **IRB.**, vol. I: 498, **ḤRR[1].**, vol. III, bb. 87, n. 3655: 280, vol. XI, bb. 51, n. 15489: 542, **MĞL.**, vol. XII, bb. 9,

tone of grief and encouraged weeping as a form of participation in Karbalâ' for all the adherents of the *ahl al-bayt*. For every believer who weeps copiously for the sufferings of the *ahl al-bayt*, ʿAlî b. al-Ḥusayn pledged a dwelling place for countless ages in the mansions of Paradise, while for those who suffer injury for the sake of the *ahl al-bayt* and weep for it, he promised that God will remove all their pain and protect them from His wrath and from the Fire.[14]

3.1.1. The Weeping of the Prophets

This *leitmotif* of grief and lament does not start on the day of Karbalâ', nor is it exclusively a result of its aftermath; it resonates deeply in the *aḥâdîṯ* and pious stories of the prophets, each of whom shared in the anguish of the *ahl al-bayt* by weeping in anticipation over al-Ḥusayn long before the Karbalâ' event. When Adam was given the names of the 'holy five' by which to pray, he was overwhelmed with anguish at the fifth name, that of al-Ḥusayn, and in his tears, turned to Ǧibrîl for an explanation:

> He said: "My brother Ǧibra'îl, in the remembrance of the fifth my heart is broken and my tears flow." Ǧibra'îl said: "This son of yours will be stricken by a calamity besides which all calamities will pale." Adam said: "My brother, what is it?" He replied: "He will be killed thirsty, a stranger and as one all alone, with no helper..." Adam and Ǧibra'îl wept tears, as a mother bereaved of her child.[15]

All the prophets who succeed Adam share in these tears; Nûḥ, whose very name means 'to lament', weeps over one of the nails brought him by Ǧibrîl for the construction of the ark, for unlike the other nails, it causes him gloom and anguish.[16] Ibrâhîm is in-

---

n. 27: 264, vol. XLIII, bb. 7, n. 1: 155, vol. XLVI, bb. 5, n. 19: 61, bb. 6, nn. 1–3: 108–109, vol. LXXI, bb. 16, n. 33: 86, **NṬR.**, vol. II, bb. 74, n. 18–6479: 465.

[14] Cf. **QQM.**, bb. 32, n. 1: 201, **ṬSṬ**[6].: 9, **ḤRR**[1]., vol. XIV, bb. 66, n. 19692: 501, **MǦL.**, vol. XLIV, bb. 34, n. 13: 281, n. 21: 285.

[15] **MǦL.**, vol. XLIV, bb. 30, n. 44: 245.

[16] Cf. **MǦL.**, vol. XI, bb. 3, n. 49: 328, vol. XXVI, bb. 7, n. 14: 332, vol. XLIV, bb. 30, n. 12: 230.

formed of the impending tragedy and weeps, while his son Ismâʿîl is informed of it by his sheep, who refuse to graze at Karbalâʾ. ʿÎsâ learns of it from a group of gazelles sitting in lamentation near the place of al-Ḥusayn's death.[17] Zakariyyâʾ, father of Yaḥyâ, is taught the five names and laments over the fifth.

The lament is not restricted to human beings. The Shîʿa regard the death of al-Ḥusayn as a 'cosmic' event, touching all of human history, of nature and of the universe. The entire history (and even pre-history) of the world revolves around the divinely preordained Karbalâʾ event. It was with the Imâms that the primordial history of creation began, and with them it will be judged and consummated. In the interim, all of humankind and the whole of creation participate in the lament over al-Ḥusayn's death. The Shîʿa insist that all creation, the sky, the earth, the angels, the *ǧinn*, the birds and all beasts weep and grieve over al-Ḥusayn.

3.1.2. The Weeping of the Angels and the *Ǧinn*

The angels, as noted, played a significant role in the annunciation and birth of al-Ḥusayn, as well as in the harrowing predictions of his death. Now, they join their lament to the tears of the Shîʿa, standing watch in tears over his tomb until the Day of Resurrection, as articulated in a widely-diffused *ḥadîṯ*:

> Abû ʿAbd Allâh[18] said that forty thousand angels descended, wanting to fight with al-Ḥusayn b. ʿAlî, but they were not permitted to fight, and when they returned to seek permission and descended again, al-Ḥusayn had been killed. Now, at his tomb, dishevelled and in dust, they weep until the Day of Resurrection, and their leader is an angel said to be al-Manṣûr.[19]

---

[17] **ṢDQ¹**., n. 5: 597, **ṢDQ²**., vol. II, bb. 47: 531, bb. 48: 532, **RWD¹**., vol. III: 1143, **MǦL**., vol. XIV, bb. 18, n. 56: 258, vol. XVII, bb. 6: 257, vol. XLIV, bb. 31, n. 2: 252, vol. LII, bb. 25: 201.

[18] The sixth Imâm.

[19] **RṬB¹**.: 71, 243, **KLY**., vol. IV, Book 15 (*Kitâb al-ḥaǧǧ*), bb. *al-nawâdir*, nn. 6–8: 587–589, **NUM**., bb. 19, nn. 4–5: 309–310, **QQM**., bb. 27, n. 2: 171–172, bb. 77, n. 1: 349–350, **ṢDQ¹**., n. 5: 129, n. 7: 238, **ṢDQ²**., vol. II, bb. 58, n. 22: 671, **ṢDQ³**., vol. II, n. 3203, **ṢDQ⁵**., vol. I,

Like ʿAlî b. al-Ḥusayn, the angels were prevented from fighting alongside al-Ḥusayn, so that, like ʿAlî b. al-Ḥusayn, their ensuing participation in his suffering is expressed in their lament and tears. Those who surrounded the dead al-Ḥusayn wept with extreme anguish, while others supplicated God in heaven for him.[20]

The *ğinn* too mourn with disturbing songs and poems:

> The *ğinn* wept for al-Ḥusayn b. ʿAlî, saying: "What will you say when the Prophet says to you, What have you done, you, the last of the generations, to the people of my house, my brothers, my noble traits? From between my ascending and my killing, you were stained with blood."[21]

In his *Kâmil al-ziyârât*, al-Qummî dedicates a complete chapter to the lament of the *ğinn* for al-Ḥusayn.[22] These consist of concise, pithy verses, always put by al-Qummî in the mouth of the *ğinn*, a number of which are transmitted on the authority of Umm Salama.[23] Al-Qummî remarks in a footnote that these *aḥâdîṯ* are to be

---

bb. 28, n. 58: 299, **ṬFA¹**., vol. VI, n. 21: 116, **ṬSṬ³**.: 544, **KFM¹**.: 490, **KFM²**.: 275, **ḤRR¹**., vol. XIV, bb. 37, 19476: 409, n. 19501: 420, n. 19505: 421, n. 19523: 427, bb. 45, n. 19586: 453, **MĞL**., vol. XLIV, bb. 34, n. 23: 275, vol. XLV, bb. 41, n. 2: 220, n. 8: 222, nn. 10–15: 222–223, n. 21: 226, vol. LVI, bb. 27, n. 30: 325, n. 38: 328, vol. XCVIII, bb. 1, n. 29: 7, bb. 5, n. 60: 40, bb. 9, n. 16: 55, bb. 14, n. 9: 102, **NṬR**., vol. X, bb. 26, n. 23–11933: 242, n. 29–11939: 245, n. 3–11963: 257, n. 3–12155: 349.

20 **QQM**., bb. 28, n. 23: 187, **SHB**., vol. IV, bb. *fî âyâti-hi baʿda wafâti-hi*: 70, **MĞL**., vol. XLV, bb. 41, n. 19: 226.

21 **QQM**., bb. 29, n. 6: 193, **MĞL**., vol. XLV, bb. 43: 237. It should be noted that this verse, generally believed to have been recited after Karbalâʾ, is more usually put into the mouth of a human reciter, Zaynab bt. ʿAqîl. Cf. for e.g. **BLḎ¹**., vol. III: 4120, **HAY**., vol. IX, bb. 95 (*Manâqib al-Ḥusayn*), n. 15183: –234235.

22 **QQM**., bb. 28, n. 23: 187, bb. 29, nn. 1–10: 189–197.

23 "I heard the *ğinn* lamenting over al-Ḥusayn," Umm Salama is reported to have said, and, in another version: "Since the death of the Prophet, I never heard the lament of the *ğinn* except at night…" What did Umm Salama hear on the night air? It is not unreasonable to imagine that she heard what a number of others reported having heard; unidentified

found in other works – specifically, *Shayḫ* al-Ṣadûq in his *Kitâb al-amâlî fî al-aḥâdîṯ wa-l-aḫbâr*, Ibn Shaḥrâshûb in his *Manâqib âl Abî Ṭâlib* and al-Mağlisî in his *Biḥâr al-anwâr*. While this is essentially true, these transmitters do not always put these laments in the mouth of the *ğinn*. Many of these same transmitters narrate identical verses, but this time put into the mouths of humans – on occasion Zaynab bt. ʿAqîl, or Zaynab bt. ʿAlî, or her nephew ʿAlî b. al-Ḥusayn or an unnamed poet or spokesperson.[24] Al-Qummî notes further that these *aḥâdîṯ* are also to be found in some of the Sunnî authors, such as Ibn ʿAsâkir[25] and al-Hayṯamî.[26] The Shîʿî author of *The Revolution of al-Husayn. Its Impact on the Consciousness of Muslim Society* is critical of these verses placed into the mouths of the *ğinn*, suggesting that they are in fact written by individuals who wanted to be part of al-Ḥusayn's 'revolution', but preferred to remain anonymous for fear of the authorities.[27] However, this is not finally

---

voices crying out in lament in the night. Cf. for e.g. **AKR**., vol. XIV, bb. 1566: 242 for a *ḥadîṯ* in which similar lamentation poetry is put into the mouth of "a caller who cried out at night." Cf. also **MFD⁵**., n. 7: 350, **ṬBR²**., vol. II: 305, **ṬFA²**., bb. 3, n. 50–131: 91, **SHB**., vol. IV, bb. *fî âyâti-hi baʿda wafâti-hi*: 69–70, **MĞL**., vol. XLIV, bb. 37: 378, vol. XLV, bb. 39: 147, bb. 43: 236–237, bb. 44: 276 for similar accounts of unidentified speakers.

[24] Cf. for e.g. **MFD¹**., vol. II, bb. *fî wuṣûl ḫabar istishhâd al-Imâm al-Ḥusayn*: 124, **FNR**., vol. I: 193, **ḤWZ**., Part 2, bb. *fî maqtal al-Ḥusayn*: 71, 84, **AKR**., vol. LXIX, bb. 9353 (*Zaynab al-Kubrâ bt. ʿAlî b. Abî Ṭâlib b. ʿAbd al-Muṭṭalib b. Hâshim b. ʿAbd al-Manâf*): 178, **ṬBR²**., vol. II: 305, **SHB**., vol. IV, bb. *fî maqtali-hi*: 115, **ṬSṬ⁶**.: 99, **NAM**., Part 2: 95, **IRB**., *Kashf al-ġumma fî maʿrifat al-aʾimma*, vol. II: 68, **KṮR¹**., *al-Bidâya wa-l-nihâya*, vol. XI: 567, **SQL⁴**., vol II, (*Ḥusayn b. ʿAlî b. Abî Ṭâlib*): 353, **MĞL**., vol. XLV, bb. 39: 123, 136, 164, **SHL**., 202.

[25] **AKR**., vol. XIV, bb. 1566: 240–242, mostly on the authority of Umm Salama.

[26] **HAY**., vol. IX: 199, narrating the experience of Umm Salama as well as of Maymûna.

[27] "In the literature of lamentation for al-Ḥusayn, there has arisen an element known as the poetry of the Jinn in lamentation for al-Ḥusayn…it seems to us that most of this poetry is by unknown human poets who

the point: these *aḥâdîṯ* aim at clarifying the death of al-Ḥusayn as a cosmic event, impinging upon every creature, and even inanimate creation, so that every creature, without exception, participates in a universal lament.

3.1.3. The Weeping of the Heavens and the Earth

The universal lament is encapsulated by *aḥâdîṯ* that tell of the weeping of the heavens and the earth.[28] This weeping is predicted by ʿAlî b. Abî Ṭâlib, upon the foundation of Q. 44: 29:

> I heard the Commander of the Faithful speaking in a public square, and he recited this verse: "*And the heaven and the earth wept not for them, nor were they reprieved*". Then al-Ḥusayn came out to him from one of the doors of the mosque, and he said: "Truly, this one will be killed, and the heaven and the earth will weep over him."[29]

The Qur'ânic citation serves to prove the capacity of the heavens and the earth to weep. In the context of this particular verse, they refuse to weep for the recalcitrant Egyptians; but for the righteous

---

wanted to spread propaganda on behalf of the revolution and who wanted to take part in one of the cherished acts of piety without endangering themselves and exposing themselves to the punishment of the authorities. Therefore they composed these verses and attributed them to the Jinn. Perhaps some of this poetry was the work of the women who used to devote themselves to exclamations of grief at the women's rites of remembrance for al-Ḥusayn; they might have wanted to create wonder and amazement by attributing their exclamations of grief to creatures who were not human." Cf. HOWARD I.K.A., (trans.), *The Revolution of al-Husayn. Its Impact on the Consciousness of Muslim Society*, The Muhammadi Trust, London 1985: 88.

[28] **KLY.**, vol. IV, Book 15 (*Kitâb al-ḥaǧǧ*), bb. *ziyârat qabr Abî ʿAbd Allâh al-Ḥusayn*, n. 2: 575–576, **ṢDQ¹.**, n. 5: 219, **ṢDQ⁵.**, vol. I, bb. 28, n. 58: 299, **BṬQ.**, nn. 835–836: 405, **ṬSṬ².**, vol. I, n. 293: 203, **ṬSṬ³.**: 544, **ḤLL¹.**: 257, **KFM¹.**: 741, **MǦL.**, vol. XLIV, bb. 34, n. 23: 285, vol. XCVIII, bb. 1, n. 22: 5.

[29] **QMM.**, bb. 28, n. 1: 179–180, n. 21: 186, **MǦL.**, vol. XIV, bb. 15, n. 6: 167, vol. XLV, bb. 40, n. 1: 201, nn. 15–16: 209, n. 29: 212.

martyr al-Ḥusayn, the report of their weeping serves to incorporate all of creation.

This cosmic grief is described in eschatological language; the skies, which last wept at the murder of Yaḥyâ,[30] wept for forty days[31] at the death of al-Ḥusayn, raining down blood or red dust,[32] turning the sky and earth to red,[33] while the sun rose and set red, like a clot of blood.[34]

---

[30] A number of Shîʿî *aḥâdîṯ* insist that the heavens and the earth have only ever wept for two people: for Yaḥyâ, son of Zakariyyâʾ, when he was murdered, and for al-Ḥusayn at Karbalâʾ. Cf. **QMM.**, bb. 28, n. 4: 181, n. 6: 181, nn. 8–10: 182, nn. 11–12: 183, n. 15: 184, n. 22: 186, n. 27: 188, **RWD³.**, bb. 3, n. 293: 220, **SHB.**, vol. IV, bb. *fî maqtali-hi*: 61, **MǦL.**, vol. XIV, bb. 15, n. 7: 168, n. 25: 182, n. 27: 183, vol. XLV, bb. 40, n. 2: 201, nn. 20–21: 210, nn. 23, 27: 211, n. 31: 213, vol. XCVIII, bb. 5, n. 44: 35. This strand of thought hearkens back to the *aḥâdîṯ* that only two people have ever been born after six months in the womb: ʿÎsâ (or, alternatively, Yaḥyâ) and al-Ḥusayn and that like Yaḥyâ, nobody before al-Ḥusayn received that name. These narratives serve to elevate al-Ḥusayn above the ordinary run of people.

[31] **QMM.**, bb. 28, n. 6: 181, n. 10: 182–183, n. 20: 185–186, **SHB.**, vol. IV, bb. *fî maqtali-hi*: 61, **MǦL.**, vol. XIV, bb. 15, n. 25: 182, vol. XLV, bb. 40, n. 13: 206, n. 18: 210, n. 23: 211, n. 38: 215, **NṬR.**, vol. I, bb. 22, n. 1–952: 391, vol. X, bb. 49, n. 6–12077: 313. A number of transmitters hold that the angels too wept for a period of forty days: cf. **QQM.**, bb. 26, n. 8: 167–169, **MǦL.**, vol. XIV, bb. 15, n. 25: 182, vol. XLV, bb. 40, n. 13: 206, n. 45: 218, **NṬR.**, vol. X, bb. 49, n. 6–12077: 313.

[32] **QMM.**, bb. 28, n. 13: 183, n. 14: 183–184, n. 25: 188, **BṬQ.**, nn. 835–836: 405, **ṬSṬ².**, vol. I, n. 293: 203, **ḤLL¹.**: 257, **MǦL.**, vol. XLV, bb. 40, n. 13: 206, n. 20: 217, n. 25: 211; **NṬR.**, vol. X, bb. 49, n. 6–12077: 313.

[33] **QMM.**, bb. 28, n. 4: 181, n. 9: 182, **SHB.**, vol. IV, bb. *fî maqtali-hi*: 61–62, **BṬQ.**, n. 832: 405, **MǦL.**, vol. XLV, bb. 40, n. 21: 210, n. 31: 213, n. 38: 215.

[34] **QMM.**, bb. 28, n. 6: 181, n. 7: 181–182, n. 10: 182–183, n. 18: 185, n. 19: 185–186, **MǦL.**, vol. XLV, bb. 40, n. 13: 206, n. 28: 212.

3.1.4. The Weeping of All Created Things

Finally, as if to underscore this spectacle, the Shîʿî books of *aḥâdîṯ* pronounce that all created things – human beings, *ğinn*, birds and wild beasts – join in the cosmic lament for al-Ḥusayn. Already, this is witnessed in the weeping of the prophets – the sheep of Ismâʿîl and the gazelles that weep in front of ʿÎsâ. Together with the angels and *ğinn*, the earth and the sky, al-Qummî devotes a chapter of his *Kâmil al-ziyârât* to this exhibition of grief.[35]

> On the authority of Abû Ğaʿfar,[36] who said: Mankind, the *ğinn*, the birds and the wild beasts wept over al-Ḥusayn b. ʿAlî, until their tears welled forth.[37]

The reports that tell of this great and universal lament are not, with rare exceptions, transmitted by the major Shîʿî transmitters. The vast majority of them are pious traditions recorded by al-Qummî, since his *Kâmil al-ziyârât* is primarily a handbook of spirituality. Al-Mağlisî transmits from him, but as noted earlier in this work, al-Mağlisî is an encyclopedist; he gathers all the *aḥâdîṯ* he can find, but pays little attention to critical elaboration or grading. Nevertheless,

---

[35] **QMM.**, bb. 26: 165–171.

[36] The fifth Imâm.

[37] **QQM.**, bb. 26, n. 1: 165, **MFD**[2].: 144, **SHB.**, vol. IV, bb. *fî âyâti-hi baʿda wafâti-hi*: 61–62, **MĞL.**, vol. XL, bb. 91, n. 117: 97, vol. XLV, bb. 39, n. 22: 184, bb. 40, n. 8: 205. Of these creatures, a special qualification is given to the birds; among other things, the doves, frightened by his death, supplicate God and curse the killers of al-Ḥusayn (cf. **KLY.**, vol. VI, Book 27 (*Kitâb al-dawâğin*), bb. *al-ḥamâm*, n. 13: 547, **QQM.**, bb. 30, nn. 1–3: 197–198, **ḤRR**[1]., vol. XI, bb. 33, n. 15427: 519, **MĞL.**, vol. XLIV, bb. 36, n. 19: 305, vol. XLV, bb. 40, nn. 32–33: 213, **NṬR.**, vol. VIII, bb. 26, n. 1–9455: 284), while the owls lament and are stricken by his death: "Has any of you ever seen an owl during the day?" is the question put by the *ḥadîṯ*. The answer is in the negative, and the *ḥadîṯ* elucidates: "They never failed to shelter in built-up areas, but when al-Ḥusayn was killed, they decided only to take shelter in deserted ruins. During the day they never stop fasting and grieving, until night covers them, and then they never cease to wail for al-Ḥusayn until morning comes." Cf. **QQM.**, bb. 31, n. 1: 199, **MĞL.**, vol. XLV, bb. 40, n. 34: 213, vol. LXI, bb. 14, n. 1: 239.

the collective sorrow forms an indispensable part of the grief of the Shîʿa, and these stories and *aḥâdîṯ* serve to accentuate Karbalâʾ as a cosmic event. Its cosmic proportions, and the collective grief, are encapsulated in a tradition from the sixth Imâm Ǧaʿfar al-Ṣâdiq:

> Abû ʿAbd Allâh[38] said: "O Zurâra, heaven wept blood over al-Ḥusayn for forty mornings; the earth wept blackness for forty mornings, the sun wept for forty mornings with an eclipse and with redness, the mountains were dismembered and dispersed, and the oceans burst forth. The angels wept over al-Ḥusayn for forty mornings, and there is not a woman among us who will use dye, anoint herself, colour her eyes or comb her hair until the head of ʿUbayd Allâh b. Ziyâd,[39] may God curse him, comes to us, nor will we cease weeping after him. My uncle, whenever he remembered him, wept until his eyes overflowed onto his beard, and to the point that whoever saw him wept in mercy for his tears. The angels around al-Ḥusayn's tomb weep, and the angels that are in the air and in heaven weep for their tears, until (he) remembered the wrath of Hell against his killers. He said: The angels weep for him and bewail him and burn with anger against his killers. And were there not on the earth one of the Proofs of God, the earth would be destroyed and those in it overturned; nor are the number of earthquakes increased until the approach of the hour. There is no eye dearer to God, no tear from an eye which has wept and shed tears over him, except that he is joined and helped by Fâṭima and joined by the Messenger of God…"[40]

At the centre of this cosmic mourning are the *ahl al-bayt*, comprising Muḥammad, Fâṭima and the twelve Imâms, who have become

---

[38] The sixth Imâm.

[39] Governor residing in Kûfa at the time of al-Ḥusayn's death. In Shîʿî piety, according to Ayoub, he has become the arch-symbol of evil and infidelity. Cf. AYOUB M., *Redemptive Suffering in Islam. A Study of the Devotional Aspects of ʿAshura in Twelver Shiʿism*, 1978: 100.

[40] **QQM.**, bb. 26, n. 8: 167–168, **MĞL.**, vol. XLV, bb. 40, n. 13: 206, **NṬR.**, vol. X, bb. 49, n. 6–12077: 313.

the 'house of sorrow' (*bayt al-aḥzân*). At the heart of this house stands Fâṭima.

3.2. THE SORROW OF FÂṬIMA

> All things weep in emulation of her tears, and the tears of the faithful here on earth are but a way of sharing in her sorrows and a means of bringing consolation to her broken heart.[41]

Over this house of sorrows, Fâṭima reigns supreme as mistress of grief. Lammens is scathing, comparing her to 'Niobe',[42] characterizing her "a sad creature, perpetually in mourning",[43] wondering how the Shîʿa attempted to make this "ghost of a wailing woman interesting"[44] and declaring that weeping was Fâṭima's most "suitable role."[45] However, Lammens has apparently not grasped the sublime theological significance of weeping asserted by the Shîʿa, the context in which Fâṭima's tears must be read.

What has been posited of Fâṭima may by the same token be posited of al-Ḥusayn; for just as, at her approach, her siblings fade and vanish into history, so too, despite the Shîʿî claim that her eldest son al-Ḥasan was himself murdered, the whole thrust of Fâṭima's grief centers around the murder of al-Ḥusayn. In reality, her grief, like the entire grief of the Shîʿa, is inextricably tied to the life and death of this second son of hers; already forewarned of his death, she bears him in sorrow, and long dead before his murder at

---

[41] Ibid.: 144.

[42] LAMMENS H., "Fatima and the Daughters of Muhammad" in Ibn Warraq (ed. and trans.), *The Quest for the Historical Muhammad*, 2000: 227. In Greek mythology, Niobe was the daughter of Tantalus. Her large brood of children was killed by Apollo and Artemis, and Niobe exhausted herself with weeping, becoming the symbol of grief and everlasting sorrow. Cf. PRICE S. and KEARNS E., (eds.), *The Oxford Dictionary of Classical Mythology*, 2004: 375.

[43] LAMMENS H., "Fatima and the Daughters of Muhammad" in Ibn Warraq (ed. and trans.), *The Quest for the Historical Muhammad*, 2000: 227.

[44] Op. cit.: 228.

[45] Op. cit.: 241.

Karbalâʾ, she continues to grieve ceaselessly for him until the Day of Judgment. All the other injustices, grievances and sorrows that befell her merely intensified this singular and colossal grief.

Al-Mağlisî devotes the seventh chapter of the forty-third volume of his work to the iniquity suffered by Fâṭima. Fifty *aḥâdîṯ* recount the injustices perpetrated against her, her tears, sorrow and grievances, her final sickness, death and the reason for her secret burial, and earnestly pray the curse of God on all who ill-treated her. He begins by placing Fâṭima on a sure footing. There are only five weepers,[46] he claims:

1. Adam, who wept over Paradise until his cheeks became like a valley

2. Yaʿqûb, who wept over his son Yûsuf until he lost his sight[47]

3. Yûsuf, who wept so copiously in prison over his father Yaʿqûb, that his annoyed fellow prisoners asked if he could not weep by day and keep silent by night, or *vice versa*[48]

4. Fâṭima, whose weeping over her father caused the irritated citizens of Medina to complain to ʿAlî that they were unable to sleep

---

[46] **ṢDQ¹**., n. 5: 140, **ṢDQ⁴**., vol. I, n. 15: 272, **FNR**., vol. I: 170, vol. II: 450, **ṬBR³**.: 315, **IRB**., vol. I: 498, **DAY**., vol. I: 95, **MĞL**., vol. XI, bb. 4, n. 2: 204, vol. XII, bb. 9, n. 27: 264, vol. XLIII, bb. 7, n. 1: 155, vol. XLVI, bb. 6, n. 2: 109, vol. LXXIX, bb. 16, n. 33: 86, **ḤRR¹**., vol. III, bb. 87, n. 3655: 280. Al-Mağlisî transmits a strand from Ibn Shaḥrâshûb's *Manâqib âl Abî Ṭâlib* which names eight weepers, adding Nûḥ, Shuʿayb and Dâwûd to the five already mentioned. Cf. **SHB**., vol. III, bb. *manâqib Fâṭima al-Zahrâʾ*: 369, **MĞL**., vol. XLIII, bb. 3, n. 32: 39.

[47] Cf. Q. 12: 84. The word 'whitened' in the text is a suggestion that all his weeping made him blind. Cf. also Q. 12: 93, 96, where this blindness is healed («*and he became a seer once more*«) by the torn and bloodied shirt of his son Yûsuf.

[48] This anecdote is not in the Qur'ânic account of Yûsuf's imprisonment, where his two fellow prisoners ask him to interpret their dreams (Q. 12: 35–42).

on their beds for the noise she was making, so that she was forced to go to the tombs of the martyrs to weep[49]

5. ʿAlî b. Ḥusayn, the fourth Imâm and son of al-Ḥusayn, who, as noted earlier, wept for twenty or forty years over the Karbalâʾ event, and who never failed to weep whenever food was placed before him.

Al-Mağlisî then proceeds to demonstrate that the injustices and grievances over which Fâṭima wept were no figment of her imagination, but were clearly predicted by her father:

> On the authority of ʿAbd Allâh b. al-ʿAbbâs, who said: "When death approached the Messenger of God, he wept until his beard was wet with tears. Some said to him: O Messenger of God, why this weeping? He said: I am weeping for my progeny, and the evil that my community after me will do to them; it is as if I see my daughter Fâṭima will be treated unjustly after me, and she will cry out 'O father!', but not one of my community after me will look out for her. Fâṭima, peace be upon her, heard this and wept. The Messenger of God said to her: My daughter, do not weep! She said: I am not weeping over what will be done to me after you, but I am weeping over your departure, Messenger of God…"[50]

In another report, Muḥammad addresses Fâṭima directly with a grim warning:

> Ğâbir b. ʿAbd Allâh al-Anṣârî reported, saying: "Fâṭima came to the Messenger of God, who was in the agony of death. She leaned over him, weeping, and he opened his eyes and awoke. Then he said: My daughter, you are the tyrannized and the op-

---

[49] **ṢDQ[1]**., n. 5: 140, **ṢDQ[4]**., vol. I, n. 15: 272, **FNR**., vol. I: 170, **ṬBR[3]**.: 315, **SHB**., vol. III, bb. *manâqib Fâṭima al-Zahrâʾ*: 369, **IRB**., vol. I: 498, **DAY**., vol. I: 95, **MĞL**., vol. XLIII, bb. 3, n. 39: 32, bb. 7, n. 1: 155, n. 15: 177, n. 27: 196, vol. XLVI, bb. 6, n. 2: 109, vol. LXXIX, bb. 16, n. 33: 86.

[50] **ṬFA[2]**., bb. 7, n. 18–316: 188, **MĞL**., vol. XXVIII, bb. 2, n. 4: 41, vol. XLIII, bb. 7, n. 2: 156.

> pressed after me. Whoever harms you, harms me; whoever angers you, angers me; whoever gladdens you, gladdens me; whoever reverences you, reverences me; whoever turns from you, turns from me; whoever unites himself to you, unites himself to me; whoever snubs you, snubs me; whoever treats you justly, treats me justly; and whoever treats you unjustly, treats me unjustly…"[51]

The Shîʿî texts take note of her weeping over a number of incidents and individuals; over the death over her mother Ḫadîǧa,[52] over her marriage to ʿAlî, over her hunger and poverty,[53] at the grave of her sister Zaynab[54] where Muḥammad tried to comfort her, at the grave of her uncle Ḥamza, killed at Uḥud[55] as well as over the death of Ǧaʿfar b. Abî Ṭâlib,[56] husband of Asmâʾ bt. ʿUmays,[57] a woman who would play a key role in Fâṭima's own sickness and death. Fâṭima's grief over these events and individuals is a portent of things to come. Her father, the ill-treatment he received and the opposition he faced (recounted, as noted earlier, by the Sunnî

---

[51] **IRB.**, vol. I: 497, **MĞL.**, vol. XXVIII, bb. 2, n. 34: 76, vol. XXXIV, bb. 35: 338, vol. XXXVI, bb. 41, n. 110: 288.

[52] **YQB.**, vol. II: 35, **ṢDQ⁴.**, vol. II, n. 116: 404, **RWD¹.**, vol. II; 529, **MĞL.**, vol. XVI, bb. 5, n. 6: 3, vol. XLIII, bb. 3, n. 31: 27–28.

[53] **SHB.**, vol. III, bb. *manâqib Fâṭima al-Zahrâʾ*: 319, **MĞL.**, vol. XXIV, bb. 36, n. 6: 99, vol. XLIII, bb. 5, n. 30: 120.

[54] Among the Sunnî, who say it was not Zaynab but Ruqayya, cf. **ḤNB.**, vol. I, *Musnad ʿAbd Allâh b. al-ʿAbbâs b. ʿAbd al-Muṭṭalib*, n. 3103: 717–718. Among the Shîʿa, who say it was Zaynab, cf. **RṬB².**: 273.

[55] **RQM.**: 197, **ṢDQ³.**, vol. I, n. 537: 180, **ṬFA¹.**, vol. I, bb. 23, n. 168: 465, **ḤDI.**, vol. XV: 17, **ḤRR¹.**, vol. III, bb. 55, n. 3468: 224, **MĞL.**, vol. XXXVI, bb. 41, n. 224: 352, vol. XLIII, bb. 4, n. 13: 90, vol. LXXIX, bb. 20, n. 3: 169, vol. XCIX, bb. 6, n. 27: 300, **NṬR.**, vol. II, bb. 46, n. 1–2203: 365.

[56] **MĞL.**, vol. XXII, bb. 5, n. 25: 276.

[57] Muḥammad ordered Fâṭima to see to the needs, especially domestic, of Asmâʾ bt. ʿUmays after the death of her husband: cf. **ṢDQ³.**, vol. I, n. 549: 182, **ḤRR¹.**, vol. II, bb. 27, n. 3506: 273, **MĞL.**, vol. LXXIX, bb. 16, n. 21: 83.

transmitters)[58] as well as his imminent death, was a primary reason for Fâṭima's tears. Many of the *aḥâdîṯ* recount her visiting her father during the illness that would finally kill him, where he comforts her with promises that she will very soon follow him and will be the first to do so.

In spite of these promises, her grief at his death and in fear of a future without him is enormous; seeing his frailty, she is choked with tears, which stream down her cheeks. "How can I not weep, looking at your frailty?" she asks, as he attempts to comfort her sorrow and her fear of what is to come ("who will we have when you are gone?"), instructing her to trust in God and to be patient, as her fathers the prophets and her mothers, the wives of the prophets, were patient in tribulation. [59]

After the death of her father, her grief continues unabated.[60] The texts tell us that she never laughed again,[61] that her weeping

---

[58] Cf. **ḤNB.**, vol. I, *Musnad ʿAbd Allâh b. al-ʿAbbâs*, n. 2762: 649–650, n. 3485: 788.

[59] **RQM.**: 36, 62, 124, **ṢDQ²**., vol. I, bb. 24, n. 10: 262, **ĞQM.**: 121, **ṬFA²**., bb. 6, n. 8–256: 154, **ḤDI.**, vol. IV: 107, **IRB.**, vol. II: 468, **DAY.**, vol. II: 419, **MĞL.**, vol. XXVIII, bb. 2, n. 21: 52, vol. XXXVI, bb. 41, n. 110: 288, n. 146: 307, n. 184: 328, vol. XXXVII, bb. 50, n. 16: 41, vol. XLIII, bb. 7, n. 49: 218, bb. 8, n. 2: 218, vol. LI, bb. 1, n. 37: 78; vol. LXXVIII, bb. 10, n. 56: 391, **NṬR.**, vol. II, bb. 34, n. 3–1995: 290.

[60] Although lamentation poetry would only develop at a later period, and would be centered chiefly upon al-Ḥusayn, a number of transmitters place on Fâṭima's lips what could qualify as poems of lamentation over her father. These are varied and of differing lengths, and one example, which unfortunately loses its rhythm in the translation, will suffice here: "My strength has been eliminated, my steadfastness has betrayed me, and my enemies have been haughty towards me. O father, sadness is killing me. I remain grief-stricken and abandoned, dismayed, alone. My voice is stifled, my back broken, my life made loathsome, my destiny troubled. After you, father, I find no one close in my desolation, or to stop my tears or to support my weakness. Precise revelations have come to an end after you, as have the coming down of Ğibraʾîl and the place of Mîkâʾîl. After you, father, motives have changed, and doors have been shut before me. I hate this world after you. My longing for you will not waver, nor will my

increased, and continued interminably, day and night, and she intensified her visits to the graveyard.[62] This was, in part, a response to the people of Medina, who had complained to ʿAlî that she was keeping them from their rest. Writes al-Mağlisî:

> Her sorrow was renewed and increased, and her tears became intense. She sat for seven days, her groaning not subsiding and her yearning not abating. Every day that came, her weeping was more than the first day.[63]

She asked for her father's shirt, in which he had been washed after death, fainting when she smelled it, so that ʿAlî had to take it from her and hide it.[64] Even Bilâl[65] was caught up in her sorrow; having refused, after Muḥammad's death, to sing the *aḏân* for anyone else, he did so when Fâṭima expressed a desire to hear it again. She was

---

desire for you or my grief over you be exhausted. (Cf. **MĞL.**, vol. XLIII, bb. 7, n. 15: 174).

[61] **KLY.**, vol. III, Book 11 (*Kitâb al-ğanâ'iz*), bb. *ziyârat al-qubûr*, n. 3: 228, vol. IV, Book 15 (*Kitâb al-ḥağğ*), bb. *ityân al-mashâhid wa-qubûr al-shuhadâ'*, n. 3: 561, **ḤRR[1].**, vol. III, bb. 55, n. 3467: 223, vol. XIV, bb. 13, n. 19380: 356, **MĞL.**, vol. XLIII, bb. 7, n. 24: 195, vol. XCVII, bb. 7, n. 12: 216. Among the Sunnî, cf. **IṢH.**, vol. II, bb. 133: 42–43, **KṮR[1].**, vol. VI: 333.

[62] **KLY.**, vol. III, Book 11 (*Kitâb al-ğanâ'iz*), bb. *ziyârat al-qubûr*, n. 3: 228, vol. IV, Book 15 (*Kitâb al-ḥağğ*), bb. *ityân al-mashâhid wa-qubûr al-shuhadâ'*, n. 3: 561, **RQM.**: 197, **ṢDQ[3].**, vol. I, n. 537: 180, **TFA[1].**, vol. I, bb. 23, n. 168: 465, **ḤRR[1].**, vol. III, bb. 55, nn. 3467–3468: 223–224, vol. XIV, bb. 13, n. 19380: 356, **MĞL.**, vol. XXXVI, bb. 41, n. 224: 352, vol. XLIII, bb. 4, n. 13: 90, bb. 7, n. 24: 195, vol. LXXIX, bb. 20, n. 3: 169, vol. XCVII, bb. 7, n. 12: 216, vol. XCIX, bb. 6, n. 27: 300, **NṬR.**, vol. II, bb. 46, n. 1–2203: 365. The texts imply that up until the death of her father, she was accustomed to visit the graves of the martyrs (including Ḥamza) every Saturday afternoon. After her father's death, these visits increased to twice every Friday.

[63] **MĞL.**, vol. XLIII, bb. 7, n. 15: 174–177.

[64] Op. cit., n. 6: 157.

[65] An African and ex-slave, freed by Abû Bakr, and whose fine singing voice made him the first to sing the 'Call to Prayer' (*aḏân*). Cf. LINGS M., *Muhammad, his life based on the earliest sources*, 1983: 79, 131.

convulsed with sorrow upon hearing the familiar words, and the people attempted to persuade Bilâl to cease, but Fâṭima insisted that he continue.[66] So overwhelming is her sorrow, that assistance is sent from heaven:

> Abû ʿUbayda on the authority of al-Ṣâdiq,[67] said: "Fâṭima wept over her father for seventy-five days, and Ǧibraʾîl used to come to her and inform her about the situation of her father, and console her, and inform her about what would happen after her. ʿAlî would write this down, and this is like His words, may He be exalted: «*Then (one) cried unto her from below her, saying: Grieve not!*»"[68]
>
> While in heaven the angels themselves weep for the tears and grief of Fâṭima,[69] Ǧibrîl is sent to dictate consoling words to her. These words, written down by ʿAlî, comprise what the Shîʿa term the 'scroll' (*muṣḥaf*) of Fâṭima, an esoteric text passed down from one Imâm to the next.

The loss of her father is only exacerbated by the injustice she perceives in the one who has succeeded him:

> Umm Salama came to call on Fâṭima, and said to her: "How did you wake from your night, daughter of the Messenger of God?" She said: "I awoke between grief and sorrow, the loss of the Prophet and the iniquity of the trustee. By God, he has torn aside his veil, from the beginning of his Imamate, taking possession of other than what God prescribed in His Revela-

---

[66] **ṢDQ³**., vol. I, n. 907: 297, **MĞL**., vol. XLIII, bb. 7, n. 7: 107.

[67] The sixth Imâm.

[68] **KLY**., vol. I, Book 4 (*Kitâb al-ḥuǧǧa*), bb. *fî-hi ḏikr al-ṣaḥîfa wa-l-ǧafr wa-muṣḥaf Fâṭima*, n. 2: 240, n. 5: 241, bb. *mawlid al-Zahrâʾ Fâṭima*, n. 6: 460, **SHB**., vol. III, bb. *manâqib Fâṭima al-Zahrâʾ*: 385, **MĞL**., vol. XXII, bb. 2, n. 63: 545, vol. XXVI, bb. 1, n. 72: 41, vol. XLIII, bb. 3, n. 67: 79, bb. 7, n. 4: 106, n. 22: 194. Cf. Q. 19: 23.

[69] **MĞL**., vol. XXII, bb. 1, n. 38: 492.

> tion and the Prophet, may God bless and save him and his family, established in his interpretation…"[70]

All her grief and anger pours out during her final illness, in a lengthy tirade spoken to the women of the emigrants and the helpers who have gathered around her bed, and as transmitted by her granddaughter:

> On the authority of ʿAbd Allâh b. al-Ḥasan, on the authority of his mother, Fâṭima bt. al-Ḥusayn, who said: "When the illness of Fâṭima, the daughter of the Messenger of God, grew worse and overcame her, the women of the emigrants and of the helpers gathered around her and said: Daughter of the Messenger of God, how have you become in your illness? She replied: I have reached a state, by God, of loathing your world and hating your menfolk, whom I have discarded before even putting them to the test and whom I have hated after having probed them. Shame on the dents of sword, the lassitude of the lance, the foolish prattle of the decision, and miserable «*that which they themselves send on before them: that Allah will be wroth with them and in the doom they will abide*»,[71] which has already invested them with her rope and attacked them with her incursion, a mutilation, a barrenness, a crushing for the people who do wrong…"[72]

This injustice is encapsulated chiefly in the *Saqîfa* event, in which the claim of ʿAlî was usurped and the *ahl al-bayt* particularly badly treated, and in the denial of her claim to Fadak. Both events, already examined earlier in this work, continue to loom large in the Shîʿî psyche, and persist as polemical issues. Fâṭima's vain attempts

---

[70] **SHB.**, vol. II, bb. *fî ẓulâmat ahl al-bayt*: 234, **MĞL.**, vol. XLIII, bb. 7, n. 5: 156–157.

[71] Cf. Q. 5: 80.

[72] **RṬB¹.**: 39, 41, **ṢDQ⁶.**, n. 1: 354, **ṬBR².**, vol. I: 108, **ḤDI.**, vol. XVI: 233, **IRB.**, vol. I: 492, **MĞL.**, vol. XLIII, bb. 7, n. 8: 109–109, nn. 9–10: 159–170, vol. LXXIII, bb. 99, n. 2: 15. There are a number of discrepancies between the transmitters.

to claim her rightful inheritance, primarily from Abû Bakr,[73] drive her in tears to her father's grave, where she weeps with impotent fury over the treatment she has received:[74]

> After you there have been tidings and happenings which, had you witnessed them, the affair would never had become so great. We have missed you the way the earth misses its heavy rains. Your people have become disordered. Look at them, how they have deviated. Ǧibrîl use to delight us with the verses: now they are hidden from us, and every good is concealed. You were a moon and light which illuminated. To you were sent down the books from the Lord of might. Men have regarded us with displeasure and made light of us since you were hidden from us. Today we have been usurped! We will weep for you as long as we live, and as long as there remain with us eyes welling up with tears."[75]

Fâṭima's tears of grief on earth become tears of intercession in Paradise:

> On the authority of Abû Baṣîr, who said: "I was with Abû ʿAbd Allâh,[76] talking to him, when his son came to him. He said: Welcome, and embraced and kissed him. Then he said: God despise those who despise you, and take revenge on those who wrong you, and God abandon those who abandon you and curse those who slay you. God is a Supporter, and Guardi-

---

[73] **RṬB**[1].: 75, **BṬQ**., nn. 776–777: 390, **ḤDI**., vol. VI: 46, vol. XVI: 217, **ṬSṬ**[2]., vol. I, nn. 356–357: 257–258, **IRB**., vol. I: 474, **ḤLL**[1].: 359, **MǦL**., vol. XXVIII: 533, vol. XXIX, bb. 11: 111, 200, 202, 245, 329.

[74] **MFD**[5]., n. 8: 30, **ṬBR**[2]., vol. I: 90, **ḤDI**., vol. I: 198, **MǦL**., vol. XXIX, bb. 11: 27, bb. 11: 107.

[75] **RṬB**[1]., 35, **KLY**., vol. VIII, Book 35 (*Kitâb al-rawḍa*), bb. *ḫuṭbat amîr al-muʾminîn*, n. 564: 375–376, **MFD**[5]., n. 8: 31, **ṬBR**[2]., vol. I: 96, 106, **SHB**., vol. II, bb. *faṣl fî ẓulâmat ahl al-bayt*: 208, **ḤDI**., vol. I: 43, vol. XVI: 212, 251, **ṬSṬ**[2]., vol. I: 265, **IRB**., vol. I: 489, **MǦL**., vol. XXIX, bb. 11: 108, 130, 233, 239, 307–308, vol. XLIII, bb. 7, nn. 25, 27: 196, vol. LIII, bb. 28: 18. It is to be noted that there are substantial discrepancies in the wording of the transmitters, as well as some errors in the transcription.

[76] The sixth Imâm.

an and Helper for you. Prolonged is the weeping of the women, and the weeping of the prophets and the holy ones and the martyrs and the angels of heaven! Then he wept, and said: Abû Baṣîr, when I look at the offspring of al-Ḥusayn, I would not want to happen to them what happened to their father. Abû Baṣîr, Fâṭima weeps for him,[77] and Hell sobs and sighs deeply, and were it not that its guards hear her tears and are roused by them, there is a fear that evil would go out from it, or that its

---

[77] The concept of Fâṭima, weeping over the murder of her son until the Day of Resurrection, as well as the *ḥadît*, already examined, that she will be the first to enter Paradise, leads us to ask: where exactly is Fâṭima now? Going strictly according to Shîʿî theology, she is not in Paradise, but in the place between this world and the Resurrection called the 'barrier' or 'interval' (*barzaḫ*). Writes one Shîʿî author: "The first stage of the soul's life in the Bazarkh begins with the withdrawal of the spirit from the body. At the time that man is buried, according to many hadiths, the angels question him on *Tawḥīd*, Prophecy, and a series of other principles pertaining to belief and religion. Obviously, the answers given by a believer will differ from those given by a disbeliever, and in consequence the grave and the Barzakh will be places wherein divine mercy manifests for the believer, and divine wrath, for the disbeliever…the grave constitutes the beginning of 'Barzakhī' life, which will persist unto the Day of Resurrection." (SHAH-KAZEMI R., (trans.), *Doctrines of Shiʿi Islam. A Compendium of Imami Beliefs and Practices*, I.B. Tauris, London 2001: 126). This helps to clarify the seeming contradiction, that Fâṭima could weep in Paradise, a place of bliss and felicity. It is, in fact, in the *barzaḫ* that she weeps, waiting for the Day of Resurrection, when God will punish those who harmed her and her family. According to the Qur'ân, the *barzaḫ* is «*a barrier until the day when they are raised*» (Q. 23: 100), that is, a place of temporary happiness for the good, for this pleasure will end on the Day of Resurrection. That day, when, according to the Qur'ân, a trumpet blast will bring every living creature standing before God (Q. 39: 68), will mark entrance into the domain of the Resurrection, from whence some will proceed to Paradise and some to Hell, each according to the record of his or her deeds. Thus does the *barzaḫ* "represent a small portion of the reward or punishment that man will receive after resurrection." Cf. LARI M.M., "Man's Situation in the Intermediate Realm (Barzakh)" in *Al-Tawḥīd*, vol. X, nn. 2 & 3 Rabī' al-Thānī – Ramaḍān 1413.

> smoke would escape and burn the people of the earth. They restrain it as long as she continues to weep, and hold it back and make its doors solid, fearing for the people of the earth, nor will Hell settle down until the voice of Fâṭima is stilled. The seas are on the point of being torn apart and flowing into each other, and there is not a single drop which does not have a commissioned angel. Whenever the angel hears her voice, he smothers her fire with his wings and confines one from the other, fearing for the world and those in it and those on the earth. The angels, commiserating, do not cease weeping for her tears; they pray to God and implore Him, and the people of the Throne and those around it implore Him, and the voices of the angels are raised in sanctifying God, fearing for the people of the earth. And were one of their voices to reach the earth, it would strike the people of the earth, the mountains would be uprooted and the earth with its people shaken. I said: May I be your sacrifice, this is a serious matter! He replied: I have heard of none more serious. Then he said: Abû Baṣîr, does it please you to be among those who degrade Fâṭima? I wept as he said it, and in weeping had no power over my speech or my words. Then he went to the place of prayer and prayed, and I left him in that position. I had no use for food, and sleep would not come to me. I became a faster, fearful…"[78]

The intimate correlation between Fâṭima's great sorrow, the grievances suffered by the *ahl al-bayt*, the reward for weeping over these sufferings and Fâṭima's exalted, intercessory status is patently encapsulated in words spoken to her by her father:

> When the Prophet informed his daughter Fâṭima about the killing of her son al-Ḥusayn, and about the tribulations that would befall him, she wept copious tears and said: "My father, when will this happen?" He said: "In a time devoid of me and you and ʿAlî." Her weeping became passionate and she said: "Father, who will weep for him, and who will undertake to

---

[78] **QQM**., bb. 26, n. 9: 169–171, **MĞL**., vol. XLV, bb. 40, n. 14: 208, **NṬR**., vol. X, bb. 49, n. 7–12078: 314.

perform the ceremony of mourning for him?" The Prophet said: "Fâṭima, the women of my community will weep for the women of the people of my house, and their men will weep for the men of the people of my house. They will repeat the ceremony of mourning every year, generation after generation; and on the Day of Resurrection you will intercede for the women and I will intercede for the men. Each one of them who wept over the calamity of al-Ḥusayn, we will take by his hand and we will lead him to Paradise. Fâṭima! On the Day of Resurrection, every eye will weep except for the eye that that wept over the calamity of al-Ḥusayn, because they will be laughing, happy in the felicity of Paradise."[79]

[79] **MĞL.**, vol. XLIV, bb. 34, n. 37: 292.

CHAPTER THREE. PART TWO: THE INTERCESSORY PREROGATIVES OF FÂṬIMA

3.1. THE POSSIBILITY OF INTERCESSION IN ISLAM

The belief that there are precise intercessors who, on the Day of Resurrection and specifically with God's permission, can make intercession for the faithful, is a central principle of Shîʿî Islamic theology and piety.[1] Nonetheless, it remains a highly disputed and debated question within Islam in general; for while the Shîʿa, and some groups within the Sunnî, uphold not merely the possibility but also the reality of intercession, others disallow it, insisting that those who believe in it negate their Islam.[2] This subject has been clearly dealt with scholars such as Bowker and Fitzgerald;[3] what follows is a summary of their findings.

> «*Ask forgiveness for them (O Muhammad) or ask not forgiveness for them; though thou ask forgiveness for them seventy times Allah will not forgive them. This is because they disbelieved in Allah and His messenger, and Allah guideth not wrongdoing folk*» (Q. 9: 80).

---

[1] SHAH-KAZEMI R., (trans.), *Doctrines of Shiʾi Islam. A Compendium of Imami Beliefs and Practices*, 2001: 132.

[2] So say, for example, the Salafiyya, a reform movement started in Egypt by Muḥammad ʿAbduh (1849–1905). Cf. al-QAHTÂNÎ M. S., *al-Walâʾ wa-l-Barâʾ*, al-Firdous Ltd., London 1993: 99.

[3] Cf. BOWKER J., "Intercession in the Quran and the Jewish Tradition" in *Journal of Semitic Studies* XI (1966): 69–70, FITZGERALD M.L., "Mediation in Islam" in *Studia Missionalia*, vol. XXI, 1972: 185 – 206.

Ostensibly, the Qur'ân rebuffs any prospect that intercession can help wrong-doers; in reality, the issue is more ambiguous than this. Certainly, the dismissal of intercession occurs more than once, as in, for example Q. 40: 18, Q. 6: 51, 70. As Bowker notes, there is a twofold argumentation in the text; the first refutes any false security that the wickedness one has done could somehow be annulled on Judgment Day (Q. 2: 48, 123), while the second warns that there exist no beings on such equal terms with God that they can convince him to change His mind or one of His just decisions, principally in terms of *shirk* (Q. 6: 94, Q. 10: 18, Q. 30: 13, Q. 36: 23).[4]

Nonetheless, there remain Qur'ânic passages that suggest the opposite – that not only do intercessors exist, but that intercession is a possibility: Q. 4: 85 (where Pickthall renders the traditional verb for 'intercede' – *shafaʿa* – as 'intervene'), Q. 2: 255, Q. 10: 3, Q. 20: 109 and Q. 34: 23 (all of which introduce the concept on intercession by God's permission)[5] and Q. 39: 43–44 (introducing the idea that all intercession belongs to God alone). Alternatively, Q. 43: 86 suggests that only those who knowingly bear witness to the truth have any intercessory power. In terms of groups of intercessors, the angels can intercede, but only with the requisite divine permission (Q. 53: 26, Q. 21: 28). It is hard to discern who precisely has received God's permission to intercede: Q. 43: 86 has suggested only those who knowingly bear witness to the truth, while Q. 19: 87 posits only the one who has made a covenant with God. Bowker wonders if this is one person or more than one, and if this could perhaps be a reference to Ibrâhîm.[6]

The thrust of Bowker's argument is, as he notes, that "it is possible, therefore, that these passages mean no more than that intercession is allowed for those who are already acceptable before God, but who have offended in some minor way" (Q. 40: 7).[7] The Arabic is not always entirely clear as to whether God allows intercession 'for' (in the sense of 'on behalf of') whomever He permits, it or 'to' whomever He permits. Q. 34: 23 seems to be the former.

---

[4] BOWKER J., "Intercession in the Quran" (1966): 69–70.

[5] Op. cit.: 71.

[6] Ibid.

[7] Op. cit.: 72.

What is clear is that intercession is of no benefit for those who are categorized as evil because of their works (Q. 7: 53, Q. 26: 100, Q. 74: 48) – those, for example, who reject God and His messenger (Q. 9: 84) – not even Muḥammad's intercession will be of any use for these. What seems clear is that despite those passages that appear to rule it out entirely, some prospect of intercession is permitted, albeit controlled and limited.

A curious Qur'ânic exception to this appears to be the intriguing figure of Ibrâhîm. The text knows of two traditions of Ibrâhîm interceding, both of them well known in Judaism. Q. 11: 74 alludes to the famous story of his intercession for Sodom, using the 3RD form verb *ğâdala-yuğâdilu*, meaning 'to wrangle' or 'argue' – specifically, to 'argue on behalf of' in the sense of being an advocate for someone – cf. Q. 40: 4–5 and particularly Q. 4: 107, where Pickthall renders it as 'plead'. In Q. 11: 76 Ibrâhîm is informed that his intercession will not avail the people of Lûṭ, for God's command has already gone forth, and the threatened doom cannot be stopped. The Qur'ân also alludes to Ibrâhîm's intercession for his idolatrous father; in Q. 9: 47–8 he assures his father not only of his prayers for him but also of God's graciousness to him (Ibrâhîm), which has not left him without blessing.

But Q. 9: 113 is less positive: «*It is not for the Prophet, and those who believe, to pray for the forgiveness of idolaters even though they may be near of kin (to them) after it hath become clear that they are people of hell-fire*». The following verse makes clear that Ibrâhîm's prayer his father is made only because of a promise he made, and that discovering that his father is an enemy to God, Ibrâhîm separates from him. In Q. 60: 4 this is clearly underscored. «*There is a goodly pattern for you Abraham and those with him, when they told their folk; Lo! we are guiltless of you and all that ye worship beside Allah. We have done with you. And there hath arisen between us and you hostility and hate for ever until ye believe in Allah only save that which Abraham promised his father (when he said): I will ask forgiveness for thee, though I own nothing for thee from Allah Our Lord*».

The Qur'ân mentions prayers that Ibrâhîm prayed (such as Q. 14: 41 «*Our Lord! Forgive me and my parents and believers on the day when the account is cast*» and Q. 26: 86 «*And forgive my father. Lo! he is of those who err*». However, as Bowker notes, "in two places a passage about

Abraham is preceded or followed by a statement that intercession is unavailing" (Q. 26: 100, following a story and Q. 2: 123 preceding one).[8]

Therefore, at the level of the Qur'ânic text, the issue of intercession (*shafâ'a*) is taken up in a general manner on three levels. There are, to begin with, texts which ostensibly repudiate the possibility of intercession. These include, for example, Q. 2: 123 («*And guard [yourselves] against a day when no soul will in aught avail another, nor will compensation be accepted from it, nor will intercession be of use to it; nor will they be helped*») and Q. 6: 70 («*And forsake those who take their religion for a pastime and a jest, and whom the life of the world beguileth. Remind [mankind] hereby lest a soul be destroyed by what it earneth. It hath beside Allah no protecting ally nor intercessor, and though it offer every compensation it will not be accepted from it*»).

On a second level, there are the verses which strongly contend that intercession is indeed possible, but that it remains wholly the prerogative of God, who alone has the ability to intercede. These verses include Q. 39: 43–44 («*Or choose they intercessors other than Allah? Say: What! Even though they have power over nothing and have no intelligence? Say: unto Allah belongeth all intercession*»).

Finally, there are those verses which appear to combine the first two classifications and give a more holistic picture of intercession in Islam. These propose that while intercession does indeed belong properly to God alone, God may, should He wish it, extend the possibility of intercession to others. These verses include Q. 10: 3 («*There is no intercessor [with Him] save after His permission*») and Q. 34: 23 («*No intercession availeth with Him save for him whom He permitteth*»). Further examples include Q. 2: 255, Q. 19: 87, Q. 20: 109 and Q. 21: 28.

Accordingly, there are ostensibly certain chosen ones, such as the prophets, the Imâms, the holy ones (*awliyâ'*) and even the angels, who could receive permission from God, and would then be able, by reason of their standing with God and, more crucially, the divine acquiescence, to assist people by their prayers. Without this divine consent, no intercession would be possible or accepted. It is notable that even in the course of their earthly lives, God's proph-

---

[8] Cf. BOWKER J., "Intercession in the Quran" (1966): 74.

ets had the capacity to intercede on behalf of those who, by their repentance, sought forgiveness and a return to the path of God. This is attested to by Qur'ânic verses such as Q. 4: 64, in reference to Muḥammad («*We sent no messenger save that he should be obeyed by Allah's leave. And if, when they had wronged themselves, they had but come unto thee and asked forgiveness of Allah, and asked forgiveness of the messenger, they would have found Allah Forgiving, Merciful*») and Q. 12: 97–98, in reference to Ya'qûb («*They said, O our father! Ask forgiveness of our sins for us, for lo! we were sinful. He said: I shall ask forgiveness for you of my Lord. Lo! He is the Forgiving, the Merciful*»).

At the level of the Qur'ânic text then, there are specifically eight features we could underscore concerning intercession. The first is that it is, ostensibly, an impossibility. The Children of Israel (Q. 2: 48) and the general mass of believers (Q. 2: 254) are warned to stand ready for this day when no intercession will be accepted. The idolaters especially are warned that the Day of Judgment is a day on which no intercession will be accepted, and especially from those whom the idolaters mistakenly set up as intercessors. On that day, «*the mediation of no mediators will avail them*» (cf. Q. 10: 18, Q. 74: 48). The second feature is that intercession is established, categorically and in absolute terms, as belonging to God alone (cf. Q. 39: 43–44, cited above). The third feature is the opening of the possibility that intercession could permitted for others than God, but only by His permission; so, for example, Q. 2: 255 («*Who is he that intercedeth with Him save by His leave?*«), as well as Q. 10: 3, Q. 19: 87, Q. 21: 28 and Q. 43: 86.

A fourth feature of the Qur'ân is the suggestion that intercession, but only on behalf of those for whom God wills it (and these are among the believers) is permitted for the angels. So, for example, Q. 40: 7 («*Those who bear the Throne, and all who are round about it, hymn the praises of their Lord and believe in Him and ask forgiveness for those who believe [saying]: Our Lord! Thou comprehendest all things in mercy and knowledge, therefor forgive those who repent and follow Thy way. Ward off from them the punishment of hell*») and Q. 42: 5 («*Almost might the heavens be rent asunder while the angels hymn the praise of their Lord and ask forgiveness for those on earth*») – notable in this latter verse is the absence of any delineation that it is for believers alone that the angels pray.

A fifth feature of intercession is that it is overtly and recurrently attributed to Muḥammad in his lifetime, not only by his prayers but also by his presence (such as Q. 8: 33); so, for example,

Q. 47: 19 («*So know [O Muhammad] that there is no God save Allah, and ask forgiveness for thy sin and for believing men and believing women*»). This intercession appears to be only for believers (highlighted, for example, by Q. 4: 107 and Q. 9: 113); in fact, his intercession for the non-believers will be of no use to them (Q. 9: 80, 84 and Q. 63: 5–6 – «*whether thou ask forgiveness for them or ask not forgiveness for them is all one for them; Allah will not forgive them*»). See also Q. 3: 159, Q. 4: 64, 106–107, Q. 9: 103, Q. 24: 62 and Q. 60: 12.

A sixth feature is that intercession is suggested with reference to Muḥammad and his distinctive position in the afterlife; the intercession and mediation of Muḥammad on the Day of Judgment has been established by the consensus of scholars (*iǧmâʿ*), based upon the Qur'ânic text and the books of *aḥâdîṯ*, and is an article of belief in Islam. The specific reference to Muḥammad's station in the afterlife is found in Q. 17: 70 («*It may be that thy Lord will raise thee to a praised estate*»). A number of the texts of Sunnî *aḥâdîṯ*, such as al-Buḫârî and Muslim, link this 'praised estate' with Muḥammad's prerogatives of intercession in Paradise.[9]

A seventh feature is the prospect of intercession by the prophets, based as always on the possibility of divine permission, and in particular because the prophets made a covenant with their Lord (Q. 33: 7, 3: 81) and knowingly bore witness to the truth. A number of Qur'ânic verses uphold the prophets' intercession during their lifetime: for example, the intercession of Ibrâhîm, seen already and recorded in Q. 60: 4 and in Q. 19: 47 («*Abraham promised his father: I will ask forgiveness for thee, though I own nothing for thee from Allah – our Lord*»), of Yaʿqûb (Q. 12: 97–98 cited above).

A final feature concerns verses that deal with the believers' intercession in their lifetime; so, for example, in Q. 59: 10 («*And those who came (into the faith) after them say: Our Lord! forgive us and our brethren who were before us in the faith*»).

Within the books of *aḥâdîṯ*, Muḥammad speaks of his own intercession; a few examples from the books of Sunnî *aḥâdîṯ* will suffice. These texts establish clearly that God will bring out of the Fire those whom He wishes, whose sins have placed them there provi-

---

[9] **BUḪ[1]**., vol. II, bk. 24 (*Kitâb al-zakât*), bb. 51, n. 553: 321–322, **MSL**., vol. I, bk. 1 (*Kitâb al-îmân*), bb. 84, n. 320: 179–180.

sionally, and that He will do this by intercession.[10] The agent of this intercession is named (primarily) as Muḥammad, whose intercession the transmitters link with his 'praised estate' (so-named in the Qur'ân).[11]

A number of basic strands of thought underscoring the issue of Muḥammad's own intercession in the books of Sunnî *aḥâdîṯ*. According to Muḥammad, it is indeed intercession that is meant by his 'praised estate' (Q. 17: 79),[12] and indeed, people will be brought of the Fire and into Paradise by his interceding for them.[13] Muḥammad makes intercession specifically for members of his community who have committed serious sin,[14] although Ibn Mâǧa carries a *ḥadîṯ* that says Muḥammad's intercession will be for every Muslim.[15] It is noted that each prophet has been given a special prayer, and Muḥammad is reserving his prayer to be intercession for his followers on the Day of Resurrection.[16] There are other strands of *aḥâdîṯ* that appear to contradict this one; one, recorded by al-Buḫârî and Muslim, has Muḥammad saying that he has been given five things that no one before him has been given and that one of these is intercession.[17] Various others – those who pray in groups (of forties or, in other places, one hundreds) for the dead,

---

[10] **BUḪ[1].**, vol. VIII, bk. 81 (*Kitâb al-riqâq*), bb. 51, n. 563: 367, **MSL.**, vol. I, bk. 1 (*Kitâb al-îmân*), bb. 83, n. 306: 172–173, bb. 84, n. 318: 178.

[11] **BUḪ[1].**, vol. II, bk. 24 (*Kitâb al-zakât*), bb. 51, n. 553: 321–322, **MSL.**, vol. I, bk. 1 (*Kitâb al-îmân*), bb. 84, n. 320: 179–180. Cf. Q. 17: 79.

[12] **BUḪ[1].**, vol. II, bk. 24 (*Kitâb al-zakât*), ch. 52, n. 1475: 323, vol. VI, bk. 65 (*Kitâb al tafsîr*), ch. 11, n. 4718: 193, vol. IX, bk. 97 (*Kitâb al-tawḥîd*), ch. 19, n. 7440: 325–8, **NSA[1].**, vol. I, bk. 7 (*Kitâb al-aḏân*), ch. 38, n. 681: 400–1, **MĞA.**, vol. I, bk. 3 (*Abwâb al-aḏân*), ch. 4, n. 722: 477.

[13] **BUḪ[1].**, vol. VIII, bk. 81 (*Kitâb al-riqâq*), ch. 51, n. 6558: 299, n. 6566: 3, **ADD.**, vol. V, bk. 39 (*Kitâb al-sunna*), ch. 20–1, n. 4740: 233, **MĞA.**, *Abwâb al-zuhd*, ch. 37, n. 4315: 408.

[14] **ADD.**, vol. V, bk. 39 (*Kitâb al-sunna*), ch. 20–1, n. 4739: 233, **MĞA.**, vol. V, bk. 37 (*Abwâb al-zuhd*), ch. 37, n. 4310–11: 404.

[15] **MĞA.**, vol. V, bk. 37 (*Abwâb al-zuhd*), ch. 37, n. 4317: 410.

[16] **BUḪ[1].**, vol. IX, bk. 97 (*Kitâb al-tawḥîd*), ch. 31, n. 7474: 346.

[17] **BUḪ[1].**, vol. I, bk. 8 (*Kitâb al-ṣalât*), ch. 56, n. 438: 280–1, **NSA[1].**, vol. I, bk. 4 (*Kitab al-ġusl wa-l-tayammum*), ch. 26, n. 432: 254 .

those who are martyrs or those who have memorized the Qur'ân can make intercession and their intercession will be heard. This intercession is either for the dead person, or for a certain number of their family members who were destined for the fire. Angels too are numbered among these who can intercede (al-Nasâ'î), as are other, unnamed intercessors.[18] Muḥammad is pre-eminent among the descendants of Adam and his is the first intercession to be accepted;[19] the other prophets will, in the final analysis, deflect their own intercessory prerogatives in favour of those of Muḥammad. An example of one of these *ḥadîṯ*, which is carried by numerous transmitters and with varied details, reads:

> On the Day of Resurrection, the people will surge with each other like waves, and then they will come to Adam and say: "Please intercede for us with your Lord." He will say: "I am not fit for that, but you had better go to Ibrâhîm, as he is the friend of the Beneficent." They will go to Ibrâhîm and he will say: "I am not fit for that, but you had better go to Mûsâ, as he is the one to whom God spoke directly." So they will go to Mûsâ and he will say: "I am not fit for that, but you had better go to ʿÎsâ as he is a soul created by God and His Word." They will go to ʿÎsâ and he will say: "I am not fit for that, but you had better go to Muḥammad." They will come to me and I will say: "I am fit for that." Then I will ask for my Lord's permission, and it will be given, and then He will inspire me to praise Him with such praises, as I do not know now. So, I will praise Him with those praises, and will fall down prostrate before

---

[18] **MSL.**, vol. II, bk. 11 (*Kitâb al-ğanâ'iz*), ch. 18, n. 947: 479, ch. 19, n. 59, 479–80, **ADD.**, vol. III, bk. 15 (*Kitâb al-ğihâd*), ch. 26, n. 2522: 217, *Awwal kitâb al-ğanâ'iz*, ch. 40–1, n. 3170: 591, **NSA[1].**, vol. II, bk. 12 (*Kitâb al-taṭbîq*), ch. 81, n. 1141: 164–5, vol. III, bk. 21 (*Kitâb al-ğanâ'iz*), ch. 78, nn. 1993–5: 106–7, **MĞA.**, vol. II, bk. 6 (*Abwâb mâ ğâ' fî al-ğanâ'iz*), ch. 19, n. 1489: 388–9, *Abwâb al-zuhd*, ch. 37, n. 4313: 408, n. 4316: 409, n. 4323: 413

[19] **ADD.**, vol. V, bk. 39 (*Kitâb al-sunna*), ch. 13, n. 4673: 195, **MSL.**, vol. VI, bk. 43 (*Kitâb al-faḍâ'il*), ch. 2, n. 3: 134, **MĞA.**, vol. V, bk. 37 (*Abwâb al-zuhd*), ch. 37, n. 4308: 402.

> Him. Then it will be said: "Muḥammad, raise your head and speak, for you will be listened to, and ask, for your request will be granted, and intercede, for your intercession will be accepted." I will say: "Lord, my followers! My followers!" Then it will be said: "Go and take out of Hell (Fire) all those who have faith in their hearts, equal to the weight of a barley grain." I will go and do so and return to praise Him with the same praises, and fall down (prostrate) before Him. Then it will be said: "Muḥammad, raise your head and speak, for you will be listened to, and ask, for your request will be granted, and intercede, for your intercession will be accepted." I will say: "Lord, my followers! My followers!" It will be said: "Go and take out of it all those who have faith in their hearts equal to the weight of a small ant or a mustard seed." I will go and do so and return to praise Him with the same praises, and fall down in prostration before Him. It will be said: "Muḥammad, raise your head and speak, for you will be listened to, and ask, for your request will be granted, and intercede, for your intercession will be accepted." I will say: "Lord, my followers!" Then He will say: "Go and take out (all those) in whose hearts there is faith even to the lightest, lightest mustard seed. (Take them) out of the Fire." I will go and do so.[20]

Even the believing Muslims on earth can intercede for others,[21] and Muḥammad's intercession is itself not restricted to the Day of Judgment; he speaks, for example, of the intercession he makes on earth for his uncle Abû Ṭâlib.[22] Muḥammad also assures his inter-

---

[20] **BUḪ¹.**, vol. VI, bk. 65 (*Kitâb al-tafsîr*), ch. 1, n. 4476: 23, vol. VIII, bk. 81 (*Kitâb al-riqâq*), ch. 51, n. 6565: 302–3, *Kitâb al-tawḥîd*, ch. 19, n. 7410: 304–6, n. 7440: 325–8, ch. 36, n. 7510: 362–5, **MSL.**, vol. I, bk. 1 (*Kitâb al-îmân*), ch. 84, n. 322: 315–7, n. 326: 319–323, n. 327: 323–6, **MĞA.**, vol. V, bk. 37 (*Abwâb al-zuhd*), ch. 37, n. 4312: 405–7.

[21] **MSL.**, vol. II, bk. 11 (*Kitâb al-ğanâ'iz*), bb. 18, nn. 58–59: 654–655. These reports speak specifically of Muslims (one hundred or, alternatively, forty), whose intercession at the grave of a deceased believer will be accepted.

[22] **BUḪ¹.**, vol. VIII, bk. 81 (*Kitâb al-riqâq*), n. 569: 369.

cession for those who ask for him *al-wasîla* (described as a rank in Paradise fitting only for one of God's servants).[23]

In reality then, as one author points out, the weight of Islamic teaching falls on the side of intercession rather than against it.[24]

Within their theological tradition and piety, the Shîʿa have no reservations about intercession, and uphold not merely the possibility but also the reality of the intercession of the prophets and the Imâms on behalf of their communities. Most especially, it is the intercession of the *ahl al-bayt* that is a protection felt to be hugely valuable by the Shîʿa. At the heart of this *ahl al-bayt*, sometimes called the 'house of sorrows' (*bayt al-aḥzân*) for the sufferings inflicted upon it, stands Fâṭima; and it is within their comprehensive belief in intercession, and the permissibility of seeking such intercession, that the Shîʿî theologians situate her extraordinary intercessory prerogatives.

3.2. FÂṬIMA'S TRIUMPHAL ENTRY INTO PARADISE

> On the Day of Resurrection, a herald will call from the middle of the throne: "O people of the Resurrection, lower your gaze, for Fâṭima the daughter of Muḥammad is crossing…"[25]

---

[23] **MSL.**, vol. I, bk. 4 (*Kitâb al-ṣalât*), bb. 7, n. 11: 288–289.

[24] FITZGERALD M.L., "Mediation in Islam" in *Studia Missionalia*, vol. XXI, 1972: 196.

[25] Among the Shîʿa, cf. **FRT.**, n. 435: 321, **RṬB¹.**: 57, **RṬB².**: 18, **ṢDQ¹.**, n. 4: 17, **ṢDQ⁵.**, vol. II, n. 55: 32, **ǦQM.**: 10, **FNR.**, vol. I: 147, **SHB.**, vol. III, bb. *manâqib Fâṭima al-Zahrâʾ*: 374, **IRB.**, vol. I: 450, 457, 506, **ABḎ.**: 599, **MǦL.**, vol. VIII, bb. 21, n. 62: 53, vol. XXII, bb. 4: 235, vol. XXIV, bb. 63, n. 60: 274, vol. XLIII, bb. 3, n. 48: 52, n. 54: 62, bb. 8, n. 1: 219, n. 2: 220, n. 12: 224, n. 13: 225, vol. LXV, bb. 15, n. 109: 59. Among the Sunnî, cf. **ḤNA.**, vol. III, bk. 31 (*Kitâb maʿrifat al-ṣaḥâba*), *Manâqib Fâṭima bt. rasûl Allâh*, n. 4791, p. 180, n. 4821: 190, **BĠD.**, vol. VIII, n. 4234: 141, **ḤWZ.**, Part 1, bb. *faḍâʾil Fâṭima al-Zahrâʾ bt. rasûl Allâh*, n. 11: 94–95, **ǦWZ¹.**, vol. I, bb. *fî ḏikr tazwîǧ Fâṭima bi-ʿAlî*: 423, **ATH².**, vol. V, bb. *ḥarf al-fâʾ*: 523, **HAY.**, vol. IX, bb. *fî faḍli-hâ wa-tazwîǧi-hâ bi-ʿAlî*: 212, **MTQ.**, vol. V: 96, **RḤB.**: 48, **SHL.**: 42–43.

A number of the Shîʿî transmitters clarify that it is precisely as Fâṭima is crossing the Bridge[26] that the call arises for gazes to be lowered in deference to her exalted status.[27] A further amplification is found in some of the Sunnî transmitters: "She will be wearing two green mantles…"[28] Still other Sunnî transmitters add a different element: "She will pass by with seventy thousand servants from the black-eyed maidens of Paradise, like brilliant lightening…"[29]

Within the large corpus of Shîʿî *aḥâdîṯ* which concern eschatology, and particularly in terms of Fâṭima, two basic strands are dominant: the first concerns the entry of Fâṭima into Paradise, and the second details her status there.

In terms of the first strand, al-Mağlisî carries a *ḥadîṯ* which at once causes some difficulty:

> From *Kitâb al-firdaws* of Ibn Shîrawayh al-Daylamî, on the authority of Abû Hurayra, who said: The Messenger of God said: The first person to enter Paradise will be Fâṭima. She is to this community what Maryam was to the children of Israel.[30]

---

[26] The Bridge (*al-ṣirâṭ*) denotes the bridge that traverses Hell. This concept is not articulated in the Qur'ân, but abounds in the Shîʿî and Sunnî books of *aḥâdîṯ*. Cf. MONNOT G., "Ṣirāṭ" in H.A.R Gibb et al. (eds.), *EI*², 1971, vol. IXb: 670–671.

[27] **RṬB**¹.: 50, 65, **MFD**⁵., n. 6: 130, **SHB**., vol. III, bb. *manâqib Fâṭima al-Zahrâʾ*: 374, **IRB**., vol. I: 457, **ḤLL**².: 352, **ÂML**., vol. I: 171, **ABḎ**.: 472, **MĞL**., vol. VIII, bb. 22, n. 12: 68, vol. XVII, bb. 2: 242, vol. XXVII, bb. 4, n. 144: 139, vol. XXXVII, bb. 50: 70, vol. XLIII, bb. 3, n. 48: 53, bb. 8, nn. 9–11: 222–224.

[28] **ḤNA**., vol. III, bk. 31 (*Kitâb maʿrifat al-ṣaḥâba*), *Manâqib Fâṭima bt. rasûl Allâh*, n. 4821: 190 (who notes that some texts read 'red' rather than 'green'), **HAY**., vol. IX, bb. *fî faḍli-hâ wa-tazwîği-hâ bi-ʿAlî*: 212, **SHL**.: 42–43 (who notes, as does al-Nîsâbûrî, that some texts read 'red' rather than 'green').

[29] **ḪWZ**., Part 1, bb. *faḍâʾil Fâṭima al-Zahrâʾ bt. rasûl Allâh*, n. 11: 94–95, **MTQ**., vol. V: 96.

[30] **MĞL**., vol. XXXVII, bb. 50, n. 38: 70, vol. XLIII, bb. 3, n. 44: 44.

Ibn Shaḥrâshûb transmits it in his *Manâqib âl Abî Ṭâlib* from Abû Ṣâliḥ al-Mu'aḏḏin in his *al-Arbaʿîna.*[31] Al-Mağlisî transmits it twice: once from one Ibn Shîrawayh al-Daylamî in his *Kitâb al-firdaws*, and then from Abû Ṣâliḥ. Among the Sunnî, al-Ḏahabî also carries it from Abû Ṣâliḥ,[32] but it is found in no other major transmitter, Shîʿî or Sunnî. This *ḥadîṯ* appears to gainsay a number of others; it contradicts the report examined earlier in this work, carried by large numbers of Shîʿî and Sunnî transmitters, in which Muḥammad assures Fâṭima that she will be the first to follow him. Presumably, she is therefore the second, and not the first to enter into Paradise, unless one interprets Muḥammad's words strictly in the sense that she will be the first to follow him in death, without any allusion to an entry into Paradise (or interprets them as referring to her as the first of his community). It also contradicts a body of *aḥâdîṯ* carried by Shîʿî scholars (besides al-Mağlisî) in which Muḥammad maintains that he himself will be the first to enter Paradise, and that ʿAlî, Fâṭima, al-Ḥasan and al-Ḥusayn will follow after him;[33] and some *aḥâdîṯ* in which Muḥammad claims that he, ʿAlî, Fâṭima, al-Ḥasan and al-Ḥusayn will enter Paradise together.[34] Finally, there are a number of *aḥâdîṯ* in which it is ʿAlî, and not Fâṭima, who is given the promise of being first. ʿAlî will be, with Muḥammad, the first for whom the tombs split open, the first, with Muḥammad, to stand on the Bridge, the first, with Muḥammad, to be robed with heavenly garments, the first, with Muḥammad, to stand on the right of the throne, the first, with Muḥammad, to knock on the door of Paradise and the first, with Muḥammad, to drink the sweet nectar of heaven.[35]

---

[31] **SHB.**, vol. III, bb. *manâqib Fâṭima al-Zahrâ'*: 377.

[32] **ḎHB²**., vol. II, bb. *ḥarf al-ʿayn*, n. 5057: 618.

[33] **ṬFA²**., bb. 12, n. 66–726: 351, **ÂML.**, vol. II, bb. 16: 87, **MĞL.**, vol. XXVIII, bb. 2, n. 8: 45, vol. XXXVII, bb. 50, n. 54: 191, vol. LXV, bb. 18, n. 56: 127.

[34] **RṬB²**.: 46, **IRB.**, vol. I: 398, **ḤLL²**.: 466.

[35] **ṬBR³**.: 444, **ṬFA²**., bb. 32, n. 21–1335: 641, **MĞL.**, vol. XL, bb. 91, n. 70: 35, vol. XLIII, bb. 5, n. 11: 99, vol. LXXIV, bb. 3: 62.

3.3. THE RIDERS OF PARADISE

A further strand focuses upon Fâṭima's mount on the Day of Resurrection:

> ʿAlî b. ʿAbd Allâh b. al-ʿAbbâs, on the authority of his father, who said: "I heard the O Messenger of God saying: People, we will be four riders (mounted) in the Resurrection, and none besides us." Somebody said to him: "May my father and mother be ransomed for you, Messenger of God; who are those mounted?" He said: "I will be on al-Burâq, and my brother Ṣâliḥ on the she-camel of God, which his people hamstrung,[36] and my daughter Fâṭima on my she-camel al-ʿAḍbâʾ,[37] and ʿAlî b. Abî Ṭâlib on one of the she-camels of Paradise…"[38]

3.4. SUPPLEMENTARY THEMES

Other *aḥâdîṯ* which specify her entrance into Paradise are infused with themes of the magnificent vestments of Paradise, of light and of angelic activity.

> In the three chains of transmission on the authority of al-Riḍâ,[39] on the authority of his forefathers, who said that the Messenger of God said: "My daughter Fâṭima will be gathered wearing the garment of esteem soaked in the water of Life.[40] The creatures will look at her and marvel over her. Then she

---

[36] According to the Qur'ânic text, the prophet Ṣâliḥ was sent to the people of Ṯamûd, to whom were also sent the camel of God as a sign. Ṣâliḥ instructed the people not to harm the creature, but they hamstrung it (Q. 7: 73–77, 11: 64–65, 17: 59, 26: 155–157, 54: 27–29, 91: 13–14).

[37] Al-ʿAḍbâʾ is the name of Muḥammad's own she-camel. Cf. **KLY.**, vol. IV, bk. 15 (*Kitâb al-ḥaǧǧ*), bb. *nawâdir al-ṭawâf*, n. 16: 429. Cf. also **YṬB**[2]., vol. IX, n. 1806: 174.

[38] **RṬB**[2].: 61, **ṢDQ**[1]., n. 7: 206, **ṢDQ**[4]., vol. I, n. 20: 204, **MFD**[5]., n. 3: 271, **ṬFA**[2]., bb. 2, n. 4: 34, **MǦL.**, vol. VII, bb. 8, nn. 1–2: 230–231, vol. XI, bb. 6, n. 6: 380, vol. LXV, bb. 18, n. 25: 112. It is of note that in other accounts, the four riders are named as Muḥammad, Ṣâliḥ, Ḥamza and ʿAlî: cf. **MǦL.**, vol. XLIII, bb. 6, n. 6: 149.

[39] The eighth Imâm.

[40] Cf. Q. 29: 64.

> will also be clothed with the garments of Paradise, one thousand garments, and written on each garment in green script; 'let the daughter of Muḥammad enter Paradise in the most beautiful form, the most beautiful esteem and the most beautiful appearance'. She will be led into Paradise as a bride is led, and seventy thousand servants will be assigned to her."[41]

The golden thread running through all the narratives about Fâṭima on the Last Day is that God vindicates her; in the preceding narrative, this vindication is noticeably articulated. Apparently scorned and neglected on earth, Fâṭima now wears the vestments of esteem. All of creation must now lower their gaze before the one who on earth suffered such ill-treatment at the hands of some of her father's own followers. This woman, who experienced the humility of a meagre dower and such poverty in her married life, is now clothed in heavenly garments and enters Paradise like a bride. After years of hard and painful toil on earth, she has numerous servants entrusted to her.

The Shîʿî transmitters develop this theme:

> On the authority of Ǧaʿfar b. Muḥammad,[42] on the authority of his father, who said: "On the Day of Resurrection, a herald will call before the throne: Assembly of creatures, lower your gaze until Fâṭima the daughter of Muḥammad has passed by! She will be the first to be vested, and twelve thousand maidens of Paradise from *al-Firdaws*[43] will meet her, and with them, fifty thousand angels on thoroughbreds of sapphire, their flanks of

---

[41] **RṬB[1]**.: 57–58, **ṢDQ[5]**., vol. II, bb. 31, n. 38: 30, **ABḎ**.: 599, **MǦL**., vol. XXIII, bb. 63, n. 60: 274, vol. XLIII, bb. 8, n. 6: 221, n. 12: 224.

[42] The sixth Imâm.

[43] Ayoub writes of obscure words that have been taken up by the Arabic language "to convey an aspect of mystery and myth beyond their generally accepted meaning. Firdaws, for example, which means 'paradise', becomes a specific place in paradise with a special significance." Al-Firdaws is described as a mountain higher than the entire Paradise. Cf. AYOUB M., *Redemptive Suffering in Islam. A Study of the Devotional Aspects of ʿAshura in Twelver Shiʿism*, 1978: 202.

chrysolite and their halters of fresh pearl, wearing saddle bags of pearls, on each saddle bag a cushion of silk brocade. She will cross the Bridge with them, and they will come to *al-Firdaws*. The people of Paradise will welcome her, and she will sit on a throne of light and they will sit around her. In the middle of the throne will be two palaces, a white one and a yellow one, made of pearl from one stock. In the white palace there will be seventy thousand houses, dwellings of Muḥammad and the family of Muḥammad, and in the yellow palace there will be seventy thousand houses, dwellings of Ibrâhîm and the family of Ibrâhîm.

God will send to her (an angel) not sent to anyone before her or after her, and he will say to her: Your Lord greets you with peace and says to you: Ask Me what I can give you. She will say: I am complete by His favour, His Paradise has been permitted to me, His generosity delights me, and He has given me preference over the women of His creation. I ask Him to let me intercede for my offspring and my progeny and for those who are affectionate to them after me and who defend them after me. He said: God will reveal to that angel, without him having moved from his place, to inform her: I have allowed her to intercede for her offspring and her progeny and those who are affectionate to them and love them and defend them after her. He said: She will say: Praise be to God who has removed the grief from me and gladdened my eyes.

Then Ǧaʿfar said: whenever my father remembered this report, he would recite this verse: «*And they who believe and whose seed follow them in faith, We cause their seed to join them (there), and We deprive them of nought of their (life's) work. Every man is a pledge for that which he hath earned*»" (Q. 52: 21).[44]

Although we have seen *aḥâdîṯ* in which Muḥammad promises ʿAlî that he will be the first, with Muḥammad, to be robed with heavenly garments, this *ḥadîṯ* patently names Fâṭima as the recipient of that

[44] **RṬB**¹.: 57, **IRB.**, vol. I: 506, **MǦL.**, vol. XXIV, bb. 23, n. 60: 274–275.

honour. Once more, the important elements are present; entering Paradise in untold glory, all her long sorrow is wiped away by God, who has favoured her above all other women, and now gifts her with the power of intercessory prayer.

3.5. INTERCESSION AS THE DOWER OF FÂṬIMA

Within their comprehensive belief in intercession, and the permissibility of seeking such intercession, the Shîʿî theologians situate the intercessory prerogatives of Fâṭima.

> When Fâṭima heard that her father was to give her in marriage, and had given dirhams for her as a dower, she said: "My father, the girls of the rest of mankind are given in marriage with dirhams and dinars, and what is the difference between you and the rest of mankind? I will ask God, may He be exalted, to make my dower intercession for the sinners of your community." Instantly, Ǧibrâʾîl descended, holding in his hand a piece of silk on which was written: God, may He be exalted, has made the dower of Fâṭima the Radiant, daughter of Muḥammad the Chosen One, intercession for his sinful community. Fâṭima ordered at the time of her departure from the world that the piece of silk be placed on her shroud. She said: "When I am gathered on the Day of Resurrection, I will present this in my hand, and I will intercede for the sinners of my father's community."[45]

This is not a report found in any of the major books of Shîʿî *aḥâdîṯ*, but forms part of a genre of pious stories, told in different ways but always with an analogous theme. The account serves the constant theme of Fâṭima's vindication by God, replacing her poor earthly dower with a remarkable power, and using the recurring premise of God intervening in her life in a singular way. This theme of vindication, and of God giving Fâṭima untold power as a reward for her suffering, is articulated in a *ḥadîṯ* in which her intercession, expressed in terms of her ability to judge His creatures, is patently established by God. This narrative, not found in any of the major

---

[45] SHÎRÂZÎ Ḥ., *Kalimat Fâṭima*, Dâr al-ʿUlûm, Beirut 2000: 68, 187.

books of the Shîʿî corpus, recounts words spoken by God to Muḥammad during his 'night journey':

> As to your daughter, I will make her stand near My Throne, and she will be told: God has made you judge over His creation. Whoever harmed you and harmed your offspring, judge them as you wish, and I will sanction your judgment concerning them…[46]

Other such stories tell of how Fâṭima's hearing the voices of the sinners of Muḥammad's community crying out is enough to cause God to release them from their torment:

> All the people of grave sins cried out with the testimony of faith (*shahâda*): There is no god but God, and Muḥammad is the Messenger of God. Their voices ascended, and our mistress Fâṭima heard their voices and said: I can hear the voices of the community of my father between the strata of the sun and the moon. Ǧibraʾîl heard the words of Fâṭima and said: Let Muḥammad be informed. Then the Truth, lofty His splendour, called out to him: Ǧibraʾîl, the cry of the sinful of the community of my beloved Muḥammad has ascended to Me (in the word of *al-tawḥîd*). Ǧibraʾîl, go to Mâlik, keeper of the Fire, and order him to reduce the chastisement for them. He said: Ǧibraʾîl came to Mâlik and said to him: Mâlik, your Lord says: Open the door of the Fire for the people of grave sins of the community of Muḥammad and reduce the chastisement for them.[47]

The narrative blends elements of the pious stories and accepted reports about Fâṭima's intercessory powers as well as of Islamic theology already seen in the Sunnî *aḥâdîṯ* about intercession; that God can bring people out of the Fire at His will and that some people are affected only temporarily by the chastisement of the Fire. Fâṭima's hearing the distressed voices of the sinners is enough for her intercessory prerogatives to be honoured and her 'dower' to be fulfilled; that she would intercede specifically for the sinners of

---

[46] **QQM.**, n. 10: 334.

[47] SHÎRÂZÎ Ḥ., *Kalimat Fâṭima*, 2000: 79.

her father's community. In fact, as we shall see, her intercessory powers are somewhat wider than that, and contain elements that are both active and passive, both positive and negative.

3.6. FÂṬIMA'S NEGATIVE INTERCESSION

Fâṭima's intercessory prerogatives start with a plea for justice, in a genre comprising three basic strands, of which a short example of each will suffice. In the first, in a theme already encountered, Fâṭima holds before God the bloodied shirt al-Ḥusayn as a means of beseeching justice. In the second, she is confronted with her murdered son, blood streaming from his jugular vein. In the third, she is confronted with his headless body, and fails at first to recognize him.

3.6.1. The Bloodied Shirt

The *leitmotif* of al-Ḥusayn's blood-stained shirt held before God by Fâṭima has already been seen in a number of *aḥâdîṯ*. This moment marks the zenith of all her mourning and grief:

> On the authority of Abû ʿAbd Allâh,[48] who said: "On the Day of Resurrection, God will gather the first and the last on an equal footing, and a herald will call: Lower your gaze and bow your heads, until Fâṭima the daughter of Muḥammad has crossed the Bridge." He said: "The creatures will cast down their gaze, and Fâṭima will arrive on one of the thoroughbreds of Paradise, accompanied by seventy thousand angels, and she will halt in a noble place of the places of the Resurrection. Then she will descend from her thoroughbred, and she will take the shirt of al-Ḥusayn b. ʿAlî, stained with his blood, in her hand, and she will say: Lord, this is the shirt of my son. You know what was done to him!"[49]

---

[48] The sixth Imâm.

[49] **MFD**[5]., n. 6: 130, **ḤDI**., vol. III: 226, **MĞL**., vol. XLIII, bb. 8, n. 11: 224.

3.6.2. The Bleeding al-Ḥusayn

> On the authority the Commander of the Faithful, who said: "One day the Messenger of God went to see Fâṭima, and she was mourning, and he spoke to her concerning the circumstances of the Resurrection, concerning which he said: You will say: Show me al-Ḥasan and al-Ḥusayn, and they will come to you, al-Ḥusayn's jugular vein of streaming with blood. He will say: Lord, obtain for me today my due from those who mistreated me..."[50]

This *ḥadîṯ* is noteworthy because it is al-Ḥusayn, and not Fâṭima, who pleads for justice from God; however, it is transmitted by al-Mağlisî only from Furât al-Kûfî and is found in none of the major Shî'î books.

3.6.3. The Headless Corpse

This strand is found in the *ḥadîṯ* we have already examined, in which all living creatures are called upon to lower their gaze as Fâṭima passes by. In some accounts, transmitted by al-Mağlisî only from Furât al-Kûfî, she is holding the bloodied shirt of her dead son. In others, it is her son who comes to meet her:

> And Fâṭima my daughter will pass by, wearing two green mantles, surrounded by seventy thousand maidens of Paradise. When she arrives at the door of her palace, she will find al-Ḥasan standing there, and al-Ḥusayn standing there, the head severed. She will say to al-Ḥasan: Who is this, and he will say: My brother. The community of your father killed him and cut off his head.[51]

This report, found in none of the major Shî'î books, presupposes that Fâṭima knows nothing of al-Ḥusayn's murder and decapitation, and is first appraised of this by al-Ḥasan. In fact, the whole

---

50 **FRT.**: 222, **MĞL.**, vol. VIII, bb. 21, n. 62: 53, b. 23, n. 116: 172, vol. XLIII, bb. 8, n. 13: 225.

51 **FRT.**: 269, 437, **MĞL.**, vol. V, bb. 17, n. 21: 335, vol. XLIII, bb. 3, n. 54: 62, vol. LXV, bb. 15, n. 109: 59.

thrust of Shîʿî tradition posits her ceaseless mourning until the Day of Resurrection precisely because the Karbalâʾ event.

3.7. FÂṬIMA'S PASSIVE INTERCESSION

An examination of the name Fâṭima brought to light that God named her so because, among other reasons, her followers (*shîʿa*) have been 'separated' or 'weaned' from the Fire, and her enemies have been 'separated' from her love. A further *ḥadîṯ* revealed that God saved her offspring from the Fire because Fâṭima was chaste. Already in these two strands – her name and her chastity – is prefigured the power of her intercession; both strands stress that God has saved people from Hell because of Fâṭima. In these cases, she is a somewhat passive agent of intercession, with God acting because of her. In fact, this passive intercession of Fâṭima is, according to the books of Shîʿî *aḥâdîṯ*, not only a factor of her name and her chastity, but also of her pre-existence. For our purposes, a number of specific reports are of note, all of them transmitted by al-Mağlisî and mentioned by al-Mûsawî in his biographical work.[52]

3.7.1. The Prophets and Holy Ones

The prophets and holy ones asked for firmness of purpose through Fâṭima as a member of Muḥammad's family. In response to a question put to him by a member of the Jewish community – "Are you more excellent than Mûsâ b. ʿImrân, the prophet to whom God spoke, and to whom He sent down the *Tawrât* and the staff, and for whom He split the sea, and whom He shaded with the clouds?" – Muḥammad replied:

> When Adam incurred sin, his repentance was to say: "God, I ask You by the truth of Muḥammad and the family of Muḥammad, if You would not forgive me," and God forgave it him. Nûḥ, when he boarded the ark and feared drowning, said: "God, I ask You by the truth of Muḥammad and the family of Muḥammad, if You would not deliver me from drowning," and God delivered him from it. Ibrâhîm, when he was

[52] al-MÛSAWÎ M., *al-Kawṯar fî aḥwâl Fâṭima bt. al-nabî al-aṭhar*, 2000, v. I: 189–198, 205–209, 210–212, 215–218, 219–224.

cast into the fire, said: "God, I ask You by the truth of Muḥammad and the family of Muḥammad, if You would not deliver me from it," and God made it coolness and peace for him.[53] Mûsâ, when his staff was cast down and he was filled with a sense of foreboding, said: "God, I ask You by the truth of Muḥammad and the family of Muḥammad, if You would not safeguard me," and God, lofty His splendour said: "Do not fear! You are the higher."[54]

3.7.2. Iblîs[55]

Iblîs desired redemption and asked God for it by the truth of Fâṭima. In the course of a narrative concerning a female *ǧinn* said to be called ʿAfrâʾ, the following dialogue occurs:

> ʿAfrâʾ came, and the Prophet said to her: "ʿAfrâʾ, where were you?" She said: "I was visiting a sister of mine." He said: "Happy those who love one another in God and visit each other, ʿAfrâʾ! What did you see?" She said: "I saw many marvels." He said: "What marvels did you see?" She said: "I saw Iblîs in the green sea on a white rock, his hands stretched out to the heavens, and he was saying: My God, when You have fulfilled Your oath and made me enter the Fire of Hell, I will ask You by the truth of Muḥammad, and ʿAlî, and Fâṭima, and al-Ḥasan and al-Ḥusayn if You would not liberate me and gather me with them." I said: "Ḥâriṯ,[56] what are these names by which you plead?" He said: "I saw them on the leg of the Throne seven thousand years before God, powerful and lofty,

[53] Cf. Q. 21: 69.

[54] **ṢDQ¹**., n. 4: 218, **FNR**., vol. II: 272, **ṬBR²**., vol. I: 47, **ABḎ**.: 53, **ḤRR¹**., vol. VII, bb. 37, n. 8846: 100, **MǦL**., vol. XVI, bb. 11: 366, vol. XXVI, bb. 7, n. 1: 319. Cf. Q. 21: 69, Q. 20: 67–68.

[55] One of the Islamic names denoting Satan.

[56] One of the names given to Satan before his fall. Cf. WENSINCK A.J., "Iblis" in H.A.R Gibb et al. (eds.), *EI²*, 1995: 145–146. In his transmission of the text, al-Mûsawî writes 'Abû Ḥâriṯ', but the 'Abû' is not found in the original transcripts (cf. al-MÛSAWÎ M., *al-Kawṯar fî aḥwâl Fâṭima bt. al-nabî al-aṭhar*, 2000, v. I: 211).

> created Adam, and I perceived that they were the most distinguished of the creation for God: and I am pleading by them." The Prophet said: "By God, were the people of the earth to entreat by these names, God, may He be exalted, would answer them."[57]

3.7.3. Yûsuf

The prayer of the prophets and the prayer of Yûsuf in prison were answered through Fâṭima. In a group of *aḥâdîṯ*, elements of which have widespread occurrence throughout the Shî'î corpus, we find God instructing Mûsâ to strike the sea with his staff[58] with the words "O God, by the standing of Muḥammad and his noble family" as he does so,[59] as well as a story of Yûsuf in prison, in which he is instructed to say this prayer:

> He who is Great of all the great, He who has neither partner nor vizier, Creator of the sun and the luminous moon, protection of the necessarily blind, breaker of every obdurate tyrant, enricher of the misery of the poor, mender of the broken bone, releaser of the shackles of the prisoner, I ask You by the truth of Muḥammad and his family, to create for me in my situation a release and a way out, and to bestow upon me what I anticipate and what I do not anticipate.[60]

3.7.4. The Resolution of God

It is incumbent upon God to answer and not refuse the prayer of whoever asks by the truth of Fâṭima (*bi-ḥaqqi Fâṭima*). A final group of *aḥâdîṯ* reveals that Fâṭima's is among the five names most loved

---

[57] **ṢDQ⁴**., vol. II, n. 13: 638, **IRB**., vol. I: 465, **MĞL**., vol. XVIII, bb. 9, n. 1: 83, vol. XXVII, bb. 11, n. 1: 13, vol. LX, bb. 2, n. 36: 80, vol. XCI, bb. 28, n. 15: 20; **NṬR**., vol. V, bb. 35, n. 9–5765: 232.

[58] Cf. Q. 20: 77.

[59] Examples of this *ḥadîṯ* may be found in **MĞL**., vol. XIII, bb. 4, n. 54: 138, vol. XCI, bb. 28, n. 8: 2, **NṬR**., vol. V, bb. 35, n. 10–5766: 233.

[60] **AYY**., vol. II, bb. 12, n. 88: 198, **MĞL**., vol. XII, bb. 9, n. 147: 319, vol. XCII, bb. 106, n. 23: 193.

by God,[61] and that He cannot but answer prayer made through these names.

> On the authority of Abû Ğaʿfar,[62] on the authority of his father, on the authority of his grandfather, who said: "The Messenger of God said: On the Day of Resurrection, when the people of Paradise are settled in Paradise and the people of the Fire in the Fire, a servant who remained in the Fire for seventy autumns – and an autumn is seventy years – will ask God, powerful and lofty, and will cry out to Him, saying: Lord, I ask You by the truth of Muḥammad and the people of his house if You would not have mercy on me! He said: And God, lofty His splendour, will reveal to Ğibraʾîl: descend to My servant and lead him out. Ğibraʾîl will say: Lord, how is it possible for me to descend into the Fire? God, may He be blessed and exalted, will say: I have ordered it to be coolness and peace for you. He said: Ğibraʾîl will say: Lord, what information have I about his location? God will say: He is in a pit of imprisonment. Ğibraʾîl will descend and find him, recognizing him by his face, and will lead him out and stand him before God, powerful and lofty. God, powerful and lofty, will say: My servant! How long did you abide, imploring me in the Fire? He will say: Lord, I cannot count it. God, powerful and lofty, will say: By My might and My splendour, had not someone asked Me by their truth with Me, I would have looked upon his despicableness in the Fire. But it is My resolution that no servant would ask me by the truth of Muḥammad and the people of his house, except that I would forgive him what was between us. Today I have forgiven you. Then he will be ordered into Paradise."[63]

---

[61] **MFD²**.: 222, **MĞL**., vol. XXII, bb. 10, n. 63: 347, vol. XXXVII, bb. 50, n. 43: 76, vol. XCI, bb. 28, n. 16: 21, **NṬR**., vol. V, bb. 35, n. 1–5757–14: 228.

[62] The fifth Imâm.

[63] **RṬB²**.: 210, **ṢDQ¹**., n. 4: 672, **ṢDQ⁴**., vol. II, n. 9: 584, **ṢDQ⁶**., n. 1: 226, **MFD⁵**., n. 6: 218, **ṬFA²**., bb. 37, n. 4–1425: 675, **FNR**., vol. II: 271, **MĞL**., vol. VII, bb. 24, n. 4: 282, vol. XXVII, bb. 9, n. 5: 312, vol.

All of these *aḥâdîṯ* make Fâṭima's intercession contingent upon her membership of the pre-existent 'holy family', but it is a mode of intercession nonetheless, even if in a passive form.

3.8. FÂṬIMA'S ACTIVE AND POSITIVE INTERCESSION

In the following *aḥâdîṯ*, Fâṭima's intercession ceases to be passive and becomes active, changing from a negative plea for the punishment of those who have done evil to a positive cry for those in need. Having effectively pled with God for justice to be done, she now turns her mediatory powers to four main groups of people.

3.8.1. Her Progeny and Those who Love Them

The large majority of *aḥâdîṯ* recounting the intercession of Fâṭima make her progeny and those who love them the primary recipients (and first two groups) of her intercessory powers. These recipients are named as her own adherents (*shîʿa*), her offspring and all who loved and supported the *ahl al-bayt* (a love that may be expressed merely by grieving for them). These groups are clarified by Fâṭima herself as she pleads before the Throne:

> I heard Ǧâbir b. ʿAbd Allâh al-Anṣârî saying: "The Messenger of God said: On the Day of Resurrection, my daughter Fâṭima will approach on a she-camel of Paradise, the two flanks of its muzzle embellished with fresh pearls, its legs with green emerald, its tail with pungent musk, its eyes two rubies, and over it a dome of light, its exterior perceived from its interior and its interior from its exterior, its inside the pardon of God and its outside the mercy of God. On her head, a crown of light, and for the crown seventy supports, each studded with pearls and sapphire, which will shine the way the glittering star shines in the horizon of heaven. On her right will be seventy thousand angels and on her left seventy thousand angels.
>
> Ǧibra'îl will take halter of the camel, shouting at the top of his voice: Lower your gaze, while Fâṭima the daughter of

---

XCI, bb. 28, n. 1: 1, **NṬR.**, vol. V, bb. 35, n. 3–5759: 228. The text, as it is transmitted by al-Mûsawî, contains a number of errors.

> Muḥammad is crossing. There will not remain at that time a prophet or a messenger or a righteous one or a martyr but that they will lower their gaze while Fâṭima is crossing. She will journey until she is facing the Throne of her Lord, lofty His splendour. She will throw herself from her she-camel and say: My God and my Master, judge between me and those who harmed me. O God, judge between me and those who killed my son. Then the call will come from God, lofty His splendour: My beloved and daughter of my beloved, ask me your desire and make your intercession before me, and by my might and my splendour the wickedness of the oppressor will not pass me. She will say: My God and my Master, my progeny, and my adherents, and the adherents of my progeny, and those who love me and the lovers of my progeny. Then the call will come from God, lofty His splendour: Where are the progeny of Fâṭima, and her adherents, and those who love her and the lovers of her progeny? They will draw near, encircled by the angels of mercy, and Fâṭima will go before them until she has led them into Paradise."[64]

In another report, Fâṭima's arrival is described in much a similar vein, but when she reaches the gates of Paradise, she hesitates and turns around, eliciting a question from God:

> And God will say: "O daughter of My beloved! Why do you turn around, when I have bade you enter my Paradise?" She will say: "Lord! I desired that my standing be known on a day like this." God will say: "Daughter of my beloved! Return and see who has in his heart love for you or one of your progeny, take him by the hand and lead him into Paradise." Abû Ǧaʿfar[65] said: "By God, Ǧâbir, on that day she will pick out

[64] **FRT.**, n. 587: 446, **RṬB**²: 18, **ṢDQ**¹., n. 4: 17, **FNR.**, vol. I: 148, **SHB.**, vol. III, bb. *manâqib Fâṭima al-Zahrâ*ʾ: 374–375, **MǦL.**, vol. VIII, bb. 21, n. 62: 53, vol. XLIII, bb. 8, n. 1: 219, n. 13: 227.

[65] The fifth Imâm.

> her adherents and those who love her the way a bird picks out the good seed from the perishable seed."[66]

The texts employ other images, besides that of a bird picking out good seed; one set of *aḥâdîṯ* narrates that those who love Fâṭima will cling to the hem of her cloak[67] and will be delivered by her from the Fire, while another strand tells us that:

> Fâṭima has a position at the gate of Hell. On the Day of Resurrection, between the eyes of every man will be written 'believer' or 'rejecter of faith'.[68] A lover whose sins were many will be ordered to the Fire, and she will read between his eyes, 'lover'. Then she will say: My God and my Master! You have named me Fâṭima and by me have weaned from the Fire those who support me and support my progeny. Your promise is true and You never fail to keep Your promise. God, powerful and lofty, will say: You have spoken the truth, Fâṭima! I named you Fâṭima and by you weaned from the Fire those who love and support you and love and support your progeny. My promise is true and I never fail to keep my promise. But I ordered this servant of mine to the Fire that you might intercede for him, and I will accept your intercession, that I might make manifest to my angels, my prophets, my messengers and the people of the gathering your standing and place with me. Whoever you read between his eyes 'believer', draw him out by his hand and make him enter paradise.[69]

---

[66] **FRT.**, n. 403: 298, **MĞL.**, vol. VIII, bb. 21, n. 59: 51, vol. XLIII, bb. 3, n. 57: 64.

[67] **MĞL.**, vol. VIII, bb. 22, n. 12: 68, vol. XVII, bb. 2, n. 2: 242.

[68] The Arabic *kufr* and its derivatives are difficult to render; its basic meaning carries the sense of being irreligious or ungrateful. English translators and interpreters such as Pickthall fluctuate between 'unbeliever', 'misbeliever' and 'disbeliever', but I have chosen, following Ayoub, to render it 'rejection of faith', with the passive participle as 'rejecter of faith'. Cf. AYOUB M., *The Qur'an and Its Interpreters*, vol. II, *The House of ʿImran*, Albany 1992: 40.

[69] **ṢDQ⁸.**, vol. I, bb. 142, n. 6: 179, **IRB.**, vol. I: 463, **MĞL.**, vol. VIII, bb. 21, n. 57: 50, vol. XLIII, bb. 2, n. 11: 14.

About this report, Ayoub writes:

> This Tradition provides one of the clearest expressions of the concept of redemption in Shīʿī piety…Fāṭimah's role, as depicted in the Tradition we have just cited, is more than that of an intercessor. She is given the authority to counteract the divine judgment. She does not intercede on the behalf of a believer that his punishment may be lightened, but rather saves a sinner from the torment of hell altogether.[70]

Striking in the narrative is the juxtaposition of the word 'lover' (of the *ahl al-bayt*) with the word 'believer'. The two are used interchangeably, suggesting that they are one and the same thing. A believer is tantamount to one who loves and supports Fâṭima and her progeny.

3.8.2. Non-Shîʿa who Love her Progeny

A rare *ḥadîṯ* offers a place in Fâṭima's prayers for those who were not her adherents, always understood as members of the Shîʿa, but who loved her and her progeny nonetheless:

> There will come to her the call from God: Daughter of the beloved of God, I have related to you what the community of your father did to him, because I have stored up for you with me consolation in your calamity concerning him; indeed, I have arranged for your consolation in your calamity. I will not consider calling humanity to account until you enter Paradise, you and your progeny and your adherents and those who were not your adherents but who supported you in a friendly manner, before I consider calling humanity to account. And so Fâṭima my daughter will enter Paradise, and her progeny and her adherents and those who were not her adherents but who supported her in a friendly manner. For these are the words of God, may He be exalted, in His Book: «*the Supreme Horror will not grieve them*»:[71] He said: This is the Day of Resurrection:

---

[70] AYOUB M., *Redemptive Suffering in Islam. A Study of the Devotional Aspects of ʿAshura in Twelver Shiʿism*, 1978: 214.

[71] Cf. Q. 21: 103.

> «*while they abide in that which their souls desire*»:[72] this, by God, is Fâṭima, and her progeny and her adherents and those who were not her adherents but who supported her in a friendly manner.[73]

This *ḥadîṯ*, transmitted by al-Mağlisî only from Furât al-Kûfî, is a continuation of the one already related, in which Fâṭima is confronted with the headless body of al-Ḥusayn. In reality, it revisits the theme of a passive intercession; those who are described entering Paradise do so because, even if they were not her progeny or her adherents, they supported her. Al-Mûsawî, who relates this report with a number of textual errors, argues that it implies her effective intercession; that Fâṭima will actively cause those mentioned in the narrative, including non-adherents who supported her, to enter Paradise.[74] However, a careful reading of the extant text does not convey this meaning. Nevertheless, the element of her intercession remains vital.

3.8.3. A Number of Women

> On the authority of Ibn ʿAbbâs, on the authority of the Prophet, who said: "It is as if I am looking at my daughter Fâṭima, and she has entered the Day of Resurrection on a thoroughbred of light, seventy thousand angels on her right, seventy thousand angels on her left and seventy thousand angels behind her. She will conduct the women believers of my community into Paradise. Whichever woman prayed, day and night, the five prayers, and fasted in the month of Ramaḍân, and made the Pilgrimage to the holy house of God, and gave of her money in almsgiving, and obeyed her husband, and

---

[72] Cf. Q. 21: 102.

[73] **FRT.**, n. 362: 269, n. 578: 437, **MĞL.**, vol. VII, bb. 17, n. 21: 335, vol. XLIII, bb. 3, n. 54: 62, vol. LXV, bb. 15, n. 109: 59.

[74] Cf. al-MÛSAWÎ M., *al-Kawṯar fî aḥwâl Fâṭima bt. al-nabî al-aṭhar*, 2000, v. VII: 390.

> supported ʿAlî after me, will enter Paradise through the intercession of my daughter Fâṭima."[75]

It is of note that the Shîʿî transmitter al-Ṭabarsî, in his *Ḫâtimat mustadrak al-wasâʾil*, reproduces this *ḥadîṯ* word for word, but omits the name of Fâṭima or any mention of her intercession,[76] making the entry of the women into Paradise dependent rather upon their faithful living out of the Islamic faith.

3.8.4. The Narratives of Popular Piety

The majority of *aḥâdîṯ* giving details about Fâṭima's intercession are rare, transmitted mostly by Furât al-Kûfî, and by al-Mağlisî from him. Firmly entrenched both among the Shîʿî and the Sunnî transmitters is the call to all creatures to lower their gaze as Fâṭima crosses the Bridge; the subsequent details are less decisive, even among the Shîʿî transmitters. While her intercession for her progeny, as well as the prayer of Iblîs and some of the prophets through Fâṭima and the *ahl al-bayt* find a fairly strong resonance in the Shîʿî books, a number of the narratives examined – such as those concerning the bleeding al-Ḥusayn or his headless corpse – are not well-substantiated.

All of these themes, from the *aḥâdîṯ* of both the Shîʿa and the Sunnî, are gathered together in a lengthy narrative found in popular Shîʿî piety:

> I heard the Commander of the Faithful, ʿAlî b. Abî Ṭâlib saying: "The Messenger of God came to call on Fâṭima one day, and she was sorrowful. He said to her: What is this sorrow of yours, my child? She replied: My father, I was thinking of the place of congregation and the people standing, denuded on the Day of Resurrection. He said: My child, a truly momentous day! But Ğibrâʾîl has already informed me from God, powerful and lofty, that He said: The first for whom the world will burst asunder on the Day of Resurrection will be me, then my father Ibrâhîm, then your husband ʿAlî b. Abî Ṭâlib. Then God will

---

[75] **RṬB²**.: 177, **ṢDQ¹**., n. 18: 468, **MĞL**., vol. VIII, bb. 21, n. 76: 58, vol. XXXVII, bb. 50, n. 52: 84, vol. XLIII, bb. 3, n. 20: 24.

[76] Cf. **NṬR**., vol. XIV, bb. 71, n. 9–16646: 258.

dispatch Ǧibrâ'îl to you with seventy thousand angels, who will fashion seven domes of light upon your tomb. Then Isrâfîl[77] will bring you three vestments of light, and standing at your head, will call to you: Fâṭima, daughter of Muḥammad, betake yourself to your place of congregation. You will rise, your soul at peace, your privacy concealed. Isrâfîl will offer you the vestments and you will put them on. Rûfâ'îl[78] will bring to you a thoroughbred of light, its halter of fresh pearls and upon it, a litter of gold. You will mount it, and Rûfâ'îl will lead it by its halter. In front of you will be seventy thousand angels, bearing in their hands banners glorifying God. When the procession has hastened with you, seventy thousand black-eyed maidens of Paradise will welcome you, rejoicing because of you; in the hand of each one of them, a censer of light, from which rises a wind of intensity, without fire, and adorning them, garlands of jewels adorned with pieces of iron of the deepest green. They will journey on your right.

When you have proceeded another distance, as far from the one from your grave to the place of meeting the maidens of Paradise, Maryam daughter of ʿImrân will welcome you, with a similar number of those who are with you of the maidens of Paradise; she will greet you and will journey, she and those who are with her, on your left. Then your mother Ḫadîǧa, daughter of Ḫuwaylid, the first of the believers in God and His Messenger, will welcome you. With her will be seventy thousand angels, banners of exaltation in their hands. When you have approached through the gathering, you will be welcomed by Ḥawwâ', amid seventy thousand maidens of Paradise, and with her, Âsiya, the daughter of Mazâḥim, who will journey with you, she and those who are with her. When you stand in the middle of the gathering – in other words, God will gather the creatures without distinction – they will stand upright (on

[77] The angel who sounds the last trumpet. Cf. WENSINCK A.J., "Isrāfīl" in H.A.R Gibb et al. (eds.), *EI*[2], 1995: 184.

[78] One of the angels of the seven heavens. Cf. MURATA S., "The Angels" in S. H. Nasr (ed.), *Islamic Spirituality. Foundations*, 1997: 328.

their feet) (before you). Then a herald will call from beneath the throne, in the hearing of the creatures: Lower your gaze until Fâṭima the righteous, the daughter of Muḥammad, and those who are with her have crossed. On that day, no-one will look at you except Ibrâhîm, the friend of the Merciful, and ʿAlî b. Abî Ṭâlib. Adam will look for Ḥawwâʾ, and will see her in front of you, with your mother Ḫadîǧa.

Then a pulpit of light will be set up for you, comprising seven layers, with ranks of angels between each layer, holding in their hands banners of light, and with the black-eyed maidens of Paradise standing in formation on the right of the pulpit and on its left. The nearest of the women to you will be Ḥawwâʾ, and Âsiya on your left. When you have reached the uppermost part of the pulpit, Ǧibrâʾîl will come to you and say to you: Fâṭima, ask what you desire! You will say: My Lord show me al-Ḥasan and al-Ḥusayn! They will come to you, the jugular vein of al-Ḥusayn streaming with blood. He will say: Lord, obtain for me today my due from those who mistreated me. Thereupon, the Majestic will grow angry, and because of His anger, Hell and all the angels will grow angry, and thereupon Hell will sigh deeply, with a great sigh. Then a detachment will go out from the fire, and they will gather the killers of al-Ḥusayn and their sons, and the sons of their sons, and these will say: Lord, we did not take part (in the killing of) al-Ḥusayn! God will say to the violent thrusters of Hell:[79] Seize them by their mark! By the blueness of eye[80] and the blackness of face! Seize them by their forelocks and fling them into the bottom of the lowest part of the Fire! For indeed they were severer against the supporters of al-Ḥusayn then were their fathers

[79] The guards of Hell, named in Q. 96: 18 as *al-Zabâniyya*, literally 'violent thrusters'.

[80] A feature "considered unfortunate by the ancient Arabs" and which "finds an echo in Q 20: 102, according to which the wicked will rise on the day of resurrection with shiny (or blue) eyes." Cf. BAR-ASHER M.M., "Shīʿism and the Qur'ān" in J.D. McAuliffe (ed.), *Encyclopaedia of the Qurʾān*, vol. 4, Brill, Leiden 2004: 599

who fought against al-Ḥusayn and killed him! Their groaning will be heard in Hell!

Then Ǧibrâʾîl will say: Fâṭima, ask what you desire! You will reply: My Lord, my adherents! God, powerful and lofty, will say: I have already pardoned them. And you will say: My Lord, the adherents of my son! And God will reply: I have already pardoned them. You will say: My Lord, the adherents of my adherents! And God will say: Be free, and whoever adheres to you will be with you in Paradise; and thereupon, the creatures will wish that they had been supporters of Fâṭima. You will journey forward, and your adherents with you, and the adherents of your son, and the adherents of the Commander of the Faithful, their souls in peace, their privacies concealed; calamities will vanish from them, and for them the places of destination will be made smooth. The people will fear, but they will not be afraid; the people will thirst, but they will not thirst. When you have reached the gate of Paradise, twelve thousand maidens of Paradise, who did not receive anyone before you and who will not receive anyone after you, will receive you: in their hands, lances of light, on thoroughbreds of light, their saddles of the yellowest gold and of sapphires, their halters of fresh pearls, on each thoroughbred, a saddle pad of layered silk.

When you have entered Paradise, its people will attend to you, setting up for your adherents tables of jewels on columns of light. They will eat from them with the people of the Redeeming, «*They will not hear the slightest sound thereof, while they abide in that which their souls desire*».[81] When the holy ones of God come to dwell in Paradise, Adam and those ranking after him of the prophets will come to visit you. In the middle of *al-Firdaws*, two pearls of one stock, a white pearl and a yellow pearl, and within them, palaces and habitations, seventy-thousand habitations in each one – in the white one, the habitations for us and for our adherents, and in the yellow one, habitations for Ibrâhîm and the family of Ibrâhîm.

---

[81] Cf. Q. 21: 102

> She said: My father, I would not like to see the day of your death or to remain behind after you. He said: My child, Ǧibrâ'îl has already informed me from God that you will be the first to join me from the people of my house; affliction for all those who mistreated you, and the great victory for those who assisted you." [82]

As it stands, this narrative is found only in the work of Furât al-Kûfî[83] (and is transmitted from him by al-Maǧlisî), although fragments of its elements can be discerned in other Shîʿî books of *aḥâdîṯ*. As a pious narrative, it serves a number of didactic purposes; it dramatically augments the glory of Fâṭima's entry into Paradise, already seen some of the Shîʿî and Sunnî transmitters, in terms of her vestments, her mount, the themes of light and angelic activity, as well as in those who meet her in welcome. It also clearly exemplifies the subservience of all the other women of Paradise to Muḥammad's daughter, and initiates her work of intercession. This began as a negative mediation, pleading punishment for the killers of al-Ḥusayn, and when this had been accomplished, moved to a positive prayer for all who support her, articulated as her adherents (*shîʿa*), the adherents of her son al-Ḥusayn, and the adherents of her adherents.

---

[82] **MǦL.**, vol. VIII, bb. 21, n. 62: 53–55.

[83] **FRT.**, n. 587: 334–335.

Chapter Four.
Part One: Notes on the Catholic Theology of Mary

As a context in which to examine the feasibility of parallels between Fâṭima in Shîʿî theology and Mary in Catholicism, this chapter presents a framework of the most important Catholic teachings about Mary. Since this is not primarily a work of Mariology, these will be necessarily concise, proposing only the most important elements of each doctrine.

Within Catholic dogma, the life and doctrine of the Virgin Mary might be encapsulated in four basic categories (delineated by Scripture, theology and popular piety):

1. Her conception without sin in the womb of her mother and the supernatural intervention embedded in the stories of her conception and birth.

2. The miracle stories surrounding the virginal conception and birth of Jesus.

3. Mary's grief and suffering, intimately connected with the life and mission of her Son.

4. Her intercessory prerogatives in heaven on behalf of the people of God.

4.1. The Immaculate Conception of Mary in Catholic Tradition

> The most Blessed Virgin Mary was, from the first moment of her conception, by a singular grace and privilege of almighty

> God and by virtue of the merits of Jesus Christ, Saviour of the human race, preserved immune from all stain of original sin.[1]

Thus does the term 'Immaculate Conception', applied in the theology of the Catholic Church to Mary alone and held *de fide definita*,[2] signify that, while all of mankind inherits at birth a human nature tarnished by sin – namely 'Original Sin' – as the consequence of Adam's fall, Mary was, by an extraordinary act of God, set free from this flaw in the very instant of her conception.[3] Preserved from contracting Original Sin, she is thus said to have inherited human nature in its initial, unsoiled condition, and this by the merits of the future redemptive act of her Son. His redeeming and salvific act, although occurring within a moment of time, has no temporal bounds, but extends both retrospectively and progressively into history. Consequently, theology defines God as the efficient cause, Christ's salvific act as the meritorious cause and Mary herself as the final cause of this singular grace.[4] Theologians concede that the doctrine is found only implicitly in Scripture, quoting Gen. 3: 15 in its most literal sense,[5] as well as the angelic salutation 'full of grace' (*kécharitôménê*) recorded in Lk. 1: 28. This title, insists Pope

---

[1] *Declaramus, pronuntiamus, et definimus, doctrinam, quae tenet, beatissimam Virginem Mariam in primo instanti suae conceptionis fuisse singulari omnipotentis Dei gratia et privilegio, intuiti meritorum Christi Iesu Salvatoris humani generis, ab omni originalis culpae labe praeservatam immunem* (Pope Pius IX, *Ineffabilis Deus*, 8TH December 1854). Cf. DENZ., n. 2803: 776.

[2] That is, a truth defined by a solemn judgment of faith, either by the Pope or by a General Council, and which must be believed with full assent.

[3] Ott notes that by 'conception' is meant her passive conception, expressly, that moment in time in which her soul "was created by God and infused into the bodily matter prepared by her parents." Cf. OTT L., *Fundamentals of Catholic Dogma*, Mercier Press, Cork 1960, Book III, Part 3, ch. 2, n. 1: 199.

[4] Ibid., Book III, Part 3, ch. 2, n. 2: 201.

[5] The so-called *Proto-evangelium*, so named because, in its most literal sense, it foretells, after the Fall, the ongoing struggle between humanity and sin, and promises triumph over sin in terms of the salvation brought by the Redeemer, born of a woman.

John Paul II, was used in the sense of a proper name, expressing a characteristic quality.[6] According to the oldest extant texts, 'full of grace' is not a rigorously exact interpretation of the angel's salutation. The word used signifies a change affected in the person of whom it is used, and in Mary's case, the past perfect participial form means a change already effected. De la Potterie suggests that herein lies her sanctity and immaculate state; she is purified in advance, God preparing her by inspiring her with a desire for or orientation towards virginity.[7] This 'transformation by grace' means she was purified and sanctified from an early age; St. Bernard of Clairvaux (d. 1153)[8] entitles this the 'grace of virginity', seen as a desire for virginity.[9]

Nor did the Greek and Latin Fathers of the Church teach it explicitly, but rather, alluded to it in the fundamental proposition of Mary's most perfect purity and holiness, seen especially when she is contrasted with Eve.[10] Mary is, in the words of St. Ambrose of Milan (d. 397):

> "...a Virgin not only undefiled but a Virgin whom grace has made inviolate, free from every stain of sin."[11]

These words, while bordering on the doctrine, do not represent an unambiguous statement, any more than do the words of St. An-

---

[6] OTT L., *Fundamentals of Catholic Dogma*, Mercier Press, Cork 1960, Book III, Part 3, ch. 2, n. 2: 200. Cf. also DONDERS J.G., (ed.), *John Paul II. The Encyclicals in Everyday Language*, Orbis, New York 1996, n. 8: 111.

[7] DE LA POTTERIE I., *Mary in the Mystery of the Covenant*, Alba House, New York 1997: 19.

[8] He wrote much about Mary but, as in the case of his near contemporary St. Anselm, it is evident that he did not accept the Immaculate Conception.

[9] DE LA POTTERIE I., *Mary in the Mystery of the Covenant*, 1997: 145.

[10] OTT L., *Fundamentals of Catholic Dogma*, 1960, Book III, Part 3, ch. 2, n. 2: 201.

[11] JURGENS W.A., *The Faith of the Early Fathers*, Liturgical Press, Collegeville 1970–1979, vol. II, n. 1314: 166.

drew of Crete (d. 740), who sings, "O Virgin undefiled, undefiled is your birth."[12]

Even by the medieval period, the doctrine of the Immaculate Conception had not been definitively fixed in the Catholic Church. While it was believed that the principle was part of the deposit of faith entrusted to the Apostles, admittedly imprecise and veiled, and while the Scriptural references to such a status for Mary are oblique, it became gradually but steadily more explicit through a comprehension of the doctrine of Mary's exceptional holiness, clearly shown in the first chapter of Matthew's Gospel and the first two chapters of Luke. All the indications, such as God choosing her to be the mother of Jesus and preserving her virginity even while calling her to parturition, are indications of this holiness, extant not only in the moment of the Annunciation of her motherhood by the archangel Gabriel, but from the beginning of her life. In the writings of the early Fathers of the Church, we find no reference to the Immaculate Conception, since those early theologians did not believe her to be sinless; Origen (d. 253 or 254)[13] and others presumed her to be imperfect like the rest of humanity. With time, the theology being constructed around her person became more characterized by the keynote of great holiness, a factor stimulated in the East with the sanction of her title *Theotokos* ('Mother of God') by the Council of Ephesus in 431.[14] But it was only by the 8TH century that belief in her inestimable and flawless holiness was firmly established in the Eastern Church.

---

[12] Ibid., vol. III, n. 2336b: 326.

[13] The foremost theologian of the early Greek Church, he described Mary as *Theotokos*, thus pre-empting the official declaration of the Council of Ephesus. But while he patently affirmed the perpetual virginity of Mary, he quite clearly did not regard her as sinless.

[14] An Ecumenical Council convoked in 431 by Emperor Theodosius II as a response against Nestorius and his heretical teaching. It was this Council that defined Mary as *Theotokos*, meaning 'God-bearer' or 'Mother of God'.

In the West, the development was even more unhurried, although by the end of the 11TH century St. Anselm (d. 1109)[15] was proposing his famous argument that Mary's being enrobed in an incomparable holiness was fitting, considering the status to which she had been called. Almost spontaneously, and appearing first in the Eastern Church, the amplification of Mary's never having been tainted by sin sprang from this slow development, although it was often expressed vaguely and indirectly. By 1125 it had reached the Western Church, since by then arguments were ensuing about the precise character of her conception. While in the mid-12TH century St. Bernard of Clairvaux was proposing his classic condemnation, by the mid-13TH century the French scholastic theologians were debating whether Mary had been set free from sin before, during or after the infusion of her soul into her body. They concurred, generally, with the third option; St. Thomas Aquinas (d. 1274)[16] held that anything else would detract from the doctrine of the Christ as the Saviour of all people. For St. Thomas, Mary had indeed contracted Original Sin, but had been cleansed from it before her birth. It was the elimination of this great problem – the jeopardizing of the universal redemption by Christ – that finally brought about the acceptance of the Immaculate Conception; the Oxford Franciscan John Duns Scotus (d. 1308)[17] argued that Mary's being set free from Original Sin did not lessen her dependence upon Christ as Saviour, but increased it, since she would indeed have contracted Original Sin had the Saviour not prevented this. A later commentator, Thomistic theologian Tommaso de Vio Cajetan (d. 1534), enhanced this argument by insisting that in Mary, as in every human,

---

[15] While he defended the unsurpassed holiness of Mary, it is evident from his works (such as *Cur Deus Homo* and those dealing with the virginal conception and Original Sin) that he did not accept the Immaculate Conception.

[16] An Italian Dominican theologian and prodigious writer.

[17] Blessed John Duns Scotus was probably the first to defend the Immaculate Conception in Paris. Insisting that Mary would have great need of Christ as Redeemer so as not to contract Original Sin through human propagation, he taught that Mary was thus preserved from all sin by reason of Christ's Redemption.

there was an inherent tendency towards Original Sin (even if she was untainted by it), so that, as Duns Scotus had argued, she would have contracted it were it not for the grace of the Redeemer.

It took eighteen hundred years before the doctrine was defined as a dogma of faith by Pope Pius IX in 1854. And while the doctrine clarifies her particular spiritual status, we remain uninformed about practically all the details of Mary's birth and childhood; the few details that have passed into popular piety (such as Joachim and Anne as the names of her parents, and the event of her presentation in the Temple) are gleaned from the so-called 'Apocryphal Gospels'[18] and from works of mystics and saints, like Anne Catherine Emmerich (d. 1824).[19]

Concurrent with the doctrine of the Immaculate Conception are two further teachings of the Church; the first, defined by Ott as *sententia communis*,[20] is that from the moment of her conception, Mary was free from the motions of inordinate desire, or concupiscence. Concupiscence is regarded as one of the bodily defects resulting from the fall of Adam, since by its very nature it excites a person to commit acts that are contrary to the Law of God. Such a

---

[18] Comprising a large number of documents, either whole or in fragments, these gospels, letters and revelations have been rejected by the Church, and thus do not find a place in the Canon of the Scriptures, as opposed to the four 'Canonical' Gospels of Matthew, Mark, Luke and John). They contain countless details, many of them regarded as spurious, about Jesus, Mary and various Apostles. While the word 'apocryphal' has come to denote a text which is spurious or untrue, an 'apocryphal' book was, originally, a book deemed too sacred or esoteric to be in the hands of the common believer, reserved instead for the hands of the initiate or inner circle, suggesting a strong Gnostic trait.

[19] A German mystic and stigmatist who wrote her 'Life of the Blessed Virgin Mary' as a result of her interior locutions and visions. The work gives much detail, otherwise unknown, about the birth and childhood of Mary.

[20] 'Common teaching'. This denotes a doctrine which in itself belongs to the realm of true opinions, but which is generally held by theologians. Cf. OTT L., *Fundamentals of Catholic Dogma*, 1960, Book III, Part 3, ch. 2, n. 5: 202.

phenomenon would be entirely contrary to Mary's fullness of grace, her perfect and immaculate purity.

Secondly, Mary is held, in consequence of a special privilege, to be free of every personal sin throughout her life, in a teaching held by Ott to be *sententia fidei proxima.*[21] This teaching was expressed by the Council of Trent,[22] as well as by Pope Pius XII in his Encyclical Letter *Mystici Corporis*, who declared Mary "immune from all sin, personal or inherited."[23]

4.2. THE CONCEPTION AND BIRTH OF MARY IN CATHOLIC TRADITION

The words "in Catholic Tradition" at once limit us considerably; aside from the dogma of the Immaculate Conception, we know none of the details of Mary's conception and birth, except what has filtered into popular piety and the details given in some of the Apocryphal Gospels. A number of such documents describe Mary's conception and birth in terms that are remarkably close to the Qur'anic description given in Q. 3: 35–37, but not, curiously, in Q. 19.

In the 2ND century Apocryphal Protevangelium of James,[24] the childless Joachim and Anna pray for a child, promising that he or she will be dedicated to the service of God. An angel appears to both of them, promising a child and, in some texts, instructing that she be named Mary. The child is duly born, and kept in strict isolation by her parents, so that she may remain pure. At the age of three, she is left by her parents in the Temple, where she is fed by

---

[21] Ibid.: 203. This denotes a doctrine generally regarded by theologians as a truth of Revelation, but which is yet to be promulgated as such by the Church.

[22] Ibid.: 204.

[23] PIUS XII., *Mystici Corporis*, Pauline Books and Media, Boston (n.d.), n. 110: 66.

[24] The 'Protevangelium of James' exists, according to scholars such as Montague James, largely in its original form, both in the original Greek and in a number of oriental languages. It dates to the 2ND century. Cf. JAMES M.R. (trans.)., *The Apocryphal New Testament*, Clarendon Press, Oxford 1980: xix.

the hand of an angel. When she becomes too old for Temple service, she is given, by the casting of rods, into the guardianship of Joseph. These details, enumerated by almost all the Apocryphal works dealing with Mary's conception and birth, resonate in the Qur'anic account.

Suffice to say that, aside from the names of Mary's parents and Mary's presentation in the temple by her parents, none of the details recounted by the Apocryphal works have found their way into the corpus of Church teaching and piety; and while these documents remain of great value for scholars, they serve little purpose in this work. It can only be repeated that, in terms of the teaching of the Church, we know almost nothing of these details of Mary's life.

4.2.1. The Miraculous Food

The Protevangelium of James records an incident in the childhood of Mary not found in the four Canonical Gospels. Sent to dwell in the temple, she receives her food from the hand of an angel:

> And her parents went down marvelling, and praising the Lord God, because the child had not turned back. And Mary was in the temple of the Lord as if she were a dove that dwelt there, and she received food from the hand of an angel. And when she was twelve years old there was held a council of the priests.[25]

The same theme is found in the the 5TH century Apocryphal Gospel of Bartholomew: "When I abode in the temple of God and received my food from an angel."[26]

Among the Apocryphal writings, this miraculous feeding in the Temple (at the hand of an angel) is predicated of Mary by the Protevangelium of James, the 8TH/9TH century Gospel of Pseudo-

---

[25] Protevangelium of James, chapter VIII, verse 1. Cf. JAMES M.R. (trans.)., *The Apocryphal New Testament*, 1980: 46.

[26] Gospel of Bartholomew, chapter II, verse 15. Cf. JAMES M.R. (trans.)., *The Apocryphal New Testament*, 1980: 171. This text exists in three extant manuscripts: a Greek, possibly from the 5TH century, and two later Latin manuscripts.

Matthew, the Gospel of the Nativity of Mary, the Arabic Gospel of the Infancy, a number of the Coptic fragments detailing the life of the Virgin, and the Gospel of Bartholomew.

4.3. NOTES ON THE THEOLOGY OF MARY AS EVER-VIRGIN

"A Virgin conceived, a Virgin bore, and a Virgin she remains."[27] On 7TH August 1555, Pope Paul IV issued an Ecclesiastical Constitution, *Cum quorumdam hominum*, making it an article of faith that Mary, the mother of Jesus, "was a virgin before, during, and after the conception and birth of her son."[28] This was no startling innovation but was, like the declaration of her Immaculate Conception, the culmination of centuries of theological thought, sometimes flawed, first articulated by the Fathers of the Church, but which had its roots in much earlier traditions. The Church insists that Mary remained a virgin before, during (*in partu*) and after (*post partum*) the birth of Jesus. Her perpetual virginity is understood as quintessentially physical. While there are many examples in the Bible of barren and/or aged women falling pregnant and giving birth by means of a miraculous intervention by God, none of these is specified as a virgin birth. Only to Mary is imputed this singular miracle; that she conceives and bears a child without male intervention or sexual intercourse. Furthermore, she remains a *virgo post partum,* her physical 'integrity' (i.e. her intact hymen, understood as the physical indication of virginity) in no way damaged by the physical birth of Jesus.

Ott clarifies the three angles of this doctrine: he notes that the Church teaches *de fide definita* that Mary conceived by the power of the Holy Spirit, with no male, human intervention.[29] He then goes

---

[27] St. Peter Chrysologus (d. 450). Cf. JURGENS W.A., *The Faith of the Early Fathers*, 1970–1979, vol. III, n. 2177: 267. Also, Pope St. Leo I: cf. ibid., 2194: 275.

[28] "…*aut eandem beatissimam Virginem Mariam non esse veram Dei matrem, nec perstitisse semper in virginitatis integritate, ante partum scilicet, in partu et perpetuo post partum…*" DENZ., n. 1880: 590, n. 503: 230.

[29] OTT L., *Fundamentals of Catholic Dogma*, 1960, Book III, Part 3, ch. 2, n. 5: 204.

on to explain that Mary bore her son without any violation of the integrity of her virginity.[30] The dogma, he notes, states merely the fact, without any attempt at a physiological elucidation. While there was a time when theologians regarded this as referring to the non-rupture of the hymen, modern medical science has demonstrated that a ruptured hymen does not of itself negate virginity; in fact, its very rupture is understood as belonging to complete and natural motherhood, so that Mary's continued virginity is no longer understood in such physical terms, lest the concept of her perfect motherhood be diminished. Finally, the teaching upholds her virginity after the birth of Jesus. This doctrine too is held *de fide definita*,[31] although in this chapter we shall see how problematical it remains. Certainly, although the doctrine is taught only implicitly in the Scriptures, the Second Council of Constantinople (533) gave Mary the title 'perpetual virgin', a teaching confirmed by the Lateran Synod (649) and the 1555 declaration *Cum quorumdam hominum* of Pope Paul IV.[32]

Already in 649, the Lateran Synod had offered a concise definition of what was to be believed:

> If anyone does not in accord with the Holy Fathers acknowledge the holy and ever virgin and immaculate Mary was really and truly the Mother of God, inasmuch as she, in the fullness of time, and without seed, conceived by the Holy Spirit, God in the Word Himself, who before all time was born of God the Father, and without loss of integrity brought Him forth, and after His birth preserved her virginity inviolate, let him be condemned."[33]

---

[30] Ibid.: 205. This teaching he lists as *de fide definita* "on the ground of the general promulgation of doctrine."

[31] Ibid.: 206–207.

[32] Cf. DENZ., n. 427: 196 for the definition of the Second Council of Constantinople. Ott mistakenly calls it the Fifth Council.

[33] *Si quis secumdum sanctos Patres man confitetur proprie et secundum veritatem Dei genitricem sanctam semperque virginem et immaculatam Mariam, utpote ipsum Deum Verbum specialiter et veraciter, qui a Deo Patre ante omnia saecula natus est, in ultimis saeculorum absque semine concepisse ex Spiritu Sancto, et incorruptibili-*

There was further approval by the Second Vatican Council (1962–1965, henceforth Vatican II), which in the document *Lumen Gentium* repeated the word 'integrity' and gave a note referring back to this text of the Lateran Synod:

> This union of the Mother with the Son in the work of salvation is evident from the time of the virginal conception of Christ even to His death...when the Mother of God brought forth her firstborn, who did not diminish but consecrated her virginal integrity.[34]

Pope John Paul II, speaking at a General Audience on 28TH August 1996, cites further official texts:

> The Church has always professed her belief in the perpetual virginity of Mary…the early Christians expressed this conviction of faith in the Greek term *aeiparthenos* – 'ever-virgin' – created to describe Mary's person in a unique and effective manner, and to express in a single word the Church's belief in her perpetual virginity. The Second Council of Constantinople (533) took up the expression 'ever-virgin' and affirmed: the Word of God, 'incarnate of the holy and glorious Mother of God and ever-virgin Mary was born of her.' This doctrine is confirmed by two other ecumenical councils, the Fourth Lateran Council (1215) and the Second Council of Lyons (1274).[35]

Curiously, even the major Protestant Reformers persisted in their belief that Mary remained a virgin. John Calvin (d. 1564) attacked as folly the suggestion that Mary gave birth to other children after Jesus, insisting that the 'brethren' of Jesus in the Gospels referred to his relatives, and not to blood brothers and sisters by the same mother. Martin Luther (d. 1546) too insisted that Mary remained a

---

ter eam genuisse, indissolubili permanente et post partum eiusdem virginitate, condemnatus sit. DENZ., n. 503: 230.

[34] L.G., ch. 7, n. 57 in FLANNERY A. (ed.)., *Vatican Council II: The Conciliar and Post Conciliar Documents*, Dominican Publications, Dublin 1975: 416.

[35] JOHN PAUL II., *Theotókos. Woman, Mother, Disciple*, Pauline Books and Media, Boston 2000.

virgin after the parturition of Jesus, while Ulrich Zwingli (d. 1531) claimed to believe firmly that Mary remained a virgin, pure and intact, not only during childbirth but after it as well. The startling intimation is that this issue could not be settled by 'Scripture alone', the very rallying cry of those Reformers, but would have to be judged by the constant Tradition of the Church through the centuries.[36] Here, the most ancient creeds persisted in naming her 'ever-virgin' (*aeiparthenos*).

What is patently clear is that this doctrine, especially that part which denotes a perpetual virginity in Mary, has been fraught with difficulty. In July 1960 the Holy Office drew up a decree and sent it to a certain number of bishops and religious superiors. It was not published officially, although several journalists procured copies of it:

> This supreme Congregation has often observed recently, and with deep concern, that theological works are being published in which the delicate question of Mary's virginity 'in partu' is treated with a deplorable crudeness of expression and, what is more serious, in flagrant contradiction to the doctrinal Tradition of the Church and to the sense of respect the faithful have. Consequently, in its plenary session of Wednesday, the twentieth of this month, it seemed necessary to the eminent Fathers of the Holy Office, by reason of their serious responsibility to watch over the sacred deposit of Catholic doctrine, to see to it that for the future the publication of such dissertations on this problem be prohibited.[37]

The dilemma for the scholars who attempt to counter the doctrine, starts with Matthew, the solitary evangelist to make an unequivocal statement about the virgin birth; that Jesus was conceived by the power of the Holy Spirit before Mary and Joseph "*came together*" (Mt. 1: 18). He reaffirms this contention in the words of the archangel: "*that which is conceived in her is of the Holy Spirit*" (Mt. 1: 20). He

---

[36] Cf. THURIAN M., *Mary, Mother of All Christians*, 37–41, 195–197. Also, BEA A., "Mary and the Protestants" in *Marian Studies*, April 1961.

[37] LAURENTIN R., *A Short Treatise on the Virgin Mary*, AMI Press, Washington 1991: 318–329.

then underpins his assertion by quoting the celebrated Isaiah prophecy: "*Therefore the Lord himself shall give you a sign: Behold, a virgin shall conceive, and bear a son, and shall call his name Immanuel*" (Is. 7: 14). The trouble, as a number of scholars are wont to point out, is that Matthew was employing the Greek Septuagint translation of the Old Testament, where the Hebrew *ʿalmah* had been rendered in Greek as *parthenos*. The two words are not synonymous; while *parthenos* undoubtedly bears a sense of intact virginity, *ʿalmah* means a girl of marriageable age, with a primary connotation of eligibility. *ʿAlmah*, for example, is used of Rebecca before her marriage to Isaac (Gen. 24: 43) and even of the girls in the 'harem of the beloved' in the Song of Songs (Songs: 7: 3, 6, 8). A number of scholars insist that Matthew has dangerously misrepresented the Isaiah prophecy, the weight of the which lies not on the 'virginity' of the mother, but on the child, a symbol for King Ahaz of God's enduring beneficence. Numerous scholars remain adamant that the prophecy only describes events during the rule of King Ahaz.

Matthew's very affirmation of the initial virginity of Mary is seen by some critics to seriously endanger her *post partum* virginity, as he employs phrases such as "*before they came together*" (Mt. 1: 18) and "*Joseph…knew her not till she had brought forth…*" (Mt. 1: 25). Admittedly, scholars have elucidated the curious Biblical usage of words like 'before' and until', which do not automatically represent the end of a particular state or situation, but which have an extensive range of meanings. The words 'before' and 'until' for example, do not of necessity designate a change after the time point indicated. Matthew declares that Joseph 'knew not' Mary "*until* (*heos hou*) *she had given birth to a son*" (Mt. 1: 25). The expression *heos hou* does not therefore unequivocally demand that Joseph and Mary were intimate after Jesus' birth. Concomitantly, in the angelic message to Joseph, the bearer of the tidings does not use the phrase for marital union, 'go in unto' (as in Gen. 30: 3, 4, 16) or 'come together' (Mt. 1: 18) but merely a word meaning 'leading her into the house as a wife' (*paralambano gunaika*) but not necessarily cohabiting with her. Matthew affirms that Mary was found to be with child "*before they* [she and Joseph] *came together*" (Mt. 1: 18). Other scholars remain resolute that the term 'came together' (from *sunerchomai*) incorporates the concept of sexual intimacy, and that the implication is clearly that ultimately, they 'came together', making the verse irreconcilable with the doctrine of Mary's perpetual virginity.

Further critiques are raised by the Biblical usage of the word 'firstborn' to describe Jesus, and 'brethren' as a reference to his 'brothers and sisters'. Jesus is denoted as 'firstborn' in Lk. 2: 7 (and also in Mt. 1: 25 if we take the Vulgate addition to the Greek). This reflects the Hebrew *bekor* (and the Greek *prototokon*), which chiefly convey the privileged position of the firstborn among other children. Although they need not imply there were other children, some critics maintain that these terms plausibly suggest that there were. The depiction of Jesus' 'brethren' in the New Testament has persistently set scholars against each other, with such references cited as a basis for believing that Mary and Joseph, her spouse, had ordinary marital relations. Some follow the so-called 'Helvidian' view, positing that Mary and Joseph did indeed have other children, blood brothers and sisters to Jesus, thus negating Mary's perpetual virginity. A small number maintain the 'Epiphanian' explanation, that 'brethren' refers to Joseph's children from a previous marriage. The critical debate is raised by those who follow the 'Hieronymian' position; that these were brethren in point of kinship, and not brothers and sisters from the same mother. Catholic apologists appeal to the fact that the term 'brother' (*adelphos*) is sometimes used in a broader, kindred sense, e.g., 'cousins'. But the critics point out that while *adelphos* is employed loosely on occasion in some literature, it is never used in the New Testament for 'cousin', a relationship denoted by the word *anepsioi* (as in Col. 4: 10).[38]

---

[38] Strictly speaking, the argument that the 'brethren' of Jesus were later children of Mary and Joseph holds little sway. Firstly, the term 'brother' is posited of James: but one James was the son of Alphaeus (Mt. 10: 3), who was certainly never married to Mary, and the brother of Jude, who refers to himself not as the 'brother' of Jesus, but as the "servant of Jesus and brother of James" (Jude 1: 1). Another James mentioned is identified is one of the sons of Zebedee (Mt. 5: 21, 10: 3), so that he too could not be regarded as a blood brother of Jesus. A third James is, together with his brother Joseph, the son of Mary wife of Clophas (Jn. 19: 25), one of the three Mary's at the foot of the Cross, together with Mary Magdalene and Mary the mother of Jesus). Secondly, the 'brethren' of Jesus are depicted as being older than him, which would negate Mary's virginity when Jesus was born. Thirdly, Jesus alone in the Gospels is des-

Even more disconcerting for some is Mary's virginity *post partum*, specifically because it is hard to fathom why this should necessarily be so; why did Mary inevitably have to be a perpetual virgin? What is it about virginity that it is so esteemed? De la Potterie, a strenuous defender of Mary's virginity, quotes François Biot,[39] noting that the virginity of Mary is no longer seen as a privilege or singular quality, but a deficiency, something lacking in the accomplishment of the maternal function, setting her apart from normal women. He also takes note of the opinion of Vittorio Messori[40] who writes that the dogma of Mary's virginity before, during and after the birth of Jesus arouses sarcasm and even rage in certain theological circles.

Any examination of Catholic Mariology traces an inexorable path back to the Fall of Adam and Eve and raises the question of the Church's perception of sex. Despite Catholicism's methodically theological argumentation for Mary's perpetual virginity, it is apparent, starting with the Epistles of St. Paul, that virginity was exceedingly more favourably regarded in the early Church than was marriage; and if virginity was understood as a more elevated state, Mary would have had to have been a perpetual virgin, since only the highest state could be imputed to her.

As early as the 4TH century, St. Athanasius (d. c. 373) was proclaiming Mary "Ever-Virgin";[41] Didymus the Blind (d. c. 398) concurs, as does St. Epiphanius (d. 403), St. Jerome (d. 419 or 420), who claimed virginity also for Joseph, her husband, St. Augustine

---

ignated 'Son of Mary', while she herself is never called 'mother of the brethren of the Lord'. Only four 'brethren' of Jesus are actually mentioned by name: these are James, Joseph, Simon and Jude. But in terms of parentage, three of these (James, Joseph and Jude) are clearly accounted for.

[39] BIOT F., "Mary en questions" in *Témoignage chrétien*, 17–23 August 1987: 8. Quoted in DE LA POTTERIE I., *Mary in the Mystery of the Covenant*, 1997: xvi.

[40] MESSORI V., "Betlemme" in *Avvenire*, 24 December 1987: 17. Cf. DE LA POTTERIE I., *Mary in the Mystery of the Covenant*, 1997: xvi.

[41] JURGENS W.A., *The Faith of the Early Fathers*, 1970–1979, vol. I, n. 767a: 330.

(d. 430), especially in his battles against Jovinian and against a group of heretics named Antidicomarites, who contradicted Mary's perpetual virginity, and St. Cyril of Alexandria (d. 444).[42]

Critics refer back to the early Church Fathers, some of whom held that sexual union corrupted men; it took their minds off God and caused them to be preoccupied with their lower nature. At the very core of Mary's perpetual virginity lies the definition of sin and sex as articulated by the Fathers. Sexuality symbolized the gravest danger, the fatal flaw, while virginity came to be understood as the vanquisher and remedy. This early Christian correlation between sex and sin cannot be overstated in terms of its consequences for theological attitudes; to this must be added a third theological concept, spearheaded by St. Jerome and St. Augustine, of the human tendency to sin (concupiscence). These three concepts became inseparable, as did the triple conception of sex, sin and death. Sin brings sex and death into the world, and a vicious circle is initiated, as some theologians came to imagine that sin, which leads to death, is passed to all humans through the sexual, reproductive act. St. John Chrysostom (d. 407), for example, posited that through their sin, Adam and Eve lost, among other things, the beauty and honour of virginity; other theologians countered his extremist views by maintaining that while Adam and Eve did indeed have intercourse before the Fall, it was an act untainted and unflawed, and purely for the purposes of reproduction. So, St. Augustine can conclude triumphantly, by the virgin birth Christ's sinlessness is assured, for no 'coupling in lust' in order to reproduce on the part of Mary means no passing on of the inherent sinful condition of humanity to Christ.

The Fathers had no little help from St. Paul, who, caught in a worldview of an imminent end, unreservedly advocated celibacy, raising it above the married state, and even suggested marriage merely as a remedy for those who found perpetual chastity an impossible burden. Consequently, a peculiar notion of sexuality and marriage is derived from the Pauline writings and elaborated by the Fathers of the Church; virginity and chastity come to be seen as a

---

[42] Ibid., vol. II, n. 1073: 62, n. 1089a: 70, n. 1111: 76, n. 1361: 191, vol. III, n. 1518: 30, nn. 1643–1644: 71, n. 1974d: 166, n. 2133: 232.

higher and more perfect state, and Mary as Mother of God cannot have a lesser state than others.

All things considered, it appeared, as Origen so eloquently argued, only 'fitting' that if God were to be born, it should be of a virgin, unsullied by inherent human sin. For Origen, the Old Testament contains a sequence of prophecies which back up his arguments about Mary's virginal state, prophecies swiftly taken up by other Fathers; Mary's virginal womb was "*an enclosed garden…a shut spring…a fountain sealed*" (Songs 4: 12), words used by the Council of Chalcedon in 451, which held that it "was fitting for God, He sealed her womb." It was a closed gate which "*shall not be opened, and no man shall enter in by it*" (Ez. 44: 2).

The insistence that her physical integrity was undamaged by the physical birth of Jesus, a factor patently clear in the Protevangelium of James,[43] was an issue with which both Origen and Tertullian (c. 220) struggled. The latter wrote:

> Virgin because she abstained from man; non-virgin because she gave birth…Virgin when she conceived, she became a wife when she gave birth…Who really opened her maternal womb, if not the one who opened the womb that had been closed [in his conception]? Normally, conjugal relations open the womb. Therefore [Mary's] womb was all the more opened, since it had been more closed. Consequently, it is more accurate to call her non-virgin than virgin…[44]

---

[43] In the Protevangelium (XX: 1), Salome refuses to believe the midwife's assertion that Jesus' mother is still a virgin: she thrusts her finger into Mary's vagina and finds the hymen intact, but the vaginal membranes are so charged with divinity that her finger burns and she is distraught. Although the gospels (like the Protoevangelium) that contained the 'evidence' of Mary's virginity *post partum* were excluded from the final canonical compilation of the New Testament, many of the early Fathers of the Church, maintained the perpetual virginity of Mary. Cf. JAMES M.R. (trans.)., *The Apocryphal New Testament*, 1980: 47.

[44] GAMBERO L., *Mary and the Fathers of the Church*, Ignatius Press, San Francisco 1999: 65; JURGENS W.A., *The Faith of the Early Fathers*, 1970–1979, vol. I, n. 359: 147. Tertullian, at one time a Catholic, ended by

But other Fathers maintained the doctrine, even if not always overtly. St. Gregory Nazianzus (d. 389) speaks of Jesus being born of Mary in a "stainless"[45] way, while St. Ambrose of Milan wrote of a birth which "did not break the seals of virginity."[46] St. Augustine insisted that Mary remained 'integral' in her virginity[47] and fought against the heresy of Jovinian, who claimed that Mary's virginity was lost in childbirth;[48] and while St. Sophronius of Jerusalem (d. 638) speaks of her virginity being 'unblemished' before, during and after parturition,[49] both Pope St. Gregory I (d. 604) and St. John Damascene (d. 749) use the analogy of Christ passing through a closed door after His resurrection to articulate His passing through the closed womb of His mother.[50]

Nor, insisted some theologians like Francisco Suarez (d. 1617), did she suffer the pains of labour, "that troublesome weariness with which all pregnant women are burdened…" (although it must be noted that absence of pain in childbirth does not belong to the essence of virginity, anymore than does the preservation of the hymen).[51] The Council of Trent firmly maintained the *post partum*

---

supporting the heresy of Montanism. As Jurgens notes, Tertullian strenuously defended Mary's virginity *ante partum*, while denying her virginity *in partu* and, in all likelihood, *post partum*. "She was a virgin who gave birth to Christ," he wrote, "but after his birth she was married to one man, so that both ideals of holiness [namely, the virginal ideal and the married ideal] might be exemplified in the parentage of Christ, in the person of a mother who was both virgin and married to one husband only." Cf. GAMBERO L., *Mary and the Fathers of the Church*, 1999: 65.

[45] Op. cit., vol. II, n. 1014: 37.

[46] Op. cit., n. 1327: 172.

[47] Op. cit., vol. III, n. 1518: 30.

[48] Op. cit., n. 1975: 167.

[49] Op. cit., n. 2289: 307.

[50] Op. cit., n. 2331: 323; n. 2372: 340.

[51] In his book *Mary, Woman in the Work of Salvation* the Christologist Jean Galot envisages the birth of Jesus as happening in a commonplace way, like the birth of any other child. It was a wholly physical birth, with Jesus 'opening' his mother's womb and with all the customary bleeding of a birth. Galot understands normal birth as entirely compatible with virgin-

belief, already clearly stated, for example, by Pope Leo I (d. c. 461),[52] although Vatican II treated it somewhat more tentatively. The insistence of Mary's virginity is thus inextricably interwoven with the Christian view of the dangers of the flesh. Not only must Christ have been born of a spotless virgin, but she must also be a perpetual virgin, for it was fitting that she was nothing less than that.

Biblical theologian De la Potterie presents his arguments for Mary's virginity from a distinctive angle, not agreed upon by all his fellow exegetes. He begins by noting that virginity as a virtue is primarily Christian, which begins precisely with the birth of Christ; in this, he is not entirely correct, since there is, as we have seen, enough evidence of deliberate virginity from the Greco-Roman world and the mythologies of numerous cultures. Certainly, in the *weltanschauung* of the Old Testament, remaining a virgin was understood as a malediction, and without merit or praise.[53] Mary's startled response, "*I know not man*" to the angelic announcement is unique in the entire Bible. Some, including St. Gregory of Nyssa (d. 395), St. Augustine and St. Thomas Aquinas believe that Mary had made a vow of virginity;[54] but this does not coincide with the opin-

---

al integrity, without corruption or sin. Ultimately, the stress must fall, not on the physiological process of parturition, but rather upon the whole event, which was inimitable. Even so, Mary's lack of pain was of theological importance to the early Christians because in the Genesis account, Adam's curse is to work in sweat in the fields and Eve's is to bear children in pain (Gen. 3: 16–19).

[52] JURGENS W.A., *The Faith of the Early Fathers*, 1970–1979, vol. III, n. 2182: 270, n. 2194: 275. Leo had argued that Jesus was born "without injury to maternal integrity" and that Mary gave birth to Him while "preserving her virginity."

[53] DE LA POTTERIE I., *Mary in the Mystery of the Covenant*, 1997: xx.

[54] St. Gregory of Nyssa, the first to propose this idea, writes: "What is Mary's response? Listen to the voice of the pure Virgin. The angel brings the glad tidings of her childbearing, but she is concerned with virginity and holds that her integrity should come before the angelic message. She does not refuse to believe the angel; neither does she move away from her convictions. She says: I have given up any contact with man.

ion that virginity as something virtuous comes with the birth of Christ, and prior to this is a curse (and, as Brown points out, the verb is not in the future tense, thus giving no indication that virginity was Mary's avowed intent).[55] Others suggest that the words, coming from one already espoused, simply mean that she has 'not yet' slept with a man; but 'not yet' is not found in the text, and De la Potterie regards this explication as somewhat banal.[56] Still others see it as nothing but a literary formula. De la Potterie posits that the words express, not a conscious decision on Mary's part, but a desire for or orientation towards virginity, about which she could not yet make a final decision. This too concurs with St. Thomas Aquinas. Nor is it inconceivable that Mary and Joseph, even with only a small inkling of who their child really was, would agree to live in chastity and have no other children; for from the instant of the Annunciation, virginity ceased to be a curse and became a blessing. As St. Augustine argued:

> In being born of a Virgin who chose to remain a Virgin even before she knew who was to be born of her, Christ wanted to approve virginity rather than to impose it. And He wanted vir-

---

'How will this happen to me, since I do not know man?' (Lk. 1: 34). Mary's own words confirm certain apocryphal traditions. For if Joseph had taken her to be his wife, for the purpose of having children, why would she have wondered at the announcement of maternity, since she herself would have accepted becoming a mother according to the law of nature? But just as it was necessary to guard the body consecrated to God as an untouched an holy offering, for this same reason, she states, even if you are an angel come down from heaven and even if this phenomenon is beyond man's abilities, yet it is impossible for me to know man. How shall I become a mother without [knowing] man? For though I consider Joseph to be my husband, still I do not know man." Cf. GAMBERO L., *Mary and the Fathers of the Church*, 1999: 157. Gregory spoke of Mary being offered to God by her mother even before she was born, but also tends towards the view that Mary herself made a vow.

[55] BROWN R., *The Birth of the Messiah*, Doubleday, New York 1993: 303–304.

[56] DE LA POTTERIE I., *Mary in the Mystery of the Covenant*, 1997: 24–25.

ginity to be of free choice even in that woman in whom He took upon Himself the form of a slave.[57]

4.4. THE NARRATIVES OF JESUS' ANNUNCIATION, CONCEPTION AND BIRTH

The Annunciation genre is, above all, understood by De la Potterie as the announcement of the extraordinary birth of a child, and is resonant in a number of Old Testament annunciations (Gen. 18: 9–15, to Sarah, Jdg. 13: 2–7, to the wife of Manoah) as well as in Lk. 1: 8–22, (the annunciation of the birth of John the Baptist).[58] In both the Old and New Testaments there is a particular structure to it, (traces of which are discernible in the Islamic texts):

a) The apparition of a messenger from God, usually an angel

b) The reaction of the one visited; usually surprise or fear

c) The actual annunciation of the forthcoming birth by the angel

d) A difficulty or barrier, posed by the one visited

e) A proof or sign offered by the angel (for example, the dumbness of Zechariah or the miraculous conception of the ostensibly barren Elizabeth)[59]

The annunciation and nativity of Jesus, recounted in the Gospels of Matthew and Luke, is suffused with divine intervention and miraculous signs. Especially evident is the angelic activity enveloping his conception and birth. But the joy is tainted by gloom and foreboding, personified by Herod in his murderous intent and articulated by Simeon, the prophet of impending suffering. It must be noted that there are major differences in the narratives of the two Gospels; Matthew's Magi, star and murder planned by Herod are not found in Luke, while Luke's account of John the Baptist's birth, the canticles proclaimed by Zechariah and Mary, the shep-

---

[57] JURGENS W.A., *The Faith of the Early Fathers*, 1970–1979, vol. III, n. 1643: 71.

[58] DE LA POTTERIE I., *Mary in the Mystery of the Covenant*, 1997: 6.

[59] DE LA POTTERIE I., *Mary in the Mystery of the Covenant*, 1997: 6–7.

herds and the presentation of Jesus in the temple are not extant in Matthew.

In terms of the texts of the Gospels, the nativity of Jesus comprises a number of major elements or pericopes. The first of these is the annunciation to Mary by a heavenly messenger identified by the texts as the angel Gabriel. This announcement of her imminent pregnancy is made to Mary in the form of a dialogue, in which she questions the angel about the likelihood of such an occurrence. The next constituent elucidates in a succinct passage the divinely inspired acceptance of her pregnancy outside of marriage by Joseph, her betrothed. Inevitably, it is an angelic messenger, and not his betrothed, who is the principle agent in convincing him.

This is followed by an extended silence; we are told nothing of the period of pregnancy, except for Mary's hasty visit to her cousin Elizabeth. In the course of this visit, the child in Elizabeth's womb leaps joyfully in the presence of the child in Mary's, and Mary proclaims her *Magnificat*, a prophetic and revolutionary song of a God who intervenes in human history. Certainly, the texts offer no indication of any angelic ministration to Mary during the nine months. The next facet is the birth of Jesus, in trying and meager circumstances, in strong contrast to the heavenly signs accompanying his parturition. Hosts of angels are seen, glorifying God in words intimating that this birth is the catalyst for earthly peace, an allusion to the cosmic magnitude of the Incarnation. These angels announce the news of his birth, as well as the status and future accomplishments of the child, to shepherds, who are the first to receive these tidings.

A further aspect is the visit of the Magi, although historically this visitation was not necessarily immediately after his birth. Nevertheless, their visit is the catalyst for the first severe threat to the child's life, in the murderous actions of King Herod. A final component is the presentation of the child in the temple, in accordance with the prescriptions of Jewish Law, and the calamitous warnings issued about the child and his mother by Simeon, the resident prophet, who addresses Mary:

> "*This child is destined to call the falling and rising of many in Israel, and to be a sign that will be spoken against, so that the thoughts of many hearts will be revealed. And a sword will pierce your own soul too*" (Lk. 2: 34–35).

Striking in the narratives is the dominant dream *motif* in Matthew and the association of dreams with a divine announcement. Five dreams, three of them specifically of angels[60] bearing news, are recounted in the infancy narratives,[61] and Joseph is the recipient of four of them. The annunciation itself is not portrayed as a dream; but a number of the dreams are linked to the annunciation event because, like the message of Gabriel to Mary, the dreams highlight the status and future accomplishments of the child. A number of dreams to Joseph bring warnings about the child's safety, but none of them predict his death. This dream *motif* is crucial in the narratives of the conception and birth of both Jesus and, as we have seen, of al-Ḥusayn. That God communicates with humanity through dreams is plainly asserted in the Scriptures,[62] and divine revelation through dreams is a recurring theme in the Old and New Testaments, in most cases the dream being said to have come from God.[63] There are also some biblical dreams recorded which are not specifically said to have come from God,[64] although their divine origin is presumed.

4.5. NOTES ON THE CATHOLIC TRADITION OF OUR LADY OF SORROWS

> Simeon's eyes have peered into the distance and seen the salvation that this child will bring to the Gentiles and Israel alike: but, true prophet, he also sees the rejection and the catastro-

---

[60] Brown notes that most often in Old Testament usage, 'the angel of the Lord' is not a personal, spiritual being acting as intermediate between God and humanity, but simply a way of describing God's visible presence among people. Cf. BROWN R., *The Birth of the Messiah*, 1993: 129.

[61] Mt. 1: 20 (an angel to Joseph); Mt. 2: 12 (a dream to the Magi); Mt. 2: 13 (an angel to Joseph); Mt. 2: 19 (an angel to Joseph); Mt. 2: 22 (to Joseph).

[62] Cf. Num. 12: 6, Job 33: 14.

[63] Cf. Gen. 20: 3, 28: 12, 31: 10, I Kings 3: 5–15, Dan. 2: 19, 7: 1, Mt. 1: 20, 2: 12, 13, 19, 22, Acts 23: 11, 27: 23.

[64] Gen. 37: 6, 30: 5, 31: 1, Jdg. 7: 13, 2 Mach. 15: 11.

> phe. And his tragic second vision is addressed to the mother of the child, the one to whom the good news about Jesus first came; for as the first to hear the word and accept it, she must encounter in her own soul its challenge and the tragedy of its rejection...[65]

Although the image of Mary as 'Our Lady of Sorrows', with her inconsolable weeping, was eagerly seized upon by Medieval mystics such as John Tauler (d. 1360) and Henry Suso (d. 1366), it is in fact a piety that predates them and has its origins in Scripture. A sufficient number of Gospel passages propose the hardship, grief and suffering of Mary's life; primary is the dire prophecy of Simeon,[66] but no less telling are the flight into Egypt[67] and the whole Calvary event where she shares intensely in the sufferings of Jesus.[68] Other events from which her sorrows may be deduced are the physical difficulties surrounding Jesus' birth, the massacre of the children in an attempt to kill Jesus, the loss of the child Jesus for a period of three days in Jerusalem and the threats against his life. Ultimately, Brown rejects[69] the classical vision of popular Christian piety, which ties the sword that will pierce the soul of Mary, the 'mother of sorrows', with the sorrows of her Son's passion and death; he discards it on the grounds that among the Gospels, only John puts her at the foot of the cross, and there she is not portrayed as a 'mother of sorrows'. Nor is there any substantiation that Luke and his community ever imagined she was there. Brown warns of the danger of interpreting Luke's writings with non-Lucan categories.

---

[65] BROWN R., *The Birth of the Messiah*, 1993: 460.

[66] Lk. 2: 34–35.

[67] Mt. 2: 13–21.

[68] Jn. 19: 17–42.

[69] Brown's interpretation of the 'sword' piercing Mary's soul is related to the Gospel concept of Jesus bringing 'division' and, concomitantly, the distinction made between Jesus' 'natural' family and the 'family' of his disciples. His 'natural' family is in some sense replaced by this new one, with the former becoming the latter through obedience to God's word, the mark of being Jesus' brother and sister and mother. Mary's special anguish for Brown is her having to accept that Jesus' relationship with God outranks any relationship he may have with her.

Nevertheless, the image of the sorrowful mother at the foot of the cross, her soul pierced with sword-like grief, persists in popular Mariology, and cannot be discounted.

It is precisely beneath the cross that Mary's sorrows, spread throughout her life, reach their climax as, standing beneath her tortured and dying Son, she offers her suffering as a participation in the redemptive act:

> After this manner the Blessed Virgin advanced in her pilgrimage of faith, and faithfully persevered in her union with her Son unto the cross, where she stood, in keeping with the divine plan, grieving exceedingly with her only begotten Son, uniting herself with a maternal heart with His sacrifice, and lovingly consenting to the immolation of this Victim which she herself had brought forth.[70]

Long before the Medieval mystics, with their stress on suffering and asceticism, other theologians were already pondering the grief and suffering of Mary. These include the 5TH century Abbot Poeman in his 'Apothegms' ("Would that I could weep with her always"), the 4TH century St. Ephraim the Syrian (d. 373) and the 6TH century St. Romanos the Melodist (d. c. 560). Later writers and theologians who took up this image and devotion were St. Bonaventure (d. 1274), St. Albert the Great (d. 1280), Jacopone da Todi (d. 1306) and St. Alphonsus Liguori (d. 1787). Nor is this theme lacking in the contemporary Church; in recent Marian apparitions such as La Salette (1846), Fatima (1914), Sicily (1953) and Japan (1973) Mary was reported to have been weeping. Pope John Paul II, speaking in 1984, insisted that,

> Our Lady's tears belong to the order of signs: they testify to the presence of the Mother in the Church and in the world. A mother weeps when she sees her children threatened by evil, be it spiritual or physical. Mary weeps when sharing in Christ's tears over Jerusalem, or at the tomb of Lazarus or finally on the way of the Cross.[71]

---

[70] L.G., n. 58.

[71] JOHN PAUL II, homily in Syracuse, Sicily, 6TH November 1994.

4.6. MARY'S INTERCESSORY PREROGATIVES

> Taken up into heaven, she…by her manifold intercession continues to procure for us the gifts of eternal salvation. Therefore, the blessed Virgin is invoked in the church under the titles of advocate, helper, benefactress and mediatrix. This, however, is understood in such a way that it neither takes away anything from nor adds anything to the dignity and efficacy of Christ the one Mediator.[72]

This paragraph from the document *Lumen Gentium* contains two important Marian teachings: the first, is that Mary has been taken up into heaven in a singular manner, and the second is that there, she assists the Church and its members by her intercession, with a power that Pope Leo XIII (d. 1903) described as "greater than any man or angel has ever attained or could attain."[73]

4.6.1. Mary's Reception into Paradise

> [Mary]…was elevated to the right hand of her Son and the true God, and situated at the same royal throne of the Most Blessed Trinity, whither neither men nor angels nor seraphs have before attained, nor will ever attain for all eternity. This is the highest and the most excellent privilege of our Queen and Lady…[74]

In November 1950, Pope Pius XII, after consultation with bishops throughout the world, solemnly declared in his Apostolic Constitution *Munificentissimus Deus* that "Mary, the immaculate perpetually Virgin Mother of God, after the completion of her earthly life, was assumed body and soul into the glory of heaven."[75]

---

[72] L.G., n. 62. Cf. FLANNERY A. (ed.), *Vatican Council II: The Conciliar and Post Conciliar Documents*, New York, 1996, 62.

[73] LEO XIII., Encyclical Letter *Supremi Apostolatus*, 1883.

[74] Words of Spanish mystic María de Agreda, quoted in PELIKAN J., *Mary Through the Centuries*, Yale University Press, New Haven 1996: 204.

[75] *Pronuntiamus, declaramus et definimus divinitus revelatum dogma esse: Immaculatam Deiparam semper Virginem Mariam, expleto terristris vitae cursu, fuisse corpore et anima ad caelestem gloriam assumptam.*

This teaching, defined *de fide definita*, was no innovation; almost a decade earlier the same Pontiff had written of "Mary, resplendent in glory in body and soul"[76] reigning with her Son in heaven. Like the doctrine of the Immaculate Conception, that of Mary's Assumption underwent a long and slow development. Although no direct proofs are to be found in the Scriptures, the Scholastic theologians derived this doctrine, as they did the Immaculate Conception, from the fullness of Mary's purity and holiness; full of grace, she was logically preserved from the threefold curse of sin (Gen. 3: 16–19), one of which is the return to dust. The Fathers of the Church looked to passages about the incorruptible wood of the Ark of the Covenant (identified with Mary) such as Rev. 11: 19, in which the Ark is seen in God's heavenly temple. The Fathers and Scholastic theologians accentuated four foundations for this teaching: Mary's sinlessness, her divine motherhood, her perpetual virginity and her participation in the work of her Son. Wrote St. Gregory of Tours (d. 594):

> But Mary, the glorious Mother of Christ, who is believed to be a virgin both before and after she bore Him, has, as we said above, been translated into paradise, amid the singing of the angelic choirs, whither the Lord has preceded her.[77]

Two hundred or so years after St. Gregory, St. John Damascene offered a more fulsome account:

> ...but we have received from ancient and most truthful tradition that at the time of her glorious repose, all the Holy Apostles, who were then dispersed abroad in the world for the salvation of the nations, were in but a moment of time transported through the air to Jerusalem; and when they were there an angelic vision appeared to them, and the divine chanting of the supernal powers was heard. And thus in divine and heavenly glory her holy soul was delivered in a way that no word can de-

---

[76] PIUS XII., *Mystici Corporis*, (n.d.), n. 110: 66.

[77] JURGENS W.A., *The Faith of the Early Fathers*, 1970–1979, vol. III, n. 2288b: 306.

> scribe, into the hands of God…the chanting and choral singing of the angels continued without cease for three days.[78]

Historically, the dogma was both supported and rejected by a number of anonymous or falsely attributed tracts, and was the subject of numerous theological arguments. Pope Benedict XIV (d. 1758) declared it to be "a pious and probable opinion",[79] but 1849 saw the first petitions for its formal declaration begin arriving in Rome.

The position of Mary in Paradise is one of incomparable glory; raised above all the angels and saints, she reigns as Queen, as a direct consequence of her divine motherhood and intrinsic connection with her Son's redemptive work. It is this sublime dignity, notes Ott, that makes her so powerful in her intercessory prerogatives.[80]

4.6.2. Mary's Intercession

The intercessory role of Mary is clearly evident in the New Testament, in the account of the wedding at Cana,[81] where by her intercession she initiated the first of her Son's signs recorded by St. John, and in her prayerful presence in the early Church, especially with the Apostles before the day of Pentecost. Having been assumed into heaven and clothed in unsurpassed glory as Queen, far from putting aside this mediatory role, she continues to exercise a mission of intercession for the salvation of all her children. Her prayer is far inferior to that of her Son, but more powerful than that of all the angels and saints; for while there remains only one Mediator between God and humankind – Jesus Christ[82] – the Church insists that

> Mary's function as mother of humankind in no way obscures or diminishes this unique mediation of Christ…it flows forth

---

[78] Ibid., n. 2390: 350.

[79] OTT L., *Fundamentals of Catholic Dogma*, 1960, Book III, Part 3, ch. 2, n. 6: 210.

[80] Ibid.: 211.

[81] Jn. 2: 1–10.

[82] Cf. 1 Timothy 2: 5–6.

> from the superabundance of the merits of Christ, rests on his mediation, depends entirely upon it and draws all its power from it.[83]

Faith in her intercessory power is expressed from earliest Christian times – the Fathers used the word mediatrix ('go-between'), a word much used in Church documents – and is found articulated, for example, in the first extant prayer to Mary, the Greek text of the 3RD century prayer *Sub tuum praesidium*: "We fly to Thy patronage, O Virgin of virgins our Mother. Despise not our petitions in our necessities, but deliver us always from all dangers, O glorious and blessed Virgin."[84]

The theological nature of Mary's intercession is that she "co-operates in the application in the grace of Redemption to man."[85] As one author notes:

> In view of her unique rôle in saving history Mary is revered as Mediatrix of all graces – not productive mediation, like Jesus Christ's, but a receptive one of merit and intercession and, as Vatican II said, wholly dependent upon the mediation of Christ – because those who have attained salvation through the final achievement of their perfected lives intercede with God for the company of the saints on earth.[86]

Both in her theology and in her piety, the Catholic Church employs the word 'advocate' to portray Mary's intercession, as she pleads the cause of humanity before the throne of God. At times, this

---

[83] L.G., n. 60. Cf. FLANNERY A. (ed.), *Vatican Council II: The Conciliar and Post Conciliar Documents*, 1975: 85.

[84] *Sub tuum praesidium confugimus, sancta Dei genitrix, sancta Dei genitrix. Nostras deprecationes, ne despicias, in necessitatibus nostris, sed a periculis cunctis libera nos semper, Virgo gloriosa et benedicta.* The prayer has been traced back to 3RD century Egypt, and is extant in Greek on papyrus, in the John Rylands Library, Manchester.

[85] OTT L., *Fundamentals of Catholic Dogma*, 1960, Book III, Part 3, ch. 3, n. 6: 213.

[86] RAHNER K. and VORGRIMLER H., *Concise Theological Dictionary*, 2ND edn., Burns and Oates, London 1983: 295.

intercessory status has been expressed in strong language. St. Germanus of Constantinople (d. c. 733) wrote:

> No one is saved except through you, O All-Holy. No one is delivered from evils except through you, O All-Chaste. No one obtains the grace of mercy except through you, O All-Honorable…For, just as in your Son's presence you have a mother's boldness and strength, do you with your prayers and intercessions save and rescue us from eternal punishment, for we have been condemned by our sins and do not even dare even to lift our eyes to heaven above.[87]

---

[87] GAMBERO L., *Mary and the Fathers of the Church*, 1999: 387–288.

CHAPTER FOUR.
PART TWO: THE POSSIBILITY OF PARALLELS BETWEEN MARY AND FÂṬIMA

Although any deliberation about Mary in terms of Islam almost invariably relates to the person of Maryam in the Qur'ân, it is not hard to distinguish, both in Fâṭima's life and in the theology constructed around her by Shî'î tradition, teaching and popular piety, elements strongly identifiable with the Mariology that is specific to the Roman Catholic Church, leading one into the engaging temptation of drawing comparisons between the Fâṭima of Islam and the Mary of Catholicism. Although there is always the danger of pushing an analogy too far, such comparisons may be regarded as valid without necessarily being unequivocal or incontestable. However, since there remains a considerable disparity between the claims made by Catholicism about Mary and her Son, and the claims of the Shî'a about Fâṭima and hers, it is not a comparison that this chapter proposes, although sometimes this will be inevitable and useful; rather, since this work has aimed at an examination primarily of the Shî'î theology of Fâṭima, this last chapter suggests possible parallels between the Shî'î theology and the key Catholic doctrines about Mary. Consequently, there is no suggestion of equality in the lives, but rather an attempt to underscore certain common strands of thought.

It should be noted at once that the concept of such a timeless or diachronic act as the Immaculate Conception – that is, that the merits of the redemptive act of Christ reach unrestrictedly back into the past and forward into the future – is by no means foreign to the Shî'î worldview; in their attempts to determine the possibility of a redemptive *motif* in the death of al-Ḥusayn at Karbalâ', Shî'î scholars posit that it was a 'cosmic' event, surpassing history, time and space and appropriating dimensions that know no bounds, touching the whole story of humanity. This is seen is the grief and mourning centred upon Karbalâʾ long before the actual event. In this sense, at the very least, we are on common ground.

While there is a vast difference between the Mary of Catholicism and the Maryam of the Qurʾân, the Islamic texts are not without a hint of some special status for the mother of ʿÎsâ; while Maryam is still in the womb, her mother consecrates her to God (Q. 3: 35), begging God's protection for her and her offspring from Satan (Q. 3: 36). God, we are told, "*accepted her with full acceptance and vouchsafed to her a goodly growth*" (Q. 3: 37), providing the child with miraculous food and, according to Q. 3: 42, choosing her, purifying her, and choosing her above all the women of the worlds. Even more explicit is a *ḥadîṯ* carried by al-Buḫârî:

> There is none born of the children of Âdam whom Satan does not touch as soon as he is born, and who raises his voice in a cry from the touch of Satan, except for Maryam and her son.[1]

There is unquestionably no immaculate conception for Fâṭima, or at the very least, not in the sense that such a divine favour is posited of Mary by Catholic dogma. But Fâṭima is sinless, infallible (*maʿṣûm*), an eminence she shares with the other members of the *ahl al-bayt* and with the Imâms that spring from them. The nature of this divine gift (*ʿiṣma*) bears investigation, for it suggests a removal of sin from the individual and a resultant flawlessness that is astonishing. The Shîʿî theologians speak of the concept of *ʿiṣma* primarily in terms of the messengers and prophets, understanding it in the sense of inviolability and immunity. This applies to receiving, safeguarding and conveying revelation, to being immune from all disobedience and sin, and to being shielded from all error, both individually and socially.[2] This flawlessness does not apply to the

---

[1] **BUḪ[1]**., vol. IV, bk. 55 (*Kitâb aḥâdîṯ al-anbiyâʾ*), bb. 39, n. 641: 426–427.

[2] The fifth Imâm, Muḥammad al-Bâqir, for example, constructs his theology of *ʿiṣma* around Q. 33: 33 (cf. LALANI A.R., *Early Shīʿī Thought. The Teachings of Imam Muhammad al-Bāqir*, I.B. Tauris, London 2000: 69). For Maryam, it is based on Q. 3: 42, in which the eighth form verb used

prophets and messengers alone, for there are others who do not bear the prophetic status, but share in the inviolability nonetheless. Maryam is regarded as one of these, and so is Fâṭima. She is sinless, free from error, immune from wrongdoing. It is no easy thing to determine the precise timing of this sinlessness; within Catholic circles, there was much debate around the precise moment in which God removed all sin from Mary's life. The Qur'ânic Maryam is chosen and purified by God (Q. 3: 42), but the text gives no hint of the exact timing of this divine act.[3] In Fâṭima's case, the clue lies

---

of Maryam (*aṣṭafâ*), meaning 'to choose', is the same used of the prophets (Q. 3: 33).

[3] The exegetes are not entirely in accord over this. Al-Ṭabarî, in treating of Q. 3: 42, certainly links God's choice and purification of Maryam to her mother's dedication of the child, still in the womb, to the service of God – but he does not go as far as saying that she was purified whilst still a fetus. He understands the purification in the sense that Maryam's religion is purified of doubts (*rayb*) and uncleanness (*adnâs*), which form part and parcel of female religiosity (cf. **YṬB**[1]., vol. III, *sûrat âl ʿImrân*, v. 42: 262). Al-Zamaḫsharî understands God's choosing of Maryam in the same sense as al-Ṭabarî (i.e. before her birth); but her purification he takes to mean from the very impure actions of which she would be accused (cf. **ZMR**., vol. I, *sûrat âl ʿImrân*, v. 42: 429). Al-Râzî combines the thought of al-Ṭabarî and al-Zamaḫsharî, maintaining that her purification was both bodily and spiritual; Maryam is purified from rejection of faith (*kufr*), disobedience (*maʿṣiya*), the touch of men (*masîs al-riğâl*), menstruation (*ḥayḍ*), objectionable works (*al-afʿâl al-ḏamîma*), repugnant practices (*al-ʿâdât al-qabîḥa*), and from the speech of the Jews in terms of their accusation (*tuhma*) and falsehood (*kiḏb*) (cf. **RAZ**., vol. VIII, *sûrat âl ʿImrân*, v. 42: 42–43, McAULIFFE J.D., "Chosen of all Women: Mary and Fātima in Qur'anic Exegesis" in *Islamochristiana*, n. 7, 1981: 20). Al-Qurṭubî is not dissimilar, positing that her purification was from rejection of faith (*kufr*) and from all the uncleanness of menstruation (*ḥayḍ*), childbirth (*nifâs*) and the like (cf. **QRṬ**., vol. IV, *sûrat âl ʿImrân*, v. 42: 82–83). The Shîʿî exegete al-Baḥrânî merely remarks that she was purified from fornication (*sifâḥ*) and follows this with a long discourse on Fâṭima (cf. **BḤR**., vol. I, *sûrat âl ʿImrân*, v. 42: 280–281). None of these authors determine any temporal framework by stating explicitly that Maryam was purified whilst still in the womb. Concomitantly, in terms of the Shîʿî concept of

in the *aḥâdîṯ* surrounding her naming; there, we discover that she is named Fâṭima because of what God has already done for her in terms of weaning or separating her from the Fire, from evil, from polytheism and from menstruation. Fâṭima's purification, at once physical and spiritual, is accomplished by God before she is born.

In the accounts of the birth of Mary offered by the Apocryphal Gospels, we discover elements which correspond to the conception and birth of Fâṭima (and, concomitantly, the Qur'ânic account of Maryam's childhood); more precisely, this is the miracle of being fed with food from heaven, a text which, in terms of Fâṭima's childhood, has been examined earlier in this work. The naming of Mary in Catholic theology is hardly striking. The texts of the Apocryphal Gospels have the angel instructing her parents, Joachim and Anna, that she is to be called Mary. No special significance is attached to this name by the texts. The case of Fâṭima, as noted earlier in this work, could not be more dissimilar.

It is difficult to ascertain precisely how much the writers of the Christian Gospels, as well as the compilers of the Islamic reports about Fâṭima, were influenced by pagan and other pre-Christian and pre-Muslim estimations of virginity. The authors of the Protevangelium of James and of some of the other Apocryphal Gospels certainly seem to have been, as they develop their story of the curious childhood of the Virgin Mary.

The counter-attack against the thought that Christianity had merely 'borrowed' its concept of virginity from pre-existent cul-

---

ʿiṣma, it is patently clear that such a divine favour belongs, by their very nature, to the *ahl al-bayt* and the Imâms; not so much something conferred as something intrinsic. The Imâms are, according to Shîʿî theology, born circumcised and purified by God (cf. **RṬB**[2]: 222, **ṢDQ**[3]., vol. IV, n. 5914: 418, **ṢDQ**[4]., vol. II, n. 1: 527, **ṢDQ**[5]., vol. I, bb. 19, n. 1: 212, **ṢDQ**[6]., n. 4: 102, **ṬBR**[2]., vol. II; 436, **IRB**., vol. II: 290, **MĞL**., vol. XXV, bb. 4, nn. 1–2: 116–117, vol. LXXV, bb. 29: 372). The inescapable suggestion is that Fâṭima is not so much made pure as born pure, already bearing within her pre-existent nature the quality of *ʿiṣma.* As noted earlier, it is in the naming of Fâṭima that we find a clear indication that she was purified by God, at the very least, while still in the womb. In this, she takes precedence over Maryam, about whom no such statement is made.

tures is developed by Origen, in an argument taken up centuries later by John Henry Newman (d. 1890) and Karl Rahner (d. 1984), but not unanimously believed – that God meticulously prepared the world for the ultimate miracle of His Son's Incarnation, with a progression of signs, symbols and dogmas that merely presaged it. Scholars like St. Justin Martyr (d. c. 165) are quick to point out that, unlike so many of the myths of pagan gods and the children they begot, there was no such physical activity between God and Mary, making this a unique and singular case (with its careful distinction between parthenogenesis and divine impregnation); this was not a distinction articulated very clearly by Origen in his interpretation of the classical myths as a foreshadowing of the great miracle to come. Later thinkers in the Church would move away from this parallelism with pagan myths, regarding it as objectionable and finding new ways of underpinning Jesus' birth from a virgin.

Certainly, in terms of Mary and Fâṭima and their manner of giving birth, there is a curious link with the doctrine of Mary's virginity *in partu* (i.e. in the very act of parturition). Marian scholar and exegete De la Potterie maintains an important linguistic argument; that the words of Lk. 1: 35 ("*the one to be born will be holy*") have been generally mistranslated, and that 'holy' must be understood as a compliment of 'will be born', thus rendering it "will be born holy."[4] This, he argues, has a Levitical meaning, not describing the holiness of Jesus but designating the ritual purity of his parturition. He then links this with another verse he holds has been poorly translated; Jn. 1: 13, which reads "born not of blood." In almost all translations, maintains De la Potterie, 'born' is rendered in the plural and 'blood' in the singular; but in the earliest extant texts, 'born' is in the singular (referring to Jesus) and 'blood' in the plural (hard to render in most languages). The verse speaks of the birth of Jesus 'without bloods'. In Biblical usage, the plural 'bloods' is used to designate a forceful emission of blood.[5] For De la Potterie, this

[4] This, as opposed to ʿÎsâ son of Maryam, who is described in the Qur'ân as a 'pure boy' (*gulam zukî*); the 'pure' in the sentence quite clearly refers to the boy himself, and not the manner of his birth. Cf. Q. 19: 19.

[5] DE LA POTTERIE I., *Mary in the Mystery of the Covenant*, 1997: 97–111.

verse is a reference to Mary's virginity *in partu*, a birth without the shedding of blood (physical lesion or the rupture of the hymen), and, together with her virginal conception, a vital sign of the divine filiation and singularity of this birth. The insistence upon Fâṭima's not shedding blood in birth, as well as her ritual purity (freedom from menstruation) between the births of al-Ḥasan and al-Ḥusayn is echoed in such a concept.

The question remains: why is virginity such a crucial issue in the lives of Mary and Fâṭima? Two factors are at once evident. In Mary's case, there is a long and developed theology, although the early impetus (as opposed to the fact itself) appears to result from a misconstrual of sexuality in general and the sexual act in particular. This is not to deny her virginity; it merely interrogates the thrust of its early justification. With respect to Fâṭima, it is patently clear that everything that is posited of the Qur'ânic Maryam must also be posited of her, in order to substantiate her superior status in the Shî'î perception. This, by its very nature, means a manipulation of the primary meaning of the terminology; in reality, the Qur'ânic Maryam's was not a virgin birth (as is posited by the Catholic Church of Mary, *in partu*) but a virginal conception.[6] The Islamic texts do not contend that Maryam's virginity remained intact while giving birth, or that she remained a virgin *post partum*. Fâṭima's virginity is immediately and palpably different from the Mary of Catholicism and the Maryam of the Qur'ân, for hers is neither a virginity before, during and after the birth of al-Ḥusayn, nor is it a virginal conception. Mary's virginity, writes De la Potterie, as a whole has two complementary facets: there is the exterior or 'biological' virginity, and there is the interior, best expressed by St. Augustine in his distinction between 'virginity of the flesh' (*virginitas carnis*) and 'virginity of the heart' or 'of faith' (*virginitas cordis*). Mary's 'virginity of the heart' was precisely her virginal intent, which gives

---

[6] Raymond Brown prefers the term 'virginal conception' to 'virgin birth' for Mary, positing that "the precise question is not the manner of Jesus' birth or how he came forth from the womb, but the manner of his conception." Considering the insistence of the Church on Mary's virginity *in partu*, it is hard to agree with this definition. Cf. BROWN R., *The Birth of the Messiah*, Doubleday, New York 1993: 517.

a profound theological meaning to her corporeal virginity.[7] Mary's virginity is not understood as merely the moment in which she conceives and then gives birth to Jesus. Already in her early years she was purified and prepared by a profound and singular grace. At the moment of the Annunciation, she had already been filled with grace, and hence the angelic salutation.

Although there are palpable congruencies between Jesus and al-Ḥusayn,[8] it is the likeness between the mothers that concerns us here.

---

[7] DE LA POTTERIE I., *Mary in the Mystery of the Covenant*, 1997: 143.

[8] Examining the Karbalâʾ event and the type of theology and spirituality that has been constructed around it, it is difficult not to think of the life of Jesus and the Christian theological and spiritual tradition. The claims that Jesus makes and that Christians make about him go far beyond the claims of al-Ḥusayn and the beliefs of the Shîʿa about who he was. Nonetheless, in the issues of the nature of the Imamate, the atonement of al-Ḥusayn's martyrdom and his intercessory prerogatives, are powerful reminders of the things that Christians posit about Jesus. A handful of the possible parallels at once present themselves. The authors who examine the Karbalâʾ event stress the firmness of purpose in al-Ḥusayn as he makes his fateful journey from Mecca towards Kûfa. He goes with an almost certain knowledge of what lies ahead, and apparently ready to face martyrdom. This resoluteness in the face of death is posited of Jesus in the Gospel accounts. For both men, death appears to be something divinely preordained, although both are given the possibility of escape. The last moments of their lives are spent in fear, tension and a struggle with impending death. For both, death seems to be a necessary outcome that could, but should not, be shunned. The picture of Jesus in the garden of Gethsemane is not unlike that of al-Ḥusayn on the night before Karbalâʾ, a picture of lonely anguish and despair. Angelic intervention, or at least the possibility of such assistance, is traditional to the stories of both men. Both face death having been abandoned by almost all their followers: and the fickle behaviour of the citizens of Kûfa is not unlike that of those who shouted 'hosanna' and shortly after that, 'crucify him' in the Passion Narratives of Jesus. Even the story of al-Ḥusayn's faithless camel driver, who attempted to rob him after he was dead, has something of a 'Judas' ring to it. The accounts of al-Ḥusayn's last moments on the battlefield, with everyone around him killed, are not dissimilar to Jesus on the cross, feeling

the loss even of God. For the Shîʿa, al-Ḥusayn was an innocent and indeed sinless man, who was led to death like a lamb. While it is precarious to attempt to make Jesus and al-Ḥusayn alike in every respect, the designation of the concept of a lamb remains striking (although somewhat incongruous in Islamic terminology), leaving one wondering from which source it came. The Shîʿa insist that all creation, visible and invisible, weeps for al-Ḥusayn; it is hard not to be reminded of St. Paul's declaration that "*the whole of creation groans, awaiting redemption*" (Rm. 8: 22). A major incentive for this weeping, as we have seen, is that sacrificial deaths such as that of al-Ḥusayn have redemptive powers, which are rendered efficacious when the believers themselves take an active part in the suffering. Again, we are reminded of St. Paul, who writes: "*Now I rejoice in my sufferings for your sake, and in my flesh I complete what is lacking in Christ's afflictions for the sake of His body, that is, the Church*" (Col. 1: 24). Certainly, some of the poetical evocation of the martyrdom of al-Ḥusayn appears close to the Suffering Servant Songs of Isaiah (cf. 42: 1–4, 49: 1–6, 50: 4–9 and 52: 13–53: 12), while elements in the Shîʿî *maǧlis* and *taʿziya* commemorations seem to coincide with Christian commemorations during Holy Week (particularly in their more fervent expressions in some parts of the Catholic world). Some of the lamentation poetry conflicted with the traditional accounts of a brave al-Ḥusayn going valiantly to his death, presenting instead the image of a weak and helpless man. There is no doubt that the Passion Narrative of John's Gospel presents a different account of Christ's Passion when compared to the accounts of the other three Gospels. The Jesus of John is a man in control, apparently free of anguish and doubt, whose sufferings and human weakness are not highlighted as they are in the other Passion Narratives. The issues of mediation and of the intercessory prerogatives are crucial to understanding the redemptive qualities attached to the Karbalâʾ event, and indeed the martyrdom of all the Imâms. They are no less important in grasping Christ's redemptive act which, like that of al-Ḥusayn's, is perceived as something ongoing. The Shîʿa understand the Imâms as the true mediators between God and humankind, who were with God from the beginning as His first creative act. Al-Ḥusayn died for the sake of Islam, so as to free it from influences that were corrupting and distorting it. While suffering is not a good thing in itself, it can nevertheless be transformed and great good drawn from it. This, in essence, is the meaning of al-Ḥusayn's death for the Shîʿa. Having died, he now, in a manner reminiscent of the Letter to the Hebrews, 'lives

A considerable element is the angelic activity constructed around the conceptions and births of Jesus and al-Ḥusayn, as well as the cosmic rejoicing when the births occur:

1. In each case, so momentous an occasion merits a heavenly annunciation. In the Arabic texts examined in this work, the annunciation of al-Ḥusayn is made to his grandfather Muḥammad, rather than to his mother Fâṭima – curiously so, because she has merited the title *al-muḥaddaṯa* ('the one to whom the angels spoke'). In both cases too there is a questioning of the angelic herald, although for different motivations. It is worth noting that, in at least one text examined in an earlier chapter, Fâṭima's own conception, birth and future was announced to Muḥammad by an angel:

> He said to her: Ǧibra'îl announced this to me, that she is a female, and that she is a pure and auspicious person, and that God, may He be blessed and exalted will bring about my progeny from her, and He will bring about from her progeny Imâms in the community, whom He will make leaders on His earth after the termination of His revelation.[9]

Once more, as with al-Ḥusayn, the announcement is made not to the mother of the child, but in this case, to her father.

---

to intercede' for the faithful community, whose own suffering is in some sense an extension of his and joined to his. The concrete symbol of his divinely given prerogatives is the pool of *Kawṯar*, a concept drawn not as much from the Qur'ân as from the corpus of *aḥâdîṯ*. The waters of this pool cleanse the blood and tears of the *ahl al-bayt* and of all associated with them. Here, at this pool, will the faithful be gathered; and it is beside this pool that ʿAlî stands as judge, ready to turn evildoers away from its water on the 'day of thirst'. There are distinct parallels with the idea of the 'fountain of life' and of the river that flows 'from under the sanctuary,' with all the Biblical promises attached to these. Cf. CLOHESSY C., "The Face of Islām Flushed. The Karbalā' Event" in *Encounter*, n. 285, June 2002.

[9] **RṬB**[1].: 8, **ṢDQ**[1]., n. 1: 593, **FNR**., vol. I: 143; **RWD**[1]., vol. II: 524, **SHB**., vol. III, bb. *manâqib Fâṭima al-Zahrâ'*: 388, **MǦL**., vol. XII, bb. 5: 80, vol. XVI, bb. 5: 80–81.

2. The annunciation of al-Ḥusayn is blended with the forewarnings of his martyrdom, as well as with predictions about his status and future achievements. In the case of Jesus, while the predictions about his status and future achievements are distinctly present, the forewarnings are absent, and are only articulated by Simeon, when the child is presented in the temple by Mary and Joseph.[10] In fact, there is a dream motif concerning Jesus' death, but it comes long after the narratives of his birth; after his arrest, the wife of Pontius Pilate reports having "*suffered much over Him today in a dream*" (Mt. 27: 19). The content of this obviously disturbing dream is not revealed, but it is certainly within the context of the death of a man whom the wife of Pontius Pilate declares 'righteous'.

3. While we have almost no information about the months of Mary's pregnancy, those of Fâṭima are somewhat more detailed in the texts. Aside from the Annunciation, and the angelic warnings to Joseph, the Canonical Gospels record no such angelic ministration to Mary during her pregnancy. Conversely, the Apocryphal Gospels do, even if not at length; we have already examined Mary being fed by an angelic hand in the temple, recorded by the Protevangelium of James, although this feeding was prior to her pregnancy. The Gospel of Pseudo-Matthew[11] records angels defending the newly-

---

[10] In terms of the predictions of Simeon, and the blend of joy and sadness, St. Theodotus of Ancyra wrote: "To you Simeon spoke a prophecy, saying: O white, innocent dove! O holy tabernacle of our hope, in whom all holiness and magnificence reside! 'This Child' whom you have borne in a way beyond words, 'this Child is set for the downfall and rising of many in Israel, a sign that is spoken against. And a sword shall pierce through your own soul as well, that thoughts out of many hearts may be revealed' (cf. Lk. 2: 34–35). But why, O old man, do you mix sad predictions with glad tidings? Up until now you have proclaimed 'light' and 'glory', and now you announce 'downfall' and speak of a 'sword' for the Mother." Cf. GAMBERO L., *Mary and the Fathers of the Church*, 1999: 266–267.

[11] A Latin compilation of which only an 11TH century manuscript is extant (although the gospel may be as old as the 8TH or 9TH century), and which uses the Protevangelium of James and the Gospel of Thomas as its sources. Cf. JAMES M.R., (trans.), *The Apocryphal New Testament*, 1980: 70.

pregnant Mary against false accusation, comforting Joseph in his lament over the inexplicable pregnancy of Mary, and an angel guiding the couple to the cave where Jesus would be born. The Armenian Gospel of the Infancy[12] presents a long dialogue between Mary and Gabriel (after her marriage to Joseph). The light on Fâṭima's face until the birth of al-Ḥusayn is distinctively paralleled in the Apocryphal Gospels:

> And they stood in the place of the cave; and behold a bright cloud overshadowing the cave...And immediately the cloud withdrew itself out of the cave, and a great light appeared in the cave so that our eyes could not endure it. And by little and little that light withdrew itself until the young child appeared...and took the breast of its (*sic*) mother Mary.[13]

4. While there is a cosmic reaction recorded for both births, these are moderately different. In the case of Jesus, the rejoicing of heaven is represented by the angels, who proclaim the news to shepherds, representing all the people of the earth. At the birth of al-Ḥusayn, the texts depict an outpouring of joy, among the angels, the people of Paradise, the inhabitants of the earth and even those in Hell, whose punishment is lightened for the occasion.[14] As not-

---

[12] This manuscript, like the Gospel of Pseudo-Matthew, relies extensively upon the Protevangelium of James and the Gospel of Thomas, while greatly amplifying them. It comes from a Syriac text translated into Armenian, but the date of the original remains unsettled. Cf. JAMES M.R., (trans.), *The Apocryphal New Testament*, 1980: 83.

[13] Protevangelium of James, ch. XIX, vv. 1–2. Cf. JAMES M.R., (trans.), *The Apocryphal New Testament*, 1980: 46.

[14] At first sight, no such parallel – of Hell's punishment being diminished as a form of celebration – appears extant in Christian thought. In fact, there is a curious parallel, although it is not part of Catholic dogma and merits nothing more than an aside. It is a strand of thought freshly discovered by C.S. Lewis, himself not a Catholic, which he came across in the writings of a 17TH century Anglican clergyman, Jeremy Taylor, and used in his own writings. Technically, the strand is called the *Refrigerium*; the idea that, for a period of time or for a particular purpose, God may lessen the sufferings of those in Hell. Taylor claimed to have found it in a

Roman missal published in Paris in 1626, although scholars have found no such missal. In fact, what Taylor thought he had discovered was, in all likelihood, a reference to the Catholic doctrine of Purgatory, rather than Hell. But Taylor mentions a second, older source for the *Refrigerium*; the 4TH century Latin poet Prudentius Aurelius Clemens, who penned the following: "Often below the Styx holidays from their punishments are kept, even by the guilty spirits...Hell grows feeble with mitigated torments and the shadowy nation, free from fires, exults in the leisure of its prison: the rivers cease to burn with their usual sulphur." In fact, yet another source is the 9TH century *Voyage of Saint Brendan*, in which the saint meets Judas on one of his infrequent days of indulgence, free from Hell. Scholars claim that the concept of the *Refrigerium* appears to date from the late 4TH century, in a work entitled the *Apocalypse of Paul*, and in which some mitigation of their sufferings is granted to those in Hell for the sake of St. Paul, who has visited them. Such a concept is entertained by a number of Greek apocryphal texts in which Mary visits Hell and cries out to her Son for mercy; in response, Christ grants a certain respite to the sufferers there, on account of Mary's prayer. Cf. BARNSTONE W. (ed.)., *The Other Bible*, Harper Collins, San Francisco 1984: 547, PEARCE J., *C.S. Lewis and the Catholic Church*, Ignatius Press, San Francisco 2003: 102–105 and HOOPER W., *C.S. Lewis: A Companion and Guide*, Harper Collins, London 1996: 279–280. Notes one author about Mary's pleas for those in Hell: "The differences between the various Apocalypses of the Virgin are of trifling importance – embellishments of the penalties and varying lengths of reprieve gained by the Virgin. In some she obtains almost half the years as respite for the damned. In another, the Virgin does not rest content at a mere interval of relief, but begs her son on her breasts, her womb and her motherhood always to grant her prayers for sinners." Cf. WARNER M., *Alone Of All Her Sex. The Myth and Cult of the Virgin Mary*, Pan Books Ltd., London 1985: 322. Such a plea is reminiscent of Fâṭima's asking that her dower be to intercede for the sinners of her father's community. Again, it must be restated that these concepts have never been a part of Catholic teaching. Nevertheless, in a strangely ambiguous passage, St. Augustine writes: "In vain, therefore, do some men, indeed, very many, because of human sentiment, bewail the eternal punishment of the damned and their perpetual, unending torments, without really believing that it shall be so...But let them suppose, if it pleases them, that the punishments of the damned are, at certain periods of time, somewhat mitigated earlier, the whole cosmological effect of al-Ḥusayn's birth is underscored by the Shîʿî texts; in the Christian accounts of the birth of Jesus, the angels' jubilation and glorification is entirely centred upon God, and the cosmological effects of the Incarnation still lie in the future; conversely, the birth of al-Ḥusayn has an immediate consequence for those in Heaven and Hell, a portend of his martyrdom, which the Shîʿa envisage as a 'cosmic' event, touching all of human history, of nature and of the universe. It is also worth noting that, in the context of Fâṭima herself, there was general rejoicing among the maidens and other people of Paradise at her birth.[15]

5. Both Mary and Fâṭima gave birth under testing circumstances; Mary's was the physical discomfort and immense poverty of her surroundings, while Fâṭima's was psychological, her delivery of al-

---

ed. For even thus it can be understood that they remain in the wrath of God, that is, in damnation itself, - for it is this that is called the wrath of God, not some disturbance in the divine mind: - that in His wrath, that is, by their abiding in His wrath, He does not shut up His mercies; yet, He does not put an end to their eternal punishment, but only applies or interposes some relief to their torments." Cf. JURGENS W.A., *The Faith of the Early Fathers*, 1970–1979, vol. III, n. 1932: 152. The 9TH century *Voyage of Saint Brendan* has another curious sideline; Brendan comes across Judas sitting on a rock in the middle of the Atlantic, where, Judas claims, his torture in Hell has been mitigated for a certain period of time. It is also on a 'white rock' in the middle of a 'green sea' that the female *ǧinn* ʿAfrâʾ meets Iblîs, where he pleads for redemption through the names of Fâṭima and the other members of the 'people of the house'. This report was examined earlier in this work. Interestingly, the *Voyage of Saint Brendan* was in vogue shortly before the time that many of the *aḥâdîṯ* concerning Fâṭima were being collated by scholars like al-Ṣadûq, who died in 381/991.

15 This cosmic reaction is repeated in the moment of the deaths; in the texts examined in this work, it has been noted that all creation, even inanimate things, reacted violently at the death of al-Ḥusayn. At the moment of Jesus' death, apocryphal language is used by the Gospel authors to portray this global consequence: the temple curtain was split lengthwise, the earth shook, the rocks were split open, tombs were opened and dead people rose and were seen in the city. Cf. Mt. 27: 51–53.

Ḥusayn marred by the predictions of his murder. The Shîʿî texts use Qurʾânic wording to describe how she conceived and gave birth «*with reluctance*» (Q. 46: 15). In this sense too, both births were overshadowed by a sense of doom – Mary's just after the birth and Fâṭima's before it.

The Apocryphal Gospels recount a number of occasions, to which there is no allusion in the Canonical texts, when an exceptionally young Jesus converses with his mother or intervenes in a moment of crisis (such as the Gospel of Pseudo-Matthew, which records Jesus, in the lap of his mother, bidding a palm tree to lower its fruit so that she could pick it, a narrative which corresponds closely with Q. 19: 23–24).[16] St. Clair-Tisdall notes that in the first chapter of the Arabic 'Gospel of the Infancy' the infant Jesus speaks from the cradle:

> In the Book of Josephus, High Priest, who lived at the time of the Messiah (and men say he was Caiaphas), we find it said that Jesus spake when he was in the cradle, and called out to his mother Mary: 'Verily I am Jesus the Son of God, the Word…'[17]

In the Islamic texts, both Fâṭima and al-Ḥusayn speak from the womb; and while there is a highly contentious possibility that so did ʿÎsâ, the texts are more certain that, like the Jesus of the Apocryphal Gospels, he undoubtedly spoke from the cradle in defense of his mother's purity (Q. 19: 30). No such marvel is posited of Mary, even in the Apocryphal accounts, and this, in a sense, raises Fâṭima and al-Ḥusayn above Maryam and ʿÎsâ in status.

The phenomenon of the dove entering the robe of Fâṭima exists only as a fragment, but has strong echoes in a number of non-Islamic texts; in some of the Coptic Infancy Gospels, the angels that minister to Mary in the temple are in the form of doves, while in the same texts a white dove alights upon the breast of Mary's mother Anna (prior to the angelic announcement that she would

---

[16] Gospel of Pseudo-Matthew, ch. XX. Cf. JAMES M.R., (trans.), *The Apocryphal New Testament*, 1980: 75.

[17] ST. CLAIR-TISDALL W., "The Sources of Islam" in Ibn Warraq (ed.), *The Origins of the Koran*, Prometheus Books, New York 1988: 266.

have a child).[18] More striking is the Christian usage of a dove to symbolize the active presence of God in the Person of the Holy Spirit, seen most clearly in the famous Theophany at the moment of Jesus' baptism, and recorded by all four Canonical Gospels.

> "*As soon as Jesus was baptized, he went up out of the water. At that moment heaven was opened, and he saw the Spirit of God, descending like a dove and lighting on him*".[19]

Ayoub[20] advocates that the dove which entered the robe of Fâṭima is an echo of this very moment, when a dove appeared at Jesus' baptism. In reality, there was no dove at Jesus' baptism; the texts say, not that the Holy Spirit descended in the physical form of a dove, but merely that the Holy Spirit came down in the way a dove might descend from the air.

There is conceivably no area in which the theologies constructed around the Mary of Catholicism and the Fâṭima of Islam are more cohesive than in that of grief and lament. Writes Barbara Stowasser:

> In Muslim piety, and here especially Shi'i piety the connection of Mary and Fatima is such that the two figures at times appear collapsed into one…What most deeply binds Mary and Fatima together is the joint image of mistress of sorrows. In Shi'i piety, she is…the grieving mother whose short and hard life was made bitter by the foreknowledge of the future martyrdom of her son Husayn, an event of divine redemption and cosmic significance.[21]

---

[18] James records a number of Coptic fragments, mostly homilies, panegyrics or biographies, which recount the story of Mary's birth. A number of these fragments have been collected and published, for example by Forbes Robinson (Cambridge 1896). Cf. JAMES M.R., (trans.), *The Apocryphal New Testament*, 1980: xxx, 87–88.

[19] Mt. 3: 16, Mk. I: 10, Lk. 3: 22, Jn. I: 32.

[20] AYOUB M., *Redemptive Suffering in Islam. A Study of the Devotional Aspects of ʿAshura in Twelver Shiʿism*, 1978: 72.

[21] STOWASSER B., *Women in the Qurʾan, Traditions and Interpretation*, Oxford University Press, New York 1994: 80.

Although by the late 6TH century, St. Ephraim the Syrian, St. Romanos the Melodist (d. c. 560) and Jacob of Sarug (d. 521) had already penned their classic lamentations centred upon the sorrows of Mary, the concept of 'Mother of Sorrows' was really medieval development, spreading through Italy, France, the Netherlands, Spain and England between the 11TH and 14TH centuries.[22] Again, a number of parallels are significant:

1. Both Mary and Fâṭima are mothers of sons who will be killed, and regarded, each in his own unique way, as a martyr. Fâṭima knows this even before her son is born, so that her sorrow is immediate. Mary's knowledge of her Son's death comes later – the prediction of Simeon is not absolutely explicit – but her sorrow could be held to have its starting point in the extremely difficult particulars of her pregnancy – a young girl pregnant outside of marriage – and the trying circumstances of the birth. These are followed in quick succession by the threats of Herod and his murder

---

[22] The Catholic Church celebrates the feast of Our Lady of Sorrows on September 15TH, the day after the Feast of the Holy Cross, to demonstrate the intimate connection between the sufferings of Jesus and the sorrows of Mary. Such a connection is traceable in the Gospels; Jn. 19: 25 (Calvary) and Lk. 2: 35 (Mary's soul pierced with a sword). Additional sorrows can be deduced from Lk. 2: 7 (no room at the inn), Mt. 2: 6–18 (the massacre of the children), Lk. 2: 41–50 (the anxious search for the missing Jesus), Lk. 4: 28–30 (the rejection by people of Nazareth) and Lk. 11: 53–54 (the rejection by authorities of Jerusalem). This style of Marian piety reached its zenith in the 14TH century, but Mary's sorrows were highlighted at a much earlier period too, especially in the Syrian Church, with St. Ephraim, St. Romanos and Jacob of Sarug: the veneration of Mary's grief, based on the crucifixion scene, goes back to this period. Suffice it to say that the imagery of a young and suffering mother bearing a child in an unreceptive world and an older mother grieving beneath the cross of her Son as he was dying entranced generations of believers. This imagery was taken up by a succession of saints and mystics, especially between the 12TH and 14TH centuries: St. Anselm (d. 1109), St. Bernard of Clairvaux (d. 1153), St. Bonaventure (d. 1274), St. Albert the Great (d. 1280), St. Brigid of Sweden (d. 1373), St. Catherine of Siena (d. 1380), St. Peter Canisius (d. 1597) and St. Alphonsus Liguori (d. 1787).

of countless children, the forced exile of Mary, Joseph and Jesus in Egypt, and the temporary loss of Jesus, aged twelve, in Jerusalem. The salient dissimilarity between the two women is that, while Mary witnesses the arrest, trial, torture and execution of her Son, Fâṭima does not; she has been dead for almost fifty years.

2. The Biblical image of Mary's mournful stance at the foot of the cross has been captured in countless poems and hymns that now form an integral part of Catholic spirituality. Poignant examples of this *Mater Dolorosa* ('sorrowful mother') image are the *Kontákion* of St. Romanos the Melodist[23] and the famous *Stabat Mater* of Jacopone da Todi (d. 1306). She weeps in sorrow as Jesus dies and, according to a tradition captured in Michelangelo's renowned *Pietà*, receives him into her arms as he is taken from the cross. Fâṭima's son, and his small remnant, were deprived of access to water and finally, on the 10TH day of the month of Muḥarram, were massacred by the huge opposing force.[24] Al-Ḥusayn was the last to die,

---

[23] Gambero describes the *Kontákion* as the adaptation of "a Syrian poetic genre to create a new Greek language form…a sort of homily in verse form." Cf. GAMBERO L., *Mary and the Fathers of the Church*, 1999: 325–326.

[24] For readers who may not know the story, the catalyst of the affair was the caliphate of Muʿâwiya (during whose reign al-Ḥusayn received numerous pledges of support and appeals to lead a revolt) and the accession of Yazîd to the caliphate after his father Muʿâwiya's death. The motive is at once political and religious; al-Ḥusayn regarded Yazîd, with his demand for unswerving allegiance, as a licentious profligate. Both Yazîd and his father were seen as men who violated the Islamic socio-political ideal and who thus threatened the foundations of the office of the Caliphate and the very substructure of Islam. Al-Ḥusayn was uncompromising in his rejection of allegiance to Yazîd, and for this reason he could not possibly have remained inactive. Again, the commentators stress his resolution, despite the quite obvious outcome of such determination. Perhaps, as some say, he acted with disproportionate idealism and without the adroitness and versatility of a politician; but in the end, he appears to have had little choice. For one thing, all of this was preordained. The commentators see martyrdom as necessary in order to fulfill the office of Imâm. He left Medina for Mecca, where he stayed about four months. He con-

alone, undefended, stripped of his clothing. Fâṭima, who has already wept copiously for him in her lifetime, looks on from beyond the grave and continues to weep as she awaits the Day of Resurrection. The texts are quite clear; these are not only tears of sorrow, but also tears of righteous anger, tears that hope to win the wrath of God against the killers and vindication for the one slain. No such suggestion is found in the tears of Mary.

While the correspondence between the intercession of Mary and that of Fâṭima may appear conspicuous, there are a number of important differences to be born in mind:

3. Of its very nature, Mary's intercession depends on two factors; the merits of her Son's redemptive act, and the all-important theme of human repentance. While there may be legends and stories in popular piety about Mary rescuing people from Hell, these do not form part of the teaching of the Church. Her intercessory powers may be powerful, but they remain secondary to the mediation of her Son. Even in the legends, which tell of Mary intervening in various human situations – and St. Gregory of Tours for example col-

---

tinued to receive letters and emissaries from Kûfa, begging him to lead an insurrection and pledging support. He finally left Mecca without having completed the rites of Pilgrimage (seemingly having heard that enemies had arrived among the pilgrims and intended to shed his blood there). Thus began the fateful journey that would end at Karbalâ'. The group traveling with him grew smaller as many, who had been anticipating conquer, began to experience increasing doubts about his fate. With the arrival of a large group of horsemen sent to intercept him, and the warnings of its leader, al-Ḥusayn led both groups in prayer; he then insisted upon the pledges of support he had received and asked for that allegiance to now be given. He also offered to go back should the people of Kûfa give some sign that they were displeased with his coming. We are also told that he used this opportunity to articulate the reasons for his risk and the jeopardy into which he was bringing his family; an oppressive ruler was violating the sanctions of God, opposing the *sunna* of Muḥammad and ill-treating one of God's servants. To desist in fighting such a ruler would earn one a place in the Fire. Cf. CLOHESSY C., "The Face of Islām Flushed. The Karbalā' Event" in *Encounter*, n. 285, June 2002.

lates countless such stories in his *Libri Miraculorum* – repentance on the part of the individual remains a key factor for salvation.[25]

---

[25] The pious legends and stories of Mary's intercessory powers comprise a number of *genres*. The first, which flowered in the Middle Ages, but strands of which are still found in parts of Europe, is that through Mary's prayers, infertility and barrenness is defeated and women can bear children. Extant examples of this tradition are found in a number of Marian shrines famous for this aspect of Mary as mother and 'midwife' (a key role of the Qur'ânic Maryam in the life of Fâṭima) – the 'Black Madonna' of Montserrat, shrines in Chartres, Rome, Milan, Naples and Sicily (where in the frescoes and paintings, Mary is often portrayed with pomegranates or corn, symbols of fertility). Close to this theme is that of Mary miraculously providing dowers for poor and orphan girls; a classic example is the altarpiece in the church of Santa Maria Sopra Minerva in Rome. In terms of relics of Our Lady, the sash she wore around her waste (and described by various visionaries) became particularly associated with her power to give the gift of fertility (according to a legend from the Middle Ages, this sash fell into the hands of Thomas the Apostle, an event represented in medieval art found in England, Italy and the ex-Yugoslavia). There are numerous pious legends of Mary intervening, either to provide a child for an infertile devotee, or even to spirit away a child from one who ought not to be pregnant. A second *genre* is that of Mary interceding for and intervening in great and small events through the prayers and pleas of needy supplicants. "She mediates between heaven and earth, for in her glorified body she belongs in both realms. She listens to the implorations of mankind, 'groaning and weeping in this vale of tears' – as the *Salve Regina* sings – and promises to ease their pain with heavenly medicine." (Cf. WARNER M., *Alone Of All Her Sex. The Myth and Cult of the Virgin Mary*, 1985: 285). As noted before, in theological terms, Mary's intercession depends upon and is a share in the intercession of her Son, the only mediator between God and humankind; but in popular piety, Mary has unconstrained power. Primarily, she is approached as a mother who will be refused nothing by her Son, whom she asks on behalf of her devotees. Such a theme resonates in the most famous prayers to Mary: the 3RD century *Sub tuum praesidium*, and the 11TH century *Salve Regina* and *Alma Redemptoris Mater*. In addition to countless mundane favours, Mary has been petitioned in moments of serious historical crisis; so it is that, by her intercession and intervention, the Turks were held to have been defeated by

4. According to the Shîʿî texts already examined, Fâṭima's intercessory prerogatives are a result of her own great sufferings and, primarily, of her membership of the *ahl al-bayt.* Her intercession extends to her adherents, to those who loved and, in varied ways, supported her (even non-Shîʿa) and to her progeny. Strictly speaking, although Islam is not without a theology of sin and repentance, repentance does not play a major role in the intercessory role of Fâṭima; this partly due to the stark differences in the understanding of sin and repentance in Islam and Christianity.[26] The texts demar-

---

Christian forces at the Battle of Lepanto (1571), and again at Petrovaradin (1717). No less so was the fall of Communism in the late 20TH century ascribed, at least in part, to Mary's prayers. The major Marian shrines highlight yet another important intervention believed to be part of Mary's intercessory prerogatives: the healing of bodily illness and infirmity. In Lourdes (France) and Fatima (Portugal), innumerable pilgrims pray for a cure. (It is a point of note that there are groups within Catholicism who maintain that Mary appeared at a place called Fatima precisely because Muslims ought to be converted to Christianity; and groups within Islam who hold that her appearance there was to uphold the truth of Muḥammad by honouring his daughter. Neither of these viewpoints appears to be worthy of much consideration). A third *genre* is Mary's intercession for the dying, specifically that they might enter heaven. It is here most particularly that we find elements strongly resonant in the Shîʿî theology constructed around Fâṭima, although the theological differences remain stark. The same Virgin Mary whose powerful prayers can bring fertility, cures from various ills and consolation to those who pray to her, has a more important function within the theology of her intercession; to plead for the salvation of sinners at the throne of God. As noted in this chapter, the repentance of the individual concerned plays a key role in this mediation. Cf. WARNER M., *Alone Of All Her Sex. The Myth and Cult of the Virgin Mary*, 1985: 273–331.

[26] As Michel Lagarde points out, at the level of semantics, the Qur'ânic language used to articulate the cycle of sin, repentance and forgiveness follows two major directions; the first is the postulate of 'order' and 'disorder', while the second predicates the axiom of the 'veil' and 'unveiled'. Precisely, Qur'anic terminology, used for sin in general, employs five key terms: *ẓulm*, *maʿṣiya*, *iṯm*, *ǧurm* and *ḫaṭîʾa.* Each of these, in its own

cate certain groupings that benefit from her prayers; her adherents, progeny and those who love her. These can win a place in Paradise chiefly because Fâṭima asks it for them; the theme of their own repentance from sin hardly appears in the texts we have examined. Notwithstanding the strict Qur'ânic injunctions, which insist that no one intercedes except by the will and permission of God, Fâṭi-

---

way, signifies order and disorder; situating something outside of its proper sphere, resisting the effort to bring good order, situating oneself outside of the customary or legal order of things, the separating of something that was part of a whole, and the idea of leaving the original position. Within the same sphere of semantics are other terms used for particular sin (*fasâd*, *fisq*, *ḍalâl* and *shirk*); these too suggest a movement from order to disorder, from regularity to irregularity, from harmony to disharmony. Concomitantly, the concept of repentance is expressed by the terms *tawba* and *nadâma*; both suggest a movement back from disharmony to harmony, from chaos to order. At a second semantic level are words referring to sin (*ẓulm*, *dunûb*) and forgiveness (*maġfira*, *ʿawf*, *takfîr*) and which convey the sense of the veiled and the unveiled – hiding faith by sin or disguising the truth, as opposed to God's forgiveness which could be understood as a covering of sin and a veiling of punishment. Since in Islam there exists no concept of 'Original Sin', the theology of salvation and redemption (in the Christian sense) has no meaning; sin in Islam is understood as wronging oneself, and so does not touch precisely one's relationships with others or even, to some extent, with God. Cf. LAGARDE M., "Sin, Repentance and Forgiveness in the Qur'an and Tradition" in *Encounter*, n. 107, July-August 1984. For Christianity, sin is an act which separates one from God to a greater or lesser extent, for by its very nature is it a negation of God's will, law and covenant relationship of love. All sin springs from the Original Sin of Adam; both 'original sin', the state of being deprived of supernatural life, with all its effects, and in which every human is born, and 'actual sin', committed, in the final analysis through choice, by the human being. Only God can forgive sin; and God made man in Christ gives the Church the power to transmit His forgiveness. Repentance remains the chief characteristic in this: it means a rejection of sin, a turning from sinful behaviour and a return to God. In this, as in the Islamic concept examined above, there is a movement from one state to another (expressed precisely in Catholic theology by the Greek *metanoia*).

ma is given an extraordinary liberty in her intercessory role. This is patently clear in one of the texts already examined:

> ...God has made you judge over His creation. Whoever harmed you and harmed your offspring, judge them as you wish, and I will sanction your judgment concerning them..."[27]

The texts also demarcate the various grades of her intercession; passive, merely because she is a member of the *ahl al-bayt*, with a status and name so potent that it is incumbent upon God to answer the prayers of the prophets and holy ones who use it,[28] and active, by the will and permission of God; negative, in terms of which she asks punishment for the killers of her son, and positive, in terms of which she leads her progeny, loved ones and supporters (including a number of women) into Paradise. Love for Fâṭima is primary, as seen in a *ḥadîṯ*, which is remarkable close to some of the Gospel passages:[29]

> Abû Ğaʿfar[30] said: "By God, Ğâbir,[31] on that day she will pick out her adherents and those who love her the way a bird picks out the good seed from the perishable. When her Shîʿa come

---

[27] **QQM.**, n. 10: 334.

[28] The prayer of Iblîs in the name of Fâṭima is not answered, and he remains unredeemed.

[29] Specifically, the great judgment scene described in the parable of Mt. 25: 31–46. In terms of the parable, salvation depends on particular works of goodness: "*Come, O blessed of my Father, inherit the kingdom prepared for you from the foundation of the world; for I was hungry and you gave me food, I was thirsty and you gave me drink, I was a stranger and you welcomed me, I was naked and you clothed me, I was sick and you visited me, I was in prison and you came to see me*". When the recipients of this joyous news query the actual circumstances in which such good actions were performed, they are told by the King: "*Truly I say to you, as you did it to one of the least of these my brethren, you did it to me*". In a similar strand of thought, Jesus says that "*whoever gives to one of these little ones even a cup of cold water because he is a disciple, truly, I say to you, he shall not lose his reward*" (Mt. 10: 42). In Mark's version it is "*because you bear the name of Christ*" (Mk. 9: 41).

[30] The fifth Imâm.

[31] Ğâbir al-Anṣârî.

> with her to the gate of Paradise, God will direct their hearts to turn around, and when they turn around, God, powerful and lofty, will say: My beloved ones, why did you look around when Fâṭima, the daughter of my beloved one, has interceded for you? They will answer: Lord! We would have liked our standing to be known on a day like this. God will say: My beloved ones, go back and look for anyone who loved you for the love of Fâṭima. Look for anyone who fed you for the love of Fâṭima. Look for anyone who clothed you for the love of Fâṭima. Look for anyone who gave you a drink for the love of Fâṭima. Look for everyone who prevented slander against you for the love of Fâṭima. Take him by his hand and lead him into Paradise."[32]

In the final analysis, and in spite of elements, which, at first glance, appear to be strikingly similar, there are clear and major contrasts in the theologies constructed around these women by their adherents. Aside from the status of sorrowful mother, which certainly unites them (and countless other mothers throughout the course of history), they follow diverse paths. The virginity claimed for both of them is, although in both cases something essentially physical, not the same kind of virginity. The claims made about their respective sons very dissimilar. Their manner of intercession, although in both cases done only because God permits it, is disparate. Their personal histories are different.

Without blurring the arrant inimitability of each, the words of Pope Paul VI about Mary might no less be applied, at least in some of its aspects, to Fâṭima:

> The modern woman will note with pleasant surprise that Mary of Nazareth, while completely devoted to the will of God, was far from being a timidly submissive woman or one whose piety was repellent to others; on the contrary, she was a woman who did not hesitate to proclaim that God vindicates the humble and the oppressed, and removes the powerful people of this world from their privileged positions. The modern woman will recognize in Mary, who 'stands out among the poor and hum-

[32] **MĞL.**, vol. VIII, bb. 21, n. 59: 51, vol. XLIII, bb. 3, n. 57: 64–65.

> ble of the Lord,' a woman of strength, who experienced poverty and suffering, flight and exile…the figure of the Blessed Virgin does not disillusion any of the profound expectations of the men and women of our time but offers them the perfect model of the disciple of the Lord: the disciple who builds up the earthly and temporal city while being a diligent pilgrim towards the heavenly and eternal city; the disciple who works for that justice which sets free the oppressed and for that charity which assists the needy…[33]

It was ʿAli Shariati who took the Ṣafavid image of Fâṭima and refashioned her to suit the mood of an Iran on the knife edge of revolution. Shariati offers a beguiling reinterpretation of Fâṭima, in which a number of key strands of thought dominate. He begins his argument by postulating the confused state and the rapidly changing status of the contemporary woman, who stands between two other types of women – those who remain in the traditional mould and have no issue with identity crisis, and those who have accepted the innovative and foreign identity. In between are the women ('awakened', in Shariati's mind) who can neither accept their hereditary, traditional forms nor submit to this forced and innovative image, and who are desperately in need of a model in order to rediscover or 'rebirth' their true identity. The contemporary woman wants to elaborate herself, make her own choices. She cannot accept merely being the result of her ethnic heritage, but nor is she willing to assume a shallow veneer. At the same time, she can neither bypass Islam, nor remain apathetic to it.

It is Fâṭima whom Shariati proposes as this model, as an unqualified paradigm of an ideal woman whom no one has yet become, the Fâṭima whose face, Shariati posits, has remained anonymous behind the constant praise, eulogies, and lamentations of her followers. Thus he demarcates the three faces of women is Islamic societies; the face of the traditional woman, the face of the contemporary woman, who has just begun to grow and know herself, and the face of Fâṭima which has no resemblance whatsoever to that of the ethnically Muslim woman. Fâṭima is quite clearly in

---

[33] Pope Paul VI, *Marialis Cultus*, 1974, 37.

Shariati's mind, neither a traditional woman nor a contemporary and *avant-garde* woman, but something of a *via media*. She is presented as the model because, he argues, neither the traditional woman, hibernating in her archaic worldview, nor the new woman, seduced by the false and shallow worldview of the enemy, can play a vigorous role in helping the women of today to understand who they really are. As such, Fâṭima is presented as one who can form new human characteristics as well as break old and empty traditions; neither archaic advice nor modern, facile slogans interest her.

Having situated her as his ideal model for contemporary womanhood, Shariati then laments the fact that the real Fâṭima is quite unknown, hidden behind the devotion of her devotees, who know little of her real personality. In fact, he posits, she is a revolutionary personality; formed and shaped by her revolutionary father, Fâṭima's short life, filled with poverty, hardship, weakness, illness and suffering, was, all the while, nothing less than Fâṭima 'becoming' Fâṭima. For Shariati, she is inextricably linked with the mission and message of her father;[34] why was it, he asks, that while her sisters were permitted to live in relative luxury, Muḥammad would not even give Fâṭima a servant and frowned censoriously over her attempts to wear jewelry or decorate her home with a coloured curtain? Why was it that he treated her so strictly, making no exceptions for her in terms of the law of Islam (Shariati's interpretation of the *ḥadîṯ*, examined earlier in this thesis, that even were Fâṭima to steal, her hand would be cut off)? It was because Muḥammad was deliberately forming her; for her to 'become' Fâṭima obliged him to be strict with her. She would be his last-surviving child, replacing a son as the inheritor of the family name and history, the one who would maintain the values of her ancestors, and with the responsibility of being the link between prophecy and *al-Mahdî*, as well as one of the four highest women of the world and of Paradise.[35] In what Shariati describes as almost a covenant relationship,

---

[34] It is of interest that Shariati believes that Fâṭima received the title 'mother of her father' because she cared for him so tenderly and championed his cause. This is not quite the usual Shîʿî interpretation.

[35] Shariati reminds his readers that the other three were Maryam, Âsiya, and Ḫadîǧa. Following the *aḥâdîṯ* that place Fâṭima's name last in

while her father would have to bear the load of making known the revelation of God, his daughter would bear the responsibility of reflecting within herself the newly created revolutionary values. Not only was Fâṭima 'becoming' Fâṭima, but she was also, in a sense, 'becoming' everything to her father, giving him, through her marriage, replacements for the sons (and later daughters) he had lost.

Essentially it was, Shariati posits, through the intercession of Muḥammad that Fâṭima 'became' Fâṭima. He notes that in Islam, intercession is not a way of 'saving the unworthy', but rather, the means of reaching 'the most worthy of salvation'. The individual receives the intercession of an intercessor and through this change his character and behaviour in to alter his destiny.

The concept of revolution is yet another key element in Shariati's vision of Fâṭima. The very treatment she received at the hands of her father – his kissing of her – was revolutionary, striking at the roots of the inhumane treatment of their era. His Fâṭima is a weak and sickly child, beset by loneliness, hunger and poverty, surrounded by struggles and difficulties, weighed down by sorrow and sadness; but after her death, she would enliven the hearts and spirits of all who fight oppression and discrimination and strive for a truly just Islamic society, so that, even now, her memory affects a revolutionary stimulus in Muslim society. Writes Shariati:

> The memory of Fatima grew with the love and wonderful faith of the men and women, who throughout the history of Islam, fought for freedom and justice. Throughout the centuries they were punished under the merciless and bloody lash of the caliphates. Their cries and anger grew and overflowed from their

---

the list of four, he asks: why was she the last? He reasons that she was the last complete link in the chain for the all time and for all of the cycles of history, last among the saints and an ideal image of the Day of Judgment. Maryam's great value lies with ʿÎsâ, whom she bore and nurtured, Âsiya's with Mûsâ, whom she cared for, Ḫadîǧa's with Muḥammad whom she married and supported, and with Fâṭima whom she bore and cared for. Fâṭima's value is different from these three, for she manifested the essential aspects of Islam.

> wounded hearts. This is why in the history of all Muslim nations and among the deprived masses of the Islamic community, Fatima has been the source of inspiration for those who desire their rights, for those who seek justice, for those who resist oppression, cruelty, crime and discrimination.[36]

This is, in essence, Shariati's Fâṭima; the ideal Islamic woman, and a model for every dimension of womanhood, the perfect paradigm of daughter, wife and mother. Shariati presents her as one whose life is an exemplar for any woman who wishes to 'become' herself, through her own choice, and without falling into the trap of an archaic, traditional model or the model of the facile 'new woman'. Fâṭima, by her life, answers every question pertaining to what a woman should be; nor is hers a passive life, but one of constant struggle, both in the home and, in a revolutionary way, in society, in her thoughts and her behaviour. Her sadness, anger and difficulties, the poverty of her home and the pain she felt in seeing her father rejected, make her the model in the fight for justice and the battle against any form of oppression. Shariati was convinced that Fâṭima ought to be a role model, but could not serve in such a role unless liberated from the trappings of popular piety. As noted previously his view is shared by contemporary Lebanese theologian and modern reformist, Muḥammad Ḥusayn Faḍlallâh.

> Fatima acts as a halo for the visages of all the oppressed who later became the multitudes of Islam. All of the usurped, extorted, oppressed sufferers, all of those whose rights have been destroyed and sacrificed by pressure and force, and have been deceived had the name Fatima for a slogan. The memory of Fatima grew with the love, emotions and wonderful faith of men and women who throughout the history of Islam fought for freedom and justice…she inspires the seekers of justice,

---

[36] SHARIATI A., *Fatima is Fatima*, The Shariati Foundation, Tehran (n.d.).

> the resisters of oppression, cruelty, crime and discrimination. Fatima is the woman that Islam wants a woman to be.[37]

A similar debate in Catholic Mariology is seen in the parallel works of two contemporary writers. Elizabeth Johnson[38] insists upon the historical Mary; impoverished, sidelined and defenseless, a plausible and tangible woman, friend of God, prophet, and sister to all humanity. Johnson does not want Mary to be held up as the ideal woman, since few find it possible to emulate her, and because such a view is, to her mind, promulgated by a masculine worldview, depicting Mary as mute and submissive, stripped of sexuality and wholly absorbed with motherhood, rather than a complete, totally fulfilled woman of faith. Mary is not, says Johnson, a religious icon, nor yet the eternal feminine, nor yet an ideal woman. She is primarily just herself. The authoress offers a critical analysis of the apparent veneration of Mary as something more than human, under such symbolic titles as 'Mediatrix' and 'Redemptrix'.

However, the argument of a second authoress, Charlene Spretnak,[39] is almost diametrically opposed to Johnson's theology. She laments the reduction of Mary's position in the contemporary Church, positing that she be reinstated as a symbol of the 'maternal matrix', a feminine spiritual figure who links human beings with the divine. The authoress understands Mary as a quasi-divine personality, ontologically changed by her motherhood of God's Son, so that in addition to being an historical figure, Mary is a 'cosmic-transcendent' presence, proving spiritual strength to all who honour her.

This Marian debate is already seen in the deliberations of the Second Vatican Council; some bishops were strongly attached to traditional Marian piety and wanted it maintained. Others, favouring ecumenism and seeing Mariology as something of a stumbling

---

[37] SHARIATI A., *Red Shi'ism*, The Shariati Foundation, Tehran 1979: 4.

[38] JOHNSON E., *Truly Our Sister. A Theology of Mary in the Communion of Saints*, Continuum, New York 2003.

[39] SPRETNAK C., *Missing Mary. The Queen of Heaven and her Re-emergence in the Modern Church*, Palgrave Macmillan, New York 2004.

block, urged that the role of Mary be brought more clearly into line with the Scriptural texts and integrated into the total vision of the Church *vis-à-vis* salvation history.

Some contemporary authors have attempted to redefine Mary for a contemporary world:

> Mary is the woman butchered in Rwanda, the Muslim woman raped and brutalized and left pregnant by soldiers, the single mother on welfare, working at subsistence wages, raising her children without help from the church or community or her ex-husband. She is all the women, one third of the world's population always on the move, fleeing from starvation, war, and disasters of flood, earthquake, and draught. She is the woman who mourns the slaughter of the children, the executions of the state, the torture and disappearances of men and women. She is the shadow of the old ones battered or shunted aside, institutionalized or left on the streets to wander and scavenge for a living...She is the one who belongs to those who have no one else. She is the one who mourns injustice, violence, insensitivity, and selfishness. She is both victim and advocate. She is singer and crier for an end to evils and unnecessary hurt.[40]

The following text represents an example of the prayer, in litany-like form, commonly associated with a pilgrimage to a place associated with Fâṭima. As a prayer, it serves to highlight some of her titles (and some of those of her father), as well as to underscore some of the theology constructed around her:

> Peace be upon you, daughter of the Messenger of God!
>
> Peace be upon you, daughter of the Prophet of God!
>
> Peace be upon you, daughter of the beloved of God!
>
> Peace be upon you, daughter of the friend of God!
>
> Peace be upon you, daughter of the sincere friend of God!
>
> Peace be upon you, daughter of the trusted one of God!

---

[40] McKENNA M., *Mary, Shadow of Grace*, Maryknoll, 1995: 4.

Peace be upon you, daughter of the best of God's creatures!

Peace be upon you, daughter of the most excellent of God's prophets, messengers and angels!

Peace be upon you, daughter of the best of all created ones!

Peace be upon you, mistress of the women of the worlds from first to last!

Peace be upon you, wife of the holy one of God and the best of creatures after the Messenger of God!

Peace be upon you, Mother of al-Ḥasan and al-Ḥusayn, the masters of the youths of the people of Paradise!

Peace be upon you, righteous one and martyr!

Peace be upon you, satisfied one, and she who satisfies God!

Peace be upon you, outstanding and pure one!

Peace be upon you, maiden of Paradise in human form!

Peace be upon you, pious and pure one!

Peace be upon you, converser with angels, and knowledgeable one!

Peace be upon you, tyrannized and usurped one!

Peace be upon you, oppressed and subjugated one!

Peace be upon you, Fâṭima, daughter of the Messenger of God, and the mercy of God and His blessings. May God bless you, your spirit and your body.

I bear witness that you died fully aware of your Lord; and that the one who gladdens you, has gladdened the Messenger of God, and the one who turns from you has turned from the Messenger of God, and the one who harms you, has harmed the messenger of God, the one who unites himself to you has united himself to the Messenger of God, the one who snubs

> you has snubbed the Messenger of God. Because you are a part of him, and his spirit which is between his two loins.[41]

Prayers to Mary, in similar litanies, are found scattered throughout the writings of the Fathers of the Church and the saints of various ages. Possibly the most famous and profound of these Marian prayers is the Greek liturgical hymn, of unknown authorship but dating to the late 5TH or early 6TH century, and known as the *Akáthistos*.[42] The hymn is too long to reproduce in full; every strophe provides a name applied to Mary, each suggestive of a particular theology. A later, and much simpler example of such a prayer, is the Celtic litany attributed to St. Brogan. This litany too, attributes theologically rich titles to Mary:

> O great Mary, O Mary, greatest of Marys, O greatest of women, Holy Mother of God, Mother of Christ, Mother of divine grace, Mother most pure, Mother most chaste, Mother undefiled, Mother most amiable, Mother most admirable, Mother of good counsel, Mother of Christ our Creator, Mother of our Saviour, Mother most worthy, Mother more spacious than the heavens, Mother of consolation, Mother of eternal glory, Mother of the heavenly and earthly Church, Mother of fondness and forgiveness, Mother of the golden Light, Lady of the heavens, Lady of the families of the earth, O Woman full and replete with the grace of the Holy Spirit, True beauty of women, Virgin most prudent, most venerable and faithful, Virgin most powerful, most merciful and renowned, Beauty of virgins, Chief of the maidens, Mirror of justice, Seat of wisdom, Cause of our joy, Joy of all who sorrow, O cleansing of sins, O renewal of life, Spiritual vessel, Vessel of honour, Singular vessel of devotion, Holy grail, Mystical rose, Enclosed garden, Burning bush, Fountain of the gardens, Tower of David, Palace of ivory, House of gold, Ark of the Covenant, Gate of

---

[41] **ṢDQ³**., vol. II, bb. *ziyârat Fâṭima bt. Muḥammad*: 572, **ṬFA¹**., vol. VI, bb. 3: 10, **KFM¹**., 475, **KFM²**.: 278, **MĞL**., vol. XCVII, bb. 5, n. 12: 195, 199.

[42] The word means 'not seated', meaning that the hymn, an alphabetical acrostic, ought to be sung standing in honour of Mary.

heaven, Temple of the Divinity, Throne of the Eternal King, Sanctuary of the Holy Spirit, Keeper of the portal, Ladder of heaven, Virgin of the root of Jesse, Cedar of Mount Lebanon, Cyprus of Mount Sion, Purple rose of the land of Israel, O flowering like a palm, O fruitful like the olive tree, Light of Nazareth, Glory of Jerusalem, Glory of the world, Noblest born of the Christian flock, Morning star, Star of the sea, Health of the sick, Refuge of sinners, Model of saints, Searcher of the lost, Comforter of the afflicted, Breast of the infants, Solace of the wretched, Mother of the motherless, Mother of the unloved, Help of Christians, Terror of demons, Unexpected joy, Sign of tranquility, O shapely like a dove, O serene like the moon, O resplendent like the sun, O quick to hear, Queen of angels, Queen of all saints, Queen of peace, Handmaiden of God, Daughter of God the Father, Mother of God the Son, Spouse of God the Holy Spirit, O blessed and most blessed.

CONCLUSION

There is an intriguing question posed by Lammens, the question with which this work began; his dilemma is rooted in the apparent scarcity of references to Fâṭima in the earliest texts, weighed against prolific references to her in later sources, and the apparent incongruity between Fâṭima as an ordinary woman and the Fâṭima we discover in the later texts. Lammens rather contradicts himself by writing of Fâṭima in terms of "the indistinct outlines of this vague figure" who remains in a "mysterious twilight", and then goes on to state definitively:

> During her lifetime she was treated as an ordinary woman by her contemporaries, including her father, her husband and the most eminent Sahibis [Companions of the Prophet] such as Abu Bakr and 'Umar. Nowhere do we see her enjoying special privileges or greater consideration than that paid to the ordinary Bedouin women of that time...To be convinced of this, it is only necessary to measure the space allotted to her by the oldest chroniclers, such as Ibn Hisham's *Sîra*. She is only mentioned twice..."[1]

Lammens notes the small amount of space allotted to Fâṭima in the 'oldest chroniclers', and names Ibn Hishâm's *Sîrat Muḥammad Rasûl Allâh* as an example. This is an inexplicable citation; Ibn Hishâm was writing in the 3RD/9TH century, and he was by no means the only one. This was the same century in which Ibn Saʿd, Ibn Ḥanbal, al-Dârimî, al-Buḫârî, Muslim, Ibn Mâǧa, Abû Dâwûd, al-

---

[1] LAMMENS H., "Fatima and the Daughters of Muhammad" in Ibn Warraq (ed. and trans.), *The Quest for the Historical Muhammad*, 2000: 222, 226–227.

Tirmiḏî and al-Balâḏurî were all at work, producing between them the first major and substantial works of the corpus of Sunnî *aḥâdîṯ* and history. In most of these works, we find significant references to Fâṭima, even if Ibn Hishâm says little about her. The Shîʿa too were already writing in this century, in the figures of Rustam al-Ṭabarî and the historian al-Yaʿqûbî.

By the following century, the writings of al-Nasâʾî would complete the major Sunnî collections, while al-Ṭabarî would chronicle their history. It was in this 4TH/10TH century that many of the major Shîʿî works would arise, with al-Kulaynî, al-Nuʿmânî, al-Masʿûdî, al-Qummî and *Shayḫ* al-Ṣadûq. Even if Lammens had deemed the 4TH/10TH century Shîʿî works as late, it is unimaginable that he would cite Ibn Hishâm's *Sîrat* as the primary work of the preceding century, and ignore the numerous references to Fâṭima in Ibn Hishâm's many and important contemporaries.

Considering, then, that the major collectors and transmitters of the Sunnî corpus of *aḥâdîṯ* themselves lived and worked in the 3RD/9TH century, and that their very *raison d'etre* was to put a substantial earlier bulk of oral tradition into an ordered and written form, Lammens' contention holds little sway. The Shîʿî transmitters were doing the same as their Sunnî counterparts; it is impossible to judge just how early a tradition came to be, since it was only as late as the 3RD/9TH century that the collections begin to appear in written form. To examine a tradition about Fâṭima in the 4TH/10TH century works of *Shayḫ* al-Ṣadûq and declare it to be a 'late' development is to misconstrue the process of the transmission of *aḥâdîṯ* in Islam.

It seems to me that not only is Lammens decidedly mistaken in his assessment, but he also appears to have missed the point. Even a cursory examination of the Sunnî texts suggests a status for Fâṭima that is quite unlike that afforded her contemporaries. Notably:

1. Muḥammad's insistence that she was the most loved by him of his family. This is clearly articulated most particularly in the transmissions by the normally hostile ʿÂʾisha, which describe Muḥammad's kissing his daughter and the very distinctive treatment he affords her, seen for example in his visiting her before and after his travels. The strands of these reports are already found in

the 3RD/9TH century Sunnî writings of Ibn Saʿd, al-Buḫârî Abû Dâwûd and al-Tirmiḏî.

2. The arrant declaration of her precise status in Muḥammad's family, to the exclusion of others, in the 'verse of purification' and the *mubâhala* incident; this *ḥadîṯ* too is found among the earliest Sunnî authors – Ibn Ḥanbal, Muslim, al-Tirmiḏî and al-Balâḏurî.

3. The very clear promotion of Fâṭima by her father to the status of mistress of the community, of the women believers, of the worlds and of Paradise. This is one of the most widely transmitted of the *aḥâdîṯ* and arises already in the 3RD/9TH century Sunnî compilations of Ibn Saʿd, Ibn Ḥanbal, al-Buḫârî, Muslim, al-Tirmiḏî and the historian al-Balâḏurî.

4. The declaration by Muḥammad that his daughter is so much a part of him that whatever injures her must be regarded as an injury to him is found in almost all the major 3RD/9TH century Sunnî works: Ibn Ḥanbal, al-Buḫârî, Muslim, Abû Dâwûd, al-Tirmiḏî and al-Balâḏurî.

Aside from the work of the Sunnî complier al-Nasâʾî and the historian al-Ṭabarî, the 4TH/10TH century was something of a 'Shîʿî century' in terms of the compilation of *aḥâdîṯ*, and many of the ostensibly Shîʿî traditions concerning Fâṭima arise in this timeframe. These Shîʿî compilations can in no sense be deemed 'fringe' writings, for in the very next century, many of their important Fâṭima-centered themes are found in the works of their Sunnî counterparts. Notably:

1. The gentle and specific treatment she receives at the hands of her father, transmitted by ʿÂʾisha and already found in the 3RD/9TH century books, is perpetuated by the 5TH/11TH century Sunnî compilers like al-Nîsâbûrî, al-Iṣbahânî and Ibn ʿAbd al-Barr.

2. The status of Fâṭima as mistress of the community, and/or the women believers, and/or the worlds and and/or Paradise is carried by almost all the major Sunnî transmitters of the 5TH/11TH century (al-Nîsâbûrî, al-Ṯaʿlabî, al-Iṣbahânî and Ibn ʿAbd al-Barr).

3. Muḥammad's declaration that 'Fâṭima is part of me' continues in almost all the major transmitters of this period.

What is patently clear is that long before the 4TH/10TH century Shîʿî compilations, we already have a good number of fairly precise declarations about Fâṭima, declarations that give her a precise status, in the earliest compilations of Sunnî *aḥâdîṯ*. Lammens is not incorrect in insinuating that many of the reports about her arose later; his error lies in his bypassing the earlier works and their precise contents.

The 5TH/11TH century Sunnî al-Nîsâbûrî introduces new strands, not articulated by his Sunnî predecessors; one of these is that God is angry for the anger of Fâṭima, a *ḥadîṯ* transmitted copiously by the Shîʿa of the century preceding al-Nîsâbûrî, and which would be taken up again by Sunnî transmitters over the next four centuries (for example, al-Ḫawârizmî, 6TH/12TH century, Ibn al-Aṯîr, 7TH/13TH century, al-Ḏahabî, 8TH/14TH century and al-ʿAsqalânî, 9TH/15TH century).

Another of al-Nîsâbûrî's interpolations is the theme of Fâṭima being conceived as a result of her father eating mystical fruit in heaven. What is immediately striking about this *ḥadîṯ* is that those Sunnî transmitters who condemn it do so not because they think the mystical fruit a palpable fable, but but rather because they perceive the report as misdating the 'night-journey'. Al-Nîsâbûrî transmits it, but with an annotation of rejection by the 7TH/13TH century al-Ḏahabî inserted into the notes by the editor of this edition of al-Nîsâbûrî's work. The 7TH/13TH century al-Ǧawzî condemns it, as does the 9TH/15TH century al-ʿAsqalânî, but on the basis of a misdating of the 'night journey'. As noted earlier in this work, this *ḥadîṯ* is nonetheless found in a number of later Sunnî authors (for example, al-Baġdâdî, contemporary with al-Nîsâbûrî, al-Ḫawârizmî, 6TH/12TH century, al-Ṭabarî, 7TH/13TH century, al-Ṣaffûrî, 9TH/15TH century and al-Suyûṭî, 10TH/16TH century).

The declarations surrounding her marriage – that it is ordered by God and that Fâṭima is especially created by God for ʿAlî – are certainly later traditions, not found among the Sunnî much before al-Ḫawârizmî (6TH/12TH century). There are other strands of biography too, which highlight something specific about her position, and arc found in later works:

1. The patent deference that ʿAlî pays her, in his monogamy and in certain domestic matters, in spite of what some interpret as his generally harsh view of women.

2. The fact that Muḥammad's wives, conscious of her influence with her father, use her as a spokesperson and, in the same vein, that the politically astute Abû Sufyân pleads her assistance in a moment of crisis.

3. That Muḥammad makes explicit and subtle declarations about her, as, for example, in his declaration, based on a grammatical analysis, that she could never possibly steal.

We would be hard-pressed, having gleaned all these examples from the Sunnî texts alone, to go along with Lammens' assessment. The truth is that, in spite of a not uncommon presumption, Fâṭima is not simply a Shîʿî fabrication, but maintains a high standing among the Sunnî.

The theology of Fâṭima is undoubtedly associated with the Qurʾânic and Islamic view of Maryam, mother of ʿÎsâ. Nothing is said of Maryam that is not also posited of Fâṭima; this is necessarily so, since in the Shîʿî view Fâṭima, as daughter and thus 'part' of the Prophet and mother of Islam's saviour, al-Ḥusayn, is greater than Maryam and cannot therefore lack some virtue or heavenly gift bestowed upon the latter. Notably:

1. Maryam is a virgin, and consequently, so is Fâṭima; although the Qurʾân says nothing about Maryam's status after the birth of ʿÎsâ, and whether she remained a perpetual virgin, her virginity and simultaneous motherhood are perceived as a gift of God. Fâṭima, on the other hand, is a perpetual virgin, although virginity in her case is somewhat reinterpreted. God steps into her life and removes menstruation (as He may have done for Maryam, according to some scholars like al-Râzî), and this 'virginal' state is enduring.

2. Maryam heard her son speaking as an infant (Q. 19: 30 and, according to some interpretations of Q. 19: 24–26, perhaps from the womb), and Fâṭima spoke from the womb to her mother, as did her son al-Ḥusayn.

3. Maryam was fed with miraculous food from heaven, and consequently, so was Fâṭima.

4. Maryam was chosen and purified by God, and so was Fâṭima.

5. Maryam conversed with angels, and so did Fâṭima.

6. The dead body of Maryam was washed only by one worthy (ʿÎsâ) and so was Fâṭima's (ʿAlî).

7. Maryam is declared the mistress of the women, and many Shîʿî interpreters, as we have seen, regard this as a chronological designation; but Fâṭima is designated the mistress of all women, from first to last.

It is hardly surprising, therefore, that Fâṭima is given the title 'the greater Maryam' (*Maryam al-kubrâ*).

But Fâṭima's virginity is an enigma and remains nothing more than a matter of religious semantics. She must be a virgin, in the Shîʿî view, so as not to be less than Maryam; in order to achieve this, the concept of virginity is redefined, but, it has to be said, somewhat misconstrued and forced into a category in which it does not rightfully belong. The Qurʾânic Maryam was a virgin because she conceived a child without male intervention. The same applies to Mary in Catholic dogma. Fâṭima is not a virgin in the primary and physiological meaning of the word; neither physically, because she was married with children who were the result of normative sexual intercourse, and because the failure to menstruate[2] could

[2] The medical terminology for this condition is 'amenorrhea'; it is called 'secondary amenorrhea' to denote the absence of menstrual periods for six months in a woman who had previously been regular, or twelve months in a woman who had had irregular periods (normal menstruation occurs every twenty-three to thirty-five days). 'Primary amenorrhea' denotes a woman who has never had a period in her life, or who has not started to menstruate by the age of sixteen. This is a rare condition, found in about 1% of women. It is most often the result of a late puberty, a fairly common phenomenon among girls who are undernourished or very athletic. It may also be due to a genetic disorder, a birth defect, genital abnormalities, or to a number of medical conditions such as drastic weight reduction through anorexia nervosa, poverty, malnutrition or long-term illness. Two things are noteworthy in the case of Fâṭima: the first is the great stress placed on her extreme weakness, thinness and poverty. The second is that her failure to menstruate (or even shed blood in childbirth) is witnessed by others. This could well lead us to imagine that Fâṭima's lack of bleeding was a medical condition brought about by the prevalence

never technically be considered virginity, nor even because she may have been 'pure' of heart and life, for purity in this sense, while a noble value, is not the same as virginity. Non-virgins are not by nature incapable of living pure lives.

The question arises once more; what is it about virginity that is deemed so necessary? So necessary, that classical mythology insists upon labeling as 'virgins' some of its goddesses who were quite patently not, at least in the primary and technical meaning of the word? So necessary, that Islam, a religious system which, while valuing virginity before marriage, puts a great stress on conjugal relations and has little time for celibacy, follows the same path as classical mythology, reinterpreting a technical term in order to apply it? It is absolutely certain that virginity gives to a woman a particular status and, in some sense, raises her above the ordinary; but this of itself suggests an unhealthy and wrongly formed view of sexuality. In the world of classical mythology, virginity, however it may have been interpreted, was understood almost in magical terms, as bestowing power and ritual purity.[3]

---

of poverty, malnutrition and illness in her life, and that a witnessed medical phenomenon has been reinterpreted as an act of Divine intervention by Shîʿî piety. Furthermore, if we follow the Shîʿî dating of her life and marriage, she would have been pregnant and given birth almost every year of her married life: this would hardly have allowed her to return at any time to the normal cycle of menstruation after childbirth, even if such had existed.

[3] Hence the numerous stories of those, like Athena, Artemis, Juno and Hera, the wife of Zeus, who renewed their virginity by bathing in rivers. The phenomenon of virginity (and, by extension, a period devoid of sexual activity) conferring strength and power is quite patently seen, in many cultures and religious systems, in the abstinence from food, drink and sexual activity before sacred liturgies or ceremonies. Nevertheless, such an abstinence does not have moral or ethical connotations in terms of the sexual acts, but springs rather from the concept of continence or abstinence as a source of power.

The prevalence of and stress upon virginity in Catholicism is well documented and is not our concern here.[4] For Islam, however, it is difficult not to conclude that, in spite of the enormous value placed upon marriage and childbirth, something of the outlook of classical mythology has filtered down. The difference is that the great abhorrence in Islam is not for sexuality but for menstruation, so that the careful redefinition of virginity in the case of Fâṭima removes from her life something normative but deemed reprehensible. However, the attendant problem is that the innate human yearning for an 'ideal', for something 'higher' and more noble, so stressed by Plato, is here entirely frustrated, since Fâṭima the model, as she stands in traditional Shîʿî Islam, remains wholly unique and consequently unattainable. Shariati's attempt at a contemporary reinterpretation is badly restricted and limited by the context of pre-revolutionary Iran in which he is writing; he does not offer Fâṭima as a timeless and universal model, but as a model for a particular group of women in a very specific situation and timeframe.

Furthermore, the complex theology constructed around the life of Fâṭima is not of necessity nothing more than a series of 'borrowings' from an earlier Christian tradition. To maintain this would be to disallow Islam an autonomous religious understanding. There is no doubt that religions and cultures borrow from each other to some extent; but there is even less doubt that influences trickle down through the ages, filtering from one tradition into another, albeit in varied forms. Jung's archetypes, examined briefly in this work, are not without validity here. The history of pagan cultures, as well as of various religions, exhibits a plethora of virgins with children, and no shortage of heroic sons with special mothers. It would be both facile and misleading to maintain that these cultures simply stole each other's religious concepts; this would be to follow the 'Ritualistic' or 'Diffusionist' School of Sir James Frazier and others, which posits that all humans had their origin in one place and spread worldwide, carrying their cultures and myths with them, so that if distinct peoples have the same stories or gods, there must

---

[4] For a brutally honest, but at times one-sided synthesis, cf. WARNER M., *Alone Of All Her Sex. The Myth and Cult of the Virgin Mary*, 1985: 68–78.

have been contact in which the more sophisticated group passed on its ideas to the more primitive. In terms of what has been said of virginity in classical mythology, there is as much chance that Shîʿî Islam took its concepts of Fâṭima from these concepts, as it did from Christianity.

In this, Fâṭima is in fact closer to some of the pagan goddesses than she is to Mary in Catholic dogma. As numerous authors point out, in the case of such goddesses, 'virgin' and 'chastity' (not in the sense of the virtue, but in the sense of not indulging in any sexual activity) were not necessarily synonymous. Venus, Ishtar, Astarte and Anat, all love-goddesses of the Near East and of classical mythology, were all called 'virgin', and yet none of them practiced sexual chastity, but took many lovers. In the case of Artemis, Hippolyte and Athene Parthenos, their virginity was not for any reason of morality or in favour of the virtue of purity: they remained virgins, rejecting male advances because they were paramount, autonomous and alone. This, as Warner writes, "is why the title virgin could be used of a goddess who entertained lovers. Her virginity signified she had retained freedom of choice: to take lovers or to reject them."[5]

Warner goes on to cite the Vestal Virgins, whose virginity during their period of office was a matter of political expediency (so that their political status and power might in no way abused) as well as the bizarre case of Queen Elizabeth I of England, ever called the 'Virgin Queen' although she was known for her sexual prowess. But Fâṭima is different, even from these pagan goddesses, for she was married to one husband, and in that sense had no freedom of choice.

The key to understanding Fâṭima is undoubtedly Karbalâʾ and her son's death there. Certainly, she is intimately connected with her husband ʿAlî; the theological reflection upon and development of the person of ʿAlî could hardly fail to affect the standing of his wife. But to an even greater extent, Fâṭima is wholly inseparable from her son al-Ḥusayn. With the evolution of a 'Karbalâʾ consciousness' as a central tenet of Shîʿî theology and piety – the insti-

---

[5] WARNER M., *Alone Of All Her Sex. The Myth and Cult of the Virgin Mary* 1985: 47–48.

tution of public ceremonies of mourning, the pilgrimages to his tomb, the almost mythical aspect given to the soil of Karbalâʾ, and the augmentation of the theology constructed around al-Ḥusayn – one must anticipate an attendant development in the theology surrounding the person of his mother. As the figure of al-Ḥusayn grows in magnitude, so does his mother. If he is greater even than ʿÎsâ, for he is perceived as the 'saviour' and 'redeemer' of authentic Islam from the corruption of Muʿâwiya and Yazîd, then his mother must be greater than Maryam herself.

In all four major aspects of Fâṭima's life examined in this work – the miraculous nature of her own conception and birth, the conception and birth of al-Ḥusayn, the immense sorrow of Fâṭima and her powerful intercessory prerogatives – the Karbalâʾ event is all-pervading, the golden thread running through every occurrence:

1. Already in the predictions Muḥammad makes about her while she is still in the womb, based on information he receives from Ǧibrîl, her status as mother of the future Imâms is highlighted, as integral to her very identity. In the moment of her birth, she utters the traditional profession of faith, adding that her son (expressed in the singular, although in some texts it is in the plural, but oddly, not in the dual form) is 'master' of the grandsons (of Muḥammad). All of Paradise rejoices at her birth; this cannot be interpreted merely because she is the daughter of Muḥammad, for he had other daughters, but must be understood that Paradise rejoices at the birth of the mother of Islam's prospective saviour. The four heavenly visitors who attend her birth are not without a strong symbolism of the future; while people on earth may turn their backs (in this case, on Ḫadîǧa, but symbolically on the progeny of Fâṭima), heaven approves of them and supports them.

2. The zenith of angelic activity is to be found in the circumstances surrounding the conception and parturition of her second son, al-Ḥusayn, thoroughly encased in accounts of heavenly intervention. The forewarnings before his birth concentrate on the Karbalâʾ event, so that Fâṭima's pregnancy is filled with bitter sorrow. "I have no need of a child whom your community after you will kill," is her primary response to her father's ominous announcement. Karbalâʾ suffuses and colours her pregnancy and, consequently, the manner in which she looks upon this second son of hers.

3. While Fâṭima grieves over numerous issues – the death of her father, the rejection of her husband and usurping of his power, her loss of Fadak, the ill-treatment she and her family receive, the dark future of her son al-Ḥusayn – it is once again the ever-present Karbalâʾ event that dominates her mourning and sorrow, even from beyond the grave. It is over Karbalâʾ more than anything else that Fâṭima weeps incessantly until the Day of Judgment.

4. On the Day of Judgment, her intercessory prerogatives are clearly articulated in her plea before God's throne that the murderers of her son be punished and justice be done. Her grief and righteous anger fills heaven, affecting the angels and even God Himself, who responds favourably to her plea. It is only after she has dealt with the perpetrators of al-Ḥusayn's murder that she turns her attention to her progeny, adherents and those who love her.

In all this she is primarily the mother of the martyred hero and saviour of Islam. It is in theological reflection upon the tragic and lonely figure of al-Ḥusayn that a theology begins to be constructed around his mother. In this light, Lammens' critique is no less incomprehensible by reason of his having been a Catholic priest; as such, he would have had no difficulty in believing or accepting that although Mary is rarely mentioned in the Gospels, or in the earliest non-Scriptural apostolic and post-apostolic texts, a valid theology and spirituality surrounding her arose nonetheless and developed in subsequent centuries. As one author notes, in terms of the exceedingly late development and definition of Mary's Immaculate Conception:

> Such affirmations arose, not from a clear concept or definite thesis about the degree of her grace, but from an obscure yet powerful impulse of Christian hearts to attribute to her the greatest holiness and glory compatible with her status of a creature. This was not mere pious wishfulness, but the germination of the Gospel teaching…[6]

[6] O'CONNOR E D., "Immaculate Conception" in *NCE*[2], B L Marthater et al. (eds.), Thomason-Gale, Missouri 2003, vol. VII: 331–335.

In terms of the Shîʿa, the development of an elaborate theology and piety around the person of Fâṭima could hardly be deemed late. Even were we to follow the opinion of Goldziher (and some Shîʿî scholars) and reject the authenticity of al-Hilâlî's *Kitâb Sulaym b. Qays* (supposedly a work on the cusp of the 1ST/6TH and 2ND/7TH centuries),[7] many of the definitive Shîʿî statements about her are found in the writings of Rustam al-Ṭabarî, who died around 224/839, and even more so in the various works of *Shayḫ* al-Ṣadûq, who died in 381/991. Of its very nature and quite inevitably, theology, spirituality and piety develop as understanding grows, and because they are not immediately extant or apparent in no way negates their validity. Nor does such a development of necessity signify innovation, but means rather, innovative ways of articulation, an intensification in insight and an advance in the comprehension of a particular issue. By the time the twelfth Imâm went into occultation around 327/940 and the great Shîʿî dynasties began to rise, the theology of the Shîʿa had reached far beyond its initial objectives and its early radicalism. The change in the political situation and standing, especially with the rise of the Bûyid dynasty, accelerated the development of Shîʿî doctrine. These developments were, concomitantly, mirrored in popular religion, with the decisive institution of the commemoration of al-Ḥusayn's martyrdom and the increase in public mourning services for him, the construction of shrine-tombs for the Imâms, all of them understood as being the direct descendants of Fâṭima, and the upsurge in pilgrimages there.

Fâṭima is consequently not as much the 'shadowy' creature of Lammens' critique as she is a synthesis of various factors:

---

[7] While Ahmad posits that only sixteen or seventeen distinct and very early Shîʿî 'notebooks' or 'sources' (*uṣûl*) are known to be extant in manuscript form, Awliyâʾî holds that most of them are extant in the major Shîʿî collections, and that more than two-hundred have survived to the present day, often prefixed with the title *kitâb* or *nawâdir*. He names thirteen of these extant in the Tehran University library: *Kitâb Sulaym b. Qays* is not among them. Cf. AHMAD N., "Twelver Shīʿī Ḥadīṯ: From Tradition to Contemporary Evaluations" in *Oriente Moderno* XXI (LXXXII), 1 – 2002: 133; AWLIYÂʾÎ M., "Outlines of the Development of the Science of Ḥadīth" in *al-Tawḥīd*, Volume I, Number 1, Muḥarram 1404: 29.

1. The steady realization by the Shîʿa that they would never attain to the power they thought was their due, and the concomitant turning increasingly to a supernatural, other-worldly power; this would profoundly colour their conception of Fâṭima. The mystical tendency arose very soon among the early Shîʿa; it is notably, for example, that after Karbalâʾ, the Imâms moved away from political aspirations, terming themselves not 'partisans of ʿAlî' but 'friends of God' (*awliyâʾ*), with the increasingly more important theme of *wilâya* predominating.

2. The factor that Fâṭima is the only-surviving child of the Prophet of Islam. Shariati takes careful note of this; she replaces a son as the bearer of the family name and history, the one who would uphold the ancestral values, and who would provide the ultimate link between the prophecy and *al-Mahdî*. While Muḥammad would make known the revelation of God, his daughter would bear the responsibility of mirroring within herself the newly created revolutionary values of Islam.

3. The development of thought around ʿAlî; as he assumes a central role, his wife is automatically elevated to a special status.

4. The rise of the 'Karbalâʾ consciousness' as a central tenet of Shîʿî theology and piety.

5. An examination of Maryam in the Qurʾânic texts; what is posited of her must also be posited of the greater Fâṭima, in terms of God's particular blessings and gifts.

6. The development of Shîʿî theology, in three particular categories: the first is the suffering of the weak. The 'weak' are the 'people of the house', who were usurped of their rightful position. In this, Fâṭima supplies a powerful example of suffering; its inevitability and its redemptive quality. The Imâms, descendants of Fâṭima and appointed by God, are not those who have prestige, but those whom the world considers ineffectual, those rejected, scorned and maltreated, those whose very weakness is an integral part of their status. The second theological category is the sinlessness of the *maʿṣûmûn*, the pure ones, the majority of whom are sprung from the loins of Fâṭima. The third category is the powerful intercessory prerogatives given by God to these pure ones, prerogatives which

are the reward for all their suffering and weakness, and which therefore pertain to their status with God.

Ultimately, all of these factors colour and influence the person and standing of Fâṭima, and it is within these factors and theological categories that her life must be read and comprehended. Rather than being colourless or shadowy, her life becomes, for the believer, multihued. Following the caution issued by Ayoub and quoted at the very start of this work, in any reading of her life,

> It will not do…to limit ourselves to the bare facts as we see them…nor can we…take all traditions to be factual data. We must, however, choose our facts, often including those facts which, while to us they do not seem historically valid, were nonetheless considered as such by the community.[8]

[8] AYOUB M., *Redemptive Suffering in Islam. A Study of the Devotional Aspects of ʿAshura in Twelver Shiʿism*, 1978: 137.

APPENDIX A: THE NAMES OF FÂṬIMA[1]

1. AL-ḪAṢÎBÎ IN HIS *AL-HIDÂYA AL-KUBRÂ*[2]

Her names (*asmâʾ*) are: Fâṭima, and Fâṭim in an apocopate (*tarḫîm*) form.

Her *kunâ* are: mother of al-Ḥasan and al-Ḥusayn (*umm al-Ḥasan wa-l-Ḥusayn*), mother of the Imâms (*umm al-aʾimma*) and mother of her father (*umm abî-hâ*).[3]

Her *alqâb*: the radiant (*al-zahrâʾ*), the virgin (*al-batûl*), the inviolable (*al-ḥaṣân*), the maiden of paradise (*al-ḥawrâʾ*), the mistress (*al-sayyida*), the righteous (*al-ṣiddîqa*), the greater Maryam (*Maryam al-kubrâ*), mother of al-Ḥasan and al-Ḥusayn (*wâlidat al-Ḥasan wa-l-Ḥusayn*), mother of the pure (*umm al-naqî*), mother of the pious (*umm al-taqî*), mother of the daybreak (*umm al-balǧa*), mother of pity (*umm al-raʾfa*), mother of the gift (*umm al-ʿaṭiyya*), mother of the places of mourning (*umm al-mawâniḥ*), mother of the two lights (*umm al-nûrayn*), mother of exaltedness (*umm al-ʿulâ*), mother of created things (*umm*

[1] For a contemporary list drawn from the Shîʿî sources, cf. al-MÛSAWÎ M., *al-Kawṯar fî aḥwâl Fâṭima bt. al-nabî al-aṭhar*, 2000, vol. I, bb. 9, 10: 349–355. While the *asmâʾ*, *kunâ* and *alqâb* of Fâṭima are found diffused throughout the Shîʿî corpus, longer listings can be accessed in a number of works, three of which are consulted here.

[2] **ḪAṢ.**, bb. 14: 417.

[3] Cf. for e.g. **ATH**[2]., vol. V, bb. *Ḥarf al-fâʾ*: 520, **BRR.**, vol. IV, *Kitâb al-nisâʾ*, bb. *al-Fâʾ*, n. 4057: 1899.

al-bariyya),[4] esteemed mother of the curtain (*umm al-riwâq al-ḥasîba*), mother of the martyrs of Badr (*umm al-badriyîna*)[5]

Among the names (*asmâʾ*) of the father of al-Ḥasan (ʿAlî) for her, are: mother of blessings (*umm al-barakât*), mother of the guide (*umm al-hâdy*) and mother of magnanimity (*umm al-raḥba*).

2. IBN SHAḤRÂSHÛB IN HIS *MANÂQIB ÂL ABÎ ṬÂLIB*[6]

Her *kunâ* are: mother of al-Ḥasan (*umm al-Ḥasan*), mother of al-Ḥusayn (*umm al-Ḥusayn*), mother of al-Muḥassin (*umm al-Muḥassin*), mother of the Imâms (*umm al-aʾimma*), mother of her father (*umm abî-hâ*).

Her names (*asmâʾ*), going by what was mentioned by Abû Ğaʿfar al-Qummî, are: Fâṭima, the virgin (*al-batûl*), the inviolable (*al-ḥaṣân*), the free (*al-ḥurra*), the mistress (*al-sayyida*), the virgin (*al-ʿaḏrâʾ*), the maiden of paradise (*al-ḥawrâʾ*), the blessed (*al-mubâraka*), the pure (*al-ṭâhira*), the chaste (*al-zakiyya*), the satisfied (*al-râḍiyya*), the one who satisfies God (*al-marḍiyya*), the one to whom the angels spoke (*al-muḥaddaṯa*), the greater Maryam (*Maryam al-kubrâ*), the greater righteous one (*al-ṣiddîqa al-kubrâ*).[7]

It is said that in heaven she has: the luminary (*al-nûriyya*), the heavenly (*al-samâwiyya*), the affectionate (*al-ḥâniyya*).[8]

---

[4] The text of al-Ḫaṣîbî reads *badiyya* (بدية); this may be a mistranscription of *al-bariyya* (برية), as in al-Baḥrânî's text, in which case it could be rendered as 'mother of created beings' (*umm al-bariyya*).

[5] The battle of Badr, fought in 2/624, although a decisive victory for the Muslim forces, resulted in the martyrdom of around fourteen Muslims.

[6] **SHB**., vol. III, *faṣl fî ḥilyati-hâ wa-tawârîḫi-hâ*: 357.

[7] To distinguish her from her daughter Zaynab, known as *al-ṣiddîqa al-suġrâ*.

[8] An editor's note defines this as a 'mother affectionate to her children'. Lane notes that it is applied to a woman who "undertakes the care and maintenance of her children, or acts affectionately towards them, and does not marry again after [the loss of] their father." Cf. LANE E. W., *An Arabic-English Lexicon*, 1997, vol. II: 660. The essence is of one

We say: the righteous in words (*al-ṣiddîqa bi-l-aqwâl*), the blessed in circumstances (*al-mubâraka bi-l-aḥwâl*), the pure in deeds (*al-ṭâhira bi-l-afʿâl*), the chaste in integrity (*al-zakiyya bi-l-ʿadâla*), the satisfied in speech (*al-râḍiyya bi-l-maqâla*), the one who satisfies God in leadership (*al-marḍiyya bi-l-dalâla*), the one to whom the angels spoke in solicitude (*al-muḥaddaṯa bi-l-shafaqa*), the free in charitable giving (*al-ḥurra bi-l-nafaqa*), the mistress in almsgiving (*al-sayyida bi-l-ṣadaqa*), the inviolable in dignity (*al-ḥaṣân bi-l-makân*), the virgin and time and in favour (*al-batûl bi-l-zamân wa bi-l-iḥsân*), the greater Maryam in seclusion (*Maryam al-kubrâ fi-l-sitr*), the one who weans in mystery (*fâṭim bi-l-sirr*), the one who weans in reverence (*fâṭima bi-l-birr*),[9] the luminary in the attestation of faith (*al-nûriyya bi-l-shahâda*), the heavenly on worship (*al-samâwiyya bi-l-ʿibâda*), the affectionate in moderateness (*al-ḥâniyya bi-l-zahâda*),[10] the virgin in childbirth[11] (*al-*

---

who bends or curves towards someone or something. I have chosen to render it 'affectionate', although this does not capture the depth of meaning.

[9] As noted by Lane, *fâṭim* or the name *fâṭima* refers to one who weans a child, who is *fiṭâm* or *maftûm* ('weaned'). Cf. LANE E. W., *An Arabic-English Lexicon*, 1997, vol. VI: 2473. It is of note that the weaning associated with Muḥammad's daughter has a depper theological and spiritual significance, extending beyond the physical act, to weaning people from the punishment of the Fire. Lane refers his reader to a tradition found in *Tâğ al-ʿarûs*, in which 'al-Fâṭima' is rendered as 'death': cf. LANE E. W., *An Arabic-English Lexicon*, 1997, vol. III: 1098, al-Zabîdî., *Tâğ al-ʿarûs min ğawâhir al-qâmûs*, al-Maṭbaʿat al-Ḫayriyya, Cairo 1306/1888, vol. V: 356.

[10] Lane clarifies that *zahâda* refers to abstinence specifically in worldly things; the sense of this title is that even in deprivation, Fâṭima remained caring and affectionate towards her children. Cf. LANE E. W., *An Arabic-English Lexicon*, 1997, vol. III: 1266.

[11] This appellation could be read in two ways. In the first, it is a simple afirmation that when Fâṭima gave birth, she was a virgin in the sense explained early in this work. In the second, it may echo the virginity of Mary in Catholic theology, and specifically her virginity *in partu*, that even in the actual birth of her son, her virginity was kept intact and the hymen remained unruptured (understood, physiologically incorrectly, as

ʿaḏrâʾ bi-l-wilâda), the abstemious (*al-zâhida*), the serene (*al-ṣafiyya*), the worshiper (*al-ʿâbida*), the satisfied (*al-râḍiyya*), the one who satisfies God (*al-marḍiyya*), the keeper of vigils (*al-mutahaǧǧida*), the distinguished (*al-sharîfa*), the humble (*al-qânita*), the modest (*al-ʿafîfa*), mistress of the women (*sayyidat al-niswân*), beloved of the beloved of the Most Merciful (*ḥabîbat ḥabîb al-raḥmân*), the one veiled from keepers of the Garden (*al-muḥtaǧaba ʿan ḫuzzân al-ǧinân*),[12] sincere friend of the Most Merciful (*ṣafiyyat al-raḥmân*), daughter of the best of those sent (*ibnat ḫayr al-mursalîn*), consolation of the eye of the master of all created beings (*qurrat ʿayn sayyid al-ḫalâʾiq aǧmaʿîn*), intermediary of the bond between the mistresses of the women of the worlds (*wâsiṭat al-ʿaqd bayna sayyidât nisâʾ al-ʿâlamîn*), the ill-treated one before the throne on the Day of Judgment (*mutaẓallima bayna yadayi al-ʿarsh yawm al-dîn*), fruit of the prophethood (*ṯamarat al-nubuwwa*), mother of the Imâms (*umm al-aʾimma*), brightness of the heart of the intercessor of the community (*zuhra fuʾâd shafîʿi al-umma*).

The revered (*al-muḥtarama*), the beautiful (*al-ġarrâʾ*), the modest (*al-muḥtashama*), the venerated under the dome (*al-makarrama taḥta al-qubba*), the verdant (*al-ḫaḍrâʾ*), the maiden of Paradise in human form (*al-insiyya al-ḥawrâʾ*), the virgin (*al-batûl*), the virgin (*al-ʿaḏrâʾ*), mistress of the women (*sitt al-nisaʾ*),[13] heir of the master of the prophets (*wâriṯa sayyid al-anbiyâʾ*), spouse of the master of the trustees (*qarîna sayyid al-awṣiyâʾ*), Fâṭima, the greater righteous one (*al-ṣiddîqa al-kubrâ*), comfort of the chosen one's spirit (*râḥa rûḥ al-muṣṭafâ*), bearer of affliction with neither fear nor complaint (*ḥâmilat al-balwâ min ġayri fazʿ wa lâ shakwa*), companion of the tree Ṭûbâ[14] and the one sent down concerning her, and concerning her hus-

---

the sign of virginity). Since the virginity of Mary in Catholicism and the virginity of Fâṭima in Shîʿî theology are explained differently, it seems that the first explanation is more logical. This topic is treated at length earlier in this work.

[12] Cf. Q. 39: 73, Q. 40: 49, Q. 47: 8.

[13] Cf. LANE E. W., *An Arabic-English Lexicon*, 1997, vol. IV: 1304.

[14] The mystical tree of Paradise. Cf. Q. 13: 39 for the only use of the word in the Qur'ân, where it is rendered as 'blessedness' or 'bliss'.

band and children (*ṣâḥiba shağara Ṭûbâ wa-man unzila fî sha'ni-hâ wa-sha'ni zawği-hâ wa-awlâdi-hâ*), (*sûrat hal atâ*),[15] daughter of the prophet (*ibnat al-nabî*), companion of the trustee (*ṣâḥibat al-waṣy*), mother of the generous (*umm al-sabaṭîn*), grandmother of the Imâms (*ğaddat al-a'imma*), mistress of the women of this world and the hereafter (*sayyidat nisâ' al-dunyâ wa-l-âḫira*), spouse of the approved one (*zawğat al-murtaḍâ*), mother of the chosen (*wâlidat al-muğtabâ*), daughter of the chosen (*ibnat al-muṣṭafâ*), the mistress (*al-sayyidat*), the bereft (*al-mafqûda*), the generous (*al-karîma*), the tyrannized (*al-maẓlûma*), the martyr (*al-shahîda*), the mistress (*al-sayyidat*), the rightly-guided (*al-rashîda*), sister of Maryam (*shaqîqa Maryam*), daughter of the most noble Muḥammad (*ibnat Muḥammad al-akram*), the one weaned from every evil (*al-mafṭûma min kulli sharr*), known for every good thing (*al-ma'lûma bi-kulli ḫayr*), described in the gospel (*al-man'ûta fî-l-inğîl*), attributed with reverence and veneration (*al-mawṣûfa bi-l-birr wa-l-tabğîl*), pearl of the one entrusted with revelation and the sending down (*durrat ṣâḥib al-waḥy wa-l-tanzîl*), her forefather the friend (*ğadd-hâ al-ḫalîl*),[16] her eulogist the exalted (*mâdiḥ-hâ al-ğalîl*),[17] her preacher the approved one[18] by order of the protector Ğabra'îl (*ḫâṭib-hâ al-murtaḍâ bi-amri al-mawlâ Ğabra'îl*)

3. AL-BAḤRÂNÎ IN HIS *'AWÂLIM AL-'ULÛM WA AL-MA'ÂRIF AL-AḤWÂL MIN AL-ÂYÂT WA-L-AḪBÂR WAL-AQWÂL*[19]

Mother of the immaculate Imâms (*umm al-a'imma al-ma'ṣûmîn*), mother of the righteous (*umm al-abrâr*), mother of her father (*umm abî-hâ*), mother of the excellent (*umm al-aḫyâr*), mother of the radiant (*umm al-azhâr*), mother of the pure (*umm al-aṭhâr*);

---

[15] A reference to the opening line of Q. 76: 1, «*Hath there come upon man (ever) any period of time in which he was a thing unremembered*».

[16] The epithet of Ibrâhîm is *ḫalîl Allâh* ('friend of God'); cf. Q. 4: 125.

[17] While *al-ğalîl* is one of the names of God, it means 'the exalted', the same meaning as the name 'Alî.

[18] 'Alî b. Abî Ṭâlib.

[19] **BAḤ.**, vol. XI, bb. *abwâb asmâ'i-hâ wa-alqâbi-hâ wa-kunâ-hâ*: 66–93.

Mother of lights (*umm al-anwâr*), mother of the martyrs of Badr (*umm al-badriyîna*), mother of the reverent (*umm al-barara*), mother of created beings (*umm al-bariyya*), mother of the daybreak (*umm al-balğa*), mother of the pious (*umm al-taqî*), mother of al-Ḥasan (*umm al-Ḥasan*);

Mother of al-Ḥusayn (*umm al-Ḥusayn*), mother of the good (*umm al-ḫayra*), mother of pity (*umm al-ra'fa*), esteemed mother of the curtain (*umm al-riwâq al-ḥasîba*), mother of the two 'sweet basils' (*umm al-rayḥânatayn*),[20] mother of the generous (*umm al-sabaṭîn*);

Mother of the gift (*umm al-ʿaṭiyya*), mother of exaltedness (*umm al-ʿulâ*), mother of knowledge (*umm al-ʿulûm*), mother of virtues (*umm al-faḍâ'il*), mother of the book (*umm al-kitâb*),[21] mother of al-

---

[20] Pet names given to al-Ḥasan and al-Ḥusayn.

[21] The phrase *umm al-kitâb* ('mother of the book', although *umm* can also mean 'root', 'foundation' or 'source') occurs three times in the Qur'ân: «*He it is Who hath revealed unto thee (Muhammad) the Scripture wherein are clear revelations – they are the substance of the Book – and others (which are) allegorical*» (Q. 3: 7), «*Allah effaceth what He will, and establisheth (what He will), and with Him is the source of ordinance*» (Q. 13: 39), «*And Lo! in the Source of Decrees, which We possess, it is indeed sublime, decisive*» (Q. 43: 4). At a first level, the Qur'ân itself understands *umm al-kitâb* as a reference to the clear or literal (*muḥkamât*) verses as opposed to the allegorical (*mutashâbihât*) ones in the text (cf. for e.g. **MSL**., vol. VII, bk. 47 (*Kitâb al-ʿilm*), bb. 1, n. 2665: 41). However, others regard the *umm al-kitâb* as the Qur'ân itself, or the pre-existent text present with God before creation (suggested by Q. 13: 39; cf. also **TRM**., vol. IV, bk. 30 (*Abwâb al-qadr*), bb. 17, n. 2155: 216, **BUḪ¹**., vol. IX, bk. 97 (*Kitâb al-tawḥîd*), bb. 37, n. 7517: 371, **NSA¹**., vol. IV, bk. 27 (*Kitâb al-ṭalâq*), bb. 54, n. 3529: 282) or as *sûrat al-Fâtiḥa*, which begins, prefaces and is believed to summarize the whole Qur'ân (**TRM**., vol. V, bk. 44 (*Abwâb al-tafsîr*), n. (3) 3124: 433, **BUḪ¹**., vol. VI, bk. 65 (*Kitâb al-tafsîr*), bb. 1: 21, bb. 3, n. 4704: 181, **ADD**., vol. II, bk. 8 (*Kitâb al-witr*), bb. 15, n. 1457: 186). Once again, this name is applied analogically to Fâṭima; as the first mother of the *ahl al-bayt* who stands at the very center of the house and, through ʿAlî, generates all the Imâms, but also in reference to her own pre-existence as noted in the *ashbâḥ ḥadîṯ* and to the fact that Fâṭima is, in her life, actions and sufferings, a clear sign from God

Muḥassin (*umm al-Muḥassin*), mother of the believers (*umm al-mu'minîn*);

Mother of the places of mourning (*umm al-mawâniḥ*), mother of those of noble descent (*umm al-nuǧabâ'*), mother of the pure (*umm al-naqî*), mother of the two lights (*umm al-nûrayn*), servant of God (*ammat Allâh*), sign of God (*âyat Allâh*), greatest sign of God (*âyat Allâh al-ʿaẓmâ*).

Tearful of eye (*bâkiyyat al-ʿayn*), the virgin (*al-batûl*), interval of the prophethood and the guardianship (*barzaḫ al-nubuwwa wa-l-wilâya*),[22] part of the Messenger of God (*biḍʿat rasûl Allâh*), residue of the prophethood (*baqiyyat al-nubuwwa*), splendour of the heart (*bahǧat al-fu'âd*), splendor of the white and tender-skinned (*bahǧat bayḍâ' biḍḍa*).

Apple of Paradise (*tuffâḥat al-firdaws*),[23] the pious (*al-taqiyya*);

Third of the sun and the moon (*ṯâliṯat al-shams wa-l-qamar*), fruit of the prophethood (*ṯamarat al-nubuwwa*).

Origin of glorious deeds (*ǧurṯûmat al-mafâḫir*), beauty of the fathers (*ǧamâl al-âbâ'*), beautiful one of high standing (*ǧamîla ǧalîla*).[24]

Bearer of affliction (*ḥâmilat al-balwâ*), the affectionate (*al-ḥâniyya*), germinating seed (*al-ḥabba al-nâbita*), love for whom is the best work (*ḥubbu-hâ ḫayr al-ʿamal*), beloved of the chosen one (*ḥabîbat al-muṣṭafâ*), lowered curtain of God (*ḥiǧâb Allâh al-murḫî*), greater proof of God (*ḥuǧǧat Allâh al-kubrâ*), the free (*al-ḥurra*), the inviolable (*al ḥaṣân*), enclosure of holiness (*ḥaẓîrat al-qudus*), the maiden of paradise (*al-ḥawrâ'*).

---

[22] In Ṣûfî thought, the 'interval' (*barzaḫ*) is traditionally thought to lie between death and resurrection. It is something that stands between two things, and is this context refers to Fâṭima as standing between Muḥammad, who represents the prophethood, and ʿAlî, who represents the one given authority (*wilâya*).

[23] A reference to the Shîʿî belief that Fâṭima was conceived in the womb of Ḫadîǧa after Muḥammad had eaten fruit from Paradise.

[24] In al-Baḥrânî's text these are not written as two separate names.

Fifth of the people of the cloak (*ḫâmisat ahl al-ʿabâʾ*),[25] best of the best (*al-ḫayrat min al-ḫayr*).

Pearl of divine unity (*durrat al-tawḥîd*), string of pearls (*al-durra al-munaḍḍada*),[26] answered prayer (*daʿwat mustağâba*).

The lofty summit (*al-ḏurwa al-shâmiḫa*), the summit of the Shîʿa (*ḏurwat al-shîʿa*).

The satisfied (*al-râḍiyya*), foster daughter of Mecca (*rabîbat Makka*), the rightly-guided (*al-rashîda*), support of religion (*rukn al-dîn*), spirit between the chosen one's two loins (*rûḥ bayna ğanbay al-muṣṭafâ*),[27] sweet basil of the Prophet (*rayḥânat al-nabî*), vessel of revelation (*zuğâğat al-waḥy*), the chaste (*al-zakiyya*), wife of God's greatest holy man (*zawğat walî Allâh al-ʿaẓm*), embellishment of the weaned (*zayn al-fawâṭim*).

The greater veil of God (*sitr Allâh al-kubrâ*), ship of deliverance (*safînat al-nağât*),[28] descendant of good will (*sulâlat al-riḍwân*), descendant of honour (*sulâlat al-faḫar*), heaven of the glittering stars (*samâʾ al-kawâkib al-durriyya*), the mistress (*al-sayyida*), mistress of the daughters of Adam (*sayyidat banât Âdam*), mistress of the women from first to last (*sayyidat nisâʾ al-awwalîn wa-l-âḫirîn*), mistress of the women of the Garden (*sayyidat nisâʾ al-ğanna*), mistress of the wom-

---

[25] A reference to the 'tradition of the cloak' (*al-kisâʾ*), which gathers Muḥammad, ʿAlî, Fâṭima, al-Ḥasan and al-Ḥusayn together as a single and exclusive family unit.

[26] Lane notes that *munaḍḍada* has an intensive signification, carrying the sense of household good arranged in good order. Cf. LANE E. W., *An Arabic-English Lexicon*, 1997, vol. VIII: 2808.

[27] A reference to a tradition in which Muḥammad says: "Fâṭima is my heart and my spirit between my two sides…" Cf. **RṬB**[2].: 197, **ṢDQ**[1]., n. 2: 112, **IRB**., vol. I: 466, 497, **MĞL**., vol. XXVII, bb. 1, n. 21: 62, vol. XXVIII, bb. 2, n. 1: 37, n. 34: 86, vol. XLIII, bb. 3: 54, bb. 7, n. 13: 176.

[28] As already noted, I have a certain hesitancy in using 'salvation' or 'redemption' to translate the Arabic *nağât* (نجاة), since in the realm of theology and spirituality, these have taken on a substantial Christian significance that is foreign to Islamic theology; hence the use of 'deliverance'.

en of this community (*sayyidat nisâ' hâḏihi al-umma*), mistress of the women (*sayyidat al-niswân*).

Nobility of the sons (*sharaf al-abnâ'*), intercessor of the community (*shafi*ʿ*at al-umma*), the intercessor on the Day of Resurrection (*al-shafî*ʿ*a yawm al-qiyâma*), the luminous sun (*al-shams al-muḍî'a*), the martyr (*al-shahîda*).

The one who fasted in the day (*al-ṣâ'ima fî al-nahâr*), the patient in tribulations (*al-ṣâbirat fî-l-miḥan*), companion of prolonged sorrows (*ṣâḥibat al-aḥzân al-ṭawîla*), companion of the exalted Garden (*ṣâḥibat al-ğanna al-sâmiyya*), companion of the scroll (*ṣâḥibat al-muṣḥaf*),[29] the truthful in the secret and the overt (*al-ṣâdiqa fî-l-sirr wa-l-*ʿ*alan*), the most glorious pearl (*al-ṣadaf al-faḫḫâr*), the righteous (*al-ṣiddîqa*), the greater righteous one (*al-ṣiddîqa al-kubrâ*), best of the nobility (*ṣafwat al-sharaf*), the best prayer (*ṣalât al-wusṭâ*);[30]

---

[29] The word may be used to refer to the Qur'ân or, specifically in the case of Fâṭima, to the esoteric text known as her *muṣḥaf*.

[30] The phrase is found in Q. 2: 238 («*Be guardians of your prayers, and of the midmost prayer, and stand up with devotion to Allah*»); however, as noted by the editors of 'The Study Qur'an' there appears to be little consensus on the precise meaning of the phrase *al-ṣalât al-wusṭâ* (cf. NASR S.H., et al, (eds.), *The Study Quran*, 2015: 104). While some hold it to be the morning prayer (*ṣalât al-fağr*) (cf. for e.g. **TRM**., vol. I, bk. 2 (*Kitâb al-ṣalât*), bb. 19, n. 182: 205), the majority push for the afternoon prayer (*ṣalât al-*ʿ*aṣr*) (cf. for e.g. **MSL**., vol. I, bk. 5 (*Kitâb al-masâğid wa-l-mawâḍi*ʿ *al-ṣalât*), bb. 36, n. 1425: 128, n. 1426: 129, n. 1428: 29–30, **ADD**., vol. I, bk. 2 (*Kitâb al-ṣalât*), bb. 5, n. 409: 255, **ADD**., vol. I, bk. 2 (*Kitâb al-ṣalât*), bb. 5, n. 411: 256, **TRM**., vol. I, bk. 2 (*Kitâb al-ṣalât*), bb. 19, n. 181: 204, n. 2983: 303, n. 2985: 304, **BḌW**., vol. I, Part 1: 147). Others say the noon prayer (*ṣalât al-ẓuhr*) (cf. for e.g. **TRM**., vol. I, bk. 2 (*Kitâb al-ṣalât*), bb. 19, n. 182: 205, **BḌW**., vol. I, Part 1: 147), which lies between dawn and afternoon, or merely suggest that it is not *ṣalât al-*ʿ*aṣr*, without offering an alternative (cf. for e.g. **MSL**., vol. I, bk. 5 (*Kitâb al-masâğid wa-l-mawâḍi*ʿ *al-ṣalât*), bb. 36, n. 1427: 129, **ADD**., vol. I, bk. 2 (*Kitâb al-ṣalât*), bb. 5, n. 410: 256, **TRM**., vol. V, bk. 44, (*Kitâb al-tafsîr*), bb. 2, n. 2982: 302- 303, **NSA**[1]: vol. I, bk. 5 (*Kitâb al-ṣalât*), bb. 14, n. 473: 283). This is presuming that is in in fact one of the five daily prayers. A stronger sense is that *al-ṣalât al-wusṭâ* is the

Guarantor of intercession (*ḍâmin al-shafâʿa*).

The pure (*al-ṭâhira*), the pure in deeds (*al-ṭâhira fî-l-afʿâl*), the pure born (*al-ṭâhirat al-mîlâd*), the outstretched shadow of God (*ẓill Allâh al-mamdûd*).

The pious worshiper (*al-ʿâbida al-taqiyya*), the conversant with things (*al-ʿârifa bi-l-ashyâʾ*), the cognizant of what was and what is (*al-ʿâlima bi-mâ kâna wa-mâ yakûnu*), the high-minded (*ʿâliyat al-himma*), equal to the greater Maryam (*ʿadîlat Maryam al-kubrâ*),[31] the virgin (*al-ʿaḏrâʾ*), the firm handhold (*al-ʿurwat al-wuṯqâ*),[32] the modest (*al-ʿafîfa*),

---

most important prayer and consequently the best prayer (cf. for e.g. **BḌW**., vol. I, Part 1: 147). Pickthall in Q. 68: 28 translates *awsaṭu-hum* as «*the best of them*», and this ties up with Lane's explanation, that *al-ṣalât al-wusṭâ* could also mean 'the best prayer', perhaps referring to the Friday prayer which is the best of all prayers (Cf. LANE E. W., *An Arabic-English Lexicon*, 1997, vol. VIII: 2942). I have chosen to render it thus, as a name of Fâṭima, bearing in mind her powerful intercessory prerogatives. Notably, the root *w-s-ṭ* comprises the sense of 'mediator' or 'intermediary' (as in *wâsiṭa* – cf. WEHR H., *A Dictionary of Modern Written Arabic*, 1980: 1251). As Abû Dâwûd notes, *al-ṣalât al-wusṭâ* is encased by two prayers on either side of it; this too might be a symbol of Fâṭima, at the heart of the house of sorrows, surrounded and enshrouded by Muḥammad, ʿAlî, al-Ḥasan and al-Ḥusayn (cf. **ADD**., vol. I, bk. 2 (*Kitâb al-ṣalât*), bb. 5, n. 411: 256).

[31] Although she herself is also called 'Maryam the greater'.

[32] Cf. Q. 2: 256, Q. 31: 22. The concept of *al-ʿurwat al-wuṯqâ* (العروة الوثقى) is diversely attributed; the general sense given by the Sunnî scholars is that it refers to Islam itself or to the Islamic faith (cf. for e.g. **BUḪ¹**., vol. V, bk. 63 (*Kitâb manâqib al-anṣâr*), bb. 19, n. 3813: 95, vol. IX, bk. 91 (*Kitâb al-taʿbîr*), bb. 19, n. 7010: 100, bb. 23, n. 7014: 102, **MSL**., vol. VI, bk. 44 (*Kitâb faḍâʾil al-ṣaḥâba*), bb. 33, nn. 6381–2: 348–349) or even to the *shahâda* (cf. al-Zabîdî., *Tâğ al-ʿarûs min ğawâhir al-qâmûs*, 1306/1888, vol. XIX: 669). Their Shîʿî counterparts offer other possibilities: the Qur'ân (**BḤR**., vol. I, *sûrat al-Baqara*, n. 565: 288), the Imâms or Imamate (**QQM**., bb. 79, n. 3: 202, bb. 104, n. 2: 317, **BḤR**., vol. I, *sûrat al-Baqara*, n. 1410: 523, vol. IV, *sûrat Luqmân*, n. 8441: 379), the *ahl al-bayt* (**FUR**., n. 230: 178, n. 412: 307), ʿAlî (**FUR**., n. 117: 115, n. 503: 372, **KLY**., vol. IV, bb. *Duʿâʾ âḫir ʿinda qabr amîr al-muʾminîn*, n. 1: 570, **ṢDQ¹**., *mağlis* 8, n. 4:

the best of the message (*ʿaqîlat al-risâla*), depository of the secrets of knowledge (*ʿayyibat al-ʿilm*),[33] source of the proof (*ʿayn al-ḥuğğa*), source of life (*ʿayn al-ḥayât*), most fair of complexion (*al-ġurra al-ġarrâʾ*).

The most excellent benefaction (*al-fâḍila al-fuḍlâ*),[34] glory of the Imâms (*faḫr al-aʾimma*), the chosen one's own child (*filḏdat kabid al-muṣṭafâ*).

The one who rose in the night (*al-qâʾima fî-l-layl*), the humble (*al-qânita*), the content (*al-qâniʿa*), the rightly directed exemplar (*al-qudwa al-musaddada*), abode of the heart (*qarâr al-qalb*), consolation of the eye of created things (*qurrat ʿayn al-ḫalâʾiq*), necklace of existence (*qilâdat al-wuğûd*).

The downcast (*al-kaʾîba*), generous in charity (*al-karîma fî al-nafaqa*), perfect word of God (*kalimat Allâh al-tâmma*), word of piety (*kalimat al-taqwâ*), the pleasant word (*al-kalima al-ṭayyiba*), the abundance (*al-kawṯar*),[35] glittering star (*al-kawkab al-durrî*), night of power (*laylat al-qadr*).

31, *mağlis* 10, n. 6: 39, **BḤR.**, vol. I, *sûrat al-Baqara*, n. 1413: 524, vol. II, *sûrat al-Mâʾida*, n. 2912: 239, *sûrat al-Tawba*, n. 4434: 736, vol. IV, *sûrat al-Aḥzâb*, n. 8603: 451), the *wilâya* of ʿAlî (**BḤR.**, vol. I, *sûrat al-Baqara*, n. 1415: 524, vol. IV, *sûrat Luqmân*, n. 8442: 380), al-Ḥusayn (**KLY.**, vol. IV, bb. *Ziyârat qabr Abî ʿAbd Allâh al-Ḥusayn*, n. 1: 571), affection for the family of Muḥammad (**BḤR.**, vol. IV, *sûrat Luqmân*, n. 8439: 379), or love for ʿAlî, al-Ḥasan and al-Ḥusayn (**QQM.**, bb. 14, n. 6: 51). Here, it is applied analogically to Fâṭima (apart from her membership of the *ahl al-bayt*), possibly in reference to the assurance that she will win Paradise by her intercession for all who adhere to her.

[33] Cf. LANE E. W., *An Arabic-English Lexicon*, 1997, vol. V: 2206.

[34] In al-Baḥrânî's text, these are not written as two separate names.

[35] The interpretation of the verse: «*Lo! We have given thee Abundance*» (Q. 108: 1) varies according to interpreters; a popular understanding is that *al-kawṯar* (the literal sense is 'abundance' or 'abundant benevolence') is a heavenly pool or basin (*ḥawḍ*) or "a river that flows from under the Throne of God, its waters whiter than milk, sweeter than honey and softer than butter" (**FUR.**, n. 766: 609), and which will be given to Muḥammad on the Day of Resurrection. On that day, ʿAlî will take his

The blessed (*al-mubâraka*), messenger of the holy ones (*mubashshirat al-awliyâ'*), the fatigued in the world (*al-mat'ûba fî al-dunyâ*), the keeper of vigils (*al-mutahağğida*), aflame of heart (*muḥtariqat al-qalb*), the one to whom the angels spoke (*al-muḥaddaṯa*), the one who satisfies God (*al-marḍiyya*), the greater Maryam (*Maryam al-kubrâ*), the one married among the heavenly host (*al-muzawwağa fî-l-malâ' al-a'lâ*), niche of lights (*mishkât al-anwâr*), the oppressed (*al-muḍṭahada*), the tyrannized (*al-maẓlûma*), treasure trove of wisdom (*ma'din al-ḥikma*), the one known in heaven (*al-ma'rûfa fî-l-samâ'*), turbaned (crowned) of head (*mu'aṣṣabat al-ra'is*),[36] the immaculate (*al-ma'ṣûma*), usurped of her rightful possession (*al-maġṣûba ḥaqqa-hâ*), she whose fetus was murdered (*maqtûlat al-ğanîn*), thwarted of affection (*maksûrat al-ḍal'*), the tested (*al-mumtaḥana*),[37] forbidden her inheritance (*al-mamnû'a irṯa-hâ*), the one aided by God (*al-manṣûra*), described in the gospel

---

place by this river, distributing its water to Muḥammad's friends and denying it to his enemies (**QQM**., bb. 108, n. 9: 102). While in his exegesis of this verse, the Shî'î al-Ṭabarsî makes reference to Fâṭima in terms of the abundance of her offspring (**ṬBR**[4]., vol. VI, Part 30, *sûrat al-Kawṯar*: 252), no reference to her is found in the exegesis of the same passage by the Shî'î exegete al-Baḥrânî. He does, however, suggest that *al-kawṯar* represents intercession (**BḤR**., vol. V, *sûrat al-Kawṯar*, n. 11945: 776), so that 'Alî's dispensing or refusal of its waters takes on this precise meaning. Analogically therefore, because of her extraordinary intercessory prerogatives, Fâṭima could be called *al-kawṯar*. Furthermore, since scholars of the 'occasions of revelation' (*asbâb al-nuzûl*) suggest that the context of this verse was that of Muḥammad being mocked for his lack of offspring, *kawṯar* in the sense of 'abundance' is justifiably applied to his daughter Fâṭima, from whom so many descendants would spring. This sense is noted, for example, by al-Râzî in his *tafsîr* (**RAZ**., vol. XXXII, *sûrat al-Kawṯar*: 124), although he does not mention Fâṭima's name.

[36] The precise sense, according to Lane, is to be attired with a turban, and thus crowned as a chief or a king. Cf. LANE E. W., *An Arabic-English Lexicon*, 1997, vol. V: 2060.

[37] The title of Q. 60, rendered by Pickthall as 'She that is to be examined'.

(*al-manʿûta fî-l-inğîl*), weakened of strength (*al-munhaddat al-rukn*),[38] attributed with reverence and veneration (*al-mawṣûfa bi-l-birr wa-l-tabğîl*), habitat of mercy (*mawṭin al-raḥma*), life-blood of the world (*muhğat al-ʿâlam*), life-blood of the heart of the chosen one (*muhğat qalb al-muṣṭafâ*), the blessed (*al-maymûna*).

Emaciated of body (*nâḥilat al-ğism*), speaker of the twofold declaration of faith at birth (*al-nâṭiqa bi-l-shahâdatayn ʿinda al-wilâda*), the sublime (*al-nabîla*), star of the crown of prophethood (*nağmat iklîl al-nubuwwa*), chosen part of her father (*nuḫbat abî-hâ*), lofty favour (*al-niʿma al-ğalîla*), light of lights (*nûr al-anwâr*), the luminary (*al-nûriyya*).

Mother of the proofs (*wâlidat al-ḥuğağ*),[39] mother of al-Ḥasan and al-Ḥusayn (*wâlidat al-Ḥasan wa-l-Ḥusayn*), grief-stricken and bereaved mother (*al-wâliha al-ṯaklâ*), the incomparable solitary one (*al-waḥîda al-farîda*), entrusted to the Messenger (*waḍîʿat al-rasûl*), vessel of knowledge (*wiʿâʾ al-maʿrifa*), greatest holy one of God (*waliyyat Allâh al-ʿuẓmâ*), born in Islam (*al-walîda fî-l-islâm*).

Al-Baḥrânî then transmits another long list, many of them arranged and listed in a didactic poem, although not all of these are found in the major transmitters.[40] He notes that she has many *alqâb*, some of

---

[38] The phrase *munhaddat al-rukn* is used by a number of authors to describe Fâṭima's physical and mental state after the death of her father (cf. for e.g. **FNR**., vol. I, 150, **SHB**., vol. III, *faṣl fî wafâti-hâ*: 362, **BAḤ**., vol. XI, bb. 2, n. 3: 800, **MĞL**., vol. XLIII, bb. 7, n. 16: 181). Lane suggests that the meanings of *rukn* range from 'corner', 'strength' or 'support', though 'kinsfolk' or 'nearest relations' to 'a noble or high person', 'might' or 'resistance' or 'an affair of great magnitude' (cf. LANE E. W., *An Arabic-English Lexicon*, 1997, vol. III: 1149). The verb *hadda-yahuddu* carries a sense of being weakened, broken down or undermined, as, notes Lane, in the phrase *hadda ruknî* ('the thing distressed and broke or crushed me') (cf. LANE E. W., *An Arabic-English Lexicon*, 1997, vol. VIII: 2882). Using this concept of being deprived of a strength or support, I have chosen to render this name 'weakened of strength'. In most texts it appears in the possessive (*munhaddat al-rukn*); in al-Baḥrânî, it appears as *al-munhaddat al-rukn*.

[39] A reference to the Imâms who would spring from her.

[40] **BAḤ**., vol. XI, bb. *ğawâmiʿ alqâbi-hâ wa-kunâ-hâ*, nn. 1–3: 93–96.

them laid down in writing and some of them mentioned in the description of her of the scholars (*ʿulamâʾ*) and the orators (*ḫuṭabâʾ*):

Mistress (*sayyida*), maiden of Paradise in human form (*ḥawrâʾ insiyya*), luminary (*nûriyya*), affectionate (*ḥâniyya*), virgin (*ʿaḏrâʾ*), generous (*karîma*), merciful (*raḥîma*), martyr (*shahîda*), modest (*ʿafîfa*), content (*qâniʿa*), rightly-guided (*rashîda*), distinguished (*sharîfa*), beloved (*ḥabîba*), venerated (*muḥtarama*), patient (*ṣâbira*), flawless (*salîma*), noble (*mukarrama*), serene (*ṣafiyya*), cognizant (*ʿâlima*), learned (*ʿalîma*), immaculate (*maʿṣûma*), unjustly usurped (*maġṣûba*), tyrannized (*maẓlûma*), blessed (*maymûna*), aided by God (*manṣûra*), decorous (*muḥtashama*), beautiful (*ğamîla*), lofty (*ğalîla*), sublime (*muʿaẓẓama*), bearer of affliction without complaint (*ḥâmilat al-balwâ bi-ġayri shakwa*), one who cleaves to worship and piety (*ḥalîfat al-ʿibâda wa-l-taqwâ*), beloved of God and daughter of the best (*ḥabîbat Allâh wa-l-ibnat al-ṣafwa*), support of the right way and sign of the prophecy (*rukn al-hudâ wa-l-âyat al-nubuwwa*), intercessor of sinners (*shafîʿat al-ʿuṣât*), mother of the good (*umm al-ḫayra*), apple of the Garden (*tuffâḥat al-ğanna*), the pure (*al-muṭahhara*), mistress of the women (*sayyidat al-nisâʾ*), daughter of the chosen (*bint al-muṣṭafâ*), best of her Lord (*ṣafwa rabbi-hâ*), habitat of guidance (*mawṭin al-hady*), consolation of the eye of the chosen and part of him (*qurrat ʿayn al-muṣṭafâ wa biḍʿati-hu*), lifeblood of his heart and thus his residue (*muhğat qalbi-hi wa kaḏâ baqiyyati-hi*), wise (*ḥakîma*), discerning (*fahîma*), the best (*ʿaqîla*), grief-stricken (*maḥẓûna*), sorrowful (*makrûba*), ailing (*ʿalîla*), worshiper (*ʿâbida*), abstemious (*ẓâhida*), guardian (*qawwâma*), tearful (*bâkiyya*), patient (*ṣâbira*)[41] ardent practitioner of fasting (*ṣawwâma*), affectionate (*ʿaṭûfa*), benevolent (*raʾûfa*), compassionate (*ḥannâna*), the benevolent (*al-birra*), the solicitous (*al-shafîqa*), the lamenter (*al-annâna*), mother of the generous (*wâlidat al-sabaṭîn*), great tree of the prophet (*dawḥat al-nabî*), heavenly light (*nûr samâwî*), wife of the one entrusted (*ẓawğat al-waṣy*), full moon (*badr tamâm*), best (*ġurra*), beautiful (*ġarrâʾ*), spirit of her father (*rûḥ abî-hâ*), white pearl (*durra bayḍâʾ*), intermediary of the necklace of existence (*wâsiṭat qilâdat al-wuğûd*), pearl of the ocean of nobility and generosity (*durrat baḥr al-sharaf wa-l-ğûd*), holy woman

[41] Occurs twice in the poem.

of God (*waliyyat Allâh*), mystery of God (*sirr Allâh*), custodian of revelation (*amîna al-waḥy*), choice of God (*ʿayn Allâh*), firmly established in the heavenly world (*makîna fî ʿâlam al-samâʾ*), beauty of the fathers (*ǧamâl al-âbâʾ*), nobility of the sons (sharaf *al-abnâʾ*), pearl of the ocean of knowledge and perfection (*durrat baḥr al-ʿilm wa-l-kamâl*), jewel of power and sublimity (*ǧawharat al-ʿizza wa-l-ǧalâl*), axle of the mill of the proud (*quṭba raḥy al-mufâḫir*), the exalted (*al-saniyya*), collection of glorious deeds (*maǧmûʿat al-mâʾṯir*), the exalted (*al-ʿaliyya*), niche and vessel of God's light (*mishkât nûr Allâh wa-l-zuǧâǧa*), *kaʿba* of hopes for the destitute (*kaʿba al-âmâl li-ahl al-ḥâǧa*), night of power (*laylat al-qadr*), blessed night (*laylat mubâraka*), daughter of the one upon whom the angels invoke blessing (*ibna man ṣallat bi-hi al-malâʾika*), abode of the heart (*qarâr al-qalb*), whose mother was the sublime (*ummu-ha al-muʿazzama*), exalted of position (*ʿâliyya al-muḥall*), mystery of exaltedness (*sirr al-ʿazama*), thwarted of affection (*maksûrat al-ḍalʿ*), crushed of heart (*raḍîḍ al-ṣadr*), usurped of (her) right (*maġṣûba al-ḥaqq*), her tomb unknown (*ḫafî al-qabr*).

He transmits from al-ʿAllâma *al-shayḫ* Ḍabîḥ Allâh al-Maḥallâtî's *Rayâḥîn al-sharîʿa*, which repeats many of the titles already listed, but adds:

Daughter of the best (*ibnat al-ṣafwa*), one of great standing (*iḥdâ al-kubr*), origin of origins (*arûmat al-ʿanâṣir*), most mighty of creation (*aʿazz al-bariyya*), mother of names (*umm asmâʾ*).[42]

---

[42] **BAḤ.**, vol. XI, bb. *mustadrak sayyidat al-nisâʾ*, n. 1: 46 (from al-Maǧlisî), n. 3: 90 (from al-Ḫawârizmî); cf. also **MĞL.**, vol. XLIII, bb. 1, n. 12: 8 (who elucidates approximately twenty names, naming Fâṭima as the 'mistress of *alqâb*').

APPENDIX B: THE PROTEST OF FÂṬIMA

This text, in English translation from the Arabic transmission in al-Ṭabarsî's *Kitâb al-iḥtiğâğ ʿalâ ahl al-liğâğ*,[1] represents the protest (*iḥtiğâğ*) ostensibly lodged by Fâṭima in the presence of a gathering of women in the Medina mosque, after the *Saqîfa* event and Abû Bakr's refusal to hand over the property of Fadak. As a text, it is a beguiling document; part exhortation, part catechism on the Islamic creed, part angry reproach, part appeal for assistance and part threat of future punishment for perceived injustices. The protest is carried by Ibn Abî Ṭayfûr in his *Balâğât al-nisâʾ*[2] and, two and a half centuries later, by al-Ṭabarsî in his *Kitâb al-iḥtiğâğ*; these texts carry the most complete version (and al-Mağlisî transmits from them both), but clearly, fragments of the protest are found in other classical Shîʿî authors.[3] As may be noted in the Arabic original, the text contains a number of singularities; idiom that is hard to render in another language, the use, at times, of language that has acquired a technical import in Islam (and especially among Ṣûfî adherents) and discrepancies in various transmissions (where the transmitter offers an alternative in parentheses). Also of note is the substantial number of quotes from the Qurʾân, not yet compiled (in the Sunnî but not the Shîʿî view) as a written document at the time of the protest, and thus suggesting that Fâṭima had memorized significant portions.

---

[1] **ṬBR**[2]., vol. I, bb. *iḥtiğâğ Fâṭima al-Zahrâʾ*: 99–104.

[2] **ṬAY**., bb. *kalâm Fâṭima bt. Rasûl Allâh*: 27–31.

[3] Cf. also **RṬB**[1].: 111–117, **IRB**., vol. I: 480–489, **MĞL**., vol. XXIX, n. 8: 220–230.

The protest contains a developed and at times technical theology; the reader's first reaction might be to wonder if the text represents a precise record of the words spoken by Fâṭima, or a redaction and embellishment of what was perhaps originally a much simpler appeal for justice by the justifiably distraught young women.

> "Praise be to God for all He has granted, and thanks be to Him for all He has inspired, and praise for all He has offered, from the sum of the benefits He brought into being, the abundance of blessings He conferred, the perfection of the favours He rendered. Their number has become too abundant to count, their scope far from any recompense, and their eternity remote from comprehension. He charged (His people) to desire more of them by gratitude for their continuity, and demanded the praise of created beings by giving them munificently, and repeated the charge to the people like them.
>
> I bear witness that there is no god but God, who is one and has no partner, an utterance whose explanation is the pronouncement of sincerity, attachment to which is the guarantee of hearts, comprehension of which has thrown light upon reflection.
>
> Seeing Him is forbidden to the gaze, as is His quality to the tongue and His nature to conjecture. He devised everything, not from anything that was before them, and brought them into being without copying a pattern. He ordered them, bringing them forth by His power and creating them by His will. Without necessity for Him their fashioning; nor was there gain for Him in their shaping, except a consolidation of His wisdom, an awakening of obedience to Him, a manifestation of His power, a veneration for His creation and a strengthening of His call. Then He appointed the reward for obedience to Him and laid down the punishment for disobedience to Him, a protection

for His servants from His retribution and the gathering[4] of them into His Garden –

I bear witness that my father Muḥammad is His servant and His Messenger. He chose him before sending him, and named him before electing him, and selected him[5] before delegating him,

a sign from God, may He be exalted, in consequence of the affairs,

a communication in the calamities[6] of the ages,

a knowledge in congruence with the affairs,

– since created beings were concealed in conjecture, well-guarded by the covering of darkness (*ahâwîl*) and affiliated with the utmost degree of privation. God sent (Muḥammad), a completion of His command, a decision for the realization of His judgment, an enforcment of the degrees of His mercy. He observed the nations, in groups in their religions, addicted to their fires, adorers of their idols, deniers of God with their knowledge.

By my father Muḥammad, God

illuminated their darkness,

removed from hearts their ambiguities,

cleared from perceptions their perplexities,[7]

---

[4] The Arabic *ḥiyâsha*; al-Ṭabarsî's editor likens it to the rounding up of camels, their being gathered and driven.

[5] This verb (*iṣṭafâ*) is used twice of Maryam in Q. 3: 42. Pickthall renders it as 'to choose' and then as 'to prefer'. Three times in this sentence Fâṭima insists upon her father's divine election, using three different verbs (*iḫtâra*, *iğtabâ*, *iṣṭafâ*).

[6] The Arabic *ḥawâdiṯ*; cf. LANE E. W., *An Arabic-English Lexicon*, 1997, vol. II: 528.

[7] According to al-Ṭabarsi's editor, this refers to what is obscure and vague, but in some texts reads as 'their blindness'.

accomplished guidance among the people,

delivered them from error,

made them see the folly,

guided them to the correct religion,

and called them to the straight path.

Then God took (Muḥammad) to Himself, a death of graciousness and choice, of desire and preference. Muḥammad is at rest from the toil of this abode, surrounded by reverent angels, the satisfaction of the Lord, the Ever Forgiving[8] and the proximity of the King,[9] the Strong.[10] God bless my father, His Prophet and faithful one, His choice from creation and His sincere friend, and peace be upon him and the mercy of God and His blessing.

Then she turned to the people of the assembly and said: You, servants of God, are the standard of His command and His prohibition, the bearers of His religion and His revelation, the faithful ones of God as regards your souls and His eloquent speakers to the nations, the guarantor of what is His due among you. He extended a covenant to you and He appointed as successor over you; the speaking book of God, the truthful Qur'ân, the radiant light, the lustrous glow. Its insights are a clear proof, its secrets disclosed, its literal meanings revealed, its adherents delighted by it; leading its followers to satisfaction, furnishing its listeners for deliverance.[11] The shining proofs of God are conferred by it, His intentions elucidated, His taboos cautioned, His declarations made manifest, His

---

[8] *al-Ġaffâr.*

[9] *al-Malik.*

[10] *al-Ǧabbâr.*

[11] Although *naǧât* (نجاة) can mean 'salvation' or 'redemption', these terms have a certain dominant Christian theological content that does not fit in with Islamic theology; I prefer to render the word as 'deliverance'.

proofs sufficient, His excellent qualities approved, His permissions granted and His laws written. God has made[12]

Faith, a purification from polytheism for you

Prayer, a declaration from presumption for you

Almsgiving, a chastening for the soul and an increase in subsistence

Fasting, a consolidation of sincerity

Pilgrimage, a firm construction for religion

Justice, an ordering for hearts

Obedience to us, a regime for the religious community[13]

---

[12] In this 'catechetical litany', Fâṭima, having established the centrality of the divine unity (*tawḥîd*) and the prophethood of her father (*nubuwwa*), now names the five pillars (*arkân*) of Islam, replacing the first, the 'declaration of faith' (*shahâda*) with 'faith (*îmân*), and then listing prayer (*ṣalât*), almsgiving (*zakât*), fasting (*ṣawm*), and pilgrimage (*ḥağğ*). To these, she adds two tenets specific to Shîʿî Islam: *ʿadl* (that God is just in a manner that can be understood rationally) and *imâma* (belief in the divinely-inspired leaders descended from Muḥammad, and whose existence is essential for the clarification and preservation of revelation). While *tawḥîd*, *nubuwwa* (and belief in the last day, which will also find an echo in Fâṭima's protest) are foundational to Islam, so that anyone who accepts them is unquestionably a Muslim, acceptance of *ʿadl* and *imâma* establishes that an individual is a Shîʿî Muslim. While the five *arkân* form some of the duties expected of a Shîʿî Muslim, Fâṭima specifies two more; the righteous struggle against vice (*ğihâd*), and the enjoining others to do good (*amr bi-l-maʿrûf*). She does not explicitly mention further precepts intrinsic to Shîʿî Islam; *ḫums* (almsgiving), forbidding others from doing evil (*naḥî ʿan al-munkar*), loving Muḥammad's family, emulating their deeds (*tawallâ*) and disassociating from the enemies of that family (*tabarrʾa*). These, however, resonate in various parts of the text.

[13] The Arabic *milla*, which has a wider range of meaning ('religious community', 'religion', 'creed', 'faith' or 'denomination') than the more customary *umma*. Cf. WEHR H., *A Dictionary of Modern Written Arabic*, Librairie du Liban, Beirut 1980: 1077.

Our Imamate, a safeguarding from disunion

Striving, a strength for Islam

Patience, an aid to the meriting of recompense

The enjoining of that which is good, a common benefit for the public

Reverence for parents, a protection from wrath

Union with kin,[14] a means of multiplying the span of life[15] and an augmentation of the number

Retaliation,[16] a sparing of blood[17]

The keeping of the vow, an intimation of pardon

The fulfillment of measures and weights, an altering of neglect

The prohibition on drinking wine, a declaration from filth

The avoidance of defamation,[18] a protection from the curse

The relinquishment of theft, a commitment to virtuousness.

God has forbidden polytheism as sincerity to Him in the Divinity. So, «*observe your duty to Allah with right observance, and die not save as those who have surrendered (unto Him)*«.[19] Submit to God

---

[14] The word *arḥâm* literally means 'wombs', but could also signifiy relatives or kin.

[15] Cf. LANE E. W., *An Arabic-English Lexicon*, 1997, vol. VIII: 2786.

[16] The principle of 'retaliation' (*qiṣâṣ*) is laid down in Q. 2: 178–179; cf. also Q. 2: 194, Q. 5: 45.

[17] The word occurs here in the plural: 'bloods'. Although unusual in English, this poses little problem for the Semitic languages. In both Hebrew and in Greek, for example, the word 'blood' is used in the plural to describe the discharge of blood after an act of violence, as in murder or battle.

[18] The word *qaḏf* refers especially to the defamation of a chaste women in an accusation of fornication (*zinâ*).

[19] Q. 3: 102.

in what He has commanded you and prohibited for you, for «*the erudite among His bondsmen fear Allah alone*».[20]

Then she said: You people, know that I am Fâṭima and my father is Muḥammad. I say it all over again; I do not say what I say in error, or do what I do excessively. «*There hath come unto you a messenger, (one) of yourselves, unto whom aught that ye are overburdened is grievous, full of concern for you, for the believers full of pity, merciful*».[21] If you assert relationship to him and recognize him, know that he is my father, to the exclusion of your women, and the brother of the son of my uncle, to the exclusion of your men.[22]

How excellent the relationship to him! He conveyed the message, manifesting the warning,[23] inclining from the route of the polytheists, striking their necks,[24] seizing their throats,[25] inviting to the path of his Lord with wisdom and beautiful exhortation. He agitated[26] the idols, and disunited the illustrious so that the throng was put to flight and turned (their) backs; until the night was split lengthwise by his dawn and the truth un-

---

20 Q. 35: 28.

21 Q. 9: 128.

22 A declaration that Fâṭima's is the primary human relationship with Muḥammad, as his only surviving child.

23 al-Ṭabarsî's editor notes that *ṣad*ʿ means a 'disclosure', 'manifestation' or 'demonstration', while *niḏâra* (*inḏâr*) is a 'warning' or 'admonition' that should lead to fear (of God).

24 The word *ṯabağ* has, according to Lane, a fairly price anatomical meaning; somewhere between the base of the neck and the back, or the part between the shoulder blades and the base of the neck (among others). Cf. LANE E. W., *An Arabic-English Lexicon*, 1997, vol. I: 330.

25 The verb *kaẓama-yakẓimu* relates to the being filled with anger or the suppressing or restraining of anger, remaining silent from anger or grief: as regard *akẓâm*, al-Ṭabarsî's editor relates the word to *taḥrîk* ('stirring', 'provoking' or 'putting in a state of commotion'), like the escaping of the breath from the throat.

26 al-Ṭabarsî's editor notes that in other texts it is 'smashed' (*kasara*) and in still others 'cut off' (*ǧadda*).

covered by his genuineness. The leader of the religion spoke and the silly prattle of the demons was muted, the rabble[27] of religious hypocrites came to nothing, and the knot of unbelief in God[28] and of hardships was untied; you uttered a word of sincerity in the group of the empty egg,[29] «*and (how) ye were upon the brink of an abyss of fire*»,[30] the watery milk of the drinker,[31]

---

[27] Hava renders the word *washîẓ* as 'rabble', although this meaning is not extent in Wehr or Lane. Cf. HAVA J.G., *Arabic English Dictionary for Advanced Learners*, Goodword Books, New Delhi 2008: 863. Lane refers his reader to *ṣamîm*, the sense of which is the best or most excellent of the people, and thus the opposite of *washîẓ*. Cf. LANE E. W., *An Arabic-English Lexicon*, 1997, vol. VIII: 3054, vol. IV: 1723. Al-Ṭabarsî's editor relates *washîẓ* to the riffraff and contemptible among the people.

[28] From the verb *kafara-yakfuru*, ('to veil, conceal, hide or cover something, to deny or refuse to acknowledge a favour or benefit, to be ungrateful or unthankful, to deny, refuse to acknowledge, conceal or cover the favours or benefits of God, to disbelieve, to become an unbeliever or infidel, to deny God, to be remiss, to fall short of one's duty with respect to the law, to neglect the gratitude to God incumbent upon one') (cf. LANE E.W., *An Arabic-English Lexicon*, 1997, vol. VII: 2620). The Arabic *kufr* in its most basic sense means 'ingratitude, to refuse a gift, to deny the gentleness of the giver, to deny or to refuse to acknowledge favours and benefits, especially those conferred by God'. The greatest *kufr* is the denial of the unity of God or of the prophetic status of Muḥammad (or other prophets). It does not carry the meaning of 'idolater'; and although some translators render it as 'misbelief' or 'disbelief', there is a subtle difference between the two terms (the first of the two refers to one who does believe, but whose belief is in some way disordered)

[29] al-Ṭabarsî's editor notes that this expression is directed to the 'people of the house'. The palpable meaning is of something that will come to nothing, or not be born.

[30] Q. 3: 103.

[31] The Arabic *maḏqa*, signifying milk that has been mixed with too much water, carries the connotation of being insipid or disgusting; the root *maḏaqa* also includes the sense of simulating friendship (cf. STEINGASS F., *Learner's Arabic English Dictionary*, Hippocrene Books, New York 1993: 978).

the opportunity of the avaricious, the firebrand of the hasty,[32] a foot of ground. You drank the stagnant water[33] and subsisted on strips of untanned skin, contemptible outcasts, «*in fear lest men should extirpate you*».[34] But God, may He be blessed and exalted, delivered you by Muḥammad, after much ado, and after he was afflicted by the army of the men, the jackals of the Arabs, the recalcitrant of the 'people of the book', «*As often as they light a fire for war, Allah extinguisheth it*»,[35] or the horn[36] of Satan appeared, or the mouths of the polytheists opened wide and they slandered his brother[37] in their mouths.[38] He would not be turned aside until, with the sole of his foot, he had trampled underfoot their side and extinguished their flame with his sword; worn out in the way[39] of God, diligent in the command of God, close to the Messenger of God, master of the holy ones of God, vigorous, sincere, assiduous, toiling, irreproachable in God by the censure of a critic, while you lived comfortable lives, peaceful, merry and secure, awaiting calamity for us, anticipating the reports, recoiling from the battle, fleeing from the fighting.

When God chose for His prophet the house of His prophets and the abode of His friends, the thorns of hypocrisy appeared among you, the garment of religion became tattered, the silent

---

32 In the sense of *istiğâl*, 'impelled', 'driven', 'wishing to expedite'. Al-Ṭabarsî's editor relates 'a foot of ground' to one renown in defeat and humility (perhaps 'a step for the feet').

33 Cf. LANE E. W., *An Arabic-English Lexicon*, 1997, vol. V: 1846 for *ṭaraq*, stagnant water which has collected and in which animals have waded.

34 Q. 8: 26. All of this appears to be a lyrical although obscure description of the condition of the people before the advent of Muḥammad, and thus in that period termed the *ğâhiliyya*.

35 Q. 5: 64.

36 A reference, says al-Ṭabarsî's editor, to Satan's people and followers.

37 ʿAlî b. Abî Ṭâlib.

38 Literally, with their uvulas, at the very back of their throats.

39 Cf. LANE E. W., *An Arabic-English Lexicon*, 1997, vol. III: 985.

among the erring spoke, the undistinguished[40] of the insignificant emerged, the stallion camel[41] of those who speak untruths brayed and strutted in your courtyards, Satan raised his head from his hole,[42] calling to you and found you susceptible to his call, and regardful of the strength in him. Then he incited you and found you possessed of agility,[43] stirred you and found you wrathful. You branded other than your camels and showed up at other than your drinking place;[44] this, while the era was still near, the gash still wide, the wound barely healing, the Messenger not yet buried – hastily, you alleged, for fear of dissension. «*Surely it is into temptation that they (thus) have fallen. Lo! hell verily is all around the disbelievers*».[45]

How far from the mark you are! How wrong you are, that you lie, when the book of God was in your midst, its matters manifest, its judgments luminous, its characteristics dazzling, its restrictions apparent, its commands lucid. You have left it behind your backs! Do you covet some desired thing as a substitute for it, or to rule by something other than it? «*Calamitous is the exchange for evil-doers*»,[46] «*And whoso seeketh as religion other than*

---

[40] al-Ṭabarsî's editor notes that this is one whose reputation is obscure or hidden and whose station in life either vile or forgotten.

[41] A stallion (camel) that is highly regarded, and neither ridden or maltreated. Cf. LANE E. W., *An Arabic-English Lexicon*, 1997, vol. VI: 2450.

[42] al-Ṭabarsî's editor relates this to a hiding place or a place into which something is stuck, like the hole in the ground used by a hedgehog, which pokes its head out only when it does not fear to do so.

[43]The Arabic *ḫifâf*, from the singular *ḫafîf*, in this context meaning 'light' in the sense of possessing quickness, acuteness, sharpness or intelligence. Cf. LANE E. W., *An Arabic-English Lexicon*, 1997, vol. II: 771.

[44] An allusion not only to the rejection of ʿAlî's candidacy for leadership in favour of Abû Bakr, but also of the refusal to hand over to Fâṭima her rightful property (Fadak).

[45] Q. 9: 49.

[46] Q. 18: 50. This same verse would be quoted by Fâṭima's daughter Zaynab in her famous protest against Yazîd.

the Surrender (to Allah) it will not be accepted from him, and he will be a loser in the Hereafter».[47]

Moreover, it did not take you long before aversion to it settled and became docile; you took up kindling its fire, you stirred up its embers, you responded to the call of Satan the tempter, to the extinguishing the lights of the clear religion and to the disregard of the practices of the pure Prophet. You drank small sips in froth[48] and proceeded towards his family and offspring in the covert of trees,[49] in the bare and open place;[50] but he was patient[51] with you despite it being like the incision of the knife, the piercing of the spearhead in the intestines. Now you maintain that there is no inheritance for us; «*Is it a judgment of the time of (pagan) ignorance that they are seeking? Who is better than Allah for judgment to a people who have certainty (in their belief)?*».[52] Do you not understand? Surely, it is as evident to you as the forenoon sun that I am his daughter!

Muslims! Will I be robbed of my inheritance? Son of Abû Quḥâfa! Is it in the book of God that you inherit from your father and I do not inherit from mine? You have brought forth a thing unheard of! Do you mean to relinquish the book of God and fling it behind your backs, when it says «*And Solomon was David's heir*"?[53] And in what it relates of the story of Yaḥyâ b. Zakariyyâʾ, when it says: «*Oh, give me from Thy presence a successor*

---

[47] Q. 3: 85.

[48] According to Lane, a proverb applied to one who pretends one thing when meaning or desiring another. Cf. LANE E. W., *An Arabic-English Lexicon*, 1997, vol. III: 1115.

[49] Cf. LANE E. W., *An Arabic-English Lexicon*, 1997, vol. II: 809.

[50] Or, an alternative reading suggested by Lane: 'a place covered with trees', 'a valley of tangled trees': cf. LANE E. W., *An Arabic-English Lexicon*, 1997, vol. V: 1777.

[51] al-Ṭabarsî's text reads *yaṣîru* (يصير), with a footnote from his editor adding that some texts read *yaṣbiru* (يصبر).

[52] Q. 5: 50.

[53] Q. 27: 16.

who shall inherit of me and inherit (also) of the house of Jacob».[54] He said: «*And the owners of kinship are closer one to another in the ordinance of Allah*».[55] And He said: «*Allah chargeth you concerning (the provision for) your children: to the male the equivalent of the portion of two females*».[56] And He said: «*...if he leave wealth, that he bequeath unto parents and near relatives in kindness. (This is) a duty for all those who ward off (evil)*».[57] You maintain that there is no precedence for me, and that I do not inherit from my father, and that there is no kinship between us! Did God favour you with a verse from which He excluded my father? Or do you say: the people of two religious communities do not inherit? Am I not, my father and I, from the people of one religious community? Are you more knowledgeable with respect to the Qur'ân and its affairs than my father and the son of my uncle?

Here it is (for you), roped and saddled![58] It will meet you on the day of your gathering: and how excellent an arbitrator God is, how excellent a leader Muḥammad is, how excellent the appointed resurrection; at the hour, those who speak untruths will incur loss, and it will not benefit you if repent, «*For every announcement there is a term*»[59] and «*...thus ye will come to know who it is unto whom cometh a doom that will abase him, and on whom there falleth everlasting doom*».[60]

Then she aimed her glance at the 'helpers' and said: You gathering of intellect,[61] strength of the religious community[62] and

---

[54] Q. 19: 5–6.

[55] Q. 33: 6.

[56] Q. 4: 11.

[57] Q. 2: 180.

[58] A reference to a she-camel with the halter (*ḫiṭâm*) fastened around her nose and jaw, and saddled up. Cf. LANE E. W., *An Arabic-English Lexicon*, 1997, vol. II: 768, vol. III: 1055.

[59] Q. 6: 67.

[60] Q. 39: 39–40.

[61] While the text of al-Ṭabarsî transmits 'intellect', al-Mağlisî reads 'youths' (الفتية), (النقيبة).

[62] *Milla.*

helpers of Islam, what is this failing in respect of my right, this paralysis[63] in the face of the injustice done to me? Was not the Messenger of God, my father wont to say: one is remembered in one's offspring? How quickly you have innovated, how speedily possessed of disrespect. But you have strength in what I am attempting and power in what I am requesting and pursuing. Or do you say: Muḥammad is dead? A momentous situation, its weakness increased, its breach widened, its mending ripped open. The earth became tenebrous for his vanishing, the sun and the moon were ecliped, the stars were dispersed for his calamity, hopes were trodden, the mountains were humbled, the sanctuary was lost and the sacred vanished with his death. This, by God, is the greatest mishap, the most terrible calamity; there is no mishap like it, nor misfortune so swift. The book of God, powerful His praise, made it known in your courtyards, in your evenings and your mornings, calling in your courtyards a shout, a cry, a recitation, a corrective,[64] just as what befell the prophets of God and His messengers before him, a decisive judgment, a final Divine decree: «*Muhammad is but a messenger, messengers (the like of whom) have passed away before him. Will it be that, when he dieth or is slain, ye will turn back on your heels? He who turneth back on his heels doth no hurt to Allah, and Allah will reward the thankful*».[65]

---

[63] The Arabic *al-sinna* is problematic to translate; al-Ṭabarsi's editor relates it to the sleep or slumber that overtakes those who are fearful, leading me to render it as 'paralysis'.

[64] The Arabic *ilḥân*, the verbal noun (*maṣdar*) of the 4TH form *alḥana-yulḥinu* suggests a correction of a misreading or mispronouncing of the Qur'ân. Lane omits the 4TH form (Cf. LANE E. W., *An Arabic-English Lexicon*, 1997, vol. VIII: 3009), while Wehr does not mention the verbal noun (WEHR H., *A Dictionary of Modern Written Arabic*, 1980: 1011). Steingass renders it as 'to make one understand' (STEINGASS F., *Learner's Arabic English Dictionary*, 1993: 913). Kazimirski suggests a 'melody' (KAZIMIRSKI A., *Dictionnaire Arabe-Français*, vol. IV, Maisonneuve, Paris 1860: 167).

[65] Q. 3: 144.

You Banû Qayla?[66] Will the inheritance of my father be withheld,[67] while you are convened and gathered in sight and earshot of me? The appeal has enveloped you, the experience engulfed you, and you are possessed of number and equipment and power; you have the weapons and the shields. The appeal comes to you and you do not answer! The cry comes to you and you do not help! You are characterized by contention, known for charity and righteousness, the elite who were chosen, the best who were selected (for us the 'people of the house'). You fought the Arabs, bore trouble and hardship, butted the nations, combatted the army.[68] We did not withdraw; rather, you withdrew: we ordered you and you conspired: so that when Islam broke out among us, and the milk of the days flowed copiously,[69] the stronghold of polytheism yielded, the flare-up of falsehood was stilled, the fires of unbelief[70] subsided, the call to disorder abated, the arrangement of religion became possible. And yet you wavered[71] after the elucidation, concealed (matters) after the declaration, recoiled after boldness, committed polytheism[72] after faith! Misery for «*a*

---

[66]As al-Ṭabarsî's editor notes, a reference to the two tribes of the *anṣâr*, al-Aws and al-Ḫazraǧ.

[67] Penrice 154: *haḍama-yahḍimu* as 'the withholding of that which is due'.

[68] I am following Lane in this translation. Cf. LANE E. W., *An Arabic-English Lexicon*, 1997, vol. I: 268.

[69] LANE vol. II: 624. Lane makes note of a proverb, "The milch camel of the Muslims has yielded a copious supply of milk", meaning that the dues of the government treasury are in good state. The proverb, has quoted here in a slightly altered state, seems to suggest an analogous meaning: that things began to go well.

[70] *Kufr.*

[71] Al-Maǧlisî transmits the verb *ḥarra* (حرّ): I have followed al-Ṭabarsî, who transmits *ḥazza* (حزّ), a verb, Lane claims "of anything making an impression in, or upon, the bosom, and causing one to waver or scruple…" Cf. LANE E. W., *An Arabic-English Lexicon*, 1997, vol. II: 558.

[72] That is, the sin of associating partners with God (*shirk*).

folk who broke their solemn pledges» (after their oath) «*and purposed to drive out the messenger and did attack you first? What? Fear ye them? Now Allah hath more right that ye should fear Him, if ye are believers*».[73]

But I have seen that you have tended to ease and have banished the one who is worthier of the expansion[74] and the taking possession;[75] you have isolated yourselves with meekness and saved yourselves with miserliness from abundance. You have rejected what you know by heart and you have repelled the one who was permitted for you, and «*though ye and all who are in the earth prove thankless, lo! Allah verily is Absolute, Owner of Praise*».[76]

Surely, I have said what I have said with knowledge of the antagonism[77] which has seized you, and the treachery of which your hearts are conscious. But this is the overflowing of the

---

[73] Q. 9: 13, but not a complete transmission of the verse.

[74] In Ṣûfî parlance, the concept of 'expansion' (*basṭ*) is regarded as one of the mystical states (*ḥâl*, pl. *aḥwâl*), corresponding to the stage (*maqâm*) of hope (*rağâ'*). As such, it is not the result of human effort, but is a sense of joy and exaltation given by God in accordance with the definition of the states.

[75] Contrasted with 'expansion' is 'contraction' (*qabḍ*), a state corresponding to the stage of fear (*ḫawf*). God seizes and contracts the heart of the mystic, inducing within him a desolation, not unlike the 'dark night' depicted by the Spanish Catholic mystics. It remains a matter of debate whether Fâṭima had such meanings in mind when she used this terminology, which appears to come from a later period. I have chosen to render it 'spoils' following Lane. Cf. LANE E. W., *An Arabic-English Lexicon*, 1997, vol. VII: 2483.

[76] Q. 14: 8.

[77] The root *ğaḏila-yağḏalu*, aside from meanings expressing happiness, gaiety or exuberance, also carries the sense of 'antagonism' or 'contending' (Lane 396–397) or 'hostility' (Steingass 225). Al-Ṭabarsî's editor relates the word *ğiḏla* to those who have abandoned Fâṭima without rendering assistance, those who hold back through cowardice or who meddle in other's affairs.

soul, the outpouring of anger, the weakness of the spear, the revealing of the heart, the tendering of the proof. Here it is! Bag it, put it on the back of a sick, thin-humped she-camel, branded by the disgrace of eternity, bound for the «*fire of Allah, kindled, which leapeth up over the hearts (of men)*».[78] By God's witness of what you do, «*those who do wrong will come to know by what a (great) reverse they will be overturned*».[79] I am the daughter of «*a warner to you before a severe punishment*»[80] so «*…act…Lo! We (too) are acting…and wait! Lo! We (too) are waiting*».”[81]

[78] Q. 104: 7–8.
[79] Q. 26: 227.
[80] Q. 34: 46.
[81] Q. 11: 121–122.

BIBLIOGRAPHY

BOOKS

ABBOTT N., *Aishah the Beloved of Mohammed*, Saqi Books, London 1988.

AKHTAR S.W., *The Early Imāmiyyah Shi'ite Thinkers*, Ashish Publishing House, New Delhi 1988.

al-AMINE H., *Shorter Shi'ite Encyclopaedia*, Ansariyan Publications, Qum 1997.

al-ANṢÂRÎ M., *Li-kulli al-nâs al-ğawâb*, Imam Hussein Foundation, Qum 1999.

ʿAQQÂR ʿA.M., *Fâṭima al-Zahrâʾ wa-l-Fâṭimiyyûn*, Dâr al-kitâb al-ʿarabiyya, Beirut 1967.

ARMSTRONG K., *Muhammad*, Victor Gollancz Ltd, London 1992.

ʿÂSHÛR ʿA., *Fâṭima bt. Muḥammad, qudwa li-l-nisâʾ*, Dâr al-hâdî, Beirut 2002.

AYOUB M., *Redemptive Suffering in Islam. A Study of the Devotional Aspects of ʿAshura in Twelver Shiʿism*, Mouton Publishers, The Hague 1978.

——— *The Qurʾan and Its Interpreters*, vol. II, *The House of ʿImrān*, State University of New York Press, Albany 1992.

——— *The Crisis of Muslim History. Religion and Politics in Early Islam*, Oneworld, Oxford 2003.

BAR-ASHER M.B. and KOFSKY A., *The Nuṣayrī-ʿAlawī Religion. An Enquiry into its Theology and Liturgy*, Brill, Leiden 2002.

BARLAS A., *Believing Women in Islam. Unreading Patriarchal Interpretations of the Qurʾan*, Sama Editorial and Publishing Services, Karachi 2004.

BARNSTONE W., (ed.), *The Other Bible*, Harper Collins, San Francisco 1984.

BEINHAUER-KÖHLER B., *Fāṭima bint Muḥammad. Metamorphosen einer frühislamischen Frauengestalt*, Harrassovitz Verlag, Wiesbaden 2002.

BILL J.A. and WILLIAMS J.A., *Roman Catholics and Shi□i Muslims*, University of North Carolina Press, Chapel Hill 2002.

BOSWORTH C.E., (ed.), *Iran and Islam*, Edinburgh University Press, Edinburgh 1971

BROWN R., *The Birth of the Messiah*, Doubleday, New York 1993.

CAMPBELL J., *The Hero with a Thousand Faces*, Fontana Press, London 1993.

——— *The Masks of God: Occidental Mythology*, Souvenir Press, London 2001.

——— *The Masks of God: Creative Mythology*, Souvenir Press, London 2001.

CHANNON J., *The Concept of Intercession in Hadith Qudsi*, Pontifical Institute for Arabic and Islamic Studies, Rome 1985.

CHIRI M.J., *The Brother of the Prophet Mohammad*, 2 vols., The Islamic Center of America, Michigan 1979, 1982

CHITTICK W.C., *A Shi'ite Anthology*, Muhammadi Trust, London 1980.

COLE J., *Sacred Space and Holy War. The Politics, Culture and History of Shi'ite Islam*, I. B. Tauris, London 2002.

COOK M., *Commanding Right and Forbidding Wrong in Islamic Thought*, Cambridge University Press, Cambridge 2000.

DAFTARY F., *Ismâ'îlis. Their History and Doctrine*, Cambridge University Press, Cambridge 1990.

DE LA POTTERIE I., *Mary in the Mystery of the Covenant*, Alba House, New York 1997.

DONDERS J.G., (ed.), *John Paul II. The Encyclicals in Everyday Language*, Orbis, New York 1996.

ELLIOTT J.K., (ed.), *The Apocryphal Jesus. Legends of the Early Church*, Oxford University Press, Oxford 1996.

FADLULLAH M.H., *Fatimah al-Ma`sumah (as): A Role Model for Men and Women*, Al-Bakir Cultural & Social Center, London (n.d.).

al-FAYRÛZÂBÂDÎ M., *Faḍâʾil al-ḫamsa min al-ṣiḥâḥ al-sitta*, 3 vols., al-Mağmaʿ al-ʿâlamâ li-ahl al-bayt, Qum 2004.

GAMBERO L., *Mary and the Fathers of the Church*, Ignatius Press, San Francisco 1999.

GAMBERO L., *Mary in the Middle Ages*, Ignatius Press, San Francisco 2000.

GHADANFAR M. A., *Great Women of Islam*, Darussalam Publishers, Riyadh 2001

GUILLAME A., *The Life of Muhammad. A Translation of Ibn Ishaq's Sirat Rasul Allah*, Oxford University Press, Oxford 2006.

HALM H., *Shiism*, Edinburgh University Press, Edinburgh 1991.

HOWARD I.K.A., (trans.), *Kitāb al-Irshād. The Book of Guidance by Shaykh al-Mufīd*, Balagha Books, West Sussex 1981.

——— *The Revolution of al-Husayn. Its Impact on the Consciousness of Muslim Society*, The Muhammadi Trust, London 1985.

JAFFER A.M.M., (trans.), *Al-Amali. The Dictations of Sheikh al-Mufid*, World Federation of KSIMC, London (n.d.) and reproduced with the permission of the Ahlul Bayt Digital Islamic Library Project.

JAFRI S.H.M., *The Origins and Early Development of Shiʾa Islam*, Oxford University Press, Oxford 2003.

JAMES M.R., (trans.), *The Apocryphal New Testament*, Clarendon Press, Oxford 1980.

JOHN PAUL II., *Theotókos. Woman, Mother, Disciple*, Pauline Books and Media, Boston 2000.

KAZI A.K. and FLYNN J.G., *Muslim Sects and Divisions. The Section on Muslim Sects in Kitāb al-Milal wa ʾl-Niḥal*, Kegan Paul International, London 1984.

KENNEDY H., *The Prophet and the Age of the Caliphates*, Longman, London 1986.

KRAMER M., (ed.), *Shiʾism, Resistance and Revolution*, Westview Press, Colorado 1987.

LALANI A.R., *Early Shīʾī Thought. The Teachings of Imam Muhammad al-Bāqir*, I.B. Tauris, London 2000.

LINGS M., *Muhammad, his life based on the earliest sources*, Inner Traditions International Ltd, New York 1983.

MADELUNG W., *The Succession to Muḥammad. A study of the early Caliphate*, Cambridge University Press, Cambridge 1997.

MERNISSI F., *Women and Islam. An Historical and Theological Enquiry*, Women Unlimited, New Delhi 2004.

MOIN B., *Khomeini. Life of the Ayatollah*, I.B. Tauris, London 1999.

MOMEN M., *An Introduction to Shiʾi Islam. The History and Doctrines of Twelver Shiʾism*, Yale University Press, New Haven 1985.

MOTZKI H., (ed.), *The Biography of Muḥammad. The Issue of Sources*, E.J. Brill, Leiden 2000.

MUIR W., *The Caliphate: Its Rise, Decline and Fall*, Khayats, Beirut 1963.

al-MÛSAWÎ M., *al-Kawṯar fî aḥwâl Fâṭima bt. al-nabî al-aṭhar*, 7 vols., Qum 2000

al-MUZAFFAR M.R., *The Faith of Shiʾa Islam*, The Muhammadi Trust of Great Britain and Northern Ireland, Cambridge 1982.

NACHEF A., *Mary's Pope. John Paul II, Mary and the Church since Vatican II*, Sheed and Ward, Wisconsin 2000.

NAKASH Y., *The Shiʾis of Iraq*, Princeton University Press, Princeton New Jersey 1994.

NAKASH Y., *Reaching for Power. The Shiʾa in the Modern Arab World*, Princeton University Press, New Jersey 2006.

NASR S.H., *Ideal and Realities of Islam*, George Allen & Unwin Ltd, London 1966.

NEVILL A., (trans.), *Shiʾite Islam*, Blackwell, Oxford 1995.

NOMANI M.M., *Khomeini, Iranian Revolution and the Shiʾite Faith*, Furqān Publications, London 1988.

ORDONI A.M., *Fatima the Gracious*, Ansariyan Publications, Qum (n.d.).

PADWICK C., *Muslim Devotions. A Study of Prayer Manuals in Common Use*, Oneworld, Oxford 1996.

PAIDAR P., *Women and the political process in twentieth-century Iran*, Cambridge University Press, Cambridge 1995.

PELIKAN J., *Mary Through the Centuries*, Yale University Press, New Haven 1996.

PETERS F.E., *Muhammad and the Origins of Islam*, State University of New York Press, Albany 1994.

PINAULT D., *The Shiites*, St. Martin's Press, New York 1992.

PRICE S. and KEARNS E., (eds.), *The Oxford Dictionary of Classical Mythology*, Oxford University Press, Oxford 2004.

al-QAZWÎNÎ M.K., *Fâṭima al-Zahrâ᾽ min al-mahd ilâ al-laḥd*, Dâr al-Qârî, Beirut 2002.

REZA S.A., (trans.), *Peak of Eloquence. Nahjul Balagha*, Tahrike Tarsile Qur'an, New York 1996.

RICHARD Y., *Le Shi᾽isme en Iran. Imam et Revolution*, Librairie d'Amérique et d'Orient, Paris 1980.

ROGERSON B., *The Heirs of the Prophet Muhammad and the Roots of the Sunni-Shia Schism*, Abacus, London 2006.

SADR-ʿAMELÎ S.A., (trans.), *A Bundle of Flowers from the Garden of Traditions of the Prophet & Ahlul-Bayt*, Amir-ul-Mu'mineen Ali Library, Isfahan 1998.

SCHIMMEL A., *Mystical Dimensions of Islam*, University of North Carolina Press, Chapel Hill 1975.

SHAH-KAZEMI R., (trans.), *Doctrines of Shi᾽i Islam. A Compendium of Imami Beliefs and Practices*, I.B. Tauris, London 2001.

al-SHAIBI K.M., *Sufism and Shi᾽ism*, LAAM, Surrey 1991.

SHARIATI A., *Fatima is Fatima*, The Shariati Foundation, Tehran (n.d.).

SHÎRÂZÎ Ḥ., *Kalimat Fâṭima*, Dâr al-ʿUlûm, Beirut 2000.

STOWASSER B., *Women in the Qur᾽an, Traditions and Interpretation*, Oxford University Press, New York 1994.

ṬABÂṬABÂ᾽Î M., *al-Mîzân. An Exegesis of the Qur᾽ân*, 8 vols., World Organization for Islamic Services, Tehran 1974.

——— *Shi᾽ite Islam*, George Allen & Unwin Ltd, London 1975.

TRIMINGHAM J.S., *Christianity among the Arabs in Pre-Islamic Times*, Longman, London 1979.

WARNER M., *Alone Of All Her Sex. The Myth and Cult of the Virgin Mary*, Pan Books Ltd., London 1985.

WATT W.M., *The Formative Period of Islamic Thought*, Edinburgh University Press, Edinburgh 1973.

ZANJANI I.A., *Fatima (p.b.u.h.) in the Reflection of Books*, al-Hadi Publications, Iran 1996.

ARTICLES

ABBOTT N., "*Ḥadīth* Literature – II: Collection and Transmission of *Ḥadīth*" in A.F.L. Beeston et al., (eds.), *Arabic Literature to the End of the Umayyad Period*, Cambridge University Press, Cambridge 1983: 289–298.

AHMAD N., "Twelver Šīʿī *Ḥadīṯ*: From Tradition to Contemporary Evaluations" in *Oriente Moderno* XXI (LXXXII), 1–2002: 125–145.

AWLIYÂ'Ī M., "Outlines of the Development of the Science of Hadith" in *al-Tawḥīd*, vol. I, n. 1, Muḥarram 1404: 26–37, n. 2, Rabī' al-Thānī 1404: 30–42.

AYOUB M., "Towards an Islamic Christology I: An Image of Jesus in Early Shi'i Muslim Literature" in *The Muslim World*, vol. LXV1, n. 3, July 1976: 163–181.

——— "Towards an Islamic Christology II: The Death of Jesus, Reality or Illusion" in *The Muslim World,* vol. LXX, n. 2, April 1980: 91–121.

BEVAN A.A., "Mohammad's Ascension to Heaven" in K. Marti (ed.), *Studien zur semitischen Philologie und Religionsgeschichte, Julius Wellhausen zum siebzigten Geburtstag am 17. Mai 1914 gewidmet*, Giessen 1914 (Beihefte zur Zeitschrift für die alttestamentliche Wissenschaft 27): 51–61.

BECKER C.H., "Matters of Fundamental Importance for Research into the Life of Muhammad" in Ibn Warraq (ed. and trans.), *The Quest for the Historical Muhammad*, Prometheus Books, New York 2000: 330–336.

BILL J., "Shi'i Islam and Roman Catholicism: an Ecclesial and Political Analysis" in *The Vatican, Islam and the Middle East*, Syracuse University Press, New York 1987: 69–106.

BUSSE H., "Jerusalem in the Story of Muhammad's Night Journey and Ascension" in *Jerusalem Studies in Arabic and Islam*, 14 (1991): 1–40.

CHELKOWSKI P., "ʿAshura" in J. Esposito (ed.), *The Oxford Encyclopedia of the Modern Islamic World*, Oxford University Press, Oxford 1995, vol. 1: 141–142.

CLOHESSY C., "The Face of Islām Flushed. The Karbalā' Event" in *Encounter*, n. 285, June 2002.

——— "Mary and Fāṭima in the Catholic and Shīʿī Traditions" in A. Mahony et al. (eds.), *Catholics and Shiʾa in Dialogue*, Melisende, London 2004.

D'SOUZA D., "In the Presence of the Martyrs. The ʿAlam in Popular Shiʿi Piety" in *The Muslim World*, vol. LXXXVIII, n. 1, January 1998: 67–80.

ELIASH J., "The Shî'ite Qurʾân. A Reconsideration of Goldziher's Interpretation" in *Arabica* XVI, 1969: 15–24.

ELIASH J., "The Ithnâ 'Asharî-Shî'î Juristic Theory of Political and Legal Authority" in *Studia Islamica* XXIX, 1969: 17–30.

ELIASH J., "On the Genesis and Development of the Twelver-Shî'î three tenet Shahâdah" in *Der Islam* 47, 1971: 265–272.

FERDOWS A.K., "Women in Shi'i Islam and Iran" in *Oriente Moderno*, 1/1–12, 1982: 71–82.

FITZGERALD M.L., "Mediation in Islam" in *Studia Missionalia,* vol. XXI, 1972: 185 – 206.

FITZGERALD M.L., "Shi'ite Understanding of the Qurʾan" in *Encounter*, Number 178, October 1991.

FITZGERALD M.L., "Jesus in a Shiʿite Community' in *Encounter*, n. 229, November 1996.

FYZEE A.A.A., "The Ismâʾîlîs" in A.J. Arberry (ed.), *Religion in the Middle East*, vol. II, 1969: 318–329.

GEISSINGER A., "The Exegetical Traditions of ʿĀʾisha. Notes on Their Impact and Significance" in *Journal of Qurʾanic Studies*, vol. IV, Issue 1 (2004).

HALLAQ W., "The Authenticity of Prophetic Ḥadîth: a Pseudo-Problem" in *Studia Islamica* LXXXIX, 1999: 75–90.

HOROVITZ J., "Muhammeds Himmelfahrt" in *Der Islam* 9 (1919): 159–183 and HARTMANN R., "Die Himmselsreise Muhammads und ihre Bedeutung in der Religion des Islam" in F. Saxl (ed.), *Vorträge der Bibliothek Warburg*, Vorträge 1928–1929, Leipzig/Berlin 1930: 42–65.

HOWARD I.K.A., "Shīʿī Theological Literature" in M.J.L. Young et al., (eds.), *Religion, Learning and Science in the ʿAbbasid Period*, Cambridge University Press, Cambridge 1990: 16–32.

HUSTED W., "Karbala Made Immediate: The Martyr as Model in Imami Shiʿism" in *The Muslim World*, vol. LXXXIII, nn. 3–4, July-October 1993: 263–278.

JA'FARIYAN R., "Shīʿism and its Types During the Early Centuries" in *al-Tawḥīd*, vol. XIV, n. 3, Fall 1997: 155–176, n. 4, Winter 1997: 150–172.

JA'FARIYAN R., "Tadwīn al-Ḥadīth: A Historical Study of the Writing and Compilation of Ḥadīth" in *al-Tawḥīd*, vol. V, n. 2, Rabī' al-Thānī – Jamādī al-Thānī 1408: 39–70, nn. 3–4, Rajab – Dhū al-Ḥijjah 1408: 71–84, vol. VI, n. 1, Muḥarram – Rabī' al-Awwal 1408: 19–35.

JAFRI S.H., "Twelve-Imam Shiʿism" in S.H. Nasr (ed.), *Islamic Spirituality. Foundations*, Crossroad Publishing Company, New York 1997.

KOHLBERG E., "Western Studies of Shi'i Islam" in *Shi'ism, Resistance and Revolution*, Mansell Publishing Ltd, London 1987: 31–46.

KOHLBERG E., "From Imâmiyya to Ithna 'ashariyya" in *Bulletin of the School of Oriental and African Studies* 39, 1976: 521–534.

KOHLBERG E., "Shīʿī *Ḥadīth*" in A.F.L. Beeston et al., (eds.), *Arabic Literature to the End of the Umayyad Period*, Cambridge University Press, Cambridge 1983: 299–307.

LAMMENS H., "Al-Husain" in H.A.R. Gibb et al. (eds.), *Shorter Encyclopaedia of Islam*, E.J. Brill, Leiden 1995: 142.

LAMMENS H., "Fatima and the Daughters of Muhammad" in Ibn Warraq (ed. and trans.), *The Quest for the Historical Muhammad*, Prometheus Books, New York 2000: 218–329.

LAWSON T., "The Authority of the Feminine and Fatima's Place in an Early Work by the Bab" in L.S. Walbridge (ed.), *The*

Most Learned of the Shiʿa" Oxford University Press, Oxford 2001.

LEWIS B., "The Ismailites and the Assassins" in M.N. Baldwin (ed.), *A History of the Crusades*, vol. I, University of Wisconsin Press, Wisconsin 1969.

MADELUNG W., "Imamism and Mu'tazilite Theology" in *Le Shi'isme imamite*, Editeur, Paris 1970: 13–30.

MARGOLIOUTH D.S., "The Last Days of Fatima" in *Mélanges Hartwig Derenbourg*, Ernest Leroux, Paris 1909: 279–286.

MASSIGNON L., "Der Gnostische Kult der Fatima im Schiitischen Islam" in *Opera Minora* Tome I, Dar al-Maaref, Beirut 1963: 514–522.

——— "La Mubahala de Médine et l'Hyperdulie de Fatima" in *Opera Minora* Tome I, Dar al-Maaref, Beirut 1963: 550–572.

——— "La Notion de Voeu et la Dévotion Musulmane à Fatima" in *Opera Minora* Tome I, Dar al-Maaref, Beirut 1963: 573–591.

——— "L'Oratoire de Marie à l'Acqa, vu sous le Voile de Deuil de Fatima" in *Opera Minora* Tome I, Dar al-Maaref, Beirut 1963: 592–618.

McAULIFFE J.D., Chosen of all Women: Mary and Fātima in Qur'anic Exegesis" in *Islamochristiana*, n. 7, 1981: 19–28.

MILLWARD W.G., "Aspects of Modernism in Shī'a Islam" in *Studia Islamica* XXXVII, 1973: 111–128.

MUTAHHARI M., "The Meaning of ʿAshura: Popular Distortions and Our Responsibility" in *al-Tawḥīd*, vol. XIV, n. 2, Summer 1997: 27–38.

NAKASH Y., "The Visitations of the Shrines of the Imams and the Shi'i Mujtahids in the Early Twentieth Century" in *Studia Islamika: Indonesian Journal for Islamic Studies*, 81 (June), 1995/1: 153–164.

NASR S.H., "Ithna ʿashari Shīʿism and Iranian Islam" in A.J. Arberry (ed.), *Religion in the Middle East*, vol. II, 1969: 96–118.

PALLAVICINI ʿA., "Il Pianto di Maria nella Tradizione Islamica" in *Il Messaggio* IV, n. 10, Gennaio 2004: 140–148.

QARA'I A.Q., "Husayn ibn Ali the Saviour of Islam" in *al-Tawḥīd*, vol. I, n. 1, Muḥarram 1404: 39–44.

ROSINY S., "The Tragedy of Fāṭima al-Zahrā' in the Debate of Two Shiite Theologians in Lebanon" in R. Brunner and W. Ende (eds.), *The Twelver Shia in Modern Times*, Brill, Leiden 2001: 207–219.

RICE W.A., "'Ali in Shi'ah Tradition" in *The Muslim World*, vol. IV, n. 1, January 1914: 27–44.

RUBEN U., "Pre-Existence and Light. Aspects of the Concept of Nūr Muḥammadī" in *Israel Oriental Studies* 105 V (1975).

RUBIN I., "Prophets and Progenitors in the early Shī'a Tradition" in *Jerusalem Studies in Arabic and Islam*, vol. I (1979): 41–65.

SCHAEFFER K., "Suffering with Al-Husayn" in *The Bulletin of The Henry Martyn Institute*, vol. 12/1–2, January-June 1993, 74–84.

SCHRIEKE B., "Die Himmselsreise Muhammads" in *Der Islam* 6 (1916): 1–30.

SERJEANT R.B., "The Zaydis" in A.J. Arberry (ed.), *Religion in the Middle East*, vol. II, University of Cambridge Press, Cambridge 1969: 285–301.

STAFF OF *AL-TAWḤĪD*., "Ḥadīth al-Thaqalayn: A Study of its Tawātur" in *al-Tawḥīd*, vol. VIII, n. 1, Rabīᶜ al-'Awwal 1411.

ST. CLAIR-TISDALL W., "The Sources of Islam" in Ibn Warraq (ed.), *The Origins of the Koran*, Prometheus Books, New York 1988: 227–292.

VAHDAT F., "Post-Revolutionary Islamic Discourses on Modernity in Iran: Expansion and Contraction of Human Subjectivity" in *International Journal of Middle East Studies*, vol. 35, n. 4, November 2003: 599–631.

VECCIA VAGLIERI L., "Fadak" in H.A.R. Gibb et al. (eds.), *Encyclopaedia of Islam*, 2ND edn., E.J. Brill, Leiden 1965, vol. IIb: 725–727.

——— "Fāṭima" in H.A.R. Gibb et al. (eds.), *Encyclopaedia of Islam*, 2ND edn., E.J. Brill, Leiden 1965, vol. IIb: 841–850.

——— "Khaybar" in H.A.R. Gibb et al. (eds.), *Encyclopaedia of Islam*, 2ND edn., E.J. Brill, Leiden 1978, vol. IVb: 1137–1143.

WATT W.M., "Shiism under the Umayyads" in *Journal of the Royal Asiatic Society*, 1960: 158–172.

——— "Sidelights on early Imamite Doctrine" in *Studia Islamica* XXX, 1970: 287–298.

——— "Khadīdja" in H.A.R. Gibb et al. (eds.), *Encyclopaedia of Islam*, 2ND edn., E.J. Brill, Leiden 1971, vol. IVb: 898–899.

WIERINGA E., "Does Traditional Islamic Malay Literature contain Shi'itic elements? 'Al✕ and F•tima in Malay Hikayat Literature" in *Studia Islamika: Indonesian Journal for Islamic Studies*, 1996: 93–102.

PAMPHLETS

SHARIATI A., *Red Shi'ism*, The Shariati Foundation, Tehran 1979.

REFERENCE WORKS

BROCKELMANN C., *Geschichte der arabischen Literatur*, 2 vols., 3 supplementary vols., Leiden 1937–1945.

CAETANI L. and GABRIELI G., *Onomasticon Arabicum*, 2 vols., Rome 1915.

DENZIGER H. and SCHÖNMETZER A., *Enchiridion symbolorum definitionem et declarationum de rebus fidei et morum*, 39TH edn., Herder, Freiburg im Breisgau 2001.

FLANNERY A., (ed.), *Vatican Council II: The Conciliar and Post Conciliar Documents*, Dominican Publications, Dublin 1975.

JURGENS W.A., *The Faith of the Early Fathers*, 3 vols., Liturgical Press, Collegeville 1970–1979.

LANE E.W., *An Arabic-English Lexicon*, 8 vols., Librairie du Liban, Beirut 1997.

IBN MANẒÛR., *Lisân al-ʿarab*, 18 vols., Dâr Iḥyâ al-Turâṯ al-ʿArabî, Beirut 1999.

MODARRESSI H., *Tradition and Survival. A Bibliographical Survey of Early Shīʾite Literature*, vol. 1, Oneworld, Oxford 2003.

NEUNER J. and DUPUIS J., *The Christian Faith in the Doctrinal Documents of the Catholic Church*, Collins Liturgical Publications, London 1983.

OTT L., *Fundamentals of Catholic Dogma*, Mercier Press, Cork 1960.

RAHMAN H.U., *A Chronology of Islamic History 570–1000*CE, Mansell Publishing Limited, London 1989.

RAHNER K. and VORGRIMLER H., *Concise Theological Dictionary*, 2ND edn., Burns and Oates, London 1983.

SEZGIN F., *Geschichte der arabischen Schrifttums*, 9 vols., Leiden 1967–1972.

WENSINCK A. J., *Concordance et Indices de la Tradition Musulmane*, 4 vols., 2ND edn., E.J. Brill, Leiden 1962.

INDEX

Q

R

S